HEAVY WORK INVESTMENT

This book deals with the concept of Heavy Work Investment (HWI) recently initiated by Snir and Harpaz. Since its introduction the interest in the general HWI model has increased considerably. The book illustrates the development of HWI conceptualization, theory, and research. It deals with the foremost HWI subtype of workaholism. However, it also compares workaholism as a "negative" HWI subtype with work devotion/passion/engagement, as a "positive" HWI subtype. Most importantly, it addresses HWI in general, including its possible situational subtypes. In view of Snir and Harpaz's claim that the study of situational heavy work investors is relatively scarce, this certainly constitutes a promising step in the right direction. Finally, it deals with timely and important topics examined by prominent international researchers on Heavy Work Investment and such issues as personality factors of workaholism, work–life balance, cross-cultural similarities and differences in HWI, work addiction and technology, HWI and retirement, and intergenerational similarity in work investment.

Itzhak Harpaz, PhD, is Professor of Management, Dean of Graduate Studies, and Director of the Center for the Study of Organizations and Human Resource Management at the University of Haifa, Israel. He is also a Research Fellow at the Center for Human Resources and Labor Studies at the University of Minnesota.

Raphael Snir, PhD, is Senior Lecturer at the School of Management and Economics and at the School of Behavioral Sciences at the Academic College of Tel Aviv-Yaffo, Israel. He is also a Research Fellow in the Center for the Study of Organizations and Human Resource Management at the University of Haifa, Israel.

SERIES IN APPLIED PSYCHOLOGY

Jeanette N. Cleveland, Colorado State University
Kevin R. Murphy, Landy Litigation and Colorado State University
Series Editors
Edwin A. Fleishman, Founding Series Editor (1987–2010)

Winfred Arthur, Jr., Eric Day, Winston Bennett, Jr., and Antoinette Portrey
Individual and Team Skill Decay: The Science and Implications for Practice

Gregory Bedny and David Meister
The Russian Theory of Activity: Current Applications to Design and Learning

Winston Bennett, David Woehr, and Charles Lance
Performance Measurement: Current Perspectives and Future Challenges

Michael T. Brannick, Eduardo Salas, and Carolyn Prince
Team Performance Assessment and Measurement: Theory, Research, and Applications

Zinta S. Byrne
Understanding What Employee Engagement Is and Is Not: Implications for Theory, Research, and Practice

Neil D. Christiansen and Robert P. Tett
Handbook of Personality at Work

Jeanette N. Cleveland, Margaret Stockdale, and Kevin R. Murphy
Women and Men in Organizations: Sex and Gender Issues at Work

Aaron Cohen
Multiple Commitments in the Workplace: An Integrative Approach

Russell Cropanzano
Justice in the Workplace: Approaching Fairness in Human Resource Management, Volume 1

Russell Cropanzano
Justice in the Workplace: From Theory to Practice, Volume 2

David V. Day, Stephen Zaccaro, and Stanley M. Halpin
Leader Development for Transforming Organizations: Growing Leaders for Tomorrow's Teams and Organizations

Stewart I. Donaldson, Mihaly Csikszentmihalyi, and Jeanne Nakamura
Applied Positive Psychology: Improving Everyday Life, Health, Schools, Work, and Safety

James E. Driskell and Eduardo Salas
Stress and Human Performance

Sidney A. Fine and Steven F. Cronshaw
Functional Job Analysis: A Foundation for Human Resources Management

Sidney A. Fine and Maury Getkate
Benchmark Tasks for Job Analysis: A Guide for Functional Job Analysis (FJA) Scales

J. Kevin Ford, Steve W. J. Kozlowski, Kurt Kraiger, Eduardo Salas, and Mark S. Teachout
Improving Training Effectiveness in Work Organizations

Jerald Greenberg
Organizational Behavior: The State of the Science, Second Edition

Jerald Greenberg
Insidious Workplace Behavior

Itzhak Harpaz and Raphael Snir
Heavy Work Investment: Its Nature, Sources, Outcomes and Future Directions

Edwin Hollander
Inclusive Leadership: The Essential Leader–Follower Relationship

Ann Hergatt Huffman and Stephanie R. Klein
Green Organizations: Driving Change with I-O Psychology

Jack Kitaeff
Handbook of Police Psychology

Uwe E. Kleinbeck, Hans-Henning Quast, Henk Thierry, and Hartmut Häcker
Work Motivation

Laura L. Koppes
Historical Perspectives in Industrial and Organizational Psychology

Ellen Kossek and Susan Lambert
Work and Life Integration: Organizational, Cultural, and Individual Perspectives

Martin I. Kurke and Ellen M. Scrivner
Police Psychology into the 21st Century

Joel Lefkowitz
Ethics and Values in Industrial and Organizational Psychology

John Lipinski and Laura M. Crothers
Bullying in the Workplace: Causes, Symptoms, and Remedies

Manuel London
Job Feedback: Giving, Seeking, and Using Feedback for Performance Improvement, Second Edition

Manuel London
How People Evaluate Others in Organizations

Manuel London
Leadership Development: Paths to Self-Insight and Professional Growth

Manuel London
The Power of Feedback: Giving, Seeking, and Using Feedback for Performance Improvement

Robert F. Morrison and Jerome Adams
Contemporary Career Development Issues

Michael D. Mumford, Garnett Stokes, and William A. Owens
Patterns of Life History: The Ecology of Human Individuality

Michael D. Mumford
Pathways to Outstanding Leadership: A Comparative Analysis of Charismatic, Ideological, and Pragmatic Leaders

Kevin R. Murphy
Validity Generalization: A Critical Review

Kevin R. Murphy and Frank E. Saal
Psychology in Organizations: Integrating Science and Practice

Kevin Murphy
A Critique of Emotional Intelligence: What Are the Problems and How Can They Be Fixed?

Susan E. Murphy and Ronald E. Riggio
The Future of Leadership Development

Susan E. Murphy and Rebecca J. Reichard
Early Development and Leadership: Building the Next Generation of Leaders

Margaret A. Neal and Leslie Brett Hammer
Working Couples Caring for Children and Aging Parents: Effects on Work and Well-Being

Robert E. Ployhart, Benjamin Schneider, and Neal Schmitt
Staffing Organizations: Contemporary Practice and Theory, Third Edition

Steven A.Y. Poelmans
Work and Family: An International Research Perspective

Erich P. Prien, Jeffery S. Schippmann, and Kristin O. Prien
Individual Assessment: As Practiced in Industry and Consulting

Robert D. Pritchard, Sallie J. Weaver, and Elissa L. Ashwood
Evidence-Based Productivity Improvement: A Practical Guide to the Productivity Measurement and Enhancement System

Ned Rosen
Teamwork and the Bottom Line: Groups Make a Difference

Eduardo Salas, Stephen M. Fiore, and Michael P. Letsky
Theories of Team Cognition: Cross-Disciplinary Perspectives

Heinz Schuler, James L. Farr, and Mike Smith
Personnel Selection and Assessment: Individual and Organizational Perspectives

John W. Senders and Neville P. Moray
Human Error: Cause, Prediction, and Reduction

Lynn Shore, Jacqueline Coyle-Shapiro, and Lois E. Tetrick
The Employee–Organization Relationship: Applications for the 21st Century

Kenneth S. Shultz and Gary A. Adams
Aging and Work in the 21st Century

Frank J. Smith
Organizational Surveys: The Diagnosis and Betterment of Organizations Through Their Members

Dianna Stone and Eugene F. Stone-Romero
The Influence of Culture on Human Resource Processes and Practices

Kecia M. Thomas
Diversity Resistance in Organizations

Kecia M. Thomas, Victoria C. Plaut, and Ny M. Tran
Diversity Ideologies in Organizations

George C. Thornton III and Rose Mueller-Hanson
Developing Organizational Simulations: A Guide for Practitioners and Students

George C. Thornton III and Deborah Rupp
Assessment Centers in Human Resource Management: Strategies for Prediction, Diagnosis, and Development

Yoav Vardi and Ely Weitz
Misbehavior in Organizations: Theory, Research, and Management

Patricia Voydanoff
Work, Family, and Community

Mo Wang, Deborah A. Olson and Kenneth S. Shultz
Mid and Late Career Issues: An Integrative Perspective

Mark A. Wilson, Winston Bennett, Shanan G. Gibson and George M. Alliger
The Handbook of Work Analysis: Methods, Systems, Applications and Science of Work Measurement in Organizations

HEAVY WORK INVESTMENT

Its Nature, Sources, Outcomes, and Future Directions

Edited by
Itzhak Harpaz and Raphael Snir

Routledge
Taylor & Francis Group
NEW YORK AND LONDON

First published 2015
by Routledge
711 Third Avenue, New York, NY 10017

and by Routledge
27 Church Road, Hove, East Sussex BN3 2FA

Routledge is an imprint of the Taylor & Francis Group, an informa business

Library of Congress Cataloging-in-Publication Data
Heavy work investment : its nature, sources, outcomes and future
directions / edited by Itzhak Harpaz, Raphael Snir. — 1 Edition.
pages cm — (Applied psychology series)
Includes bibliographical references and index.
1. Psychology, Industrial. 2. Workaholism. I. Harpaz, Itzhak, editor of compilation. II. Snir, Raphael, editor of compilation.
HF5548.8.H3664 2014
158.7—dc23
2014005443

ISBN: 978-0-415-83505-3 (hbk)
ISBN: 978-0-415-83506-0 (pbk)
ISBN: 978-0-203-38098-7 (ebk)

Typeset in Sabon
by Apex CoVantage, LLC

CONTENTS

ABOUT THE EDITORS

Itzhak Harpaz, Professor of Management, is the Dean of Graduate Studies and director of the Center for the Study of Organizations and Human Resource Management at the University of Haifa, Israel. His main areas of expertise include: employment relations, organizational behavior, human resource management, and cross-cultural comparative management.

He is a research fellow at the Center for Human Resources and Labor Studies at the University of Minnesota. He was a visiting professor in several North American universities, including the Wharton School, University of Pennsylvania and the Centre for Industrial Relations and Human Resources at the University of Toronto. Harpaz is the author or coauthor of more than one hundred scientific publications and seven books. He has received awards and grants from prestigious institutions in the USA, Europe, and Israel. He serves on several journals' editorial boards and is a consulting reviewer for scientific foundations and agencies. Among several public positions, he currently serves as a lay judge in Israel's National Labor Court, is a member of several committees of Israel's National Council of Higher Education, and was the Chairperson of the Industrial Relations Research Association of Israel.

Raphael Snir (PhD, Behavioral and Management Sciences, Technion—Israel Institute of Technology) serves as a senior lecturer at the School of Management and Economics and at the School of Behavioral Sciences at the Academic College of Tel Aviv-Yaffo, Israel. He is also a research fellow in the Center for the Study of Organizations and Human Resource Management at Haifa University, Israel. His current research interests include workaholism (among other subtypes of heavy work investment), work/non-work relations, and work meaning and attitudes.

ABOUT THE CONTRIBUTORS

Mariya Gavrilova Aguilar is a doctoral candidate at the University of North Texas. She works in the local government sector in the area of human resources with emphasis on performance improvement and leave management. Her research focuses on organizational creativity, diversity, and commitment.

Cecilie Schou Andreassen, PhD, is currently holding a postdoctoral scholarship at the Department of Psychosocial Science, University of Bergen, Norway, and also has an affiliation with the Bergen Clinics Foundation, Norway. Her main research interest concerns work and organizational psychology, as well as chemical and nonchemical addictions. Her research has been published in journals such as the *Journal of Computer-Mediated Communication*, *Current Pharmaceutical Design*, *Stress & Health*, the *European Journal of Personality, Psychology and Health*, the *European Journal of Work and Organizational Psychology*, *Psychological Reports*, and the *Journal of Behavioral Addictions*, etc. Besides her academic interest, Andreassen is a licensed Clinical Psychologist Specialist with special training in psychological work with drug abuse and addictive behaviors, and a member of the Motivational Interviewing Network for Trainers. In addition, she has practiced as an organizational consultant for a decade, providing her with broad scientific, clinical, as well as organizational experience.

Marina Astakhova is a PhD student (ABD) at Kent State University, Ohio, USA. She received her MA and MBA degrees from Kent State University. Her research interests include person–organization fit, heavy work investment, organizational sustainability, and sexual harassment in the workplace. She conducts intercultural studies on organizational phenomena (person–organization fit and sexual harassment), as well as methodological work concerning the application of computer-based research methods (agent-based simulation) to study behavioral processes in organizations.

Shahnaz Aziz, PhD, is Associate Professor in the Department of Psychology at East Carolina University. Her area of expertise is in Industrial/Organizational (I/O) Psychology. Dr. Aziz is a published researcher and was a co-investigator on a multidisciplinary research grant from the National Science Foundation on online course delivery systems in education. Her research is on the application of psychological principles to human behavior in the workplace. In her program of research, Dr. Aziz has mainly conducted studies in the areas of workaholism, work–life balance, and work stress. The primary research goals of her lab have involved expanding upon the notion of workaholism as a syndrome, and studying workaholism, its correlates, and potential moderators. Dr. Aziz's lab has also investigated the relation of personality traits to workaholism facets, and developed a composite approach to further study of workaholism. She has also served as a consultant, developing training needs assessments and performance appraisal systems. Dr. Aziz is the 2010 recipient of East Carolina University's Board of Governors Distinguished Professor for Teaching Award. She is also a member of the American Psychological Association, the Society for Industrial/Organizational Psychology, North Carolina Industrial/Organizational Psychologists, and the Society for Occupational Health Psychology.

Arnold B. Bakker is Professor of Work and Organizational Psychology at Erasmus University Rotterdam, the Netherlands, and president of the European Association of Work and Organizational Psychology (www.eawop.org). His research interests include positive organizational behavior (e.g., flow, work engagement, happiness), burnout, crossover of work-related emotions, and internet applications of organizational psychology. His articles have been published in journals such as *Journal of Applied Psychology*, *Journal of Occupational Health Psychology*, and *Journal of Organizational Behavior*. Arnold Bakker is series editor of *Current Issues in Work and Organizational Psychology* (Psychology Press) and *Advances in Positive Organizational Psychology* (Emerald). See also: www.arnoldbakker.com

Ronald J. Burke is one of Canada's most prolific researchers. Professor Burke's work has focused on the relationship between the work environment and the individual's overall well-being, and over the past 40 years he has written articles for numerous academic and professional journals. In addition to his research and teaching activities, Professor Burke was the founding editor of the Canadian Journal of Administrative Sciences. Burke has served on the editorial board of two dozen journals and has reviewed manuscripts for a dozen more journals. He has served as a member of two grants committees for the Social Sciences and Humanities Research Council of Canada, as Director of the PhD program in the School of Business at York University, and as

Associate Dean Research with the Schulich School of Business at York University. He has participated in research conferences in North and South America, the UK, Europe, Asia, and Australia. He is a fellow of the Canadian Psychological Association.

Professor Burke previously held the Imperial Life Professorship in Organizational Behavior and was a senior research fellow at the National Centre for Management Research and Development, Ivey School of Business Administration, the University of Western Ontario. As holder of this professorship, he started the Women in Management Research Program at Ivey.

Professor Burke earned a BA from the University of Manitoba and an MA and a PhD from the University of Michigan. After completing his PhD in 1966 Professor Burke taught for two years at the University of Minnesota, following which he joined the School of Business at York University in Toronto. He has participated in over 300 management development programs as well as serving as a consultant on organizational effectiveness issues for private and public sector organizations. His views on management have also appeared in various media. An outstanding teacher, Professor Burke has been frequently nominated for MBA teaching awards, ranking first in 2001. Burke has published over 500 journal articles and book chapters and presented over 500 papers at academic conferences around the world. He has also edited or co-edited 41 books to date with McGraw-Hill, Kluwer, Blackwell, Routledge, the American Psychological Association, Sage, Edward Elgar, Cambridge University Press, Emerald, Gower, and Elsevier. In addition, he serves as co-editor of the Gower Publishers series on the psychological and behavioral aspects of risk in organizations.

Kevin Chaney is a graduate assistant at East Carolina University.

Malissa A. Clark is Assistant Professor of Industrial/Organizational Psychology and Women's Studies at the University of Georgia. She received her PhD in Industrial/Organizational Psychology from Wayne State University. Her research interests include workaholism, women and work, work and family issues, and moods and emotions in the workplace. Her research has been published in *Journal of Applied Psychology, Journal of Organizational Behavior, Journal of Vocational Behavior, Journal of Business and Psychology*, and *Personality and Individual Differences*.

Lonnie Golden is Professor of Economics and Labor Studies-Employment Relations at Penn State University, Abington College. He holds a PhD in Economics from the University of Illinois-Urbana. His research pertains to the instability of work hours and employment and effects on work–life and well-being, focusing on working hours determination, work scheduling, Fair Labor Standards Act overtime law, work hour preferences, workplace flexibility, overwork, students' time use, nonstandard jobs, the behavioral economics of labor supply, and the relation of work hours to aggregate employment. He is co-editor of the books *Working Time: International Trends, Theory and Policy Perspectives*, and *Nonstandard Work: The Nature and Challenge of Changing Employment Arrangements*. Recent articles include "Work–Life Balance, Flexibility and Instability of Work Hours: Salaried vs. Hourly Paid Workers"; "Work-Sharing and the Potential for Positive Effects on Employment Stability"; "Physical Health Risks: Extra Hours vs. Inflexible Schedules"; "Not Formally Introduced? Formal vs. Informal Flexible Daily Work Schedules among US Workers"; "A Brief History of Long Work Time and the Contemporary Sources of Overwork"; "Overemployment Mismatches in the US?"; "The Economics of Flexible Work Scheduling: Theoretical Advances and Paradoxes"; and "Is Labour More or Less Flexible? Dynamic Behavior and Asymmetries of Labour Input in US Manufacturing."

Mary Hogue received her PhD in Industrial and Organizational Psychology from the University of Akron. As an associate professor in the Management and Information Systems department at Kent State University, Mary teaches leadership to undergraduate, MBA, and PhD students. Her research focuses on how the intersection of gender and status bring differential work outcomes for women and men. She has presented and published her research in national conferences and top-level journals, has worked as a consultant, helping organizations with personnel issues from selection to performance management, and has led focus groups during organizational change. As an invited guest speaker and workshop leader, she has counseled a variety of workers in leadership development.

Nathalie Houlfort is Professor of Psychology at the Université du Québec in Montreal, Canada. Her research focuses on the motivational processes involved in workers' well-being, work–life conflicts, and knowledge transfer. Her current research interests include the determinants and consequences of passion for work, boundary work management, and the role of individual and group motivation in successful knowledge transfer strategies.

Kazumi Kubota is a visiting fellow at the Department of Mental Health, the University of Tokyo, Japan. His research interests include job stress, work engagement, workaholism, sleep quality, and job performance. His articles have been published in journals such as *Industrial Health* and *Ciencia & Trabajo*. E-mail: kazumikubota-tky@umin.net

Andréanne Laframboise earned a BA in Psychology from the University of Ottawa. She is currently a doctoral student in Industrial/Organizational Psychology at the Université du Québec à Montréal. Her research focuses on the influence of psychological needs balance between life spheres on the psychological adjustment to retirement. She is interested in work motivation, psychological health at work, work–family balance, and transfer and application of learning and knowledge.

Jesse S. Michel is Assistant Professor in the Psychology Department at Florida International University. His research interests include the dynamics between the work and family domains; leadership and supervision; and affect, mood, and personality. His research has been published in *Journal of Vocational Behavior, Journal of Organizational Behavior, Work & Stress, Journal of Business and Psychology*, and *Personality and Individual Differences*.

Kim Nimon, PhD, is an assistant professor in the Learning Technologies Department at the University of North Texas. A corporate veteran of the high-tech industry, Kim is committed to teaching and applying methods that bridge the gap between research and practice. Her research agenda focuses on improving human performance through the measurement and evaluation of employee attitudes, the development of quantitative statistical methodologies to assess human performance technology interventions, and the practice of workplace spirituality. Her work has been published in journals such as *Advances in Human Resource Development, Behavior Research Methods, Human Resource Development International, Human Resource Development Quarterly*, and the *Journal of Management, Spirituality, and Religion*. At the national level, Kim provides leadership for several professional organizations and serves on the editorial review board for a number of peer-reviewed publications.

Deborah A. Olson, PhD, earned her MA and PhD degrees in Industrial/Organizational (I/O) Psychology from Wayne State University in Detroit, Michigan. She is currently an associate professor of Management and Leadership at the University of La Verne (ULV) in La Verne, California, USA. Prior to joining ULV, she was a leadership development management consultant for over 25 years. As a consultant, she was the Vice President of Organizational Effectiveness and Management Development for Hay McBer and she also founded her own consultancy providing services to clients in the areas of executive development, training and development processes, and team effectiveness. During her time as a consultant, she worked with over 350 organizations, from both public and private sectors across North America. She has presented over 50 papers at regional, national, and international conferences and invited addresses. She has also published more than 20 refereed journal articles and book chapters. Her current research focuses on the areas of career development, leadership and team development, human resource management practices, positive organizational behavior, and the use of talents to optimize the effectiveness of older workers. She is also a co-author of the recently published book *Mid and Later Career Issues: An Integrative Perspective* (2013).

Gayle Porter is a professor of Management at Rutgers University and an author and consultant on workplace performance; she is a recognized expert in the topic of work addiction. Gayle's previous industry experience includes technical work in the oil and gas industry and finance and accounting positions with a Fortune 500 company. Her training programs and employee development work span multiple industries in both service and manufacturing environments. Gayle received her PhD in Management and Human Resources from the Ohio State University. At Rutgers she now teaches courses in Organization Change and Development, Social Responsibility of Business, International Human Resource Management, and Employee Development.

Justin Raines is a graduate assistant at Center for Survey Research—East Carolina University.

Wilmar Schaufeli received a PhD in Psychology in 1989 from the University of Groningen. After being affiliated at Groningen and Nijmegen University, he was appointed in 1994 at Utrecht University as a full professor of Work and Organizational Psychology and, since 2014, also as Research professor at the University of Leuven, Belgium. He is also visiting professor at Loughborough Business School, UK, and at Jaume I Universitat, Castellon, Spain. Schaufeli has published almost 400 articles, chapters, and books, mainly on occupational health psychology, including topics such as job stress, burnout, work engagement, and workaholism (see: www.schaufeli.com). He is a fellow of the European Academy of Occupational Health Psychology, is a licensed occupational health psychologist, and also works part-time as an organizational consultant.

Avital Sella-Dotan is a PhD student at the Faculty of Management School at Haifa University under the guidance of Professor Itzhak Harpaz, Dean of Graduate Studies Authority and head of the center of Study of Organizations and Human Resources Management. Sella Dotan received her MA in Labor Studies from Tel Aviv University in 2005 and her BA in Sociology from Haifa University. Sella Dotan's PhD concerns the relationships between work family benefits available, employees' perceptions of family support from the organization, supervisors, and coworkers, and work outcomes. She works at a major defense company in the field of human resources.

Orit Shamai is a research fellow at the Center for the Study of Organizations and Human Resource Management at the University of Haifa, Israel. She received a highly competitive PhD scholarship from the University of Haifa, as well as several monetary grants to conduct her research. Her areas of specialization are Human Resource Management, Organizational Behavior, Happiness, Heavy Work Investment, and Organizational Management. Dr. Shamai is a lecturer in Administration and Management, Organizational Behavior, and Human Resources Management at the University of Haifa and the Carmel Academic Center.

Akihito Shimazu is Associate Professor of Mental Health at the School of Public Health, the University of Tokyo, Japan. His research interests include job stress and coping, stress management at the workplace, work engagement, workaholism, work–home interface, and the application of IT for workplace intervention. He has published on a wide array of topics in journals such as *Cross-Cultural Research, Journal of Behavioral Medicine, International Archives of Occupational and Environmental Health, Social Science and Medicine*, and *Work & Stress*.

Kenneth S. Shultz, PhD, earned his MA and PhD degrees in Industrial/Organizational (I/O) Psychology from Wayne State University in Detroit, Michigan. He also completed a year-long National Institute on Aging (NIA) funded post-doctoral research fellowship in social gerontology at the University of Southern California (USC). Ken has been a professor in the Psychology Department at California State University, San Bernardino (CSUSB) for over 20 years. He has presented over 100 papers at regional, national, and international conferences, as well as invited addresses, and also published more than 50 refereed journal articles and book chapters mostly on aging and work related topics, including bridge employment and the transition to retirement. He has also co-authored/co-edited three books, including *Aging and Work in the 21st Century* (2007) and *Mid and Later Career Issues: An Integrative Perspective* (2013).

Gregory W. Stevens is a doctoral graduate student in the Industrial and Organizational Psychology program at Auburn University, where he also received his Master's degree in 2010. He is a member of the Academy of Management, Society for Industrial and Organizational Psychology, and Southern Management Association. His research interests include work engagement, organizational change, and business ethics.

Haya Stier is Professor of Sociology and Labor Studies at Tel Aviv University. Stier received her PhD in Sociology from the University of Chicago in 1990, and her BA and MA degrees in Sociology from Tel Aviv University. She served formerly as the chair of the Labor Studies Department, the head of the Institute for Social Research at Tel Aviv University, and the editor of "Israeli Sociology." She is currently the president of the research committee on stratification (ISA-RC28), serves as the head of the Welfare Policy Program at the Taub Center for Social Policy Studies in Israel, and is a member of the editorial board of several Israeli and international journals. Haya Stier's research interests include issues of work, gender and the family, poverty, and inequality.

Toon Taris received a PhD in Psychology in 1994 from the Free University of Amsterdam. In 2000 he was appointed at the Radboud University Nijmegen, the Netherlands, where he received a full professorship (in 2006) in Work and Organizational Psychology. In 2009 he moved to Utrecht University. He is currently chair of the Department of Work and Organizational Psychology of that university. Taris is interested in a wide variety of research topics, including worker well-being, (excessive) work motivation and workaholism, job stress, job insecurity, and (longitudinal) research methods. He has published extensively on these and other issues in journals and supervises several PhD students on these topics. He currently serves on the boards of several journals and is Editor-in-Chief of *Work & Stress*.

Robert J. Vallerand is Full Professor of Social Psychology and director of the Laboratoire de Recherche sur le Comportement Social at the Department of Psychology at the Université du Québec à Montréal. Professor Vallerand has served as head of the Psychology Department at his university as well as president of both the Quebec Society for Research in Psychology and the Canadian Psychological Association. He is currently president of the International Positive Psychology Association (IPPA). He has served or serves as consulting editor for several of the top international journals in the field and has supervised to completion a number of students, including 20 who are now university professors across Canada and Europe. Professor Vallerand is recognized as a leading international expert on motivational processes where he has developed theories dealing with intrinsic and extrinsic motivation, as well as passion for activities. He has written or edited six books and some 250 scientific articles and book chapters. His research has been cited over 6,000 times and he has received several millions of dollars in research grants. Professor Vallerand has received numerous awards and honors from over a dozen learned societies. Among these are his being elected Fellow of the International Association of Applied Psychology, the American Psychological Association, the Association for Psychological Science, the Society for Personality and Social Psychology, the Royal Society of Canada, and others. He has also received the Adrien Pinard Career Award from the Quebec Society for Research in Psychology, the Donald O. Hebb

Career Award from the Canadian Psychological Association (the highest research awards for a psychologist in Quebec and Canada, respectively), and the Sport Science Award from the International Olympic Committee.

Ilona van Beek received her PhD degree in the field of occupational health psychology in 2014. She conducted several empirical studies on the relation between heavy work investment (workaholism and work engagement) on the one hand, and work motivation and outcomes (job satisfaction, turnover intention, performance, and burnout) on the other hand.

SERIES FOREWORD

The goal of the Applied Psychology series is to create books that exemplify the use of scientific research, theory, and findings to help solve real problems in organizations and society. Drs. Harpaz and Snir's *Heavy Work Investment* brings together a distinguished group of scholars to help us understand and deal constructively with the growing phenomenon of unusually strong levels of involvement in work. As this book shows, heavy levels of involvement in work can have a complex mix of positive and negative effects on workers, their families, and communities and organizations.

Heavy Work Investment is divided into four sections. The first two sections challenge the common assumption that heavy involvement in work is necessarily dysfunctional (e.g., workaholism). Rather, substantial and sustained involvement in work can be the result of passion and engagement, or can reflect temporary adjustments to a variety of economic, career, or life-stage challenges. The ten chapters in the first two sections of this book discuss the nature, assessment, and outcomes of heavy work investment.

The third section of this book examines a range of special issues in heavy work investment (HWI), including its implications for work–life balance, its relationship to work transitions and retirement, and the way heavy work investment colors workers' assessments of company policies (such as providing workers with cell phones). The fourth section of this book considers future directions in HWI research and practice, including cross-cultural and intergenerational issues in HWI.

Taken together, the chapters in this volume provide an in-depth examination of an increasingly important set of issues that are defined by the relationships between people and work. They outline the complexities of HWI and the ways individuals, families, and organizations can respond to the challenges posed by heavy involvement in work. We are happy to add *Heavy Work Investment* to the Applied Psychology series.

Jeanette N. Cleveland
Kevin R. Murphy

Introduction

WORKAHOLISM, HWI SUBTYPES, AND BEYOND

Towards a General Model of Work Investment

Raphael Snir

Some people put a lot of time and energy into their work. By the term workaholics, Oates (1971) refers to people whose need to work has become so excessive that it may constitute a danger to their health, personal happiness, interpersonal relations, and social functioning. Since 1995, the number of publications on the topic of workaholism appears to have been increasing exponentially (Sussman, 2012). There is also considerable interest in related concepts, such as work engagement (e.g., Bakken & Torp, 2012), working long hours (e.g., Nakata, 2011), and overwork (e.g., Golden, 2009).

Snir and Harpaz (2009, 2010, 2012, 2013), who introduced the concept of Heavy Work Investment (HWI), maintain that *both* long hours *and* heavy effort are its core dimensions, and consider workaholism as only *one* of its subtypes. Using Weiner's (1985) attributional framework, Snir and Harpaz (2012) differentiate two major types of HWI, situational and dispositional, each with its own subtypes, *as based* on the predictors of such an investment. The first major type of HWI is situational, stemming from external (to the person) predictors. In the short term, external predictors, such as basic financial needs (food, accommodation, etc.), job demands, employer/supervisor demands, or organizational culture (e.g., the overtime culture in high-tech organizations and among hospital physicians), are uncontrollable and stable. Accordingly, these authors distinguish common subtypes of situational heavy work investors, such as the needy and the employer-directed.

According to Snir and Harpaz (2012), the second major type of HWI is dispositional, stemming from internal (to the person) predictors. They also further distinguish common subtypes of dispositional HWI. Examples are workaholism, as based on an addiction to work (an internal, uncontrollable, and stable predictor), and work devotion as an expression of a passion for work (an internal, controllable, and stable predictor). Work devotion is similar to Spence and Robbins' (1992) concept of work enthusiasm, as well as to the concept of work engagement, which refers to a positive, fulfilling, work-related state of mind characterized by vigor, dedication, and absorption (Schaufeli, Shimazu, & Taris, 2009; Schaufeli, Taris, & Bakker, 2006). Snir and Harpaz (2012), however, note that not all possible subtypes of dispositional HWI necessarily revolve around work: they may also stem from non-work avoidance. Examples may be fear of intimacy (an internal, uncontrollable, and stable predictor) and a low preference for leisure (an internal, controllable, and stable predictor).

In sum, an estimated 22 percent of the global workforce, or 614.2 million workers, work more than 48 hours per week (Lee, McCann, & Messenger, 2007). As work assumes greater importance in people's lives, a better perception of the heavy work investment phenomenon is essential. However, the existing literature deals mainly with workaholics and (to a lesser extent) work-devoted investors.

This book of readings systematically explores and sheds new light on the HWI phenomenon. It is intended for several types of people who are interested in this subject. These in particular are researchers and students in this area, as well as practitioners and professionals associated with HRM, OB, and management in general. The book has four parts: (1) the nature, sources, and measurement of HWI, (2) HWI subtypes and outcomes, (3) special issues in the study of HWI, and (4) future directions in the conceptualization and research of HWI. Its content is the work of most of the world-class researchers in this domain. Authors come from Canada, Israel, Japan, the Netherlands, Norway, and the USA. This spectrum of writers attests to the global nature of the HWI. Seventeen of the eighteen contributions in the book were written especially for it and have never been published previously.

The first part of the book has five contributions. Chapter 1, which is an updated version of Snir and Harpaz's (2012) paper, elaborates the general model of heavy work investment. In Chapter 2, Aziz and Burke discuss the relation of personality traits to workaholism and to HWI in general. They maintain that there is general support for the association of stable personality characteristics (e.g., perfectionism, obsessive-compulsive personality, Type A behavior pattern, and conscientiousness) with both workaholism (measured in various ways) and HWI. They also assert that our understanding of personality characteristics (personality traits as well as attitudes) of workaholics and heavy work investors may be enhanced not only by our focusing on one or two measures of workaholism in future studies, but also by our replicating earlier work by including the same personality measures.

In Chapter 3, Houlfort, Vallerand, and Ménard present passion as a driver of HWI, and research confirming that the type of the individual's passion will determine the effects one encounters. They claim that generally, the outcome of harmonious passion will be positive and that of obsessive passion will be negative. Hence, while both types of passion ensure a heavy investment in work, apparently only a HWI fueled by a harmonious passion can be beneficial. Certain environmental factors (e.g., adopting a transformational leadership style, and endorsing an organizational culture that supports autonomy) can be put in place to promote the development of harmonious passion, hence a more positive HWI. Workers with high levels of emotional intelligence and capable of using their signature strengths are also more apt to develop and maintain a harmonious passion for their work. Accordingly, they should be able to experience HWI more positively.

The fourth and the fifth chapters are methodological in nature. In Chapter 4, Andreassen provides a narrative overview of workaholism in terms of its definitions and assessments. She maintains that although the workaholism concept has been difficult to define, several measurements have been developed since the late 1980s. These include the Workaholism Battery (WorkBAT), the Work Addiction Risk Test (WART), the Dutch Work Addiction Scale (DUWAS), and the Bergen Work Addiction Scale (BWAS). These measures have been validated only to a limited extent against each other or against already existing potentially overlapping constructs. Andreassen asserts that only when validation is done properly will it be possible to establish accurate classifications (by using valid and reliable instruments), hence to facilitate effective treatment of affected individuals in the long run.

In Chapter 5, Nimon expands the field by focusing on two subtypes of dispositional HWI (workaholism and work-devotion) and reviews instrumentation purported to measure related constructs. Based on his analysis of assessments related to workaholism and work devotion, Nimon concludes that two instruments appear to have scales that may be useful in distinguishing addiction to from passion for work. They are the 14-item version of the Passion Scale (Vallerand, Blanchard, Mageau et al., 2003) and appropriate versions of the drive and enjoyment scales of the WorkBAT (Ersoy-Kart, 2005; Kanai, Wakabayashi, & Fling, 1996; McMillan, Brady, O'Driscoll, & Marsh, 2002; Spence & Robbins, 1992). He concludes that data from these scales have demonstrated accepted levels of construct and concurrent validity and contain items that appear to distinguish work passion as a controllable predictor of HWI from addiction to work as an uncontrollable predictor.

The second part of this book also contains five contributions. The first two deal with HWI subtypes, the last three with HWI outcomes. In Chapter 6, van Beek, Taris, and Schaufeli explore the motivational antecedents of two subtypes of heavy work investment: workaholism (as a "bad" HWI subtype) and work engagement (as a "good" HWI subtype). They discuss theory and research on this issue from two perspectives: personality-based, in which the motivation for heavy work investment is sought in stable individual differences in personality, and a situational-based, in which the motivation for heavy work investment is examined as a function of differences in the work context. They conclude that workaholism is primarily associated with an extrinsic motivation and a prevention focus, whereas work engagement is mainly linked to intrinsic motivation and a promotion focus.

In Chapter 7, Golden contributes to the discussion on HWI subtypes by distinguishing the concepts of overemployment, overwork, and workaholism from each other and from overtime or long work hours—each with similar and dissimilar consequences for worker current well-being. The last emanates mainly from the individual, the first from the employer or labor market conditions, while the middle one may be a mix of both. Golden also briefly distinguishes among various non-work-time activities that may feed back into returns from work. Focusing on overemployment, he primarily explores its sources and its distribution among workers, finding it most prevalent among certain occupations and longer work-weeks.

In Chapter 8, Shimazu, Kubota, and Bakker describe several characteristics of workaholic employees, and provide a general overview of the negative consequences of workaholism, such as psychological and physical ill-health, family and marital dissatisfaction, unhappiness, job dissatisfaction, and poor job performance. Next they go into deeper detail on the psychological mechanisms involved in the relation between workaholism and individual well-being, and discuss the underlying psychological mechanisms involved in the relation between workaholism and family members' (especially partner's) well-being. Finally, they refer to possible strategies to reduce the adverse effects of workaholism.

In Chapter 9, Clark, Michel, and Stevens maintain that both workaholics and engaged workers are heavily invested in their work, but due to different internal motives. They suggest a theoretical framework that outlines different work and non-work behaviors and consequences for each of these HWI subtypes. Central to their model is the idea that workaholics are driven to work by introjected motivation (i.e., an inner compulsion to work), while engaged workers are driven to work by intrinsic motivation (i.e., they find it fun). These authors state that due to these different motivational factors, workaholics and engaged workers are likely to experience very different state-based affective reactions, which differentially influence job attitudes and perceptions, and in turn different work and non-work behaviors and consequences.

In Chapter 10, Shamai explores the relation of work investment to employees' global happiness, in all its components: affective (both positive and negative affects) and cognitive (life satisfaction). She maintains that as against ordinary workers, heavy work investors exhibit higher levels of positive affect and life satisfaction, and lower levels of negative affect. Shamai also claims that both dispositional and situational heavy work investors exhibit higher levels of global happiness than ordinary workers.

The third part of the book has four contributions. In Chapter 11, Stier and Sella-Dotan assert that work intensification has multiplied the debates and concerns surrounding the work–life balance. Focusing particularly on the complex relations of work and family, they discuss the problems associated with balancing heavy work demands and family life, and the strategies employed by individual workers and their organizations to enhance the fit between these two life domains. Heavy work investment has the potential to undermine the work–life balance, further negatively affecting individuals, their families, their social life, and their work performance. Workers employ a variety of strategies to enhance the work-life balance, yet these strategies highlight the primacy of the workplace in affecting individual lives, as most workers would rather adjust to work demands than try to change them. Organizations also make efforts to resolve the inevitable conflict over work and non-work time, although the implemented policies are not always efficient, especially for workers in demanding positions. Stier and Sella-Dotan conclude that a combination of different coping strategies—on the personal, family, and organizational levels—are needed to achieve balance.

In Chapter 12, Aziz, Chaney, and Raines maintain that the rising number of hours in a typical work week, coupled with the expanding use of technology in organizations, have made workaholism a progressively relevant problem. Additionally, the modern workforce is becoming more diverse, so it might be difficult for employers to understand the sectors of the workforce that are at greater risk of developing workaholism. They expand on current research by describing how generation membership and career stage might affect workaholism. These authors also claim that certain professions are underrepresented in this area of study. Accordingly they describe the role of workaholism in regard to people in artistic occupations.

In Chapter 13, Shultz and Olson discuss the changing nature of mid- and late careers, as well as the changing nature of retirement, with particular emphasis on the emerging phenomenon of bridge employment. Next they integrate Snir and Harpaz's model of Heavy Work Investment (Snir & Harpaz, 2012) with the concept of worker retirement, in order to better understand workers' transition from full-time work to retirement at the end of their careers. How HWI influences the retirement process is also thoroughly examined. Both situational and dispositional types of HWI are explored in terms of how they impact the retirement transition process, as well as retirement adjustment and related outcomes. Several prominent theories and models of retirement are juxtaposed with the HWI concept, along with related theories and models such as the selective optimization with compensation (SOC) model of aging and the emphasis on the use of one's talents from the individual and leadership development literature. They conclude their chapter with several recommendations for future research in this area.

One decision facing many companies is whether it would be advantageous to supply smart phones to employees for use of this technology in their work. In Chapter 14, as a part of a larger study on smart phone usage, Porter explores the views of individuals across a range of companies and industries as to why their own company did or did not supply this type of technology. Her measures also include a perfectionism scale, as a proxy for workaholism. She reports the following: first, perfectionists seemingly gravitate to companies that are less likely to offer company-supplied smart phones. Second, only a handful of people said a "not-supply" decision was to the employees' benefit, but nearly all of them were high-perfectionists and at a high organizational level. Third, perfectionists/workaholics may be slightly harsher in expressing cost restraints as a reason for not supplying smart phones; or, at least those harsher in their comments fell into the perfectionist classification.

The fourth part of this book consists of three contributions. In Chapter 15, Porter asks whether work addiction is the proper label for certain high work investment habits. She considers historical views of addiction, along with contemporary approaches, from the perspective of how this knowledge is related to potential organizational actions to alleviate the negative side of heavy work investment. Her overall conclusion is, yes, work addiction is a proper label, but much would be gained from expanding our knowledge of research on other addictions, both substance-based and behavioral to support this stand.

Astakhova and Hogue (2013) used the bio-psychosocial framework (BPS) to distinguish Workaholic HWI, Situational HWI, and Pseudo HWI, arguing that HWI varies according to the relative influence of diverse biological, psychological, and social factors. In Chapter 16 they explore how the bio-psychosocial influences on HWI can be examined through the lens of national culture. In particular, they demonstrate how the cultural dimension of individualism/collectivism may have a contingent impact on Workaholic HWI, Situational HWI, Pseudo HWI and their associated outcomes. Astakhova and Hogue maintain that the application of the bio-psychosocial model to understand cultural influences on HWI provides a useful framework that fosters a systematic and theoretically guided approach to synthesizing existing and future research on cross-cultural HWI.

In Chapter 17, Snir explores intergenerational similarity in personality traits, values, attitudes, and behavior in general, and the two-dimensional parental role in this respect. He goes on to address specifically intergenerational similarity in work investment with the emphasis on heavy work investment subtypes, and discusses its possible implications for job-candidate selection, organizational policy on work hours, and breaking the workaholic vicious cycle. Snir also describes research dilemmas such as which parent is the more influential? What is the relative weight of social and biological parental influences?

Finally, Snir suggests future research directions concerning intergenerational similarity in work investment. An example is a longitudinal study in which the parent's work investment in his/her child's formative years is assessed at Time 1, and the adult child's work investment at Time 2.

In the epilogue, Harpaz provides a fresh and insightful view of the current state of the literature on HWI and outlines future research needs.

Since the early introduction of the general model of HWI (Snir & Harpaz, 2010, 2012), interest in this topic has increased. For example, a recent special issue of the *Journal of Managerial Psychology* (January 2014, Volume 29, Issue 1) deals empirically with types of heavy work investment. Snir and Harpaz (2013) describe the challenge that the phenomenon of HWI poses for individuals, their families, workplaces, and society alike. The present book of readings further illustrates the development of HWI conceptualization, theory, and research. Only five of the 18 contributions to the book focus primarily on the well-known HWI subtype of workaholism: Chapters 4, 8, 12, 14, and 15. Four other contributions deal with workaholism (as a "bad" HWI subtype) and work devotion/passion/engagement (as a "good" HWI subtype): Chapters 3, 5, 6, and 9.

Six additional contributions focus on HWI in general, including its possible situational subtypes: Chapters 7, 10, 13, 16, 17, and the epilogue. In view of Snir and Harpaz's (2012) claim that the study of situational heavy work investors, regardless of the specific terminology used to name them (e.g., reluctant hard workers: Buelens & Poelmans, 2004; conscripts: Drago, Wooden, & Black, 2006; unhappy workaholics: Friedman & Lobel, 2003; and the over-employed: Golden, 2006), is relatively scarce, this certainly constitutes a promising step in the right direction.

Finally, six contributions deal with timely and important topics: personality factors of workaholism and HWI (Chapter 2), HWI and work–life balance (Chapter 11), cross-cultural similarities and differences in HWI (Chapter 16), work addiction and technology (Chapter 14), HWI and retirement (Chapter 13), and intergenerational similarity in work investment (Chapter 17); the last four of these have scarcely been addressed previously.

Nevertheless, writing on HWI still needs additional development in its model building, conceptualization, empirical research, and practical implications. Specifically, the following are recommended:

1. As Porter (Chapter 15) claims, viewing workaholism in the larger picture of HWI bypasses the arguments over "good" versus "bad" workaholism, and places it clearly on the side of a behavior with negative connotation. However, greater agreement among researchers is needed concerning the differentiation between the various HWI subtypes to facilitate future research of their possible outcomes.
2. Currently there are four main workaholism (as a "bad" HWI subtype) measures: the Workaholism Battery (WorkBAT), the Work Addiction Risk Test (WART), the Dutch Work Addiction Scale (DUWAS), and the Bergen Work Addiction Scale (BWAS)—and even these measures have been validated only to a limited extent against each other (Andreassen, Chapter 4). Work engagement (as a "good" HWI subtype) is measured by a different measure, the Utrecht Work Engagement Scale (UWES: see Schaufeli, Bakker, & Salanova, 2006). Viewing HWI as an overall concept with two core dimensions (time and effort) calls for its *uniform* measurement, with the use of *different* measures for its various predictors (e.g., work addiction, passion for work). Such a measurement approach is taken by Snir (work in progress).
3. The two least explored dispositional subtypes of heavy work investors that are driven by non-work avoidance (i.e., the intimacy-avoiders and the leisure-low-interested: see Snir & Harpaz, 2012) clearly deserve more research attention in future studies.
4. According to Snir and Harpaz (2012), the needy are a group that constitutes one of the two situational subtypes of heavy work investors: those who have to support a large family, pay debt, etc. Note however that there is a different subtype of economically oriented heavy work investors—the materialists, those who strive for a high standard of living (Burke, 2006) and therefore should be regarded as a dispositional subtype. If indeed the younger generation is even more materialistic than past generations (Burke, 2013), this subtype of economically oriented heavy work investors should also enjoy more research attention in future studies.
5. Although some progress has been made (e.g., Astakhova & Hogue, Chapter 16; Baruch, 2011; Snir & Harpaz, 2006, 2009), the issue of cross-cultural/international comparison of HWI is still inadequately studied. More research is needed on differences as well as similarities between nations, in the scope, predictors, types, and outcomes of HWI, with a special emphasis on Asian nations which tend to work the longest hours and also have the highest proportion of workers who work more than 48 hours a week (Stephenson, 2012). It is important to note in this respect that according to OECD data, a negative relation

exists between annual working hours per person and productivity measured as GDP per hour worked. For instance, the Greeks put in over 2,000 hours a year on average. Germans, on the other hand, work about 1,400 hours each year. However, German productivity is about 70 percent higher than Greek (*The Economist*, 2013). Since HWI is an input measure after all, our attention should be focused on the possible different outcomes of its subtypes, for workplaces (e.g., productivity), individuals and their families (e.g., well-being) alike.

6. Stier and Sella-Dotan argue (Chapter 11) that due to pressure to devote more time to work activities gender inequality within the family and in the labor market is increasing, as women are often those who have to make concessions (e.g., women who have care responsibilities often scale back, harming their careers and income). In this light, Snir and Harpaz's (2013) recommendation that work-*effort*-based rewards and promotion should be considered, at least as regards mothers with a career, seems highly relevant.
7. Using Weiner's (1985) attributional framework, Snir and Harpaz (2012) presented the general model of HWI. This model can be further developed into a general model of work investment, which also includes average, light, and non-work investors, in addition to heavy work investors. An initial form of such model, which includes main subtypes of work investors, is presented in Table 0.1 (the updated

Table 0.1 The Two Major Types of Heavy Work Investors, Their Common Subtypes, and Their Causes

Situational Heavy Work Investors	*Dispositional Heavy Work Investors*
The needy: Those who have to support a large family, pay debts, etc. External, and in the short term uncontrollable and stable cause	Workaholics: Those who are addicted to their work. Internal, uncontrollable, and stable cause
The employer-directed: High-tech workers, hospital physicians, etc. External, and in the short term uncontrollable and stable cause	The work-devoted: Those with a high passion for their work. Internal, controllable, and stable cause
	The intimacy-avoiders: Those who see work as an escape from intimacy/close relationships. Internal, uncontrollable, and stable cause
	The leisure-low-interested: Those who see work as an alternative to tedious leisure time. Internal, controllable, and stable cause
	The materialists: Those who strive for a high standard of living. Internal, controllable, and stable cause

Table 0.2 The Three Major Types of Non-Heavy Work Investors, Their Common Subtypes, and Their Causes

Situational Non-Heavy Work Investors	*Dispositional Non-Heavy Work Investors*
The unemployed/labor market forced part-timers: Those who can't find a job at all/full-time job due to labor market conditions. External, and in the short term uncontrollable and stable cause	The disabled: Those who can't work due to poor (mental and/or physical) health condition. Internal, uncontrollable, and stable cause The voluntary unemployed: Those who prioritize non-work activates due to cultural preferences (e.g., some ultra-orthodox Jewish men) and are willing to live in poverty. Internal, controllable, and stable cause The voluntary part-timers: Those who seek an improved work–life balance due to a high leisure/family centrality. Internal, controllable, and stable cause
Non-Heavy Work Investors due to Both External and Internal Causes	
Common full-time workers: Those who work due to both financial needs (external, and in the short term uncontrollable and stable cause) and non-financial employment commitment (internal, controllable, and stable cause) The leisure-oriented very rich: Those who endorse the leisure ethic (internal, controllable, and stable cause) and can afford not to work themselves (external, partially controllable, and relatively stable cause)	

typology of heavy work investors) and Table 0.2 (a typology of average, light, and non-work investors).

In sum, there is still much to be done in the exploration of HWI subtypes and their possible outcomes, as well as work investment in general. Nevertheless, this book of readings constitutes an important step forward.

References

Astakhova, M. and Hogue, M. (2013). A Heavy Work Investment typology: A biopsychosocial framework. *Journal of Managerial Psychology*, 29(1). [Early cite article]

Bakken, B. and Torp, S. (2012). Work engagement and health among industrial workers. *Scandinavian Journal of Organizational Psychology,* 4(1), 4–20.

Baruch, Y. (2011). The positive wellbeing aspects of workaholism in cross cultural perspective: The chocoholism metaphor. *Career Development International,* 16(6), 572–591.

Buelens, M. and Poelmans, S. (2004). Enriching the Spence and Robbins' typology of workaholism: Demographic, motivational and organizational correlates. *Journal of Organizational Change Management,* 17(5), 440–458.

Burke, R. J. (2006). Work hours and work addiction. In R. J. Burke (Ed.), *Research companion to working time and work addiction* (pp. 3–35). Northampton, MA: Edward Elgar.

Burke, R. J. (2013). Materialism and its discontents. In R. Burke, S. Fox, and C. Cooper (Eds.), *Human frailties: Wrong turns on the road to success* (pp. 67–114). Farnham, Surrey: Gower Publishing.

Drago, R., Wooden, M., and Black, D. (2006). Long work hours: Volunteers and conscripts (Melbourne Institute Working Paper No. 27/06). Victoria, Australia: Melbourne Institute of Applied Economic and Social Research, the University of Melbourne.

Ersoy-Kart, M. (2005). Reliability and validity of the Workaholism Battery (Work-BAT): Turkish form. *Social Behavior and Personality: An International Journal,* 33(6), 609–618.

Friedman, S. D. and Lobel, S. (2003). The happy workaholic: A role model for employees. *Academy of Management Executive,* 17(3), 87–98.

Golden, L. (2006). How long? The historical, economic and cultural factors behind working hours and overwork. In R. J. Burke (Ed.), *Research companion to working time and work addiction* (pp. 36–57). Northampton, MA: Edward Elgar.

Golden, L. (2009). A brief history of long work time and the contemporary sources of overwork. *Journal of Business Ethics,* 84, 217–227.

Kanai, A., Wakabayashi, M., and Fling, S. (1996). Workaholism among employees in Japanese corporations: An examination based on the Japanese version of the workaholism scales. *Japanese Psychological Research,* 38(4), 192–203.

Lee, S., McCann, D., and Messenger, J. C. (2007). *Working time around the world: Trends in working hours, laws, and policies in a global comparative perspective.* London: Routledge.

McMillan, L. H. W., Brady, E. C., O'Driscoll, M. P., and Marsh, N. V. (2002). A multifaceted validation study of Spence and Robbins' (1992) Workaholism Battery. *Journal of Occupational and Organizational Psychology,* 75(3), 357–368.

Nakata, A. (2011). Effects of long work hours and poor sleep characteristics on workplace injury among full-time male employees of small- and medium-scale businesses. *Journal of Sleep Research,* 20(4), 576–584.

Oates, W. (1971). *Confessions of a workaholic: The facts about work addiction.* New York: World Publishing.

Schaufeli, W. B., Bakker, A. B., and Salanova, M. (2006). The measurement of work engagement with a short questionnaire: A cross-national study. *Educational and Psychological Measurement,* 66(4), 701–716.

Schaufeli, W. B., Shimazu, A., and Taris, T. W. (2009). Being driven to work excessively hard: The evaluation of a two-factor measure of workaholism in the Netherlands and Japan. *Cross-Cultural Research,* 43(4), 320–348.

Schaufeli, W. B, Taris, T. W., and Bakker, A. B. (2006). Dr Jekyll or Mr Hyde? On the differences between work engagement and workaholism. In R. J. Burke (Ed.), *Research companion to working time and work addiction* (pp. 193–217). Northampton, MA: Edward Elgar.

Snir, R. (work in progress). Beyond workaholism: Measurement, predictors, and outcomes of heavy work investment.

Snir, R. and Harpaz, I. (2006). The workaholism phenomenon: A cross-national perspective. *Career Development International,* 11(5), 374–393.

Snir, R. and Harpaz, I. (2009). Cross-cultural differences concerning heavy work investment. *Cross-Cultural Research,* 43(4), 309–319.

Snir, R. and Harpaz, I. (August 6–10, 2010; oral presentation at the OB divisional paper session). *Beyond workaholism: Towards a general model of heavy work investment.* The 2010 Academy of Management Annual Meeting, Montreal, Canada.

Snir, R. and Harpaz, I. (2012). Beyond workaholism: Towards a general model of heavy work investment. *Human Resource Management Review,* 22(3), 232–243.

Snir, R. and Harpaz, I. (2013). The challenge of heavy work investment. In R. Burke, S. Fox, and C. Cooper (Eds.), *Human frailties: Wrong turns on the road to success* (pp. 165–179). Farnham, Surrey: Gower Publishing.

Spence, J. T. and Robbins, A. S. (1992). Workaholism: Definition, measurement, and preliminary results. *Journal of Personality Assessment,* 58(1), 160–178.

Stephenson, W. (May 23, 2012). Who works the longest hours? www.bbc.co.uk/news/magazine-18144319 (accessed 28 February 2014).

Sussman, S. (2012). Workaholism: A review. *Journal of Addiction Research & Therapy,* S6, 1–10.

The Economist (September 24, 2013). Get a life. www.economist.com/blogs/freeexchange/2013/09/working-hours (accessed 28 February 2014).

Vallerand, R. J., Blanchard, C., Mageau, G. A., Koestner, R., Ratelle, C., Leonard, M., and Gagne, M. (2003). Les passions de l'ame: On obsessive and harmonious passion. *Journal of Personality and Social Psychology,* 85(4), 756–767.

Weiner, B. (1985). An attributional theory of achievement motivation and emotion. *Psychological Review,* 92(4), 548–573.

Part 1

NATURE, SOURCES, AND MEASUREMENT OF HEAVY WORK INVESTMENT (HWI)

1

A GENERAL MODEL OF HEAVY WORK INVESTMENT

Introduction

Raphael Snir and Itzhak Harpaz

By the term workaholics, Oates (1971) refers to people whose need to work has become so exaggerated that it may constitute a danger to their health, personal happiness, interpersonal relations, and social functioning. Since 1995, the number of publications on the topic of workaholism appears to be increasing exponentially (Sussman, 2012). Studies of workaholism resulted initially in a large volume of clinical and anecdotal data (e.g., Killinger, 1991; Machlowitz, 1980; Waddell, 1993), causing scholars to lament the lack of conceptual and methodological rigor (e.g., Scott, Moore, & Miceli, 1997). Recent studies have adopted better procedures, resulting in quantitative data that are amenable to statistical analysis (e.g., Bakker, Demerouti, & Burke, 2009; Chamberlin & Zhang, 2009; Harpaz & Snir, 2003; Russo & Waters, 2006; Schaufeli, Taris, & van Rhenen, 2008; Shimazu, Schaufeli, & Taris, 2010; Stoeber, Davis, & Townley, 2013). Yet despite the common use of the term "workaholism," little agreement exists as to its meaning beyond its core element: heavy work investment.

This chapter, which constitutes an updated version of Snir and Harpaz's (2012) paper, serves two main objectives. The first is to stress that workaholism is only one of the subtypes of heavy work investment. Namely, every workaholic is a heavy work investor, but not every heavy work investor is a workaholic. The second is to propose a model in which, using Weiner's (1985) attributional framework, we differentiate situational from dispositional types of heavy work investment, each with its own subtypes, *as based* on the predictors of such an investment.

Several writers have focused on the negative aspects of workaholism (e.g., Killinger, 1991; Porter, 1996; Robinson, 1989, 2007; Schaufeli, Shimazu, & Taris, 2009; Taris, Schaufeli, & Verhoeven, 2005). For instance, Robinson (1989) defines workaholism as a progressive, potentially fatal disorder of work addiction, leading to family disintegration and an increased inability to manage work habits and life domains. Rooted in the addiction paradigm, one of the earliest measures of workaholism is the Work Addiction Risk Test (WART; Robinson, 1989). Workaholism, as measured by WART, includes five dimensions: Compulsive Tendencies, Control, Impaired Communication/Self-Absorption, Inability to Delegate, and Self-Worth (Flowers & Robinson, 2002). Nevertheless, despite Robinson's quite extensive use of the WART, its external validity needs additional examination. With few exceptions (e.g., Taris, Schaufeli, & Verhoeven, 2005), most samples have included students (that are typically young and do not necessarily work), members of Workaholics Anonymous (which constitute a biased/range-restricted sample), or psychotherapists as expert observers (e.g., Flowers & Robinson, 2002; Robinson, 1996, 1999).

According to Schaufeli, Shimazu, and Taris (2009), workaholism is negatively conceptualized as working excessively and working compulsively. Based on this conceptualization, they propose a two-scale, ten-item workaholism measure, dubbed the Dutch Workaholism Scale (DUWAS). Satisfactory psychometric properties of the DUWAS are indicated (e.g., Del Libano, Llorens, Salanova, & Schaufeli, 2010; Schaufeli, Shimazu, & Taris, 2009).

On the other hand, some writers view workaholism positively, as involving a pleasurable engagement at work (Machlowitz, 1980; Sprankle & Ebel, 1987). For example, Machlowitz (1980:16) found that "as a group, workaholics are surprisingly happy. They are doing exactly what they love—work—and they can't seem to get enough of it." Likewise, Snir and Zohar (2008) found that workaholics experience more positive affect during work than during leisure activity, by comparison to non-workaholics. Moreover, they found no significant differences between workaholics and non-workaholics regarding the likelihood of performing work-related activities during leisure activity, or in the levels of physical discomfort and negative affect during the weekend. This suggests *no* indications of work addiction, such as the inability to stop working, and withdrawal symptoms.

Other writers differentiate negative from positive workaholism types. For example, Scott, Moore, and Miceli (1997) identify three types of workaholism patterns: compulsive dependent, perfectionist, and achievement oriented, and signify the first two as negative types, the third positive. Spence and Robbins (1992) based their characterization of workaholism on three attitudinal work-related properties: involvement, drive (due to inner pressure), and enjoyment. They define a workaholic as a person with high scores in work involvement and drive, and low scores in work enjoyment. They contrast this profile with work enthusiasm, defined as high involvement and enjoyment and low drive. Hence, instead of differentiating negative and positive types of workaholism, Spence and Robbins (1992) differentiate workaholism, being negative, from work enthusiasm, being positive. Work enthusiasm is similar to the recently introduced concept of work engagement, which refers to a positive, fulfilling, work-related state of mind characterized by vigor, dedication, and absorption (Schaufeli, Shimazu, & Taris, 2009; Schaufeli, Taris, & Bakker, 2006). Based on the above conceptualization, Spence and Robbins (1992) developed a three-scale Workaholism Battery (WorkBAT), which is a widely used measure in workaholism research. Despite apparent polarity, Spence and Robbins (1992) reported that their largest sub-group (19 percent of the sample) scored highly in all three aforementioned work-related properties (i.e., involvement, drive, and enjoyment), and therefore labeled them enthusiastic workaholics. According to this finding, work drive and work enjoyment are not opposites and can be viewed as orthogonal dimensions. Some research supports the psychometric properties of the Workaholism Battery (e.g., Burke 2001; Spence & Robbins, 1992), but its factorial structure is subject to some controversy (e.g., Huang, Hu, & Wu, 2010; McMillan, Brady, O'Driscoll, & Marsh, 2002).

Regardless of statistical properties, it is noteworthy that the Workaholism Battery is derived from three attitudinal constructs that partially overlap other well-established concepts: work involvement and drive are not entirely differentiated from work centrality and job involvement. This also holds regarding work enjoyment and job satisfaction. According to McMillan and O'Driscoll (2006), it is feasible that work drive and enjoyment are merely antecedents that trigger workaholic behavior. Finally, Spence and Robbins' Workaholism Battery does not measure the feature that we consider a conspicuous aspect of workaholism: long work hours. That is, one may exhibit high involvement and high drive but work regular workdays. In our opinion, qualifying such an individual as a workaholic is erroneous.

The Proposed Model

The foregoing short description of the state of workaholism research indicates a great need for further theoretical and methodological development. As noted above, there is little consensus concerning the meaning of workaholism, as reflected in its negative versus positive conceptualizations, and the attitude–behavior controversy. There is also an implicit, though prevalent, assumption in the popular press and among practitioners that if one invests heavily in his/her work, he/she is most likely a workaholic (e.g., Downey Grimsley, 1999; Tuckman, 2006). In the present chapter we attempt to address these shortcomings, by introducing the two-dimensional concept of Heavy Work Investment (HWI), and

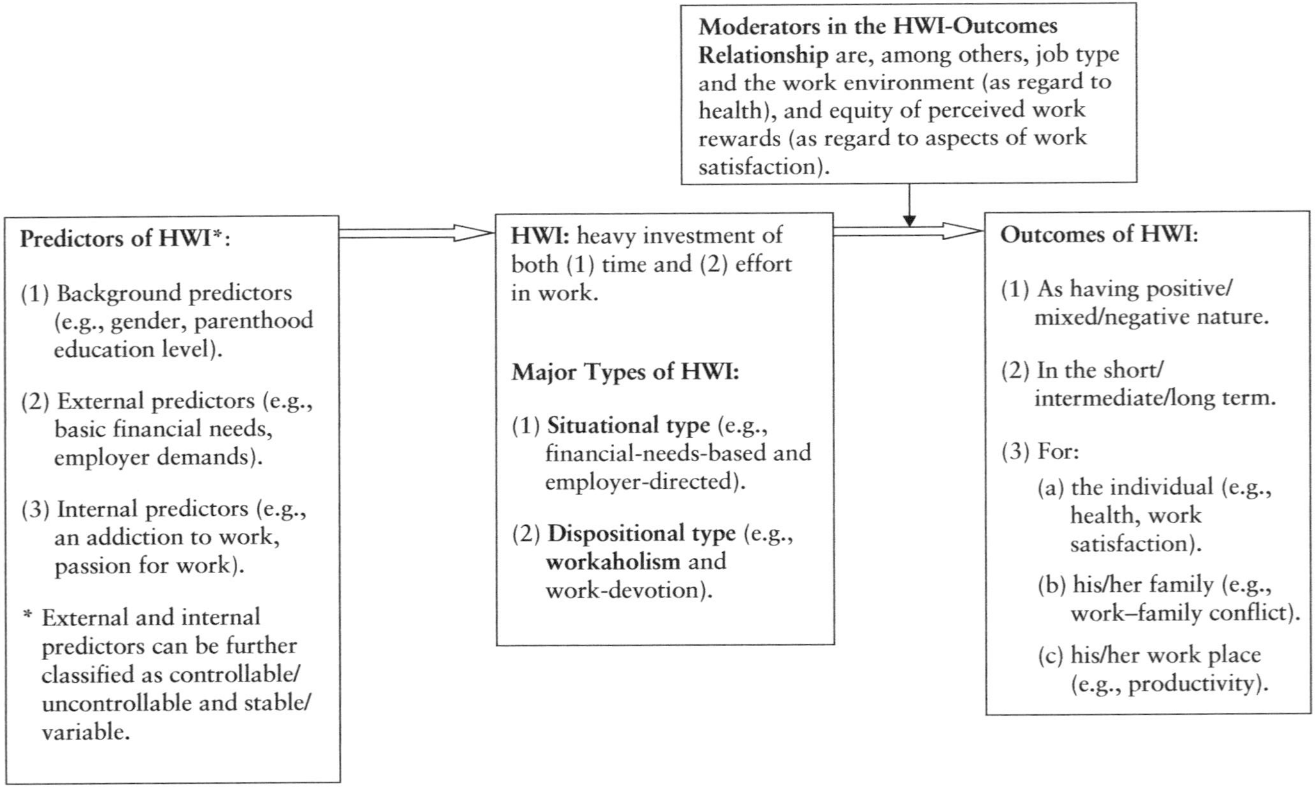

Figure 1.1 A model of Heavy Work Investment (HWI)

viewing workaholism as only one of its subtypes. Furthermore, we propose a model, presented in Figure 1.1, consisting of four main components: HWI, its possible predictors, its major types, and its outcomes.

The model shows the major sets of variables and the most straightforward relationships considered to be of primary importance in the study of HWI. The arrows indicate that an attempt should be made to determine the extent to which variables of one set predict (in a statistical sense) variables of another set. Possible moderators in relationship between HWI and its outcomes are also outlined.

Heavy Work Investment (HWI): A Two-Dimensional Concept

The shortcomings of previous workaholism research led Snir and Zohar (2008) to define workaholism as heavy time investment in work that does not stem from external demands (e.g., financial needs). This behavior-based definition does not overlap possible attitudinal predictors (e.g., work centrality, job involvement) or outcomes (e.g., job satisfaction). However, assessment of workaholism merely according to the time dimension (e.g., Harpaz & Snir, 2003; Snir & Harpaz, 2004) is somewhat simplistic, since it disregards how one acts *during* working time. According to Jacobs and Gerson (2004), the intensity of work is as important as the amount of time it takes. Thus, a second important dimension that should be considered is effort. This means the amount of either physical or mental energy allocated to work (Becker, 1985). Indeed, workaholics are intense, energetic, and competitive (Machlowitz, 1980). Naughton (1987) asserts that workaholics demonstrate endless energy in their work settings. Clark et al. (1993) also reported a positive correlation between workaholism and energy levels.

In our view, while non-stemming from external demands is a specific workaholism feature, time and effort investments in work constitute the two core dimensions of HWI in general. The HWI concept incorporates these two core dimensions while eschewing *a priori* positive or negative associations (an example of the latter being the term *workaholism*, patterned after *alcoholism*). Consequently, one can test positive and negative outcomes without risking criterion contamination.

A question may be raised, though, whether a heavy work investor has to be high on *both* dimensions in order to be classified as such. There are some indications that time and effort investments in work are positively correlated. For instance, according to an Experience-Sampling study, in which respondents provided randomly sampled self-reports over a one-week period, daily work hours were found to be strongly correlated with performing work-related activity and thinking about work-related issues (Snir & Zohar, 2008). Contradictory examples easily come to mind: staying late in the office (while in fact hardly working) just to impress the boss; or by contrast, working intensively only for a limited duration (e.g., at peak hours). However, using McMillan and O'Driscoll's (2006) terminology, we suggest that both high frequency (i.e., time) and intensity (i.e., effort) are core dimensions of HWI. Similarly, Hewlett and Buck Luce (2006) claim that Extreme Jobs demand a high number of work hours (60 or more a week), as well as having five or more out of ten specific characteristics such as fast-paced work under tight deadlines, an unpredictable flow of work, and an inordinate volume of work that amounts to more than one job.

Predictors of HWI

Broadly, there are three main categories of possible predictors of HWI: background variables, external (to the person) variables, and internal (to the person) variables.

Background Predictors

Among the most relevant background predictors of HWI are gender and parenthood. For example, in a cross-national study workaholism was found to be primarily a male phenomenon (Snir & Harpaz, 2006). Wharton and Blair-Loy (2002) state that employed women in the industrialized world continue to bear more responsibility for family and children than do their male counterparts so they are more often considered candidates for part-time work. According to a cross-national study of industrialized countries, for wives, being a parent was associated with a reduction in hours of paid work in all ten countries (Jacobs & Gornick, 2002). Rothbard and Edwards (2003) found that for women, increased time investment in either work or family reduced time invested in the other role. However, for men, increased time invested in work reduced time invested in family, but increased time investment in family did not affect time invested in work. Time invested in family was positively related to the number of children at home. In a recent study Snir, Harpaz, and Ben-Baruch (2009) found that a contrasting parenthood effect on men and women prevails even in the demanding high-tech sector, where women are expected to work long hours and play down their care-giving activities. Fathers invested more weekly hours in work than childless men, whereas mothers invested fewer weekly hours in work than childless women.

A third relevant background predictor of HWI is education level. Highly-educated people work relatively long hours (Jacobs & Gerson, 1997; Kuhn & Lozano, 2005; Maume & Bellas, 2001). This is presumably due to the opportunity provided by higher education for jobs that are more intrinsically and extrinsically satisfying, but also open-ended and demanding.

External (to the Person) Predictors

Not surprisingly, time investment in work has proved positively related to financial needs (Smith Major, Klein, & Ehrhart, 2002), as well as to holding a professional or managerial position (Jacobs & Gerson, 1997). Possible organization/industry-related external predictors of HWI are employer/supervisor demands (Clarkberg & Moen, 2001; Maume & Bellas, 2001), organizational culture (Burke, 2006a; Porter, 1996), and type of industry (e.g., Kunda, 1992; Perlow, 1998; Sharone, 2004). For example, although workers in the high-tech industry are theoretically free to work at their own pace, they tend to extend their work hours, putting in 50 to 70 hours per week (Sharone, 2004). Sharone (2004) shows how a culture of excellence and a structure of comparative performance create the individual's "choice" to work long hours. Moreover, based on a study in a large high-tech corporation, managers also use bureaucratic means to control the hours that employees work, such as imposing demands, monitoring, and penalizing employees who resist managerial control, even when they devise creative ways to schedule and complete their work (Perlow, 1998).

Finally, possible macro-level external predictors of HWI are labor-market conditions, such as labor unions policy (Alesina, Glaeser, & Sacerdote, 2005) and cross-cultural differences (Snir & Harpaz, 2009). For example, Snir and Harpaz (2009) found that time investment in work is heavier in societies where survival values are important (i.e., societies that emphasize economic and physical security) than in societies where self-expression values are important (i.e., societies that emphasize subjective well-being, self-expression, and quality of life).

Internal (to the Person) Predictors

By virtue of the Person–Situation Interaction Theory (Pervin, 1989) we recognize that internal (to the person) variables are also important for the prediction of HWI. Accepting Kanungo's (1979) recommendation not to confuse a construct and its antecedents, we view addiction to and passion for work as (the two best known) internal predictors of HWI. In our view, the difference between addiction to and passion for work is similar to the distinction of Vallerand et al. (2003) between Obsessive Passion (OP) and Harmonious Passion (HP). OP occurs when individuals feel compelled to engage in an activity because of internal contingencies that control them; HP occurs when individuals have freely accepted an activity as important to them without any contingencies attached to it.

Other possible internal predictors of HWI are a desire to stay away from intimacy and escape from private life (Seybold & Salomone, 1994); a low preference for leisure (due to experience of boredom during leisure activities: Douglas & Morris, 2006); some dimensions of obsessive-compulsive personality (namely obstinacy, orderliness, rigidity, and superego: Mudrack, 2004); materialism (striving for a high standard of living may cause one to work longer/harder: Burke, 2006b); and the work ethic, which contains elements of hard work, long hours, and pride in work and a job well done (Cherrington, 1980).

Major Types of HWI

From the above discussion, the external/internal dimension clearly constitutes a major means for classifying predictors of HWI. Nevertheless, causal locus (whether the cause is external or internal to the person) is not the only means to that end. The psychological study of casual attributions (i.e., the explanations we give for our/other people's behavior), which began with Heider's (1958) basic distinction between internal and external causes, was extended by Weiner (1985). Specifically, he defined three dimensions of causal attributions: casual locus, controllability (whether the cause is under volitional control or not), and stability (whether the cause is constant or variable over time). Weiner (1995, 2000) also recognized the importance of attribution theory in organizational behavior. In his words, "the concepts, issues, and ideas of attribution theory lend themselves so well to phenomena ingrained in organizational settings" (Weiner, 1995: 3–4). For example, attribution theory has been applied in regard to work performance (Corr & Gray, 1996), work exhaustion (Moore, 2000), and absence from work (Judge & Martocchio, 1995). Using Weiner's (1985) attributional framework, we differentiate two major types of HWI, situational and dispositional, each with its own subtypes, *as based* on the predictors of such an investment.

Situational HWI

The first major type of HWI is situational, stemming from external (to the person) predictors. In the short term, external predictors, such as basic financial needs (food, accommodation, etc.), job demands, employer/supervisor demands, or organizational culture (e.g., the overtime culture in high-tech organizations and among hospital physicians), are uncontrollable and stable. Accordingly, we can distinguish common subtypes of situational heavy work investors, such as the needy and the employer-directed. Note that even common full-time workers sometimes have to invest heavily in their work due to a temporary high workload (an external, uncontrollable, and variable predictor). However, since such occasions are exceptional, we do not consider these workers situational heavy work investors.

Dispositional HWI

The second major type of HWI is dispositional, stemming from internal (to the person) predictors. We can also further distinguish common subtypes of dispositional HWI. For instance, workaholism as based on an addiction to work (an internal, uncontrollable, and stable predictor), and work devotion as an expression of a passion to work (an internal, controllable, and stable predictor). Accordingly, we can outline our entire definition of workaholism as a subtype of heavy work investment that does not stem from external predictors or from a passion for work, but from an addiction to work. Note, however, that not all possible subtypes of dispositional HWI necessarily revolve around work: they may also stem from non-work avoidance. Examples may be fear of intimacy (an internal, uncontrollable, and stable predictor), and a low preference for leisure (an internal, controllable, and stable predictor).

Table 1.1 presents a classification of possible predictors of HWI by the dimensions of causal locus, controllability, and stability.

Table 1.1 Classification of Possible Predictors of HWI by the Dimensions of Causal Locus, Controllability, and Stability

External, Uncontrollable, and Variable
Temporary workload
External, and—in the Short Term—Uncontrollable and Stable*
Basic financial needs
Job demands (e.g., holding a professional or managerial position)
Employer/supervisor demands
Organizational culture
Type of industry
External, Uncontrollable, and Stable
Labor-market conditions (e.g., labor unions policy)
Cross-cultural differences
Internal, Uncontrollable, and Stable
Addiction to work
Fear of intimacy
Obsessive compulsive personality
Internal, Controllable, and Stable
Passion for work
Low preference for leisure
Striving for a high standard of living
Work values and attitudes (e.g., the work ethic, work centrality, and non-financial employment commitment)

Note: * A dichotomy of some predictors as controllable vs. uncontrollable or stable vs. variable is simplistic. For example, in the short term, a worker is not likely to change the characteristics/demands of a given job or organization. However, in the long term, different jobs/workplaces may be available.

Table 1.2 The Two Major Types of Heavy Work Investors and Their Common Subtypes

Situational Heavy Work Investors	*Dispositional Heavy Work Investors*
The needy: Those who have to support a large family, pay debts, etc.	Workaholics: Those who are addicted to their work
The employer-directed: High-tech workers, hospital physicians, etc.	The work-devoted: Those with a high passion for their work
	The intimacy-avoiders: Those who see work as an escape from intimacy/ close relationships
	The leisure-low-interested: Those who see work as an alternative to tedious leisure time

Table 1.2 specifies the two major types of heavy work investors and their common subtypes.

Note however that one's self-attribution (i.e., one's own grasp as to the causes) of one's HWI may be different from our attribution. A person whom we consider a workaholic may well, based on the rationale of the self-serving bias, attribute his/her HWI to job demands or employer/ supervisor demands.

Outcomes of HWI

The existing literature deals mainly with outcomes of long work hours and workaholism. Employers tend to overvalue the tendency to work long hours, particularly when objective measures of productivity are not readily available (Rebitzer & Taylor, 1995). However, work hours are not necessarily related positively to productivity (Baird & Beccia, 1980; Ben-David, 2003; Hanna, Taylor, & Sullivan, 2005). For example, Hanna, Taylor, and Sullivan (2005) reported a decrease in construction labor productivity as the number of hours worked beyond the typical 40 hours scheduled per week increased.

Moreover, there is growing evidence of the negative effects of long work hours and overtime work on health and health-related behavior (Dembe et al., 2005; Iwasaki, Takahashi, & Nakata, 2006; Raediker, Janssen, Schomann, & Nachreiner, 2006; Sparks et al., 1997; van der Hulst, 2003). For example, Raediker, Janssen, Schomann, and Nachreiner (2006) found a relation between the number of working hours per week and the frequencies of health complaints. This applies to both musculo-skeletal disorders and to psycho-vegetative complaints. There is a continuing discussion on the negative effects of long work hours concerning medical students and residents. Based on studies indicating the danger of working long hours for both residents' and patients' safety (e.g., Baldwin et al., 2003), since July 2003 most residents in the USA have been limited to 80 working hours per week (which is still twice the hours of a "regular" workweek). The data as regards the utility of limiting residents' work hours are conflicting (e.g., Goitein et al., 2005; Goldman & Fiebach, 2007; Howard, Silber, & Jobes, 2004; Lockley, Cronin, Evans, Cade et al., 2004).

Concerning workaholism, it has been found positively correlated with stress and health complaints (e.g., Andreassen, Ursin, & Eriksen, 2007; Spence & Robbins, 1992), burnout (Burke & Matthiesen, 2004; Schaufeli, Taris, & van Rhenen, 2008), work–family conflict (Bakker, Demerouti, & Burke, 2009), and work–life conflict (e.g., Aziz & Zickar, 2006; Bonebright, Clay, & Ankenmann, 2000); and negatively correlated with life satisfaction (e.g., Aziz & Zickar, 2006; Bonebright, Clay, & Ankenmann, 2000). For example, Bakker, Demerouti, and Burke (2009) report that workaholics were more inclined to think and worry about their work when at home, gave priority to their work, and neglected their domestic obligations and the relationship with their partners. In consequence, their partners were less supported, resulting in reduced relationship satisfaction.

However, a simple classification of HWI outcomes as being either positive or negative is insufficient. Workaholics were found to have lower levels of satisfaction with aspects of work (e.g., job, career), non-work (e.g., family, friends), and psychological well-being than work enthusiasts, across countries and occupations (e.g., Bonebright, Clay, & Ankenmann, 2000; Burke & Fiksenbaum, 2009a, 2009b). In a recent study, workaholism was related to an increase in ill-health and to a decrease in life satisfaction. In contrast, work engagement was related to a decrease in ill-health and to increases in both life satisfaction and job performance (Shimazu, Schaufeli, Kubota, & Kawakami, 2012). According to our HWI model, a possible explanation for the pattern is that workaholics, in contrast to work-devoted investors, are *not* in control of their HWI. The adverse effects of individuals' lack of control over long work hours on their well-being are documented (e.g., Golden & Wiens-Tuers, 2005; Sparks et al., 1997; van der Hulst & Geurts, 2001). Arguably, the needy heavy work investors, who resemble workaholics in the lack of control of their HWI, will also exhibit lower levels of satisfaction and well-being than work-devoted investors. We consider the employer-directed heavy work investors (e.g., high-tech workers, hospital physicians) a unique case. On the one hand they resemble workaholics in the lack of control of their work investment. On the other hand high-status employees reap greater material as well as social rewards from their jobs than low-status employees (Hodson, 2004), which may compensate for the lack of control of their HWI. In sum, different subtypes of dispositional and situational heavy work investors may experience different personal work/non-work outcomes. Accordingly, we expect:

- **Proposition 1a:** Negative personal work/non-work outcomes (e.g., burnout and stress) will be highest in workaholics and needy heavy work investors, lowest in work-devoted investors, and in between among employer-directed heavy work investors.
- **Proposition 1b:** Positive personal work/non-work outcomes (e.g., work and life satisfaction) will be highest in work-devoted investors, lowest in workaholics and needy heavy work investors, and in between among employer-directed heavy work investors.

Still, not all HWI outcomes are immediate, and their nature may change over time. For instance, Ng, Sorensen, and Feldman (2007) expect workaholism to have more negative consequences in the long term than in the short term.

One's family and workplace may also be affected by one's HWI, and the nature of its outcomes is not necessarily uniform. For example, one's HWI may interfere with family, which on the other hand may enjoy a high material standard of living. One may exhibit organizational citizenship behavior, but also harm the morale of one's work group, by setting unrealistic standards of face time at the office. In sum:

- **Proposition 2:** Three major issues need to be addressed as to HWI outcomes: (1) their nature (positive, mixed, or negative); (2) their term (short, intermediate, or long); and (3) the affected parties (the individual, his/her family, and the workplace). The nature of HWI outcomes may change both within and across the affected parties.

However, extreme and continuous HWI may have grave repercussions, *regardless* of its causes. Karoshi is a Japanese word meaning death from overwork. Most of its victims typically work 3,000–3,500 hours a year, commonly putting in 14-hour days and seven-day weeks; they die of subarachnoid hemorrhage or myocardial infarction (Hebrig & Palumbo, 1994).

Possible Moderators in the HWI–Outcomes Relationship

It is important to outline possible moderators in the relationship between HWI and its outcomes. The most addressed HWI outcome in the literature is health. In their comprehensive review, Sparks et al. (1997) describe a variety of moderators in the long work hours–health relationship, such as job type (e.g., the adverse effect of long work hours may be greater for jobs demanding excessive physical activity or repetitive work), the work environment (ill-effects of the work environment due to poor ergonomic design of the workstation, high level of noise, inadequate lighting, etc., may be exacerbated by working long hours), and age (employees aged over 40 may see themselves as more likely targets for redundancy, so they work longer hours under high stress). In a relatively recent survey of 372 train drivers, Tucker and Rutherford (2005) examined how the relation of long work hours to self-reported health is moderated by schedule autonomy and the degree of social support experienced. Respondents who lacked both schedule autonomy and social support showed a positive relation between the number of hours worked per week and frequency of physical health symptoms. Conversely, a negative relation was observed among respondents reporting low schedule autonomy together with high social support.

Possible moderators in the relationship between HWI and outcomes other than health are also evinced. For example, Peiperl and Jones (2001) proposed a distinction among those who put excessive time and effort into their work by introducing a second dimension, namely equity of perceived work rewards. They found that those who felt that the rewards accruing from their work were inequitably distributed—favoring the organization that employed them—were significantly less satisfied with their level of compensation and their careers than those who felt that the rewards were at least equitably distributed between themselves and the organization.

- **Proposition 3:** Possible moderators in the relationship between HWI and its outcomes are, among others, job type and the work environment (in regard to health), and equity of perceived work rewards (in regard to aspects of work satisfaction).

Dispositional and Situational Heavy Work Investors

Based on the proposed HWI model, we compare dispositional investors with situational investors regarding their HWI over time, and their affective reactions to work-related events.

HWI over Time

Different organizations attract, select, and retain different kinds of people (Schneider, 1987; Schneider, Goldstein, & Smith, 1995). Moreover, according to the dynamic interactionism approach (Ickes, Snyder, & Garcia, 1997), people actively incline to some situations and avoid others, so that the choice of situations reflects personal characteristics, such as attitudes, traits, and self-concepts. Hence, dispositional investors are more likely to be attracted to demanding jobs, to be selected by organizations for such jobs, and to keep these jobs even when less demanding jobs are available, due to their personal characteristics. Moreover, they may maintain their HWI even in the absence of financial justification to work at all. For example, Hamermesh and Slemrod (2005) found evidence that high-income, highly educated people exhibited workaholism in that they were more likely to postpone earlier plans for retirement. In another study, Arvey, Harpaz, and Liao (2004) found that individuals who won large amounts of money in the lottery were less likely to quit work if they had a high degree of work centrality.

On the other hand, situational investors are likely to reduce their HWI when they have the opportunity to do so. For instance, needy heavy work investors may work less if their financial pressures ease. Similarly, employer-directed heavy work investors may quit their current jobs during an economic upswing in favor of other, less demanding, occupational alternatives. In sum, whereas situational investors are likely to adjust their investment in work to the changing circumstances, dispositional investors are likely to disregard options of work reduction. Hence:

- **Proposition 4:** Dispositional investors are more likely to exhibit a steady HWI over time than situational investors.

A major methodological implication of this proposition is that a strict classification of an individual as a dispositional or a situational investor calls for a longitudinal research design (i.e., the examination of the work investment pattern over time). There is also a second, practical, implication. Along with the view of supportive (i.e., family-friendly) organizations, a one-size-fits-all simplistic notion of "work/life balance" has emerged (Friedman & Lobel, 2003). Dispositional investors, or at least workaholics, are less likely to approve of counseling/programs based on this notion. For them, the so-called "objective" imbalance may be in fact a subjective balance. Indeed, using the three-scale Workaholism Battery (Spence & Robbins, 1992), Russo and Waters (2006) found that workaholics, in contrast to their enthusiastic workaholic (those who score high in work involvement, enjoyment, and drive) counterparts, did not experience declining work–family conflict with increased access to flexible scheduling.

Affective Reactions to Work-related Events

Affect includes two independent dimensions: the degree of pleasantness and the degree of activation. The first dimension summarizes how well one does in terms of a positive–negative hedonic valence. Degree of activation refers to a sense of mobilization or energy and summarizes one's physiological state in terms of activation or deactivation (Feldman Barrett & Russell, 1998).

Affective processes create and sustain work motivation. Strong affective feelings are present whenever we confront work issues that matter to us and our performance at work (Barsade & Gibson, 2007). For workaholics, work is integral to and generally indistinguishable from other areas of their lives (Machlowitz, 1980). Furthermore, for workaholics, the career-self (i.e., one's corporate membership) becomes the predominant part of self-identity and the primary object of self-validation attempts (Ishiyama & Kitayama, 1994). Accordingly, we expect dispositional investors to experience a high degree of affective activation in response to work-related events, regardless of pleasantness. In detail, they are likely to experience higher degree of both positive affect (e.g., pleasure derived from a successful completion of a task, or a promotion) and negative affect (e.g., frustration due to a setback on an important project, or forced retirement) as a reaction to work-related events, than situational investors are. Indeed, those who score high on non-financial employment commitment (i.e., non-monetary motivation for working) suffer more when unemployed than do those who score low (Stafford, Jackson, & Banks, 1980; Warr, 1978). Retired or unemployed workaholics feel a loss of self-identity, which can cause grief, depression, and low self-esteem (Ishiyama & Kitayama, 1994). Therefore:

- **Proposition 5:** Affective reactions, whether positive (e.g., pleasure) or negative (e.g., frustration), to work-related events will be stronger in dispositional investors than in situational investors.

This may imply that performance appraisal is inherently more stressful for dispositional investors. Moreover, when unemployed or retired, they may need more psychological counseling than others. On the other hand, due to their supposed high non-financial employment commitment, dispositional investors are likely to be suitable candidates for participation in occupational training/reemployment programs. According to Warr and Lovatt (1977), respondents who scored high on non-financial employment commitment were significantly more likely to find new employment six months after closure of their plant than those who scored low.

Discussion

Heavy Work Investment is a significant phenomenon in contemporary life, owing to its possible important outcomes for individuals, their families, and their workplaces. In this chapter, we have outlined a preliminary model of HWI, which addresses several important issues and features hardly ever realized, or neglected previously in studies of workaholism. In the following sections, we discuss the major contributions of our chapter to the present literature, the measurement of HWI, and future research directions.

Contributions

The chapter makes several important contributions: First, it introduces a non-biased, behavior-based definition of HWI, which addresses both time and effort invested in work, does not overlap possible predictors or outcomes, and conceptualizes workaholism as only one of HWI subtypes. Every workaholic is a heavy work investor; but not every heavy work investor, or even dispositional investor, is a workaholic. One can be regarded as such only if one invests heavily in one's work not because of external demands, or a passion to work, but because of an addiction to work. Second, this chapter develops an innovative model of HWI, which constitutes a conceptual integration and extension of the present literature concerning workaholism and long work hours. Third, it presents a wide range of HWI predictors (i.e., psychological, sociological, economic, and cultural), and treats these predictors in the framework of well-established theories, such as Person–Situation Interaction Theory and Attribution Theory. Fourth, this chapter differentiates two major types of HWI, each with its own subtypes, based on the predictors of such an investment. For example, financial-needs-based and employer-directed are situational subtypes, whereas workaholism and work-devotion are dispositional subtypes. Fifth, we stress that the nature of HWI outcomes is not necessarily uniform—it may change both within and across the affected parties (i.e., the individual, his/her family, and workplace). Finally, we compare dispositional investors and situational investors regarding their HWI over time, and their affective reactions to work-related events.

HWI Measurement

We argue that individuals must be high in both the time and the effort dimensions to be classified as heavy work investors. However, several important questions remain unanswered:

1. *Should hours in a second job, work done from home, commuting time, and business travel time be considered in the calculation of time worked?*

As we define HWI in the sense of paid employment, we maintain that hours in a second job should certainly be considered in the calculation of time worked. Work done from home, paid or unpaid, should also be taken into consideration if the employer regards it as part of the worker's formal duties (e.g., a teacher grading students' exams). Commuting time and business travel time are inherently *intricate* to classify as work/non-work.

2. *What is the appropriate manner of measuring work hours (daily, weekly, monthly, or annually)?*

Daily measurement is not the preferred option due to possible considerable day-to-day variation in one's work hours. Monthly or annual work hours may vary less, but on the other hand are more complex to self-calculate/recall. So these two manners of measurement are more relevant for employer-dependent reports than for self-reports. Weekly work hours seem to vary less than daily work hours, as well as to be easier to self-report than monthly or annual work hours. In this respect, the "workweek grid" technique allows a more accurate estimation than the standard workweek question typically used in employment surveys (Robinson, Chenu, & Alvarez, 2002).

3. *How high do individuals have to be on time worked?*

Brett and Stroh (2003) define extreme work hours as 61 or more hours per week. Many researchers seem to use a 48-weekly-hours cutoff point, in line with the 1993 European Directive on working time (White & Beswick, 2003). Note however that any cutoff point is somewhat arbitrary and that labor standards vary across countries.

4. *Is there a need to use different cutoff points concerning work hours for different sexes, jobs, or industries?*

Dex, Clark, and Taylor (1995) argue that long hours should be considered differently for men (over 60 hours per week) and women (over 40 hours per week). Since certain jobs (e.g., managerial) and industries (e.g., high-tech) are more demanding than others, we agree with Ng, Sorensen, and Feldman (2007) that there is a rationale to use different cutoff points in different jobs/industries. However, implementing it could be quite cumbersome.

5. *How should we measure effort at work?*

The measurement of effort seems quite complex. One option is to determine a level of effort as high based on job requirements. For example, a job requires more effort when (1) employers establish high quantity or quality standards (Gorman & Kmec, 2007); (2) it involves strenuous physical activities (Demerouti et al., 2001) or complex cognitive tasks (Dwyer & Ganster, 1991). However, required effort is not necessarily equal to actual effort. Another option is to rely on absolute or relative (compared, e.g., with one's work colleagues) self/observer-reports.

6. *Should we rely on self-reports, observer-reports concerning the focal person (e.g., from one's family, friends, and co-workers), or objective measures?*

Objective measures of work hours, all the more so work effort, are not always available. However, there is a bias in self-reports (e.g., social desirability), as well as in observer-report (e.g., a co-worker may underestimate the worker's time and effort investment; the worker's spouse cannot see the worker at the workplace). Hence, if possible, taking a multi-source approach (e.g., using both self-reports and acquaintance reports: Aziz & Zickar, 2006) to assess interjudge agreement is strongly recommended.

Future Research Directions

Three research directions are suggested: study of situational investors, research across time and cultures, and exploration of intergenerational similarity/difference concerning HWI.

Study of Situational Investors

In total, an estimated 22 percent of the global workforce, or 614.2 million workers, work more than 48 hours per week (Lee, McCann, & Messenger, 2007). However, the existing literature deals mainly with two subtypes of dispositional investors: workaholics and (to a certain extent) work-devoted investors. Study of situational investors, regardless of the specific terminology used to name them (e.g., reluctant hard workers: Buelens & Poelmans, 2004; the conscripts: Drago, Wooden, & Black, 2006; unhappy workaholics: Friedman & Lobel, 2003; the overemployed: Golden, 2006), is scarce. It seems that even researchers in this field are prone to make the fundamental attribution error (i.e., overestimating the influence of internal factors and underestimating the influence of external factors concerning the behavior of others). In light of indications as to the considerable portion of full-time workers who want to work fewer hours (Reynolds, 2004), and of low earners, long work hours employees (Greenstein, 2000), more research on this topic is clearly needed.

Research across Time and Cultures

Longitudinal research is a necessary condition for establishing causality with regard to both predictors and outcomes of HWI, as well as for a strict classification of an individual as a dispositional or a situational investor. Furthermore, some suggest that a situational investor can become a dispositional one in the course of time. For example, a rise in work hours demanded by an employer above those preferred by the individual creates a feeling of time scarcity in the household. This in turn will lead a household to change its preferences from self-produced goods and services to those that are market-produced. The household may also shift from time-using goods and services toward the more time-saving type. Both shifts require more income. In addition, households are likely to shift preferences from time-intensive to income-intensive leisure activities. Together, all these effects ratchet upward individuals' targeted consumption levels and gradually dissipate the initial desire for shorter work hours (Rothschild, 1982). In sum, a dynamic process is triggered whereby an individual may start out involuntarily working long hours and later begin to do so voluntarily (Golden, 2006). It is also possible that due to socialization processes, organizational values of long work hours and hard work may be truly internalized and behaviorally expressed by at first a situational investor.

With the new millennium witnessing an increase in economic activity on a global scale, individuals are increasingly encountering people of different nations across real and virtual borders (Aycan & Kanungo, 2001). Hence an understanding of cross-cultural issues is becoming more critical than ever. However, except for two papers (Baruch, 2011; Snir & Harpaz, 2009), virtually no studies have been published on possible cross-cultural differences concerning HWI. More research is needed on such differences, as well as on similarities, in the scope, predictors, types, and outcomes of HWI.

Exploration of Intergenerational Similarity/Difference

If individuals see that other members in the family (e.g., parents) work excessively, they may develop a tendency to treat their own work in the same manner, because they are influenced by those important role models (Machlowitz, 1980). On the other hand, one may also claim that adult children of workaholics will do their best *not* to replicate their parents' work behavior, since they view them as *negative* role models in this respect. Anyway, research of intergenerational similarity/difference concerning workaholism or HWI in general is scarce. Statistically significant relationships were found between college students' perceived parental workaholism and their own workaholism (Chamberlin & Zhang, 2009). Compared with adult children of non-workaholics, adult children of workaholics showed a greater tendency to be workaholics themselves (Navarette, 1998; Searcy, 2000). Kravina, Falco, De Carlo, Andreassen, and Pallesen (2013) found that fathers' scores on working excessively were positively related to their adult children's level of workaholism.

According to Inglehart (1997), large intergenerational values change will be found in societies that have experienced a long period of rising economic and physical security. Young people will be much more likely to prioritize well-being values over survival values than will old people. This reflects the fact that the young have experienced greater security during their formative years than the old. Conversely, the difference between the values of young and old will be small or nonexistent in societies that have experienced relatively little increase in per capita income (Inglehart, 1997). Assuming that values affect behavior, not only psychological variables (such as parental influence) but also macro-level economic variables should be taken into consideration in the assessment of intergenerational similarity/difference in respect of HWI.

Final Words

Since the early introduction of the general model of HWI (Snir & Harpaz, 2010, 2012), the interest in this topic has increased. Relaying on the HWI model, Salanova, Del Líbano, Llorens, and Schaufeli (2013) further distinguish between heavy and soft work investors to explore employee well-being patterns. A recent special issue of the *Journal of Managerial Psychology* (Volume 29, Issue 1) deals with types of heavy work investment. One of the papers in this special issue, written by Astakhova and Hogue, applies a bio-psychosocial model to develop an integrated typology of HWI.

References

Alesina, A., Glaeser, E., and Sacerdote, B. (2005). *Work and leisure in the US and Europe: Why so different?* (NBER Working Paper No. 11278). Cambridge, MA: National Bureau of Economic Research.

Andreassen, C.S., Ursin, H., and Eriksen, H.R. (2007). The relationship between strong motivation to work, "workaholism," and health. *Psychology and Health, 22(5),* 615–629.

Arvey, R.D., Harpaz, I., and Liao, H. (2004). Work centrality and post-award work behavior of lottery winners. *The Journal of Psychology, 138(5),* 404–420.

Astakhova, M., and Hogue, M. (forthcoming). A heavy work investment typology: A biopsychosocial framework. *Journal of Managerial Psychology.*

Aycan, Z. and Kanungo, R.N. (2001). Cross-cultural industrial and organizational psychology: A critical appraisal of the field and future directions. In N. Anderson, D.S. Ones, H.K. Sinangil, and C. Viswesvaran (Eds.), *Handbook of industrial, work and organizational psychology*, vol. 1 (pp. 385–408). London: Sage.

Aziz, S. and Zickar, M.J. (2006). A cluster analysis investigation of workaholism as a syndrome. *Journal of Occupational Health Psychology, 11(1),* 52–62.

Baird, L.S. and Beccia, P.J. (1980). The potential misuse of overtime. *Personnel Psychology, 33(3),* 557–565.

Bakker, A.B., Demerouti, E., and Burke, R. (2009). Workaholism and relationship quality: A spillover-crossover perspective. *Journal of Occupational Health Psychology, 14(1),* 23–33.

Baldwin, D.C. Jr., Daugherty, S.R., Tsai, R., and Scotti, M.J. Jr. (2003). A national survey of residents' self-reported work hours: Thinking beyond specialty. *Academic Medicine, 78(11),* 1154–1163.

Barsade, S.G. and Gibson, D.E. (2007). Why does affect matter in organizations? *The Academy of Management Perspectives, 21(1),* 36–59.

Baruch, Y. (2011). The positive wellbeing aspects of workaholism in cross cultural perspective: The chocoholism metaphor. *Career Development International, 16(6),* 572–591.

Becker, G.S. (1985). Human capital, effort, and the sexual division of labor. *Journal of Labor Economics, 3 (Supplement),* S33–S58.

Ben-David, D. (2003). The labor force in Israel from the international aspect. *Riv'on Le-Kalkala, 50,* 73–90 (Hebrew).

Bonebright, C.A., Clay, D.L., and Ankenmann, R.D. (2000). The relationship of workaholism with work–life conflict, life satisfaction, and purpose in life. *Journal of Counseling Psychology, 47(4),* 469–477.

Brett, J.M. and Stroh, L.K. (2003). Working 61 plus hours a week: Why do managers do it? *Journal of Applied Psychology, 88(1),* 67–78.

Buelens, M. and Poelmans, S. (2004). Enriching the Spence and Robbins' typology of workaholism: Demographic, motivational and organizational correlates. *Journal of Organizational Change Management, 17(5),* 440–458.

Burke, R.J. (2001). Spence and Robbins' measures of workaholism components: Test–retest stability. *Psychological Reports, 88(3),* 882–888.

Burke, R.J. (2006a). Workaholic types: It's not how hard you work but why and how you work hard. In R.J. Burke (Ed.), *Research companion to working time and work addiction* (pp. 173–192). Northampton, MA: Edward Elgar.

Burke, R.J. (2006b). Work hours and work addiction. In R.J. Burke (Ed.), *Research companion to working time and work addiction* (pp. 3–35). Northampton, MA: Edward Elgar.

Burke, R.J. and Fiksenbaum, L. (2009a). Work motivations, work outcomes, and health: Passion versus addiction. *Journal of Business Ethics, 84, Supplement 2,* 257–263.

Burke, R.J. and Fiksenbaum, L. (2009b). Work motivations, satisfactions, and health among managers: Passion versus addiction. *Cross-Cultural Research, 43(4),* 349–365.

Burke, R.J. and Matthiesen, S. (2004). Short communication: Workaholism among Norwegian journalists: Antecedents and consequences. *Stress and Health, 20(5),* 301–308.

Chamberlin, C.M. and Zhang, N. (2009). Workaholism, health, and self-acceptance. *Journal of Counseling and Development, 87(2),* 159–169.

Cherrington, D.J. (1980). *The work ethic.* New York: American Management Association.

Clark, L.A., McEwen, J.L., Collard, L.M., and Hickok, L.G. (1993). Symptoms and traits of personality disorder: Two new methods for their assessment. *Psychological Assessment, 5,* 81–91.

Clarkberg, M. and Moen, P. (2001). Understanding the time-squeeze. Married couples' preferred and actual work-hour strategies. *American Behavioral Scientist, 44(7),* 1115–1136.

Corr, P.J. and Gray, J.A. (1996). Attributional style as a personality factor in insurance sales performance in the UK. *Journal of Occupational and Organizational Psychology, 69(1),* 83–87.

Del Libano, M., Llorens, S., Salanova, M., and Schaufeli, W. (2010). Validity of a brief workaholism scale. *Psicothema, 22(1),* 143–150.

Dembe, A.E., Erickson, J.B., Delbos, R.G., and Banks, S.M. (2005). The impact of overtime and long work hours on occupational injuries and illnesses: New evidence from the United States. *Occupational and Environmental Medicine, 62(9), 588–597.*

Demerouti, E., Bakker, A., Nachreiner, F., and Schaufeli, W. (2001). The jobs demands–job resources model of burnout. *Journal of Applied Psychology, 86(3),* 499–512.

Dex, S., Clark, A., and Taylor, M. (1995). *Household labour supply* (Department of Employment Research Series No. 43). Moorfoot, Sheffield: Employment Department.

Douglas, E.J. and Morris, R.J. (2006). Workaholic, or just hard worker? *Career Development International, 11(5),* 394–417.

Downey Grimsley, K. (September 7, 1999). A red, white and blue time clock: U.S. workers pass Japan in on-the-job hours, study says. *The Washington Post, financial section,* E.01.

Drago, R., Wooden, M., and Black, D. (2006). *Long work hours: Volunteers and conscripts* (Melbourne Institute Working Paper No. 27/06). Victoria, Australia: Melbourne Institute of Applied Economic and Social Research, the University of Melbourne.

Dwyer, D. and Ganster, D. (1991). The effects of job demands and control on employee attendance and satisfaction. *Journal of Organizational Behavior, 12(7), 595–608.*

Feldman Barrett, L. and Russell, J.A. (1998). Independence and bipolarity in the structure of current affect. *Journal of Personality and Social Psychology, 74(4), 967–984.*

Flowers, C.P. and Robinson, B. (2002). A structural and discriminant analysis of the Work Addiction Risk Test. *Educational and Psychological Measurement, 62, 517–526.*

Friedman, S.D. and Lobel, S. (2003). The happy workaholic: A role model for employees. *Academy of Management Executive, 17(3), 87–98.*

Goitein, L., Shanafelt, T.D., Wipf, J.E., Slatore, C.G., and Back, A.L. (2005). The effects of work–hour limitations on resident well-being, patient care, and education in an internal medicine residency program. *Archives of Internal Medicine, 165(22),* 2601–2606.

Golden, L. (2006). How long? The historical, economic and cultural factors behind working hours and overwork. In R.J. Burke (Ed.), *Research companion to working time and work addiction* (pp. 36–57). Northampton, MA: Edward Elgar.

Golden, L. and Wiens-Tuers, B. (2005). Mandatory overtime work: Who, what, and where? *Labor Studies Journal, 30(1),* 1–23.

Goldman, L. and Fiebach, N.H. (2007). Editorial. Hippocrates affirmed? Limiting residents' work hours does no harm to patients. *Annals of Internal Medicine, 147(2),* 143–144.

Gorman, E.H. and Kmec, J.A. (2007). We (have to) try harder: Gender and required work effort in Britain and the United States. *Gender and Society, 21(6),* 828–856.

Greenstein, M. (June 2000). *Employees who work long hours: Voluntarily or involuntarily?* (Manpower Planning Authority Information Text). Jerusalem, Israel: Manpower Planning Authority (Hebrew).

Hamermesh, D.S. and Slemrod, J. (2005). *The economics of workaholism: We should not have worked on this paper* (IZA Discussion Paper No. 1680). Bonn: Institute for the Study of Labor.

Hanna, A.S., Taylor, C.S., and Sullivan, K.T. (2005). Impact of extended overtime on construction labor productivity. *Journal of Construction Engineering and Management, 131(6),* 734–739.

Harpaz, I. and Snir, R. (2003). Workaholism: Its definition and nature. *Human Relations, 56(3),* 291–320.

Hebrig, P.A. and Palumbo, F.A. (1994). Karoshi: Salaryman sudden death syndrome. *Journal of Managerial Psychology, 9(7),* 11–16.

Heider, F. (1958). *The psychology of interpersonal relations.* New York: Wiley.

Hewlett, S.A. and Buck Luce, C. (2006). Extreme jobs and the dangerous allure of the 70-hour workweek. *Harvard Business Review, 84(12),* 49–59.

Hodson, R. (2004). Work life and social fulfillment: Does social affiliation at work reflect a carrot or a stick? *Social Science Quarterly, 85(2),* 221–239.

Howard, D.L., Silber, J.H., and Jobes, D.R. (2004). Do regulations limiting residents' work hours affect patient mortality? *Journal of General Internal Medicine, 19(1),* 1–7.

Huang, J., Hu, C., and Wu, T. (2010). Psychometric properties of the Chinese version of the Workaholism Battery. *The Journal of Psychology: Interdisciplinary and Applied, 144(2),* 163–183.

Ickes, W., Snyder, M., and Garcia, S. (1997). Personality influences on the choice of situations. In R. Hogan, J. Johnson, and S. Briggs (Eds.), *Handbook of personality psychology* (pp. 165–195). New York: Academic Press.

Inglehart, R. (1997). *Modernization and postmodernization: Cultural, economic and political change in 43 societies.* Princeton, New Jersey: Princeton University Press.

Ishiyama, F.I. and Kitayama, A. (1994). Overwork and career-centered self-validation among the Japanese: Psychological issues and counselling implications. *International Journal for the Advancement of counselling, 17(3),* 167–182.

Iwasaki, K., Takahashi, M., and Nakata, A. (2006). Health problems due to long working hours in Japan: Working hours, workers' compensation (Karoshi), and preventive measures. *Industrial Health, 44(4),* 537–540.

Jacobs, J.A. and Gerson, K. (1997). *The endless day or the flexible office: Working hours, work–family conflict, and gender equity in the modern workplace.* A report to the Alfred P. Sloan Foundation.

Jacobs, J.A. and Gerson, K. (2004). *The time divide: Work, family, and gender inequality.* Cambridge, MA: Harvard University Press.

Jacobs, J.A. and Gornick, J.C. (2002). Hours of paid work in dual-earner couples: The United States in cross-national perspective. *Sociological Focus, 35(2),* 169–187.

Judge, T.A. and Martocchio, J.J. (1995). Attributions concerning absence from work: A dispositional perspective. In M. Martinko (Ed.), *Attribution Theory: An Organizational Perspective* (pp. 97–124). Delray Beach, FL: St. Lucie Press.

Kanungo, R.N. (1979). The concept of alienation and involvement revisited. *Psychological Bulletin, 86(1),* 119–138.

Killinger, B. (1991). *Workaholics: The respectable addicts.* New York: Simon and Schuster.

Kravina, L., Falco, A., De Carlo, N.A., Andreassen, C.S., and Pallesen, S. (2013). Workaholism and work engagement in the family: The relationship between parents and children as a risk factor. *European Journal of Work and Organizational Psychology, (ahead-of-print),* 1–9.

Kuhn, P. and Lozano, F. (2005). *The expanding workweek? Understanding trends in long work hours among U.S. men, 1979–2004.* (NBER Working Paper No. 11895). Cambridge, MA: National Bureau of Economic Research.

Kunda, G. (1992). *Engineering culture.* Philadelphia, PA: Temple University Press.

Lee, S., McCann, D., and Messenger, J.C. (2007). *Working time around the world: Trends in working hours, laws, and policies in a global comparative perspective.* London: Routledge.

Lockley, S.W., Cronin, J.W., Evans, E.E., Cade, B.E. et al. (2004). Effect of reducing interns' weekly work hours on sleep and attentional failures. *The New England Journal of Medicine, 351(18),* 1829–1837.

Machlowitz, M. (1980). *Workaholics. Living with them, working with them.* Reading, MA: Addison-Wesley.

Maume, D.J. Jr. and Bellas, M.L. (2001). The overworked American or the time bind? Assessing competing explanations for time spent in paid labor. *American Behavioral Scientist, 44(7),* 1137–1156.

McMillan, L.H.W., Brady, E.C., O'Driscoll, M.P., and Marsh, N.V. (2002). A multifaceted validation study of Spence and Robbins' (1992) Workaholism Battery. *Journal of Occupational and Organizational Psychology, 75(3),* 357–368.

McMillan, L.H.W. and O'Driscoll, M.P. (2006). Exploring new frontiers to generate an integrated definition of workaholism. In R.J. Burke (Ed.), *Research companion to working time and work addiction* (pp. 89–107). Northampton, MA: Edward Elgar.

Moore, J.E. (2000). Why is this happening? A causal attribution approach to work exhaustion consequences. *Academy of Management Review, 25(2),* 335–349.

Mudrack, P.E. (2004). Job involvement, obsessive-compulsive personality traits, and workaholic behavioral tendencies. *Journal of Organizational Change Management, 17(5),* 490–508.

Naughton, T.J. (1987). A conceptual view of workaholism and implications for career counseling and research. *Career Development Quarterly, 35(3),* 180–187.

Navarette, S. (1998). *An empirical study of adult children of workaholics: Psychological functioning and intergenerational transmission.* Unpublished doctoral dissertation, California Graduate Institute, Santa Barbara.

Ng, T.W.H., Sorensen, K.L., and Feldman, D.C. (2007). Dimensions, antecedents, and consequences of workaholism: A conceptual integration and extension. *Journal of Organizational Behavior, 28(1),* 111–136.
Oates, W. (1971). *Confessions of a workaholic: The facts about work addiction.* New York: World Publishing.
Peiperl, M. and Jones, B. (2001). Workaholics and overworkers: Productivity or pathology? *Group and Organization Management, 26(3),* 363–393.
Perlow, L.A. (1998). Boundary control: The social ordering of work and family time in a high-tech corporation. *Administrative Science Quarterly, 43(2),* 328–357.
Pervin, L.A. (1989). Persons, situations, interactions: The history of controversy and a discussion of theoretical models. *The Academy of Management Review, 14,* 350–360.
Porter, G. (1996). Organizational impact of workaholism: Suggestions for researching the negative outcomes of excessive work. *Journal of Occupational Health Psychology, 1(1),* 70–84.
Raediker, B., Janssen, D., Schomann, C., and Nachreiner, F. (2006). Extended working hours and health. *Chronobiology International, 23(6),* 1305–1316.
Rebitzer, J. and Taylor, L. (1995). Do labor markets provide enough short-hours jobs? An analysis of work hours and work incentives. *Economic Inquiry, 33(2),* 257–273.
Reynolds, J. (2004). When too much is not enough: Actual and preferred work hours in the United States and abroad. *Sociological Forum, 19(1),* 89–120.
Robinson, B.E. (1989). *Work addiction.* Deerfield Beach, FL: Health Communications.
Robinson, B.E. (1996). Concurrent validity of the Work Addiction Risk Test as a measure of workaholism. *Psychological Reports, 79,* 1313–1314.
Robinson, B.E. (1999). The Work Addiction Risk Test: Development of a tentative measure of workaholism. *Perceptual and Motor Skills, 88(1),* 199–210.
Robinson, B.E. (2007). *Chained to the desk* (2nd ed.). New York: New York University Press.
Robinson, J.P., Chenu, A., and Alvarez, A.S. (2002). Measuring the complexity of hours at work: the weekly work grid. *Monthly Labor Review, 125(4),* 44–54.
Rothbard, N.P. and Edwards, J.R. (2003). Investment in work and family roles: A test of identity and utilitarian motives. *Personnel Psychology, 56(3),* 699–730.
Rothschild, K. (1982). A note on some economic and welfare aspects of working time regulation. *Australian Economic Papers, 21(38),* 214–218.
Russo, J.A. and Waters, L.E. (2006). Workaholic worker type differences in work–family conflict: The moderating role of supervisor support and flexible work scheduling. *Career Development International, 11(5),* 418–439.
Salanova, M., Del Líbano, M., Llorens, S., and Schaufeli, W.B. (2013). Engaged, workaholic, burned-out or just 9-to-5? Toward a typology of employee well-being. *Stress and Health, 30(1),* 71–81.
Schaufeli, W.B., Shimazu, A., and Taris, T.W. (2009). Being driven to work excessively hard: The evaluation of a two-factor measure of workaholism in the Netherlands and Japan. *Cross-Cultural Research, 43(4),* 320–348.
Schaufeli, W.B, Taris, T.W., and Bakker, A.B. (2006). Dr Jekyll or Mr Hyde? On the differences between work engagement and workaholism. In R.J. Burke

(Ed.), *Research companion to working time and work addiction* (pp. 193–217). Northampton, MA: Edward Elgar.

Schaufeli, W.B., Taris, T.W., and van Rhenen, W. (2008). Workaholism, burnout, and work engagement: Three of a kind or three different kinds of employee well-being? *Applied Psychology: An International Review, 57(2),* 173–203.

Schneider, B. (1987). The people make the place. *Personnel Psychology, 40(3),* 437–453.

Schneider, B., Goldstein, H., and Smith, D.B. (1995). The ASA framework: An update. *Personnel Psychology, 48(4),* 747–773.

Scott, K.S., Moore, K.S., and Miceli, M.P. (1997). An exploration of the meaning and consequences of workaholism. *Human Relations, 50(3),* 287–314.

Searcy, E.A. (2000). *Adult children of workaholics: Anxiety, depression, family relationships, and risk for work addiction.* Unpublished master's thesis, University of South Australia.

Seybold, K.C. and Salomone, P.R. (1994). Understanding workaholism: A review of causes and counseling approaches. *Journal of Counseling and Development, 73(1),* 4–10.

Sharone, O. (2004). Engineering overwork: Bell-curve management at a high-tech firm. In C. Fuchs Epstein and A.L. Kalleberg (Eds.), *Fighting for time: Shifting boundaries of work and social life* (pp. 191–218). New York: Russell Sage Foundation.

Shimazu, A., Schaufeli, W.B., Kubota, K., and Kawakami, N. (2012). Do workaholism and work engagement predict employee well-being and performance in opposite directions? *Industrial health, 50(4),* 316–321.

Shimazu, A. Schaufeli, W.B., and Taris, T.W. (2010). How does workaholism affect worker health and performance? The mediating role of coping. *International Journal of Behavioral Medicine, 17(2),* 154–160.

Smith Major, V., Klein, K.J., and Ehrhart, M.G. (2002). Work time, work interference with family, and psychological distress. *Journal of Applied Psychology, 87(3),* 427–436.

Snir, R. and Harpaz, I. (2004). Attitudinal and demographic antecedents of workaholism. *Journal of Organizational Change Management, 17(5),* 520–536.

Snir, R. and Harpaz, I. (2006). The workaholism phenomenon: A cross-national perspective. *Career Development International, 11(5),* 374–393.

Snir, R. and Harpaz, I. (2009). Cross-cultural differences concerning heavy work investment. *Cross-Cultural Research, 43(4),* 309–319.

Snir, R. and Harpaz, I. (August 6–10, 2010; oral presentation at the OB divisional paper session). *Beyond workaholism: Towards a general model of heavy work investment.* The 2010 Academy of Management Annual Meeting, Montreal, Canada.

Snir, R. and Harpaz, I. (2012). Beyond workaholism: Towards a general model of heavy work investment. *Human Resource Management Review, 22(3),* 232–243.

Snir, R., Harpaz, I., and Ben-Baruch, D. (2009). Centrality of and investment in work and family among Israeli high-tech workers: A bicultural perspective. *Cross-Cultural Research, 43(4),* 366–385.

Snir, R. and Zohar, D. (2008). Workaholism as discretionary time investment at work: An Experience-Sampling Study. *Applied Psychology: An International Review, 57(1)*, 109–127.

Sparks, K., Cooper, C., Fried, Y., and Shirom, A. (1997). The effects of hours of work on health: A meta-analytic review. *Journal of Occupational and Organizational Psychology, 70*, 391–408.

Spence, J.T. and Robbins, A.S. (1992). Workaholism: Definition, measurement, and preliminary results. *Journal of Personality Assessment, 58(1)*, 160–178.

Sprankle, J.K. and Ebel, H. (1987). *The workaholic syndrome*. New York: Walker.

Stafford, E.M., Jackson, P.R., and Banks, M.H. (1980). Employment, work involvement and mental health in less qualified young people. *Journal of Occupational Psychology, 53(4)*, 291–304.

Stoeber, J., Davis, C.D., and Townley, J. (2013). Perfectionism and workaholism in employees: The role of work motivation. *Personality and Individual Differences, 55(7)*, 733–738.

Sussman, S. (2012). Workaholism: A review. *Journal of Addiction Research & Therapy, S6*, 1–10.

Taris, T.W., Schaufeli, W.B., and Verhoeven, L.C. (2005). Workaholism in the Netherlands: Measurement and implications for job strain and work–nonwork conflict. *Applied Psychology: An International Review, 54(1)*, 37–60.

Tucker, P. and Rutherford, C. (2005). Moderators of the relationship between long work hours and health. *Journal of Occupational Health Psychology, 10(4)*, 465–476.

Tuckman, J. (October 13, 2006). Workaholic Adam Sandler clicks on valuable life lesson. *Daily Herald, online format.*

Vallerand, R.J., Blanchard, C., Mageau, G.A., Koestner, R., Ratelle, C., Leonard, M., and Gagne, M. (2003). Les passions de l'ame: On obsessive and harmonious passion. *Journal of Personality and Social Psychology, 85(4)*, 756–767.

van der Hulst, M. (2003). Long workhours and health. *Scandinavian Journal of Work, Environment, and Health, 29(3)*, 171–188.

van der Hulst, M. and Geurts, S. (2001). Associations between overtime and psychological health in high and low reward jobs. *Work and Stress, 15(3)*, 227–240.

Waddell, J.R. (1993). The grindstone. *Supervision, 26*, 11–13.

Warr, P.B. (1978). A study of psychological well-being. *British Journal of Psychology, 69(1)*, 111–121.

Warr, P.B. and Lovatt, D.J. (1977). Retraining and other factors associated with job finding after redundancy. *Journal of Occupational Psychology, 50(2)*, 67–84.

Weiner, B. (1985). An attributional theory of achievement motivation and emotion. *Psychological Review, 92(4)*, 548–573.

Weiner, B. (1995). Attribution theory in organizational behavior: A relationship of mutual benefit. In M. Martinko (Ed.), *Attribution theory: An organizational perspective* (pp. 3–6). Delray Beach, FL: St. Lucie Press.

Weiner, B. (2000). Attribution theory and organizational psychology: An introduction and overview. In M. Martinko (Ed.), *Attribution theory in the organizational sciences: Theoretical and empirical contributions* (pp. 1–4). Greenwich, CT: Information Age Publishing.

Wharton, A.S. and Blair-Loy, M. (2002). The "overtime culture" in a global corporation: A cross-national study of finance professionals' interest in working part-time. *Work and Occupations, 29(1)*, 32–63.

White, J. and Beswick, J. (2003). *Working long hours*. Sheffield: Health and Safety Laboratory.

2

PERSONALITY FACTORS, WORKAHOLISM, AND HEAVY WORK INVESTMENT

Shahnaz Aziz and Ronald J. Burke

Workaholism, a progressive and compulsive disorder, is a common term in popular culture that describes individuals who are addicted to work. The general media has given considerable coverage to the concept of workaholism and long work hours over the past 40 years, with research on these topics slowly emerging and increasing. Clinical and anecdotal writing has exceeded empirical research efforts (Killinger, 1991; Waddell, 1993). The dearth of empirical research on this topic is surprising given all of the interest surrounding workaholism. The primary reasons for this neglect include issues of definition and measurement, and loose theories of workaholism have hampered research efforts (Buelens & Poelmans, 2004; Ersoy-Kart, 2005; McMillan, Brady, O'Driscoll, & Marsh, 2002; Scott, Moore, & Miceli, 1997). As a result, opinions, observations, and conclusions about workaholism and heavy work investments are both varied and conflicting. We believe that more research attention needs to be devoted to better understanding workaholism and heavy work investment, especially given that workaholism is typically associated with negative individual, family, and work outcomes (Burke & Cooper, 2008).

Individuals exhibit workaholic behaviors or undertake heavy work investments. It should then come as no surprise that potential antecedents of these phenomena have included stable individual traits or predispositions. This chapter reviews what we know about personality correlates of workaholism and heavy work investment. It should be noted that, in addition to individual predispositions, situational factors also play a role in encouraging and supporting workaholism and heavy work investment. It is still important to understand the role that individual predispositions play in the etiology of workaholism, however, and research should always include measures of these variables if we are to more fully understand workaholism, its consequences, and possible reduction or treatment of this harmful syndrome.

Snir and Harpaz (2012) advanced our thinking about work hours and workaholism by developing a general model of Heavy Work Investment (HWI). It addresses the central questions of who works long hours and why. They make a useful distinction between situational and dispositional antecedents of HWI. Situational antecedents include employer-directed demands and external financial needs, whereas dispositional antecedents include workaholism and work devotion. Snir and Harpaz also propose that both dispositional antecedents (internal) and situational antecedents (external) can be further classified as controllable/uncontrollable and stable/variable. Dispositional antecedents would include obsessive-compulsive personality traits (Mudrack, 2004), greed and materialism (Burke, 2011), and work centrality, family centrality, and leisure centrality (Snir & Harpaz, 2004).

In this chapter, we first provide an overview of workaholism (including definitions and measures), as well as workaholism as an addiction, followed by a discussion on personality trait antecedents of workaholism, and, finally, a section on studies that have examined personality characteristics of workaholism and HWI.

Workaholism: An Overview

Although the word *workaholism* is commonly used in both popular culture and empirical literature, researchers have still not come to a consensus on what the term actually means. In fact, it has been suggested that perhaps workaholism is just an extreme case of established job attitudes, such as job involvement or organizational commitment. In their efforts to determine what workaholism is actually comprised of, investigators have held varying opinions over the decades. Some researchers view workaholism as a positive construct that can serve to improve organizations given that workaholics are dedicated and reliable workers (Machlowitz, 1980). Employers who espouse this stance make attraction, selection, and retention of such employees their primary goal. On the other hand, several others see workaholism through a negative lens (e.g., Burke, 2000a; Porter, 1996). If workaholics are in fact perfectionists who cannot delegate responsibilities nor work in a harmonious manner with their coworkers, then, due to the rising emphasis on teamwork, it is highly plausible they may not actually be productive in the workplace. In this sense, it might be most fruitful for employers to *not* promote workaholic behaviors and workaholism cultures in their organization. These two conflicting outlooks undoubtedly make it challenging to select an organizational strategy. Although there are different conceptualizations of workaholism and researchers seem to be at odds on whether it is a favorable or unfavorable phenomena in organizations, in this chapter we see workaholism as an addiction that interferes with one's health, happiness, and/or personal relationships (Aziz & Zickar, 2006; Burke, 2000a; Robinson, 1996).

Although many efforts have been made to define and measure workaholism and HWI, few measures have received some research attention and scrutiny. We will summarize them here since most of the research discussed in this chapter uses one of them.

Spence and Robbins's (1992) definition of workaholism appears to be the most widely used in the literature and has gained the most popularity over the years. They measured three different facets of workaholism: work involvement, work drive, and work enjoyment. Work involvement is the degree to which employees commit themselves to a project and make constructive use of their time. Work drive is the employee's intrinsic motivation to work. Work enjoyment is the pleasure employees derive from working. Spence and Robbins deemed these three dimensions to be independent of each another, because an individual could be high on one facet, yet low on another. Using a cluster analysis approach, they divided employees into six different worker types, in which three were conceptualized as workaholic types. Specifically, the Workaholic was operationalized as being high on work involvement and work drive, but low on work enjoyment; Enthusiastic Addicts score high scores on all three components; and Work Enthusiasts score high on work involvement and work enjoyment, but low on work drive. The three nonworkaholic types include: Relaxed Workers, who score high on work enjoyment, but low work drive and work involvement; Disenchanted Workers, who score high on work drive, but low on work involvement and work enjoyment; and Unengaged Workers, who score low on all three components. Despite its popularity, concerns have been raised about the work involvement facet having low reliability in some studies, particularly those undertaken in countries outside North America, and whether two or three factors best represent the measure.

On the other hand, Robinson (1999) defines workaholism as "the overindulgence in and preoccupation with work, often to the exclusion and detriment of the workaholic's health, intimate relationships, and participation in child rearing" (Flowers & Robinson, 2002, p. 517). Based on a review of the literature and his professional counselling experience, Robinson created a 25-item measure called the Work Addiction Risk Test (WART). The WART measures workaholism according to Robinson's definition and it has been regarded as a more global instrument than the WorkBAT (Brady, Vodanovich, & Rotunda, 2008). Although the WART is a considerable addition to the field of workaholism and the total scale has high reliability, it has been critiqued for its instable factor structure. Flowers and Robinson (2002) conducted a principle components analysis on the WART and found it to be comprised of five factors, three of which validly differentiated workaholics from non-workaholics (i.e., compulsive tendencies, control, and impaired communication/self-absorption)—this three factor structure has been replicated in other studies (Clark, Lelchook, & Taylor, 2010). Taris, Schaufeli, and Verhoeven (2005) called for reducing the WART to just the Compulsive Tendencies subscale, arguing that it adequately represents workaholism and has considerable overlap with the entire WART on correlates of workaholism.

Snir and Harpaz (2004) conceptualized workaholism as work hours that are independent of financial need. To measure this construct, first total work hours, including overtime, was determined. Then, financial need was established by an index including respondent marital status, whether the respondent's spouse worked, and the number of people financially dependent on the respondent. Single respondents, as well as those married with a working spouse, were assigned 0; those married with a non-working spouse were assigned 1. Finally, the number of people supported financially by the respondent was added to the previous scores.

Schaufeli, Taris, and Bakker (2006) created the Dutch Workaholism Scale (DUWAS). Based on a review of the literature, Schaufeli and his colleagues proposed a two-dimensional view of workaholic tendencies, whereby workaholism involves working excessively and working compulsively. They developed a reliable measure of these two elements, which is increasingly being used in research. Moreover, research studies have confirmed the two-factor structure and, as expected, working excessively and working compulsively are found to be significantly and positively correlated.

Vodanovich and Piotrowski (2006) elaborated on past definitions and considered workaholism to be a syndrome. The workaholism syndrome, according to these researchers, goes through particular stages that increasingly worsen over time. In its early stage, workaholic tendencies develop due to individual differences, responsibilities, and stress. Although workaholic behaviors are exhibited at this stage, they do not disrupt the individual's daily functioning. Over time, however, these behaviors become stronger and more frequent, eventually becoming maladaptive by interfering with the individual's daily functioning. When the full syndrome has emerged, work reinforces the individual's behavior, consumes the individual's life, and the individual has now become dysfunctional (Fassel, 1990). One of the key characteristics of the workaholism syndrome is that it results in individuals ignoring other aspects of their lives, including family, relationships, and health (Vodanovich & Piotrowski, 2006).

Workaholism: An Addiction

The word addiction describes excessive, persistent behavior that results in negative consequences (Porter, 1996). Workaholism in particular has often been linked to other addictions, such as drugs, gambling, and especially alcohol (Porter, 1996). Researchers are starting to gain a better comprehension of workaholism in terms of its breadth and complexity, thereby leading to a stronger connection between it and alcoholism. Commonalities between workaholism and alcoholism have been exhibited in that, similar to alcoholism, workaholism can also lead to the neglect of other interests, identity issues, rigid thinking, withdrawal, and denial (Oates, 1971; Porter, 1996).

The maladaptive behavioral patterns of workaholics stem from their compulsive need to work and their excessive desire to think about work constantly, typically at the cost of neglecting personal activities and facing health and work-related problems. It is often assumed that workaholism is strongly linked to hours worked and that a workaholic is merely someone who works a vast number of hours per week, more than an average full-time employee. For example, three decades ago, Mosier (1983) defined workaholics as individuals who worked a minimum of 50 hours per week. Findings from a study conducted by McMillan et al. (2002), however, demonstrated that hours worked did not significantly correlate with workaholism, as measured by Spence and Robbins. Therefore, based on these results, it can be presumed that workaholism is a multifaceted construct and that hours worked is not its sole indicator. It is possible that individuals work extraordinarily long hours for a variety of reasons (e.g., deadlines, pressure from a supervisor). Essentially, workaholics have an intense, internal drive to work that leads to a neglect of other interests and negative consequences—it is this intense, internal drive that is the core of workaholism.

The more they succumb to their work addiction, the more likely it is that other aspects of the workaholic's life deteriorate, leading to work–life imbalance. Work–life imbalance has recently been defined as an occupational stressor based on the amount of time spent at work, a lack of energy available after work for non-work related activities, and a strain between the demands of work life and personal life (Fisher, Bulgar, & Smith, 2009). It is not surprising that long work hours inevitably take away from time that workaholics could spend pursuing hobbies, being with family and friends, or enjoying other activities that encompass a balanced life. Work–life imbalance is a symptom of workaholism that is also part of the diagnostic criteria for other addiction disorders in the DSM-V (American Psychiatric Association, 2013). Achieving work–life balance is crucial in that it serves as a psychological and physical recovery period, which is important to circumvent health problems caused by work stress (Schaufeli, Bakker, van der Heijden, & Prins, 2009). Empirically, the positive correlation between workaholism and work–life imbalance has been shown in several studies (e.g., Aziz, Adkins, Walker, & Wuensch, 2006; Bonebright, Clay, & Ankenmann, 2000).

Personality Trait Antecedents of Workaholism

With rising interest in workaholism and HWI, there has been a growing trend in determining the personal and environmental factors that could influence their development. The number of potential antecedents that might contribute to workaholism has risen, thus we need to establish which ones are paramount, how they influence each other, and if they directly or indirectly cause workaholism. Researchers have proposed models to further understand these concepts. For example, Ng, Sorenson, and Feldman (2007) asserted that personal dispositions, socio-cultural experiences in one's family of origin and workplace, and behavioral reinforcements or rewards from the work environment directly affect workaholism. Liang and Chu (2009) proposed that personality traits, personal rewards or inducements (e.g., intrinsic work values), and organizational factors (e.g., peer competition) strongly impact workaholism and HWI.

Literature reviews undertaken by many different researchers has led to the identification of several potential dispositional or trait antecedents of workaholism and HWI. These include: obsessive-compulsion, achievement orientation, perfectionism, and conscientiousness (Liang & Chu, 2009); achievement orientation, desire for success, overcontrolling behaviors, self-efficacy, obsessive-compulsive personality traits, perfectionism, and a strong work ethic (Sussman, 2012); self-esteem and achievement-oriented traits and values (Ng, Sorensen, & Feldman, 2007); and achievement orientation, perfectionism, and compulsive-dependent personality (Scott et al., 1997).

In this section, we will review only the personality trait antecedents of workaholism, because a discussion regarding other antecedents and the nature of their interaction is beyond the scope of this chapter.

Personality traits serve as dispositions that can be triggered by certain environments or circumstances, leading to an addiction (Eysenck, 1997); workaholism is no exception to this well-established fact. Trying to establish the traits and behaviors that are most critical to the development of workaholism has been a difficult task for researchers. Perfectionism, obsessive-compulsiveness, Type A personality, and the Big 5 personality traits have been central to discussions on the relationship between workaholism and personality; therefore, we review the theoretical underpinnings and empirical findings pertaining to these traits in the paragraphs that follow.

Perfectionism

Perfectionism is associated with having high standards, a potential gap between one's hoped for performance and current performance, and a preference for order. Both perfectionism and obsessive-compulsive personality traits are similar in that they originate from a need to control the environment and lead to controlling behaviors (Robinson, 2007). In fact, Killinger (1991) states, "Perfectionism clearly is not a positive trait but a curse that leads to a compulsive need to be successful and to create a persona that broadcasts success" (p. 21)—this statement suggests that perhaps perfectionism is a precursor to obsessive-compulsiveness. Furthermore, Spence and Robbins (1992) found that perfectionism correlated more strongly with work drive than with work enjoyment and work involvement; this finding has been replicated in samples of Canadian MBA graduates (Burke & Fiksenbaum, 2009a) and Australian psychologists (Burke & Fiksenbaum, 2009b).

Obsessive-Compulsiveness

Regarding obsessive-compulsive personality traits, theoretically, Ng et al. (2007) indicate that obsessive-compulsive personality disorder (OCPD) is a key dispositional trait of workaholism. Similarly, Naughton (1987) claims that workaholism is merely OCPD expressed in the workplace. Empirical support also exists for the association between OCPD and workaholism. For instance, Aziz, Wuensch, and Brandon (2010) found that Spence and Robbins's (1992) workaholism triad, which consists of work involvement, work drive, and work enjoyment, were all predictors of obsessive-compulsive behavior. Moreover, work drive had the strongest relationship with obsessive-compulsive behavior.

Type A Personality

Achievement-oriented personality traits, such as Type A personality, are deemed antecedents of workaholism. This is not surprising given that workaholics have a strong desire for upward mobility and are receptive to external rewards. Type A behavior is associated with achievement orientation involving competition, impatience, speed, and setting performance goals. There is a great deal of overlap between individuals with Type A personality and workaholics in that both are burdened with high stress due to their hard-driving, urgent, and impatient approach to life (Robinson, 1996). Additionally, the markedly similar behavioral features displayed by Type A children and adult workaholics is interesting and suggests that perhaps Type A behaviors in childhood are temperamental antecedents to the development of workaholism in adulthood (Steinberg, 1985). Finally, in Robinson's (1999) study on work addiction risk and Type A personality, findings showed that individuals with a high risk for addiction to work scored higher on the Type A Self-report Inventory and several subscales of the Jenkins Activity Scale (e.g., hard driving and competitive) than those with a medium or low risk for work addiction.

The Big 5

Costa and McCrae's (1992) five-factor model of personality, also known as the "Big 5" personality traits (i.e., openness to experience, conscientiousness, extraversion, agreeableness, and neuroticism), are by far the most heavily researched personality traits. Openness to experience is associated with being imaginative, non-conforming, intellectual, and willing to consider new ideas. Conscientiousness is associated with persistence, dependability, being well-organized, and high performance. Extraversion is associated with sociability, assertiveness, dominance, ambition, and positive energy. Agreeableness is associated with being cooperative, likeable, and caring. Neuroticism is associated with negative moods, insecurity, depression, and higher levels of stress.

It is not surprising that potential relationships between the Big 5 and workaholism have been investigated in recent years. In fact, Burke, Matthiesen, and Pallesen (2006) stated, "Workaholism may in fact be a lower order trait that is related in a hierarchical way to higher order personality factors. There is some support for the utility of trait and personality theories in explaining workaholism" (p. 1225). Past research has studied the relationship between Big 5 and various work-related constructs that could be viewed as correlates of workaholism (e.g., job performance, Barrick & Mount, 1991; burnout, Bakker, Van Der Zee, Lewig, & Dollard, 2006). However, with the exception of the two studies discussed in the following paragraphs, to date, no studies have examined the relationship between the five-factor model of personality and the construct of workaholism itself.

Burke et al. (2006) examined the link between workaholism and the Big 5, as well as generalized self-efficacy, in a Norwegian sample of nursing home employees. Generalized self-efficacy is associated with feelings of optimism, success, competence, commitment to tasks, and satisfaction with work. Using Spence and Robbins's (1992) workaholic triad, Burke et al. found a positive relationship between extraversion and self-efficacy and work involvement. Furthermore, respondents who scored higher on neuroticism, self-efficacy, and conscientiousness, and lower on openness to experience, also had higher levels of work drive. Finally, participants who were higher on extraversion and self-efficacy were also higher on work enjoyment. In sum, personality factors were significantly related to Spence and Robbins's facets of workaholism, in which extraversion related more so to work involvement and work enjoyment, while neuroticism, openness to experience, and conscientiousness related to work drive (Burke et al., 2006).

Aziz and Tronzo (2011) partially replicated the Burke et al. (2006) study and investigated the relationship between the Big 5 personality traits and workaholism in a sample of American employees from different work settings. Replicating studies is mostly of interest to researchers whose paradigms are limited to field environments, such as organizations (for a detailed discussion, see Schafer 2001). Results showed that personality factors explained a significant amount of variance for each of Spence and Robbins's (1992) workaholism facets, above and beyond personal demographics. Specifically, conscientiousness and agreeableness were positively related to work involvement, while conscientiousness and openness to experience were positively related to work drive. Furthermore, agreeableness, conscientiousness, and openness to experience were positively related to work enjoyment, while neuroticism was negatively related to it.

While the differences are appreciated, some of the findings in the Aziz and Tronzo study (2011) were substantially different from those of the Burke et al. (2006) study (for a detailed comparison between the two studies, see Aziz & Tronzo, 2011). Although these variations could partially be the result of cross-cultural differences, it is important that in future research, participants from the same occupations and across countries are included to see if any personality differences exist. As for practical implications from these studies' findings, it has been recommended that employers not only select people who demonstrate personality traits that can positively influence the organization (e.g., conscientiousness), but also be aware of characteristics that could be harmful to the organization (e.g., neuroticism). Identifying personality traits associated with workaholism allows employers to better forecast workaholic behaviors among potential employees, which aids in the decision-making process when selecting new hires (Barrick & Mount, 1991; Tett et al., 1991). Overall, results of the Burke et al. (2006) and Aziz and Tronzo (2011) studies suggest that workaholism can be explained as a personality trait. These studies serve as the foundation to further examine the link between personality and workaholism.

Personality Characteristics of Workaholism and HWI: Research Findings

We now review findings from studies that have examined personality characteristics of workaholism and HWI. To make comparisons easier, we group these studies based on the measure of workaholism or HWI used, beginning with Spence and Robbins's (1992) WorkBAT, then Robinson's (1999) WART, leading on to Schaufeli et al.'s (2006) two workaholism factors, followed by Mudrack's (2004) two workaholic behavior factors, and, finally, hours worked (excluding those stemming from financial need) as proposed by Snir and Harpaz (2004).

Spence and Robbins's (1992) WorkBAT

Andreassen, Hetland, and Pallesen (2010), in a sample of Norwegian workers from six organizations, studied the relationship of the Big 5 personality traits and Spence and Robbins's (1992) workaholism components (i.e., work involvement, work drive, and work enjoyment). Regression analyses, controlling for personal demographics, work situation factors, and satisfaction of three basic psychological needs at work, revealed the following results. Four out of the five personality traits (not Agreeableness) were positively related to work involvement. Neuroticism and Conscientiousness were positively related to work drive, while Agreeableness was negatively related to it. Extraversion was positively associated with work enjoyment, while Agreeableness was negatively associated with it.

Burke (2000b) investigated the role of personal beliefs and fears and the workaholism types identified by Spence and Robbins (1992). Beliefs and fears are cognitions people develop about their broader environment during socialization. These beliefs and fears result from values communicated to children from parents, friends, school, and the media. Price (1982) identified three beliefs, each associated with a particular fear. The first belief was that one must consistently prove oneself through achievements, or risk the fear of being judged unsuccessful and unworthy. A second belief was that no universal moral principle exists, which is associated with the fear that "good" may not prevail. Price's last belief was that resources, things worth having, were in short supply and associated with the fear that the individual may not get their fair share of these resources. He collected data from 530 women and men MBA graduates working in a variety of organizations and functions. Spence and Robbins's three workaholism types were then compared. Work Addicts and Enthusiastic Addicts scored higher than Work Enthusiasts on two beliefs and fears—no moral principles and striving against others to get scarce resources.

Sharma and Sharma (2011) examined the relationship of the Big 5 with measures of workaholism developed by Schaufeli, Taris, and Bakker (2006). This workaholism measure has two components, working excessively and working compulsively, as well as a combined total score. The data were collected from 145 instructors from two universities in India. Regression analyses, controlling for personal demographics, indicated that both Neuroticism and Conscientiousness had significant and negative relationships with both workaholism components and their composite. These findings are at odds with much of the previously reported conclusions, which could partially be due to the fairly small sample size, very specific job, and non-Western country.

Buelens and Poelmans (2004) examined motivational correlates or antecedents of the three Spence and Robbins (1992) workaholism types. Data were collected from 5,853 full-time Flemish workers in Belgium.

Six motivational scales were included: motivation by salary, by loyalty, by one's own work rhythms, by one's self-development, by responsibility, and by relationships. Enthusiastic Addicts scored higher on motivation by pay; Enthusiastic Addicts and Work Enthusiasts scored higher on motivation by loyalty; Work Enthusiasts and Enthusiastic Addicts scored higher on motivation by self-development; Work Enthusiasts and Enthusiastic Addicts scored higher on motivation by responsibility. Work Addicts, the most negative workaholic type in the sense of having the strongest and most consistent relationship with negative work and well-being outcomes, scored low on all six sources of work motivation. No differences were found among the three workaholism types on motivation by relationships and motivation by one's own work rhythms.

Robinson's (1999) WART

Clark, Lelchook, and Taylor (2010), in a sample of 323 American working students, investigated the relationship of the Big 5 as well as Narcissism, Perfectionism, and both Positive Affect and Negative Affect as dispositional antecedents of workaholism. Narcissism is associated with a grandiose sense of self-importance, boastfulness, and exaggerated accomplishments. Positive Affect is associated with feeling energetic, joyful and excited, whereas Negative Affect is associated with fear, anxiety and anger. Workaholism was measured by Robinson's (1999) WART and included three factors (Impatience, Compulsion to Work, Polychronic Control) as well as a total score. Regression analyses were undertaken in which the Big 5 were entered first, followed by the measures of Narcissism, Perfectionism, and Positive and Negative Affect. Considering the Big 5 first, Neuroticism was positively related to all four workaholism indicators, while Agreeableness was negatively related to Compulsion to Work. Regarding the four additional antecedents, Narcissism was positively related to Compulsion to Work, Impatience, and the total WART score; Perfectionism was positively related with the three WART factors and the total WART score; and Negative Affect was positively related to Impatience, Compulsion to Work, and the total WART score. Positive Affect was independent of the four WART-based measures of workaholism. It is of note that others have found an association between Perfectionism and Spence and Robbins's three facets of workaholism and three workaholic types (Spence & Robbins, 1992; Burke, 1999).

Type A behavior (Friedman & Rosenman, 1974) is a constellation of attitudes and behaviors associated with achievement-striving. Robinson (1998) reported that Type A behavior scores were positively associated with scores on the WART. Zhdanova, Allison, Pui, and Clark (2006) reviewed the scarce but emerging literature on workaholism and concluded that Type A behavior and perfectionism served as predispositional antecedents.

Schaufeli's (2006) Two Workaholism Factors

Del Libano, Llorens, Salanova, and Schaufeli (2012) considered self-efficacy as a predictor of both positive and negative work outcomes. In a sample of 386 administrative staff at a Spanish university (65 percent female), self-efficacy, a personality characteristic, was positively related to working excessively, but unrelated to working compulsively.

Mudrack's (2004) Two Workaholic Behavior Factors

Mudrack (2004), in a U.S. sample of 278 women and men working full time, explored job involvement and obsessive-compulsive personality traits as predictors of two workaholic behavior tendencies: engaging in non-required work and efforts to control the work of others. Six traits were included in the measure of obsessive-compulsive personality: obstinacy, orderliness, parsimony, perseverance, rigidity, and superego. First, job involvement was positively correlated with five of the six obsessive-compulsive personality traits: orderliness, parsimony, persistence, rigidity, and superego. Second, undertaking non-required work was also positively correlated with four of the six obsessive-compulsive personality traits: orderliness, parsimony, perseverance, and superego, and negatively correlated with rigidity. Third, efforts to control the work of others were positively correlated with two of the six obsessive-compulsive personality traits: obstinacy and superego. Fourth, dividing the sample into high and low scores on the six obsessive-compulsive personality traits showed that correlations between job involvement and engaging in non-required work were positive for five of the six obsessive-compulsive traits among high scorers. On the other hand, only one out of the six correlations was statistically significant among those scoring low on the six obsessive-compulsive behavior traits.

Snir and Harpaz's (2004) Hours Worked

Snir and Harpaz (2004) examined attitudinal antecedents of workaholism. Workaholism was measured by hours worked/devoted to work and thinking about work not associated with external requirements or necessities. Data were collected from 942 Israeli workers. Individuals with a lower level of family centrality worked more hours, but levels of leisure centrality had no effects on hours worked.

Ng and Feldman (2008), employing meta-analytic techniques, used a social identity perspective to examine individual level antecedents of hours worked. They found support for the following: first, having higher levels of work centrality was associated with working more hours; and second, there was only weak and inconsistent support for the relationship between level of family centrality and hours worked.

Conclusions

It is possible to draw some meaningful conclusions based on this limited body of research. First, there is general support for the association between stable personality characteristics with both workaholism (measured in various ways) and HWI. Second, our understanding of personality characteristics (personality traits as well as attitudes) of workaholism and HWI would be enhanced not only by focusing on one or two measures of workaholism in future studies, but also by replicating earlier work by including the same personality measures.

As far as future research on this topic, work characteristics, in particular job profession, should be examined to investigate the relationship between personality traits with both workaholism and HWI. Perhaps certain personality types are linked to specific professions in that there are occupations inherently consistent with workaholics (e.g., surgeons, lawyers; Ng et al., 2007). Furthermore, future studies could include participants from the same occupations but across countries to see if any personality differences exist.

References

American Psychiatric Association. (2013). *Diagnostic and statistical manual of mental disorders* (5th ed.). Washington, DC: Author.

Andreassen, C. S., Hetland, J., & Pallesen, S. (2010). The relationship between workaholism, basic needs satisfaction at work and personality. *European Journal of Personality, 24,* 3–17.

Aziz, S., & Tronzo, C. L. (2011). Exploring the relationship between workaholism facets and personality traits: A replication in American workforce. *Psychological Record, 61,* 269–286.

Aziz, S., & Zickar, M. J. (2006). A cluster analysis investigation of workaholism as a syndrome. *Journal of Occupational Health Psychology, 11,* 52–62.

Aziz, S., Wuensch, K. L., & Brandon, H. R. (2010). A comparison among worker types using a composites approach and median splits. *The Psychological Record, 60,* 627–642.

Aziz, S., Adkins, C. T., Walker, A. G., & Wuensch, K. L. (2010). Workaholism and work–life imbalance: Does cultural origin influence the relationship? *International Journal of Psychology, 45,* 72–79.

Bakker, A. B., Van Der Zee, K. I., Lewig, K. A., & Dollard, M. F. (2006). The relationship between the big five personality factors and burnout: A study among volunteer counselors. *The Journal of Social Psychology, 146,* 31–50.

Barrick, M. R., & Mount, M. K. (1991). The big five personality dimensions and job performance: A meta-analysis. *Personnel Psychology, 44,* 1–26.

Bonebright, C. A., Clay, D. L., & Ankenmann, R. D. (2000). The relationship of workaholism with work–life conflict, life satisfaction, and purpose in life. *Journal of Counseling Psychology, 47,* 469–477.

Brady, B. R., Vodanovich, S. J., & Rotunda, R. (2008). The impact of workaholism on work–family conflict, job satisfaction, and perception of leisure activities. *The Psychologist-Manager Journal, 11,* 241–263.

Buelens, M., & Poelmans, S. A. Y. (2004). Enriching the Spence and Robbins' typology of workaholism: Demographics, motivational and organizational correlates. *Journal of Organizational Change Management, 17,* 440–458.

Burke, R. J. (1999). Workaholism in organizations: Measurement validation and replication. *International Journal of Stress Management, 6,* 45–55.

Burke, R. J. (2000a). Workaholism in organizations: Psychological and physical well-being consequences. *Stress & Medicine, 16,* 11–16.

Burke. R. J. (2000b). Workaholism in organizations: The role of personal beliefs and fears. *Anxiety, Stress, and Coping, 13,* 53–64.

Burke, R. J. (2011). Show me the money. In R. J. Burke, E. C. Tomlinson, & C. L. Cooper (eds.) *Crime and corruption in organizations: Why it occurs and what to do about it.* Surrey, UK: Gower Publishing.

Burke, R. J., & Cooper, C. L. (2008). *The long work hours culture: Causes, consequences, and choices.* Bingley, UK: Emerald Group Publishing Limited.

Burke, R. J., & Fiksenbaum, L. (2009a). Work motivations, satisfactions, and health among managers: Passion versus addiction. *Cross-Cultural Research, 43,* 349–365.

Burke, R. J., & Fiksenbaum, L. (2009b). Work motivations, work outcomes, and health: Passion versus addiction. *Journal of Business Ethics, 84,* 257–263.

Clark, M. A., Lelchook, A. M., & Taylor, M. L. (2010). Beyond the big five: How narcissism, perfectionism, and dispositional affect relate to workaholism. *Personality and Individual Differences, 48,* 786–791.

Costa, P. T., & McCrae, R. R. (1992). Normal personality assessment in clinical practice: The NEO Personality Inventory. *Psychological Assessment, 4,* 5–13.

Del Libano, M. D., Llorens, S. I., Salanova, M., & Schaufeli, W. B. (2012). About the dark and bright sides of self-efficacy: Workaholism and work engagement. *Spanish Journal of Psychology, 15,* 688–701.

Ersoy-Kart, M. (2005). Reliability and validity of the Workaholism Battery (Work-BAT): Turkish Form. *Social Behavior and Personality, 33,* 609–618.

Eysenck, H. J. (1997). Addiction, personality, and motivation. *Human Psychopharmacology: Clinical and Experimental, 12,* S79–S87.

Fassel, D. (1990). *Working ourselves to death.* San Francisco, CA: Harper-Collins.

Fisher, G. G., Bulgar, C. A., & Smith, C. S. (2009). Beyond work and family: A measure of work/nonwork interference and enhancement. *Journal of Occupational Health Psychology, 14,* 441–456.

Flowers, C. P., & Robinson, B. (2002). A structural and discriminant analysis of the Work Addiction Risk Test. *Educational and Psychological Measurement, 62,* 517–526.

Friedman, M., & Rosenman, R. H. (1974). *Type A behavior and your heart.* New York: Alfred Knopf.

Killinger, B. (1991). *Workaholics: The respectable addicts.* New York: Simon & Schuster.

Liang, Y. W., & Chu, C. M. (2009). Personality traits and personal and organizational inducements: Antecedents of workaholism. *Social Behavior and Personality, 37*, 645–660.

Machlowitz, M. M. (1980). *Workaholics: Living with them, working with them.* Reading, MA: Addison-Wesley.

McMillan, L. H. W., Brady, E. C., O'Driscoll, M. P., & Marsh, N. (2002). A multifaceted validation study of Spence and Robbins' (1992) Workaholism Battery. *Journal of Occupational and Organizational Psychology, 75*, 357–368.

Mosier, S. K. (1983). Workaholics: An analysis of their stress, success and priorities. Unpublished Master's thesis, University of Texas at Austin.

Mudrack, P. E. (2004). Job involvement, obsessive-compulsive personality traits, and workaholic behavioral tendencies. *Journal of Organizational Change Management, 17*, 490–508.

Naughton, T. J. (1987). A conceptual view of workaholism and implications for career counseling and research. *The Career Development Quarterly, 35*, 180–187

Ng, T. W. H., & Feldman, D. C. (2008). Long work hours: A social identity perspective on meta-analysis data. *Journal of Organizational Behavior, 29*, 853–880.

Ng, T. W. H., Sorensen, K. L., & Feldman, D. C. (2007). Dimensions, antecedents, and consequences of workaholism: A conceptual integration and extension. *Journal of Organizational Behavior, 28*, 111–136.

Oates, W. (1971). *Confessions of a workaholic: The facts about work addiction.* New York, NY: World Publishing.

Piotrowski, C., & Vodanovich, S. J. (2006). The interface between workaholism and work–family conflict: A review and conceptual framework. *Organization Development Journal, 24*, 84–92.

Porter, G. (1996). Organizational impact of workaholism: Suggestions for researching the negative outcomes of excessive work. *Journal of Occupational Health Psychology, 1*, 70–84.

Robinson, B. E. (1996). The psychosocial and familial dimensions of work addiction: Preliminary perspectives and hypotheses. *Journal of Counseling and Development, 74*, 447–452.

Robinson, B. E. (1999). The Work Addiction Risk Test: Development of a tentative measure of workaholism. *Perceptual and Motor Skills, 88*, 199–210.

Robinson, B. E. (2007). *Chained to the desk: A guidebook for workaholics, their partners and children, and the clinicians who treat them* (2nd ed.). New York: New York University Press.

Schafer, W. D. (2001). Replication: A design principle for field research. *Practical Assessment, Research & Evaluation, 15.*

Schaufeli, W. B., Taris, T. W., & Bakker, A. (2006). *Dr. Jekyll or Mr. Hyde? On the differences between work engagement and workaholism.* In R. J. Burke (Ed.), Research companion to working time and work addiction (pp. 193–217). Cheltenham: Edward Elgar.

Schaufeli, W. B., Bakker, A. B., van der Heijden, F. M. M. A, & Prins, J. T. (2009). Workaholism among medical residents: It is the combination of working excessively and compulsively that counts. *International Journal of Stress Management, 16*, 249–272.

Scott, K. S., Moore, K. S., & Miceli, M. P. (1997). An exploration of the meaning and consequences of workaholism. *Human Relations, 50,* 287–314.

Sharma, J., & Sharma, P. (2011). Workaholism and its correlates: A study of academicians. *International Journal of Management and Business Research, 1,* 151–160

Snir, R., & Harpaz, I. (2004). Attitudinal and demographic antecedents of workaholism. *Journal of Organizational Change Management, 17,* 520–536.

Snir, R., & Harpaz, I. (2012). Beyond workaholism: Towards a general model of heavy work investment. *Human Resource Management Review, 22,* 232–243.

Spence J. T., & Robbins, A. S (1992). Workaholism: Definition, measurement, and preliminary results. *Journal of Personality Assessment, 58,* 160–178.

Steinberg, L. (1985). Early temperamental antecedents of adult Type A behaviors. *Developmental Psychology, 21,* 1171–1180.

Sussman, S. (2012). Workaholism: A review. *Journal of Addiction Research and Therapy, 16,* 1–10.

Taris, T. W., Schaufeli, W. B., & Verhoeven, L. C. (2005). Workaholism in the Netherlands: Measurement and implications for job strain and work–nonwork conflict. *Applied Psychology: An International Review, 54,* 37–60.

Tett, R. P., Jackson, D. N., & Rothstein, M. (1991). Personality measures as predictors of job performance: A meta-analytic review. *Personnel Psychology, 44,* 703–742.

Vodanovich, S. J., & Piotrowski, C. (2006). Workaholism: A critical but neglected factor in O.D. *Organization Development Journal, 24,* 55–60.

Waddell, J. R. (1993). The grindstone. *Supervision, 26,* 11–13.

Zhdanova, L., Allison, L. K., Pui, S. Y., & Clark, M. A. (2006). A meta-analysis of workaholism antecedents and outcomes. Presented at the SIOP Annual Conference in Dallas, TX.

3

HEAVY WORK INVESTMENT

The Role of Passion

Nathalie Houlfort, Robert J. Vallerand, and Andréanne Laframboise

Why would someone invest vast amounts of time and energy in their work when there are so many other areas of life where that time and energy can be spent? Some might say they invest heavily in their work to increase their income, because it is expected of them, or because the nature of their job requires a heavy work investment (HWI). These types of commitment to work are often situational and diminish when the demands of the situation are no longer present. Still, Snir and Harpaz (2012) suggest that predictors that are more internal, such as addiction to work and passion for work, may fuel a more dispositional form of HWI. They propose two subtypes of dispositional HWI: workaholism and work-devotion. The former emerges from an addiction to work (Snir & Harpaz, 2012), whereas work-devotion is "an expression of passion for work" (Snir & Harpaz, 2012, p. 5). Workaholism is notorious for its negative effects on workers. For instance, workaholism is a predictor for burnout (Schaufeli, Taris, & van Rhenen, 2008) and work–life conflict (Bonebright, Clay, & Ankenmann, 2000). The question thus arises, is HWI less damaging when it is fuelled by passion for the work? We propose that when HWI is nurtured by passion, the outcomes the worker experiences may be either positive or negative, or both. It all depends on the type of passion.

This chapter presents passion as a driver of HWI. The first section presents a history of the concept of passion for work, a comparison between passion and other work-related concepts, as well as the initial studies leading to the development of the Dualistic Model of Passion. The second section presents the major empirical studies that have examined the outcomes of passion for work, followed by the studies that have investigated the determinants of passion for work. Finally, directions for future research are proposed.

A History of the Concept of Passion

Over the centuries, philosophers have devoted considerable thought to the concept of passion. Although there have been some exceptions (e.g., Kant, 1724–1804), most viewed passion more or less as we see emotions today. Two positions have emerged (see Rony, 1990). The first posits that passion entails a loss of reason and control. In line with the etymology of the word (from the Latin *passio,* meaning suffering), people afflicted with passion are seen as experiencing a kind of suffering, as if they were slaves to their passion, because it comes to control them. For instance, for Plato (427–348 BC), passion was "bad" for people because it entailed a state typically beyond one's control. Plato placed passion and reason in opposition to each other, asserting that passion could always prevail over reason and that people should thus be wary of their passions. Similarly, Spinoza (1632–1677) compared passion to a form of "bondage" to be avoided. In accordance with the Greek philosophers, Spinoza believed that reason provided the means of gaining control over such "bondage." Once reason prevailed, however, Spinoza held that passion would subside: the two could not coexist.

The second perspective presents passion in a more positive light. For instance, several of the Romantics suggested that people should seek their passions, not avoid them. Some, such as French philosopher Helvetius (1715–71), even went so far as to posit that passions can be cultivated and that such cultivation is key to intelligence: "One becomes stupid as soon as one ceases to be passionate." Similarly, Hegel (1770–1831) argued that passions are necessary to reach the highest levels of achievement. Likewise, Diderot (1713–84) held that passions are the source of much pleasure and accomplishment, positing that they are adaptive to the extent that they were in harmony among themselves (see Diderot, 1746/1998). Finally, the existentialist Kierkegaard (1813–55) wrote, "It is impossible to exist without passion, unless we understand the word 'exist' in the loose sense of a so-called existence." Thus, this second view of passion portrays passion more favorably, in that individuals may experience some adaptive outcomes when they are in control of their passions. The contrast between these two philosophical positions highlights the duality of passion: it can be seen as either adaptive or maladaptive.

Toward the end of the 19th century and the turn of the 20th century, the word "passion" disappeared from the academic literature in the United States and elsewhere. While it had been in regular use just a few years earlier in philosophical discourse, it disappeared from experimental philosophy, which would later become the field of psychology. Instead, the vast majority of psychologists followed Charles Darwin (1872) and William James (1884) in the study of "emotions" as they are defined today. Two exceptions were the French psychologists Théodule-Armand Ribot and

André Joussain. Ribot (1907) continued the work of Kant in proposing that passions are not synonymous with emotions. Indeed, Ribot proposed that the two are opposing constructs. Whereas emotions are typically seen as intense and short-lived, Ribot saw passions as less intense, highly stable, and more intellectual than affective in nature. According to Ribot, there are three main characteristics of passion: the "fixed" idea (a clear and persistent goal with regard to an object or activity), its duration (from a few months to a lifetime), and its intensity (involving some form of effort made toward the goal or objective). For his part, Joussain (1928) coined the elegant phrase: "Emotion is only a temporary state of mind; passion is a way of life" (p. 21). In line with Diderot, Joussain posited that passions should not be avoided as long as they are in harmony with each other. This notion was echoed by the American social and educational psychologist, John Dewey (1930):

> The conclusion is not that the emotional, passionate phase of action can be or should be eliminated in behalf of bloodless reason. More passions, not fewer, is the answer. [. . .] Rationality, once more, is not a force to evoke against impulse and habit. It is the attainment of a working *harmony* among diverse desires.
> (pp. 195–196; italics added by the authors)

Unfortunately, Ribot, Joussain, and Dewey did not put their perspectives on passion to the test empirically, so they have had little influence on psychology subsequently. The few psychologists who have examined the concept of passion have underscored its motivational aspect. For instance, some authors have proposed that people will spend large amounts of time and effort in order to reach their passionately held goals (see Frijda, Mesquita, Sonnemans, & Van Goozen, 1991). The first empirical studies on passion were conducted years later in research on close relationships. Hatfield and Walster (1978), for instance, studied passionate love. Here, the object of one's passion is another person. In this case, passion is conceptualized as an intense emotion associated with moments of exaltation and transcendence (see also, Baumeister & Bratslavsky, 1999; Sternberg, 1986). Once again, passion is seen as dysfunctional because it leads to some emotional suffering, especially when love is unrequited. Hatfield and Rapson (1993) posit that companionate love (a non-passionate and more cerebral form of love) is to be preferred because it is more functional.

Research on passion in the workplace has focused largely on passion as love for one's work. For instance, Baum and his colleagues (Baum & Locke, 2004; Baum, Locke, & Smith, 2001), Cardon (2008; Cardon, Wincent, Singh, & Drnovsek, 2009), as well as Lam and Pertulla (2008) define passion as simply love for one's work. Although we agree that love for the activity (work, in this case) is an important feature of passion, it is not the only key element. As will be seen below, other features of passion should be taken into consideration as well. We posit that it is crucial to distinguish between different types of passion so as to account for its inherent duality as underscored by philosophers.

A Dualistic Model of Passion

In the first conceptual analysis of passion for life activities, Vallerand et al. (2003; see also Vallerand & Houlfort, 2003) proposed the Dualistic Model of Passion. Passion is defined as a strong inclination toward a self-defining activity that one loves, finds important and meaningful, and in which one invests a significant amount of time and energy. Thus, passion is much more than motivation to do something that one loves. It is love for something that one values highly, is committed to and engages in on a regular basis. In addition, the activity one is passionate about becomes so important that it represents a central feature of one's identity. Clearly, work is central to our lives. We spend more than half our waking life at work (Vallerand & Houlfort, 2003). We come to value it deeply and at some point, our work becomes part of our identity. To the extent that we love what we do, that we value it and find it meaningful, our work will be part of our identity and we are likely to develop a passion for it.

The Dualistic Model of Passion further posits that there are two types of passion for an activity—obsessive and harmonious—that can be distinguished in terms of how the activity has been internalized into one's identity. In line with Self-Determination Theory (Deci & Ryan, 1985, 2000), the activity that one is passionate about can be internalized either through an autonomous internalization process or through a controlled internalization process, leading to two types of passion.

Harmonious passion results from autonomous internalization of the activity into the person's identity and self. Such internalization occurs when individuals have freely accepted that the activity is important to them, without any contingencies attached to it. This type of internalization stems from the intrinsic and integrative tendencies of the self (Deci & Ryan, 2000; Ryan & Deci, 2003) and engenders a sense of volition and personal endorsement to pursue the activity. With harmonious passion, individuals freely choose to engage in the activity they love. The activity occupies an important but not overpowering place in the person's identity and is in harmony with other aspects of the person's life. In other words, with harmonious passion, the authentic integrating self (Deci & Ryan, 2000) is at play, allowing the person to fully partake in the activity they are passionate about in a non-defensive (Hodgins & Knee, 2002) and mindful (Brown & Ryan, 2003) manner that is conducive to positive experiences. Consequently, people who have a harmonious passion for an activity should be able to fully focus on the task at hand and experience positive outcomes both during task engagement (e.g., positive affect, concentration, flow etc.) and after task engagement (general positive affect, satisfaction etc.). Thus, there should be little or no conflict between the activity the person is passionate about and their other life activities. Furthermore, when prevented from engaging in that activity, people who have harmonious passion should be able to adapt well to the situation and focus their attention and energy on other tasks that need to be done. Finally, with harmonious passion, the person is in control of the activity and can decide when and when not to engage in it. For instance, if a university professor has a predominantly harmonious passion for his academic work, when faced with the choice of continuing to work on a book he is writing or going home for dinner and family activities, the professor can readily go home without thinking about the missed opportunity to write some more. Thus, when the passion for the activity is harmonious, behavioral engagement in that activity is flexible.

Conversely, obsessive passion results from controlled internalization of the activity into one's identity and self. Controlled internalization originates from intra- and/or inter-personal pressure, typically because certain contingencies are attached to the activity, such as feelings of social acceptance or self-esteem (Lafrenière, Bélanger, Vallerand, & Sedikides, 2011; Mageau, Carpentier, & Vallerand, 2011), or because the sense of excitement derived from engaging in the activity is uncontrollable. At best, controlled internalization also leads to only partial internalization of the values and regulations associated with the activity into the self; at worst, they are internalized into the person's identity, but remain completely apart from the integrating self (Deci & Ryan, 2000). Consequently, people with an obsessive passion can find themselves in the position of experiencing an uncontrollable urge to engage in the activity they love. They cannot stop themselves from doing so. This places them at risk of experiencing conflicts and other negative affective, cognitive, and behavioral consequences during and after engaging in the activity. Returning to our example of the university professor writing his book, if he has an obsessive passion for his academic work instead of a harmonious one, he might not be able to stop working and may be late getting home for dinner and family activities. His obsessive passion takes over and he feels that he cannot resist the urge to pursue the writing. As he continues writing, however, he might feel upset with himself for writing instead of being at home. He might therefore have difficulty concentrating on the task at hand (writing) and he may not experience as much positive affect and flow from the act of writing as might otherwise be the case. It is thus proposed that individuals with obsessive passion come to exhibit dogged persistence with regard to the activity, as oftentimes they cannot help but engage in the activity they are passionate about. Obsessive passion for work can also lead to frustration and rumination about that work when prevented from engaging in it. Thus, if our professor somehow manages to leave the office to be on time for the family dinner, he still may end up suffering because it is difficult for him to forget about the lost opportunity of working on the ever-important book.

While it may be tempting to conclude that obsessive passion entails a higher level of passion than harmonious passion, this is not the case. Both types of passion reflect an equal level of intensity. People with a predominantly harmonious passion toward their work are thus no less passionate about it than people with a predominantly obsessive passion. The difference between the two types does not lie in the level of one's passion but rather in its quality. In line with the duality of passion seen previously, the two types of passion are qualitatively different, with harmonious passion leading one to experience a more adaptive form of passion that is in harmony with the other elements of the self and one's life and obsessive passion to a more conflicted and less adaptive form of passionate involvement.

Passion and Other Concepts

It might be useful to compare the construct of passion with other concepts used in organizational research. Although organizational scientists have addressed many concepts (see Vallerand, 2014 for a more comprehensive discussion), we will examine only the most relevant here, namely affective commitment (Meyer & Allen, 1997) and workaholism (e.g., Bonebright et al., 2000; Spence & Robins, 1992). Affective commitment is defined by Meyer and Allen (1997) as an emotional attachment to one's organization and a high level of involvement within the organization. In this definition, the authors do not refer to the love individuals have for their work, nor to the time and energy that they put into that work. Similarly, workaholism shares one conceptual aspect with the definition of passion: the time and energy that one puts into work. However, workaholism does not necessarily involve an affective component regarding the work itself (Scott, Moore, & Miceli, 1997; Spence & Robins, 1992), whereas passion for work does: passionate workers love their job (Vallerand et al., 2003; Vallerand & Houlfort, 2003). In addition, it is thought that workaholics engage in the same behavioral patterns in a variety of work settings (Scott et al., 1997), whereas passionate workers will only do so in work areas they feel passionate about. Thus, although both employees with an affective commitment toward their organization and those who exhibit workaholism are certainly heavily invested in their work (Harpaz & Snir, 2003; Spence & Robins, 1992), they do not necessarily experience passion for their work.

Passion is often discussed in relation to intrinsic and extrinsic motivation. Intrinsic motivation shares some conceptual similarities with passion, as both involve being interested in and liking (or loving) the activity. However, intrinsically motivated activities are typically not seen as being internalized in the person's identity and are best seen as emerging over the short term (Koestner & Losier, 2002). Furthermore, intrinsic motivation does not address the duality of passion, in which both adaptive and maladaptive outcomes can result from the person's love for an activity. Intrinsic motivation is hypothesized to lead to only adaptive outcomes (Deci & Ryan, 2000). On the other hand, when a person is extrinsically motivated, they do not engage in the activity out of enjoyment of the activity itself, but rather for other reasons such as external or internal pressure. Therefore, although some forms of extrinsic motivation, such as identified and integrated regulation, entail some internalization into the self of an activity that one *does not like*, a fundamental difference between extrinsic motivation and passion is the person's relative lack of liking for the activity. Thus, the concepts of integrated regulation and passion are very different because of the fundamental teleological distinction between them. The goals sought in the two constructs are completely different. With passion, one engages in the activity out of love for that activity. With integrated regulation, one does not engage in the activity out of love, but rather due to an extrinsic motivation even if there is a high level of autonomy involved. Thus, although both constructs involve internalization, the basis for that internalization differs. In one case, it is based in a profound love for the activity; in the other, it is based in an autonomous valuing of an activity that one does not intrinsically love.

Empirical research supports these distinctions between passion, intrinsic motivation, and the different types of extrinsic motivation (external, introjected, and identified regulation). Specifically, passion and the three types of extrinsic motivation are only moderately correlated, at best (Vallerand et al., 2003, Study 2). Further, controlling for intrinsic and extrinsic motivation does not change the role of harmonious and obsessive passion in the prediction of outcomes such as positive and negative affect (Bélanger, Lafrenière, Vallerand, & Kruglanski, 2013a, Study 4; Houlfort, Philippe, Vallerand, & Ménard, 2014; Vallerand et al., 2003, Study 2).

Initial Research on the Concept of Passion

As mentioned previously, the first empirical paper examining passion for activities was that of Vallerand et al. (2003). That article had three major goals: to determine the prevalence of passion for an activity in one's life, to develop a Passion Scale, and to test the validity of some of the elements of the passion constructs. In the initial study (Vallerand et al., 2003, Study 1), over 500 university students completed the Passion

Scale with respect to an activity that they loved and valued, and in which they invested time and energy (i.e., the criteria of the definition of passion), as well as other scales allowing to test predictions derived from the Dualistic Model of Passion. The participants reported being passionate about a wide variety of activities—ranging from physical activities and sports to watching movies, from playing a musical instrument to reading—and reported engaging in one specific activity for an average of 8.5 hours per week over an average period of almost six years. Of importance regarding the first goal of this study, 84 percent of the participants indicated that they had at least a moderate level of passion for a given activity in their lives, scoring at least four out of seven on an item asking whether their favorite activity was a "passion" for them. In a similar vein, a subsequent study (Philippe, Vallerand, & Lavigne, 2009) with over 750 participants ranging in age from 18 to 100 and using a more stringent criterion for passion (i.e., scoring a mean of five out of seven on items addressing the three criteria of passion seen previously) revealed that 75 percent of participants had a high level of passion for an activity in their life. It would thus appear that—at least in Quebec, Canada—the prevalence of passion is rather high and is not the exclusive province of the happy few (see also Liu, Chen, & Yao, 2011, and Stenseng, 2008 for similar results in other countries).

What is the situation in the workplace? Surprisingly, initial research on passion for work has yielded very similar findings. In a survey of workers such as teachers, managers, and technicians, Vallerand and Houlfort (2003) found that 77 percent exhibited at least a moderate level of passion for their work. Subsequent research has found that the prevalence of passion for one's work varies from over 90 percent among teachers (Carbonneau, Vallerand, Fernet, & Guay, 2008) to 78 percent among managers, professionals, and white-collar workers (Houlfort, Vallerand, & Koestner, 2013). Thus, while only a few types of jobs have been examined to date, the percentage of workers who are passionate about their job is typically quite high. One explanation may lie in the fact that, for most people, their job represents a personal choice that is, at least in part, in line with their identity and interests. However, thus far only a limited number of work activities have been assessed for their inherent level of passion and additional research is clearly needed on this issue.

The second goal of the initial paper by Vallerand et al. (2003, Study 1) was to develop the Passion Scale. The scale consists of two subscales of six items each, reflecting obsessive (e.g., "I almost have an obsessive feeling toward this activity") and harmonious passion (e.g., "This activity is in harmony with other activities in my life"). The authors conducted exploratory and confirmatory factor analyses that supported the presence of two factors corresponding to the two types of passion. The factor validity of the Passion Scale with respect to a variety of activities, including work, has since been replicated in over 15 studies (e.g., Carbonneau et al., 2008; Fernet, Lavigne, Vallerand, & Austin, in press; Vallerand & Houlfort, 2003). Furthermore, internal consistency analyses have shown that both subscales are reliable (typically, $\alpha \geq .75$). Finally, the test-retest correlations, measured over periods ranging from four to six weeks, revealed moderately high stability values (Rousseau, Vallerand, Ratelle, Mageau, & Provencher, 2002). More recently, using archival data from over 3,500 participants, Marsh et al. (2013) have shown that the Passion Scale is invariant over gender, language (English and French), and five types of activities (leisure, sport, social, work, and educational). Thus, overall, the factorial validity and reliability of the scale is well established.

Finally, with respect to their third purpose, the authors of the initial paper (Vallerand et al., 2003) found that the partial correlations (controlling for the correlation between the two types of passion) revealed that both harmonious and obsessive passions were positively associated with the passion criteria, thereby providing support for the definition of passion. These findings were replicated by Marsh et al. (2013). Thus, both types of passion were positively correlated with loving, valuing, and devoting time and energy to the activity; with perceiving the activity as being part of one's identity; and with perceiving it as a "passion." These findings support the view that both harmonious and obsessive passions are indeed "passions," as each reflects the definition of the passion construct. It should be emphasized that, in both studies, while both types of passion were similarly correlated to the criteria of the definition of passion, they were nevertheless *differentially* related to outcomes. For example, harmonious passion was positively correlated to life satisfaction whereas obsessive passion was unrelated to it (Marsh et al., 2013). Conversely, obsessive passion for an activity was positively related, and harmonious passion unrelated, to a measure of conflict between that activity and other life interests. These findings have also been replicated in the workplace (see Vallerand & Houlfort, 2003; Vallerand, Houlfort, & Forest, in press).

In sum, initial research provided support for the validity of the concepts of harmonious and obsessive passion as well as that of the Passion Scale. Since the initial research (Vallerand et al., 2003; Vallerand & Houlfort, 2003), over 100 studies have been conducted on the role of passion in a host of outcomes experienced in the context of various activities, including work (see Vallerand, 2010, 2014). Below, we focus on research on passion conducted in the workplace that is relevant to heavy work investment (see Figure 3.1).

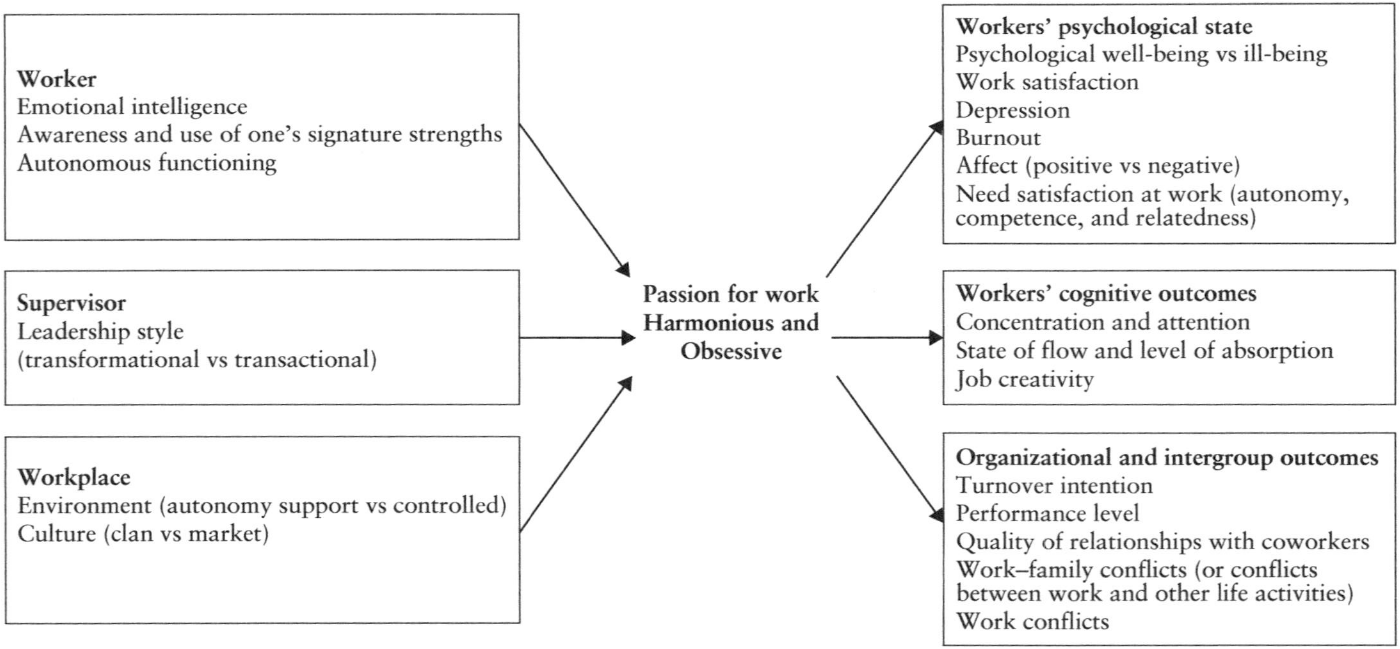

Figure 3.1 Predictors and outcomes of passion for work

Passion for Work and Its Outcomes

Numerous studies have found that psychological well-being and ill-being are both predicted by passion. Workers with a harmonious passion for their work experience greater psychological well-being, higher work satisfaction, less depression, and less ill-being; in contrast, obsessive passion for work was either unrelated or negatively related to psychological well-being, and was linked to greater ill-being, higher levels of psychological distress, and burnout (Carbonneau et al., 2008; Forest, Mageau, Sarrazin, & Morin, 2011; Houlfort, Vallerand, & Koestner, 2012; Houlfort et al., 2014; Lavigne, Forest, & Crevier-Braud, in press; Rousseau & Vallerand, 2008; Vallerand & Houlfort, 2003; Vallerand, Paquet, Philippe, & Charest, 2010). Hence, it appears that harmonious passion for one's work fosters more adaptive outcomes by promoting psychological well-being and inhibiting ill-being, while obsessive passion leads to less adaptive outcomes.

Recently, researchers have found various personal situational factors that mediate the relationship between passion and psychological well-being and ill-being. Houlfort and colleagues (2012) showed that harmonious passion for work seems to favor positive affective experiences, which, in turn, promote greater psychological well-being over a six-month period. However, obsessive passion towards work appears to limit the experience of positive affect, leading to greater ill-being and less well-being. In addition, feelings of being autonomous, competent, and connected to one's coworkers were found to mediate the relationship between harmonious passion and psychological well-being (Forest et al., 2011). Lavigne and colleagues' findings (in press, Study 2) also revealed that the experience of flow predicted by a harmonious passion for work curbs the development of burnout over time. Finally, Vallerand and colleagues (2010) found that psychological conflicts (i.e., between work and other life activities) and work satisfaction mediated the relationship between passion and burnout.

The Dualistic Model of Passion postulates that workers with harmonious passion are likely to participate in a more open-minded and attentive manner, whereas those with obsessive passion are likely to have more limited concentration, driven by outcomes or by a defensive orientation. Recent research supports this hypothesis. For example, workers from various workplaces and countries who report having a harmonious passion for their work also reported experiencing greater concentration and attention, whereas no such relationship was found for obsessive passion (Forest et al., 2011; Ho, Wong, & Lee, 2011). Another cognitive process influenced by passion for work is flow, the experience of being completely immersed in an activity (Csikszentmihalyi, Rathunde, & Whalen, 1993). Recent studies have revealed that, compared to workers with obsessive passion, those with harmonious passion not only experienced higher levels of flow in their work, but also exhibited a significant increase over a six-month period (Forest et al., 2011; Lavigne et al., in press, Studies 1 and 2). Finally, Liu and colleagues (2011) found that greater job creativity was linked to harmonious passion for work.

According to the Dualistic Model of Passion, a person's passion for work impacts their engagement in the work itself and other life activities. Recent studies showed that harmonious passion is positively related to decreased work–family conflicts, while obsessive passion is positively linked to work-related conflicts (Vallerand et al., 2010) and conflicts between work and leisure physical activities (Caudroit, Boiché, Stephan, Le Scanff, & Trouilloud, 2011). Vallerand and colleagues (2010) also reported that the two types of passion lead to different outcomes among nurses in two cultural settings (France and Quebec). Harmonious passion for their work activity was found to reduce burnout due to the nurses' ability to experience some affective rewards during task engagement (e.g., greater work satisfaction) and to fully disengage from the activity afterwards, which, in turn, created less psychological conflict. In contrast, obsessive passion appears to promote burnout and conflicts in other life activities due to a more rigid persistence in continuing the work they are passionate about.

Turnover intention refers to a worker's anticipation of continued employment and their commitment to their work and organization. When such intentions are followed by actions (i.e., quitting their job), it can translate to considerable costs for the organization (Waldman, Kelly, Arora, & Smith, 2004). Therefore, the personal feelings employees have for their work can be vital in preventing actual turnover (Griffeth, Hom, & Gaertner, 2000; Tett & Meyer, 1993). Houlfort and colleagues (in press) investigated the role of passion for work in turnover intention among teachers. Teachers with a harmonious passion reported lower turnover intentions, while those with an obsessive passion reported greater turnover intentions. The authors also examined longitudinal affect over a two-year period and found that the relationship between obsessive passion and turnover intentions was mediated by depression. Suffering from depression might generate collateral consequences at work such as diminished performance, administrative sanctions, and so on, all of which have an adverse effect on the ego. For obsessively passionate workers, passion helps in protecting the ego. When depression is experienced with threats to the ego, obsessively passionate workers may intend to leave their job in order to protect themselves. More research is definitely needed on this issue.

Recent studies conducted by Philippe, Vallerand, Houlfort, Lavigne, and Donahue (2010) addressed the role of passion for work in relationships in the workplace. The findings showed that teachers and their supervisors who exhibited harmonious passion for their work experienced greater positive emotions, which in turn predicted better relationships. However, obsessive passion did not influence work relationships or positive affect at work (Study 1). A subsequent study in the same paper examined negative emotions and the development of relationships, and found that workers with obsessive passion experienced greater negative emotions that, in turn, were related to negative relationships with colleagues; the opposite was true for harmonious passion (Study 4).

Researchers have also addressed the role of passion in work performance. Vallerand, Lafrenière, and St-Louis (2012) investigated the relationship between workers named "Personality of the Week" and their passion for work in a variety of work settings. They found that the individuals selected for the award were significantly more passionate about their work (either harmoniously or obsessively) than average workers and performed at higher levels. Additionally, Liu and colleagues (2011) found that supervisors in both a manufacturing firm and a large commercial bank assessed workers with harmonious passion as being more creative. Similar results were found in a study by Ho and colleagues (2011), showing that insurance company employees with harmonious passion reported greater levels of absorption (a concept similar to flow), which in turn positively predicted performance. However, no relationships were found between employees with obsessive passion and their experience of absorption or performance.

Passion for Work: Its Development

In light of the important role that passion plays in HWI and thereby in a variety of work outcomes, understanding how one becomes passionate about one's work is of great interest. More specifically, since harmonious and obsessive passions lead to different consequences, knowing how each passion develops is critical. Previous research in non-work settings (Mageau et al., 2009; Vallerand et al., 2003) highlighted the role of both social and personality factors in the development of harmonious and obsessive passion. For instance, in a study among children and teens, Mageau et al. (2009) confirmed the role of support for the individual's autonomy by those in their environment and the valuation of the activity in the initial development of passion. More specifically, high perceived support for the child's autonomy from close adults and high valuation of the activity by the child were conducive to the development of harmonious passion. High levels of perceived parental activity valuation and lack of autonomy support were conducive to obsessive passion. Research by Vallerand et al. (2003, Studies 1 and 3) showed that high activity valuation combined with an autonomous personality predicted harmonious passion, whereas activity valuation coupled with a controlled personality was conducive to obsessive passion.

Hence, a high valuation of the activity seems to be essential for the development of passion; however, social and personal factors pertaining to the autonomous or controlled process of internalizing the activity were found to determine the type of passion that eventually develops. Having an autonomous personality or living in an environment that is supportive of autonomy will allow one to internalize the activity in an autonomous fashion. An internalization process of this type is necessary for the development of harmonious passion. Conversely, obsessive passion develops from a controlled internalization process. A controlled personality type or a controlling social environment will lead to this type of internalization process and thereby facilitate the development of obsessive passion.

Along similar lines, recent research conducted in the workplace examined the role of social and personal factors as determinants of harmonious and obsessive passion for work. In a study among the executive directors of 55 health and social services centers, Houlfort and Rinfret (2010) found that emotional intelligence predicts harmonious passion at work. Emotional intelligence refers to a group of abilities that allow one to deal efficiently with one's emotions and those of others at the intrapersonal and interpersonal levels (Brackett & Mayer, 2003; Salovey & Mayer, 1990). Since higher levels of emotional intelligence are related to higher levels of empathy, personal insight and competence in coping, managing, and making good use of emotions (Salovey & Mayer, 1990), workers with high emotional intelligence are believed to act in a more autonomous way. This autonomy should in turn facilitate the development of harmonious passion. In contrast, individuals with low emotional intelligence are less in tune with their authentic self, which in turn should lead them to act and think in a more controlled manner. And although it was not assessed in the study by Houlfort and Rinfret (2010), it is hypothesized that they would be more likely to exhibit obsessive passion for their work.

Forest et al. (in press) have investigated the role of another personality variable: the use of signature strengths. A strength is a "pre-existing capacity for a particular way of behaving, thinking, or feeling that is authentic and energizing to the user, and enables optimal functioning, development and performance" (Linley, 2008). Forest and colleagues (in press) examined whether training in the use of one's signature strengths was related to the development of harmonious passion for work. Their results showed, first, that the training program was successful in increasing the participants' awareness of their signature strengths and increasing their use in the workplace. Second, they showed that awareness and use of one's signature strengths predicted harmonious passion for work over a two-month period. Hence, it seems that using their signature strengths allows people to function more autonomously, which in turn facilitates the development of harmonious passion for work.

Work settings are social environments that can foster the development of harmonious or obsessive passion, depending on whether the environment is supportive of autonomy or controlling. Two factors that can influence which type of environment prevails, and thereby promote the development of harmonious or obsessive passion, are leadership style and organizational culture. Houlfort et al. (2013) have examined the relationship between leadership style and passion for work in two samples of workers. Their findings show that transformational leadership—a relationship based on individual consideration, charisma, inspiration, and transcending self-interest—positively predicted harmonious passion for work. In contrast, transactional leadership—a relationship based on gratification of self-interests—positively predicted obsessive passion. Transformational leadership appears to support workers' autonomy, and thus promotes an autonomous internalization of the activity they are passionate about (i.e., work) into the self. Because transactional leadership seems to foster a more controlling work environment, the passionate activity is more likely to be internalized into the self through pressure (i.e., controlled internalization). Hence, leaders can potentially play an important role in determining which type of passion their employees will develop and sustain for their work.

Organizational culture encompasses "how things are done around here" and hints of it can be found everywhere in an organization: the values promoted, the mission and goals set by its leaders, the employees it hires, the implemented organizational structure and design; the list goes on. Organizational culture can endorse a work environment that supports autonomy or a more controlling one, consequently facilitating the emergence of either harmonious or obsessive passion, respectively. Houlfort et al. (2013) found that certain types of organizational culture can indeed predict which type of passion the workers will have. A clan culture—one in which collaboration, commitment, human development, and communication are central—was found to be positively related to harmonious passion for work. A market culture—one in which the focus is on competition, goal achievement, and profitability—was found to be positively related to obsessive passion for work. Hence, certain organizational environments promote an autonomous internalization of the passionate activity (i.e., the clan culture), whereas others promote a controlled form of internalization (i.e., the market culture).

Future Directions

Research on passion for work is still in the early stages and a number of questions remain to be addressed. For instance, more work is needed to better understand how other concepts (e.g., work commitment, HWI, workaholism, etc.) relate to the concept of passion for work. Although existing research offers preliminary answers as to how passion differs from motivation (Bélanger et al., 2013; Houlfort et al., 2014; Vallerand et al., 2003, Study 2) and flow (Lavigne et al., 2012; Vallerand et al., 2003, Study 1), the relationship between passion for work and other work-related concepts should be examined empirically.

The collective efforts of many scholars not only have demonstrated the theoretical and practical implications of passion for work but have also contributed to positioning passion for work among other well-known concepts. However, so far, research on passion for work has focused almost exclusively on its determinants and its outcomes. Future research should examine passion for work at a phenomenological level. For instance, how is passion for work experienced in day-to-day living? Is a harmonious passion for work experienced the same way for everyone? If not, what are the factors that contribute to or explain the different experiences? Answering these questions will add needed depth to our knowledge of passion for work.

A related question, one that is being addressed in ongoing research, is how individuals can foster both types of passion. The environmental context is believed to arouse one type of passion or the other (see Vallerand, 2014), even though individuals tend to have one predominant type of passion. For instance, an individual with a predominantly harmonious passion for their work may exhibit an obsessive passion for work when their organization undergoes massive personnel cuts and establishes a new pay-for-performance policy. Such a controlling environment could possibly "push" the obsessive passion "button" in an individual who is already passionate about their work, albeit harmoniously. Research is needed to confirm this possibility and understand the underlying mechanisms.

Another avenue for research is to explore the outcomes of passion in greater depth. So far, research has demonstrated that harmonious passion fosters positive outcomes whereas obsessive passion fosters negative outcomes. Is this always the case? Can an obsessive passion lead to positive cognitive, behavioral, and affective consequences for the individual? Perhaps individuals with obsessive passion for their work would fare better in competitive working environments? Amiot, Vallerand, and Blanchard (2006) found that, in highly competitive hockey leagues, hockey players who are obsessively passionate about the game are happier than those who are harmoniously passionate, while the reverse was true in less competitive leagues. These findings suggest that obsessively passionate individuals can experience positive outcomes; however, more research is needed to understand under what circumstances this takes place.

Conclusion

The research reviewed in this chapter illustrates that the concept of passion for work captures a unique experience, one that differs from motivation and workaholism. Furthermore, research confirms that the type of passion an individual has will determine the effects they encounter. Generally, harmonious passion leads to positive outcomes and obsessive passion leads to negative ones. Hence, while both types of passion ensure a heavy investment in work, it appears that only a HWI fueled by a harmonious passion can be beneficial. Certain environmental factors can be put in place to promote the development of harmonious passion and thereby a more positive HWI: adopting a transformational leadership style and endorsing an organizational culture that supports autonomy, such as a clan culture, are two such factors. Workers with high levels of emotional intelligence and who are able to use their signature strengths are also more apt to develop and maintain a harmonious passion for their work. Consequently, they should be able to experience HWI more positively. In sum, HWI can lead to either positive or negative outcomes, even when it is "an expression of passion for work" (Snir & Harpaz, 2012, p. 5). It is the type of passion that will determine whether those who invest heavily in their work will face negative outcomes or benefit from positive effects.

References

Amiot, C., Vallerand, R. J., & Blanchard, C. (2006). Passion and psychological adjustment: A test of the person-environment fit hypothesis. *Personality and Social Psychology Bulletin, 32,* 220–229.

Baum, J. R., & Locke, E. A. (2004). The relationship of entrepreneurial traits, skill, and motivation to subsequent venture growth. *Journal of Applied Psychology, 89*, 587–598.

Baum, J. R., Locke, E. A., & Smith, K. G. (2001). A multidimensional model of venture growth. *Academy of Management Journal, 44*, 292–303.

Baumeister, R. F., & Bratslavsky, E. (1999). Passion, intimacy, and time: Passionate love as a function of change in intimacy. *Personality and Social Psychology Review, 3*, 49–67.

Bélanger, J. J., Lafrenière, M.-A. K., Vallerand, R. J., & Kruglanski, A. W. (2013). Driven by fear: The effect of success and failure information on passionate individuals' performance. *Journal of Personality and Social Psychology, 104,* 180–195.

Bonebright, C. A., Clay, D. L., & Ankenmann, R. D. (2000). The relationship of workaholism with work–life conflict, life satisfaction, and purpose in life. *Journal of Counseling Psychology, 47*, 469–477.

Brown, K. W., & Ryan, R. M. (2003). The benefits of being present: Mindfulness and its role in psychological well-being. *Journal of Personality and Social Psychology, 84*, 822–848.

Carbonneau, N., Vallerand, R. J., Fernet, C., & Guay, F. (2008). The role of passion for teaching in intra and interpersonal outcomes. *Journal of Educational Psychology, 100*, 977–987.

Cardon, M. S. (2008). Is passion contagious? The transference of entrepreneurial passion to employees. *Human Resource Management Review, 18*, 77–86.

Cardon, M. S., Wincent, J., Singh, J., & Drnovsek, M. (2009). The nature and experience of entrepreneurial passion. *The Academy of Management Review, 34*, 511–532.

Caudroit, J., Boiché, J., Stephan, Y., Le Scanff, C., & Trouilloud, D. (2011). Predictors of work/family interference and leisure-time physical activity among teachers: The role of passion towards work. *European Journal of Work and Organizational Psychology, 20*, 326–344.

Csikszentmihalyi, M., Rathunde, K., & Whalen, S. (1993). *Talented teenagers: The roots of success and failure*. New York: Cambridge.

Darwin, C. (1872). The expression of the emotions in man and animals. London: John Murray.

Deci, E. L., & Ryan, R. M. (1985). The general causality orientations scale: Self-determination in personality. *Journal of Research in Personality, 19*, 109–134.

Deci, E. L., & Ryan, R. M. (2000). The "what" and "why" of goal pursuits: Human needs and the self-determination of behavior. *Psychological Inquiry, 11*, 227–268.

Dewey, J. (1930). *Human conduct: An introduction to social psychology*. New York: The modern library.

Diderot, D. (1746/1998). *Pensées philosophiques (Philosophical thoughts)*. Paris: Actes Sud.

Fernet, C., Lavigne, G., Vallerand, R. J., & Austin, S. (in press). Fired up with passion: The role of harmonious and obsessive passion in burnout in novice teachers. *Work and Stress*.

Forest, J., Mageau, G. A., Crevier-Braud, L., Dubreuil, P., Bergeron, E., & Lavigne, G. L. (in press). Harmonious passion as a mediator of the relation between signature strengths' use and optimal functioning at work: Test of an intervention program. *Human Relations*.

Forest, J., Mageau, G. A., Sarrazin, C., & Morin, E. M. (2011). "Work is my passion": The different affective, behavioural, and cognitive consequences of harmonious and obsessive passion toward work. *Canadian Journal of Administrative Sciences, 28*, 17–30.

Frijda, N. H., Mesquita, B., Sonnemans, J., & Van Goozen, S. (1991). The duration of affective phenomena or emotions, sentiments and passions. In K. T. Strongman (Ed.), *International review of studies on emotion* (Vol. 1 pp. 187–225). New York: Wiley.

Griffeth, R. W., Hom, P. W., & Gaertner, S. (2000). A meta-analysis of antecedents and correlates of employee turnover: Update, moderator tests, and research implications for the next millennium. *Journal of Management, 26*, 463–488.

Hatfield, E., & Rapson, R. (1993). Love and attachment processes. In M. Lewis & J. M. Haviland (Eds.), *Handbook of emotions* (pp. 595–604). New York: Guilford Press.

Hatfield, E., & Walster, G. W. (1978). *A new look at love*. Reading, MA: Addison-Wesley.

Harpaz, I., & Snir, R. (2003). Workaholism: Its definition and nature. *Human Relations, 56*, 291–319.

Ho, V. T., Wong, S.-S., & Lee, C. H. (2011). A tale of passion: Linking job passion and cognitive engagement to employee work performance. *Journal of Management Studies, 48*, 26–47.

Hodgins, H. S., & Knee, R. (2002). The integrating self and conscious experience. In E. L. Deci, & R. M. Ryan (Eds.), *Handbook on self-determination research: Theoretical and applied issues* (pp. 87–100). Rochester, NY: University of Rochester Press.

Houlfort, N., Philippe, F., Vallerand, R. J., & Ménard, J. (2014). On passion as heavy work investment and its consequences. *Journal of Managerial Psychology, 29*, 25–45.

Houlfort, N., & Rinfret, N. (2010). Favoriser la satisfaction au travail des directeurs généraux du réseau de la santé et des services sociaux: Impact du style de leadership adopté et de la passion envers le travail. (To facilitate the work satisfaction of general managers of health and social services: The impact of leadership style and passion for work). In B. Raveleau, & F. Ben Hassel (Eds.), *Management humain des organizations: grandeurs et misère de la fonction de dirigeant (Human management in organization: The ups and downs of the manager position)* (pp. 165–188). Paris: Éditions L'Harmattan.

Houlfort, N., Vallerand, R. J., & Koestner, R. (2012). *On the role of passion for work in psychological well-being*. Manuscript submitted for publication.

Houlfort, N., Vallerand, R. J., & Koestner, R. (2013). *On the organizational and interpersonal determinants of passion*. Manuscript in preparation.

James, W. (1884). What is an emotion? *Mind, 9*, 188–205.

Joussain, A. (1928). *Les passions humaines (The human passions)*. France: Ernest Flammarion.

Koestner, R., & Losier, G. F. (2002). Distinguishing three ways of being highly motivated: A closer look at introjection, identification, and intrinsic motivation. In E. L. Deci, & R. M. Ryan (Eds.), *Handbook of self-determination research* (pp. 101–121). Rochester, NY: University of Rochester Press.

Lafrenière, M.-A. K., Bélanger, J. J., Sedikides, C., & Vallerand, R. J. (2011). Self-esteem and passion for activities. *Personality and Individual Differences, 51*, 541–544.

Lavigne, G. L., Forest, J., & Crevier-Braud, L. (in press). Passion at work and burnout: A two-study test of the mediating role of flow experiences. *European Journal of Work and Organizational Psychology*.

Linley, A. (2008). *Average to A+: Realizing strengths in yourself and others*. Coventry: CAPP Press.

Liu, D., Chen, X. P., & Yao, X. (2011). From autonomy to creativity: A multilevel investigation of the mediating role of harmonious passion. *Journal of Applied Psychology, 96*, 294.

Mageau, G., Carpentier, J., & Vallerand, R. J. (2011). The role of self-esteem contingencies in the distinction between obsessive and harmonious passion. *European Journal of Social Psychology, 6*, 720–729.

Mageau, G. A., Vallerand, R. J., Charest, J., Salvy, S., Lacaille, N., Bouffard, T., & Koestner, R. (2009). On the development of harmonious and obsessive passion: The role of autonomy support, activity valuation, and identity processes. *Journal of Personality, 77*, 601–645.

Marsh, H. W., Vallerand, R. J., Lafrenière, M. A. K., Parker, P., Morin, A. J. S., Carbonneau, N., & Paquet, Y. (2013). Passion: Does one scale fit all? Construct validity of two-factor passion scale and psychometric invariance over different activities and languages. *Psychological Assessment, 25*, 796–809.

Meyer, J. P., & Allen, N. J. (1997). *Commitment in the workplace: Theory, research, and applications*. Thousand Oaks, CA: Sage.

Philippe, F. L., Vallerand, R. J., & Lavigne, G. (2009). Passion makes a difference in people's lives: A look at well-being in passionate and non-passionate individuals. *Applied Psychology: Health and Well-Being, 1*, 3–22.

Philippe, F. L., Vallerand, R. J., Houlfort, N., Lavigne, G., & Donahue, E. G. (2010). Passion for an activity and quality of interpersonal relationships: The mediating role of emotions. *Journal of Personality and Social Psychology, 98*, 917–932.

Ribot, T. (1907). *Essai sur les passions (Essay on passions)*. Paris: Alcan.

Rony, J.-A. (1990). *Les passions (The passions)*. Paris: Presses universitaires de France.

Rousseau, F. L., & Vallerand, R. J. (2008). An examination of the relationship between passion and subjective well-being in older adults. *International Journal of Aging and Human Development, 66*, 195–211.

Rousseau, F. L., Vallerand, R. J., Ratelle, C. F., Mageau, G. A., & Provencher, P. J. (2002). Passion and gambling: Validation of the Gambling Passion Scale (GPS). *Journal of Gambling Studies, 18*, 45–66.

Ryan, R. M., & Deci, E. L. (2003). On assimilating identities to the self: A Self-Determination Theory perspective on internalization and integrity within cultures. In M. R. Leary, & J. P. Tangney (Eds.), *Handbook of self and identity* (pp. 253–272). New York: Guilford.

Salovey, P., & Mayer, J. D. (1990). Emotional intelligence. *Imagination, Cognition and Personality, 9*, 185–211.

Schaufeli, W. B., Taris, T. W., & van Rhenen, W. (2008). Workaholism, burnout, and work engagement: Three of a kind or three different kinds of employee well-being? *Applied Psychology: An International Review, 57*, 173–203.

Scott, K. S., Moore, K. S., & Miceli, M. P. (1997). An exploration of the meaning and consequences of workaholism. *Human Relations, 50*, 287–314.

Snir, R., & Harpaz, I. (2012). Beyond workaholism: Towards a general model of heavy work investment. *Human Resource Management Review*, 22, 232–243.

Spence, J. T., & Robbins, A. S. (1992). Workaholism: Definitions, measurement, and preliminary results. *Journal of Personality Assessment, 58*, 160–178.

Stenseng, F. (2008). The two faces of leisure activity engagement: Harmonious and obsessive passion in relation to intrapersonal conflict and life domain outcomes. *Leisure Sciences, 30*, 465–481.

Sternberg, R. J. (1986). A triangular theory of love. *Psychological Review, 93*, 119–153.

Tett, R. P., & Meyer, J. P. (1993). Job satisfaction, organizational commitment, turnover intention, and turnover: Path analysis based on meta-analytic findings. *Personnel Psychology, 46*, 259–293.

Vallerand, R. J. (2010). On passion for life activities: The Dualistic Model of Passion. In M. P. Zanna (Ed.), *Advances in experimental social psychology* (Vol. 42, pp. 97–193). New York: Academic Press.

Vallerand, R. J. (2014). *The psychology of passion.* New York: Oxford University Press.

Vallerand, R. J., & Houlfort, N. (2003). Passion at work: Toward a new conceptualization. In S. W. Gilliland, D. D. Steiner, & D. P. Skarlicki (Eds.), *Emerging perspectives on values in organizations* (pp. 175–204). Greenwich, CT: Information Age Publishing.

Vallerand, R. J., Blanchard, C. M., Mageau, G. A., Koestner, R., Ratelle, C. F., Léonard, M., Gagné, M., & Marsolais, J. (2003). Les passions de l'âme: On obsessive and harmonious passion. *Journal of Personality and Social Psychology, 85*, 756–767.

Vallerand, R. J., Houlfort, N., & Forest, J. (in press). Passion for work: Determinants and outcomes. In M. Gagné (Ed.), *Oxford handbook of work engagement, motivation, and self-determination theory.* New York: Oxford University Press.

Vallerand, R. J., Lafrenière, M-A. K., & St-Louis, A. (2012). *Passion for a cause.* Manuscript in preparation.

Vallerand, R. J., Paquet, Y., Philippe, F. L., & Charest, J. (2010). On the role of passion in burnout: A process model. *Journal of Personality, 78*, 289–312.

Waldman, J. D., Kelly, F., Arora, S., & Smith, H. L. (2004). The shocking cost of turnover in health care. *Health Care Manage Review, 29*, 2–7.

4

WORKAHOLISM

The Concept and Its Assessment

Cecilie Schou Andreassen

Introduction

Work serves important functions for the individual, such as generating income, structuring the day, forming identity, establishing and developing relationships as well as creating meaning. Thus work is essential and necessary for most people. Unsurprisingly, unemployment is related to several psychological and physiological problems. Despite the positive aspects of work, however, some seem to be driven by inner and outer forces to work in a compulsive and excessive manner. These are denoted as workaholics (Schaufeli, Taris, & Van Rhenen, 2008). As workaholism may have several severe health-related and social implications, as well have implications for working life, knowledge about this topic is of vital importance. This chapter addresses the following questions: What is workaholism? How can workaholism best be conceptualized? What are the psychometric qualities of particular workaholism instruments? Does workaholism differ from other already established constructs such as work engagement, passion for work, and work overinvolvement?

This chapter aims to contribute to a better understanding of workaholism among researchers and clinicians by offering a narrative overview of the research field. In order for the reader to understand the concept and the changes that have taken place concerning its content, valence, and dimensionality, several definitions and taxonomies are discussed. In order to further aid understanding of workaholism and to guide clinicians and researchers in terms of assessment, an overview of workaholism instruments is also provided. Directions for future research efforts as well as practical implications are discussed.

The Workaholism Concept

The workaholism construct stems from the suffix –holism, meaning addiction, and derives from the term alcoholism. Workaholism often denotes "excessive working," "work addiction," and "overworking." It is not a new concept as it was introduced in psychology more than 40 years ago. Four decades later there is still no broad consensus on its definition, categorization, or even acceptance of the concept (McMillan, O'Driscoll, Marsh, & Brady, 2001; Ng, Sorensen, & Feldman, 2007; Scott, Moore, & Miceli, 1997). Although the use of the concept has become colloquially widespread, its popularity as a scientific term is not reflected in the research community. Academic interest in the concept was generally lacking until the 1990s. During the past two decades, research on workaholism has increased. Still, many of the same issues and questions remain unanswered today.

Definitions of Workaholism

"Workaholism" was initially defined as "addiction to work, the compulsion or uncontrollable need to work incessantly" (Oates, 1971). Hence, the term was rooted in the addiction paradigm. Some of the earliest approaches to its operationalization defined workaholism as working more than 50 hours per week (Mosier, 1983). Others defined workaholics in terms of persons who always devote more time and energy to work than the work situation demands (Machlowitz, 1980). This definition emphasizes an attitude towards work, rather than the number of working hours, and is more in line with current understanding of the concept. Most of the recent definitions describe workaholism as a chronic pattern of overinvolvement in work, long work days, work beyond what is expected, and being engrossed in work (Griffiths, 2011; Ng et al., 2007). Some differences in opinion still exist, however. Some argue that workaholism is primarily something positive (e.g., extra work effort) (Scott et al., 1997), while the majority of researchers today mainly emphasize the negative aspects (e.g., impaired health as a consequence) (Griffiths, 2011; Oates, 1971; Robinson, 2013; Schaufeli, Shimazu, & Taris, 2009).

Over the years, workaholism has been understood as both a trait—an obsessive and/or compulsive condition—and, as initially proposed, a behavioral addiction. In recent years the understanding of workaholism as an addictive behavior has had a renaissance (Andreassen, 2013, 2014; Sussman, 2012). Thus, when applying the perspective of an addiction, workaholism can be defined as "being overly concerned about work, being driven by an uncontrollable work motivation, and spending so much energy and effort on work that it impairs private relationships, spare-time activities, and/or health" (Andreassen, Hetland, & Pallesen, 2014, p. 7).

Workaholism Dimensions

According to Spence and Robbins (1992), workaholism can be understood as a multidimensional construct where workaholics typically score high on work involvement, high on work drive, and low on work enjoyment. This multidimensional understanding has in recent years been met with criticism, and it has been pointed out that the work enjoyment dimension is irrelevant (Mudrack, 2006). Empirically it has further been shown that the work involvement dimension is consistently invalid (Andreassen et al., 2014). Moreover, recent empirical approaches operationalize the construct primarily from dimensions that correlate highly (Schaufeli et al., 2009) or that understand the construct as unidimensional (Andreassen, Griffiths, Hetland, & Pallesen, 2012). As such, it looks like the understanding of workaholism as a multidimensional construct has given way to a more one-dimensional theoretical standpoint. There seems to be a great overlap between workaholism and constructs such as obsessive job passion (Vallerand, Paquet, Philippe, & Charest, 2010) and work overinvolvement (Lehr, Koch, & Hillert, 2010). As far as the latter is concerned, these constructs may only represent 'new wine in old bottles,' or they are actually distinctive in relation to the workaholism construct. This has yet to be clarified.

Workaholism Typologies

Existing typologies of workaholics have been anchored in theory or data only to a small extent. Scott et al. (1997) postulated three types of workaholics: the compulsive-dependent, the perfectionistic, and the achievement-oriented. Robinson (1998, 2013) proposed four different types of workaholics: "the bulimic," who does things perfectly or not at all; "the relentless," who cannot stop working, is compulsive, and is motivated to work fast and meet deadlines; "the savoring," who obsesses over details to the point of paralysis; and the "attention-deficit," who tends to start many projects but gets easily bored and needs continual stimulation. One central, empirically supported distinction is drawn between workaholics who like their work and those who do not (Bonebright, Clay, & Ankenmann, 2000). In line with this, Spence and Robbins (1992) identified "enthusiastic workaholics," who are characterized by high levels of work involvement, driven by an internal pressure to work, and who find great pleasure and satisfaction in work; and "non-enthusiastic workaholics," who also are highly work involved and driven, but who seem to lack enjoyment from doing so. The latter type was initially referred to as "real" workaholics, whereas the tag "non-enthusiastic" was later added to the label (Bonebright et al., 2000).

Six years ago, however, Ng et al. (2007) argued for the importance of distinguishing between enjoyment of the nature or content of the work and enjoyment derived from the act of working. They argued that workaholics generally enjoy the act of working, because it assuages unpleasant feelings otherwise experienced when not working (feelings of anxiety, guilt, i.e., Drive). In this regard, the Enjoyment of Work dimension measured by the Workaholism Battery (WorkBAT; Spence & Robbins, 1992), where high scores identify enthusiastic workaholics, recognizes those who really enjoy the work they do (e.g., "my job is more like fun than work"). Nevertheless, the distinction between enthusiastic and non-enthusiastic workaholism is probably better captured today by the terms work engagement and workaholism, respectively (Taris, Schaufeli, & Shimazu, 2010). The debate on how to categorize different attitudes towards work, however, is still ongoing as van Beek, Taris, and Schaufeli (2011) recently re-launched the typology distinguishing between workaholics, work engaged workaholics, and engaged workers.

Workaholism and Related Constructs

Definitions of workaholism differentiate between being passionate about work and being a workaholic. From time to time many of us work more than usual without "meeting the criteria" of workaholism. The workaholic, however, works more or less all the time, to the point where work becomes an inseparable part of life and personal identity. As with other addictive behaviors, working becomes a way of coping with stress. Workaholism is thus regarded as a stable trait of the person—a trait that certainly may be triggered by the possibilities offered by new digital devices (e.g., laptop, cell phones).

Snir and Harpaz (2012) recently placed workaholism in a broader context of heavy work investment. They distinguish between "situational heavy work investors" and "dispositional heavy work investors." In the former group they identified the needy (who are in need of money in order to fulfill different economical obligations) and the employer-directed (workers who skills and competence are in high demand). When it comes to the dispositional heavy work investors Snir and Harpaz (2012) differentiate between workaholics (who are addicted to their work), the work devoted (who have a high passion to their work), the intimacy-avoiders (who see work as an escape from intimacy/close relationships), and the leisure-low-interested (who see work as an alternative to tedious leisure time). Little research has been done on this classification.

Another construct related to workaholism is that of "passion towards work." Passion has been defined as a strong inclination of desire towards an activity that one likes, one finds important, and in which one invests time and energy (Vallerand et al., 2003, p. 757). A distinction is drawn between obsessive and harmonious passion. "Obsessive passion" stems from a controlled internalization of an activity, implying that the activity is not self-determined but rather a product of external contingencies. "Harmonious passion" on the other hand relates to an autonomous internalization of an activity, as engagement in the activity is largely self-determined and is unrelated to specific contingencies. Obsessive passion towards work seems to have a strong resemblance to workaholism, whereas harmonious passion towards work has more similarity to work engagement. In one study it was found that obsessive passion towards work, but not harmonious passion towards work, was positively related to work time (Cauroit, Boiché, Stephan, Le Scanff, & Trouilloud, 2011).

Another concept related to workaholism is "work overcommitment." Work overcommitment is regarded as a personality trait reflecting excessive ambition and the need to be approved and esteemed (van Vegchel, de Jonge, Bosma, & Schaufeli, 2005). On a conceptual basis work overcommitment seems to have striking similarities with workaholism; however, not much is known about the empirical relationship between these constructs.

From a "differential diagnostic perspective" it is overall fair to conclude that it is important to rule out other potential reasons that may cause excessive work behavior, as well as to recognize that not all excessive working is pathological.

Overall Comment

To date, we know little about the concept of workaholism. Three central reasons for this are (1) lack of consensus about how it should be defined, (2) lack of studies using representative samples, and (3) lack of consensus about the understanding of how it should be measured and where to set cut-off values between "normal" and "pathological" work behavior.

Assessment of Workaholism

So far relatively few instruments have been developed to measure workaholism. The following is a brief overview of workaholism scales developed since the 1980s to measure the phenomenon. Ten instruments were identified when narratively reviewing the literature (see Table 4.1).

Workaholism Battery (WorkBAT)

In the early 1990s, Spence and Robbins (1992) developed the workaholism measure most widely used so far—the Workaholism Battery (WorkBAT). They argued that workaholics typically are very involved in work, have an internal drive motivating them to work, and lack work enjoyment. In line with this, Spence and Robbins constructed three subscales that measure these phenomena (work involvement, work drive, and work enjoyment) tested in a randomly selected sample of 291 full-time social workers (although first administrated to students where statements referred to schoolwork). WorkBAT consists

Table 4.1 Scale Construction Key-Studies of Existing Workaholism Assessments in the Literature Presented in Reversed Chronological Order

Assessment	*Theoretical Underpinnings*	*Sample Demographics*	*Empirical Underpinnings*	*Items*	*Subscales*	*Scoring / Cut-Off*
Bergen Work Addiction Scale (BWAS) (Andreassen et al., 2012)	Based on Brown's behavioral addiction components (Brown, 1993) and Griffiths' components model of addiction (Griffiths, 2005). Assesses workaholism as a behavioral addiction	11,769 Norwegian employees (Sample 1–7,596 men; mean age 40.4 (SD=11.6)) recruited from a television broadcast, and 368 Norwegian employees (Sample 2–175 men; mean age 46.4 (SD=10.1)) from a second wave of a longitudinal web-based survey about working life. The samples represent a vast variety of professions	Item selection based on data from half of Sample 1 (n=5,932). CFA based on data from the other half of Sample 1: RMSEA=0.08, CFI=0.96, TLI=0.95. Calculation of internal consistency (Sample 1/ Sample 2): α=.84/.80. Significant and positive correlations between BWAS and WART-C (0.50), WART-CT (0.84), WART-IC/SA (0.79), WorkBAT-D (0.65), WorkBAT-WI (0.35), WorkBAT-E (0.13), and working hours (0.31–0.32). Discriminant validity (ANOVAs): workaholics scored higher on work hours, subjective health complaints, and management positions	Seven items answered along a five-point scale ranging from "never" to "always"	None	A composite score is calculated by adding the scores of the seven items. Polythetic cut-off: scoring 4 or above on at least four items. Monothetic cut-off: scoring 4 and above on all seven items

(*Continued*)

Table 4.1 Continued

Assessment	*Theoretical Underpinnings*	*Sample Demographics*	*Empirical Underpinnings*	*Items*	*Subscales*	*Scoring / Cut-Off*
Dutch Work Addiction Scale (DUWAS) (Schaufeli et al., 2009)	Based on items from WART-CT (Flowers & Robinson, 2002) and WorkBAT-D (Spence & Robbins, 1992). Assesses workaholism as an excessive obsession-compulsion	7,594 Dutch employees (48% men; mean age 36.4 (SD=9.5)) from different occupational groups (hospital workers, managers, and professionals) recruited via their organizations or the Internet, and 3,311 Japanese workers (51% men; mean age 34.4 (SD= 10.5)) (nurses, blue-collar workers, lower professionals) recruited via their organizations	EFA based on data from half of the samples: two factors emerged. CFA on data from the other half of the samples confirmed a two-factor solution (RMSEA=0.06, CFI=0.91). Calculation of internal consistencies: DUWAS WE/WC α=0.78/0.73 in Dutch sample and 0.73/0.68 in Japanese sample. Significant and positive correlations with overwork (WE/WC Dutch sample 0.40/0.23; Japanese sample 0.53/0.25). Discriminant validity: distinct from burnout and engagement	10 (or 17) items answered along a four-point scale ranging from "(almost) never/totally disagree" to "(almost) always/totally agree"	Working Compulsively (WC), Working Excessively (WE)	A composite score is calculated by adding the scores of the ten items divided by ten, and summed subscale totals. High scores on both WC and WE indicate workaholism. Cut-off=>75th percentile (2.69–3.21)

Shorter PROMIS Questionnaire–Work (SPQ-Work) (Christo et al., 2003)	Based on a comprehensive conceptual model of addiction. Assesses 16 multiple addictions, including work addiction—thus workaholism is viewed as an addiction	497 British inpatients (53% men; mean age 35.2 (SD=12.9)) from the PROMIS Recovery Centre (1995–99) and 508 British participants (39% men; mean age 30.1 (SD=11.3)) from a nonclinical community convenience sample (normative group). Retest group from a small clinical sample of 20	Calculation of internal consistency: Clinical sample α=0.84. Test-retest reliability r=0.73, ICC=0.64 Convergent and discriminant validity could not be demonstrated for all the SPQ scales, including for SPQ-Work—thus currently relying on face validity only	10 items answered along a six-point scale ranging from "not like me" to "like me"	None	A composite score is calculated by adding the scores of the 10 items (range=0–50), clinical cut-off:>90th percentile in normative group

(Continued)

Table 4.1 Continued

Assessment	*Theoretical Underpinnings*	*Sample Demographics*	*Empirical Underpinnings*	*Items*	*Subscales*	*Scoring / Cut-Off*
Non-Required Work Scale and Control of Others Scale (Mudrack & Naughton, 2001)	Based on Scott et al. (1997) conceptual definition of workaholism, and comprises two elements: non-required work and attempt to control others. Assesses workaholism as a observable behavior/ behavioral tendency (albeit may triggered by obsessive-compulsive traits)	278 U.S. heterogeneous employed (banking, health care etc.) participants (163 men; mean age 29.9 (SD=5.6); 127 managers) who attended classes in an evening MBA program	CFA confirmed a two-factor solution (RMSEA=0.08, GFI=0.95). Internal consistencies were calculated: Non-Required Work subscale/ Control of Others subscale α=0.74/0.82. Both scales correlated positively with working hours (0.20/0.14), job involvement (0.18/0.31), job stress (0.15/0.49), and work–nonwork conflict (0.19/0.38). Non-Required Work subscale also correlated with needs for achievement (0.29), autonomy (0.23), dominance (0.20), and affiliation (0.26). Control of Others subscale correlated with dominance need (0.35), self-monitoring (0.32), and role conflict (0.41)	Eight items answered along a five-point scale ranging from "none/ not applicable" to "very large amount of time and energy are spent"	Non-Required Work, Control of Others	A composite score is calculated by adding the score on the eight items, and subscale totals. High scores indicate workaholism. No cut-off suggested

Children of Workaholic Parents Screening Test (CWST) (Robinson & Carroll, 1999)	Based on WART (Robinson, 1989, 1999) and symptoms and behaviors reported by diagnosed children of workaholics, existing literature, and studies	202 U.S. undergraduate students (182 women; mean age 25.1, range 19–55 years). 158 of the sample also completed a two-week posttest	Split-half correlation coefficient: pretest 0.92, posttest 0.93. Significant correlations between scores on the CWST and depression (0.46) and parentification (0.60). Inter-item correlations yielded moderate coefficients	30 items answered along a two-choice scale (yes/no)	None	A composite score is calculated by adding all the endorsed items. A high sum score indicates parental workaholism. No cut-off suggested
Schedule for Nonadaptive and Adaptive Personality—Workaholism (SNAP-Work) (Clark, 1993, 1996)	Based on trait theory and clinical psychopathology. Assesses workaholism as a personality trait/personality disorder	163 U.S. college students (77 men; mean age 20 (SD=3.1)) receiving course credit for their participation, and 74 U.S. normal adults (40 men; mean age 34.8 (SD=9.7)) recruited via advertisements in university and community newspapers—participation was compensated	Factor-analytically (EFA) derived items. Evidence for good split-half reliability, internal consistency, test–retest stability, and strong convergent and discriminant validity	18 items answered along a two-choice scale (true/false)	None	A composite score is calculated by adding the scores of all items. A high score indicates high levels of workaholism.

(*Continued*)

Table 4.1 Continued

Assessment	*Theoretical Underpinnings*	*Sample Demographics*	*Empirical Underpinnings*	*Items*	*Subscales*	*Scoring / Cut-Off*
Workaholism Battery (WorkBAT) (Spence & Robbins, 1992)	Based on workaholism attributes in the literature and the authors' own hypotheses. Assesses workaholism as an attitude/ obsessive-compulsive tendency	291 U.S. social workers (134 men; median age 43 (range 35–49) for men, 40 for women (range 31–47)) with academic positions participated in a national mail survey (after testing the scales among students). The sample was randomly selected by computers from a National Association of Social Workers database	Calculation of internal consistencies (male/ female): WorkBAT-WI α=0.69/0.67, WorkBAT-D α=0.81/0.67, WorkBAT-E α=0.86/0.86. Cluster-analyses: Six worker groups. ANOVAs: Workaholics scored higher than work enthusiasts and others on perfectionism, non-delegation of responsibility, job stress, and health complaints	25 (24, 20 or 14) items answered along a five-point scale ranging from "strongly agree" to "strongly disagree"	Work Involvement (WI), Drive (D), Work Enjoyment (E)	A composite score is calculated by adding all the endorsed items, as well as summed subscale totals. Scores above the mean on WI and D, and below mean on E indicate non-enthusiastic workaholism. Scores above mean on all subscales indicate enthusiastic workaholism

Workaholic Adjective Checklist (WAC) (Haymon, 1992)	Based on reviews of the literature of shared attributes and behaviors of workaholics. Assesses workaholism as an attitude and observable behavior	253 U.S. male students enrolled in a general psychology course	EFA based on a subset sample (n=146): five factors emerged, explaining 74% of the variance. Calculation of internal consistencies of these five factors: α=0.61–0.83, mean 0.71. Second subsample (n=107) was used for cross validation. Regressions: WAC factors were related to depression, state anxiety, trait anxiety, state anger, and trait anger. Significant differences between respondents scoring within the upper third and those who scored within the lower third of total scores on the WAC with respect to all emotional characteristics, except trait anger	72 items (42 behavioral items / 28 attitudinal items) answered along a rating format	Anxiety, Obsessive-Compulsiveness, Mania, Intolerance, Self-Doubt	A composite score is calculated by adding all the endorsed items. High scores indicate workaholism. No cut-off score suggested

(*Continued*)

Table 4.1 Continued

Assessment	*Theoretical Underpinnings*	*Sample Demographics*	*Empirical Underpinnings*	*Items*	*Subscales*	*Scoring / Cut-Off*
Work Addiction Risk Test (WART) (Robinson, 1989)	Based on symptoms reported by clinicians treating workaholics. Assesses workaholism as Type-A behavior rather than an addiction	363 U.S. university students (107 male; mean age 22) (Robinson, 1999)—reliability and concurrent validity were tested. Two-week test-retest reliability tested in 151 U.S. students (Robinson, Post, & Khakee, 1992). Split-half reliability tested in 442 U.S. respondents (students and Workaholic Anonymous) (Robinson & Post, 1995)	Calculation of internal consistency (α=0.88) (Robinson, 1999), split-half reliability (0.85) (Robinson & post, 1995), and test–retest reliability (0.83) (Robinson, Post, & Khakee, 1992). Concurrent validity: WART scores correlated with generalized anxiety (0.40) and Type-A behavior (0.37–0.50) (Robinson, 1999). Satisfactory face and content validity (Robinson & Phillips, 1995)	25 items answered along a four-point scale ranging from "never true" to "always true"	Compulsive Tendencies (CT), Control (C), Impaired Communications/ Self-Absorption (IC/SA), Inability to Delegate (ID), Self-Worth (SW)	A composite score is calculated by adding all the endorsed items (range 25–100). A score between 57 and 66 indicates moderate work addiction; between 67 and 100 indicates severe work addiction. Fifteen items from WART-CT, -C and -IC/SA have been demonstrated to adequately discriminate workaholics from non-workaholics (Flowers & Robinson, 2002)

Work Attitudes Questionnaire (WAQ) (Doty & Betz, 1981)	Based on available descriptions of work commitment, Type-A behavior, and workaholism, and through discussions with individuals reporting high levels of work involvement and commitment or identifying themselves as workaholics. Assesses workaholism as an attitude	93 U.S. male managers in a large pharmaceutical firm	Calculation of internal consistency: Work commitment subscale $\alpha=0.80$, Psychological health subscale $\alpha=0.85$, total scale $\alpha=0.90$. Significant and positive correlations between WAQ and career salience (0.62), and hours worked per week (0.36)	45 items answered along a five-point scale ranging from "strongly disagree" to "strongly agree"	Work Commitment, Psychological Health	A composite score is calculated by adding all the endorsed items, as well as summed subscale totals. A score >69 on the Commitment scale indicates highly committed workers + a score >66 on the Psychological health subscale indicates workaholism

EFA = Explorative factor analysis, CFA = Confirmatory factor analysis of 25 statements that collectively measure whether a person's work habits are regarded as workaholic (see Table 4.2). By cluster analyzing the sample, they identified several types of workers (six clusters). Thus, scores above mean on Work Involvement and Drive, and below the mean on Enjoyment of Work, characterized what they called non-enthusiastic workaholics; those with scores above mean on all three subscales were deemed enthusiastic workaholics. Several versions of the WorkBAT exist (14-item and 20-item short scale, as well as a 24-item Chinese version) (Buelens & Poelmans, 2004; Huang, Hu, & Wu, 2010; McMillan, Brady, O'Driscoll, & Marsh, 2002). Controversy arose over its dimensionality. The Work Involvement subscale has failed several times to show acceptable psychometric properties (Kanai, Wakabayashi, & Fling, 1996; McMillan et al., 2002). In addition, the Enjoyment of Work subscale has been criticized by several researchers because they do not regard work enjoyment to be a defining workaholism trait (Mudrack, 2006).

Work Addiction Risk Test (WART)

The first well-established quantitative measure of workaholism, however, was the Work Addiction Risk Test (WART) developed by Robinson (1989, 1998). Studies have suggested WART to be a reliable and valid measure (Flowers & Robinson, 2002; Robinson, 1999; Robinson & Phillips, 1995; Robinson & Post, 1995; Robinson, Post, & Khakee, 1992). The scale items were based on symptoms reported by clinicians treating workaholics and their families. The total WART score has shown to be positively associated with scores on anxiety and Type-A behavior (Robinson, 1999). WART consists of 25 items and has been considered as a one-dimensional scale; thus, often only a single composite score has been used. An overall score of 67–100 indicates high workaholic tendencies; an overall score of 57–66 indicates moderate workaholic tendencies; whereas an overall score of 25–56 suggests no workaholic tendencies. A factor analysis showed that the items were distributed along five factors (Flowers & Robinson, 2002): (1) Compulsive Tendencies (CT), (2) Control (C), (3) Impaired Communication/Self-Absorption (IC/SA), (4) Inability to Delegate (ID), and (5) Self-Worth (SW) (see Table 4.3). Follow-up studies demonstrated, however, that only 15 items, distributed on the first three factors, were suitable to discriminate between workaholics and a control group (Flowers & Robinson, 2002). WART has been criticized for having too little relevance with modern definitions of workaholism (Mudrack, 2006) and it has been argued that the WART on a theoretical basis more seems to reflect Type-A personality than workaholism.

Table 4.2 Workaholism Battery (WorkBAT; Spence & Robbins, 1992)

Item	*Wording*	*Original Subscale*[b]
1	When I have free time I like to relax and do nothing serious[a]	WI
2	I like my work more than most people do	WE
3	I feel guilty when I take time off work	D
4	My job is more like fun than work	WE
5	I often wish I weren't so committed to my work	D
6	I like to relax and enjoy myself as often as possible[a]	WI
7	My job is so interesting that it often doesn't seem like work	WE
8	I really look forward to the weekend—all fun, no work[a]	WI
9	I do more work than is expected of me strictly for the fun of it	WE
10	Most of the time my work is very pleasurable	WE
11	I seldom find anything to enjoy about work[a]	WE
12	Wasting time is as bad as wasting money	WI
13	I spend my free time on projects and other activities	WI
14	I feel obliged to work hard even when it is not enjoyable	D
15	I like to use my time constructively, both on and off the job	WI
16	I lose track of time when I'm involved in a project	WE
17	Sometimes when I get up in the morning I can hardly wait to get to work	WE
18	It is important to me to work hard, even when I don't enjoy what I'm doing	D
19	When I get involved in an interesting project it's hard to describe how exhilarated I feel	WE
20	I often find myself thinking about work, even when I want to get away from it for a while	D
21	Between my job and other activities I'm involved in I don't have much free time	WI
22	I often feel there is something inside me that drives me to work hard	D
23	Sometimes I enjoy work so much I have a hard time stopping	WE
24	I get bored and restless on vacations when I haven't anything productive to do[a]	WI
25	I seem to have an inner compulsion to work hard	D

All items are scored along following scale: "strongly disagree"=1, "sometimes true"=2, "often true"=3, "always true"=4, "strongly agree"=5; a) originally reversed items, b) WI=Work Involvement, D=Drive, WE=Work Enjoyment.

Table 4.3 Work Addiction Risk Test (WART; Robinson, 1989, 1998)

Item	*Wording*	*Original Subscale*[a]
1	I prefer to do most things myself rather than ask for help	ID
2	I get very impatient when I have to wait for someone else or when something takes too long, such as long-slow moving lines	C
3	I seem to be in a hurry and racing against the clock	CT
4	I get irritated when I am interrupted while I am in the middle of something	C
5	I stay busy and keep many irons in the fire	CT
6	I find myself doing two or three things at one time, such as eating lunch and writing a memo, while talking on the telephone	CT
7	I overly commit myself by biting off more than I can chew	CT
8	I feel guilty when I am not working on something	CT
9	It is important that I see the concrete results of what I do	SW
10	I am more interested in the final result of my work than in the process	SW
11	Things just never seem to move fast enough or get done fast enough for me	C
12	I lose my temper when things don't go my way or work out to suit me	C
13	I ask the same question over again, without realizing it, after I've already been given the answer once	IC/SA
14	I spend a lot of time mentally planning and thinking about future events while tuning out the here and now	
15	I find myself still working after my co-workers have called it quits	CT
16	I get angry when people don't meet my standards of perfection	C
17	I get upset when I am in situations where I cannot be in control	C
18	I tend to put myself under pressure with self-imposed deadlines when I work	CT
19	It is hard for me to relax when I'm not working	CT
20	I spend more time working than on socializing with friends, on hobbies or on leisure activities	CT
21	I dive into projects to get a head start before all the phases have been finalized	IC/SA
22	I get upset with myself for making even the smallest mistake	C
23	I put more thought, time, and energy into my work than I do into my relationships, with my spouse (or lover) and family	IC/SA

Item	*Wording*	*Original Subscale*[a]
24	I forget, ignore, or minimize important family celebrations such as birthdays, reunions, anniversaries, or holidays	IC/SA
25	I make important decisions before I have all the facts and have a chance to think them through thoroughly	IC/SA

All items are scored along following scale: "never true"=1, "sometimes true"=2, "often true"=3, "always true"=4; a) ID=Inability to Delegate, C=Control, CT=Compulsive Tendencies, SW=Self-Worth, IC/SA=Impaired Communication/Self-Absorption.

Reprinted from © Bryan Robinson. (2013). *Chained to the Desk: A Guidebook for Workaholics, Their Partners and Children, and the Clinicians Who Treat Them.* (3rd Edition). New York: New York University Press.

Dutch Work Addiction Scale (DUWAS)

Relatively recently, Schaufeli et al. (2009) developed a new workaholism scale in a sample of Dutch and Japanese workers (N = 10,905). From a theoretical perspective, they argued that workaholics typically spend much time on work, and additionally that they are obsessed by it. On this background, they constructed the Dutch Work Addiction Scale (DUWAS). DUWAS comprises two subscales, one consisting of five items from the WART-CT subscale (Flowers & Robinson, 2002) ("Working Excessively") and the other consisting of four items from the WorkBAT-Drive subscale (Spence & Robbins, 1992) and one from the WART-CT subscale ("Working Compulsively") (see Table 4.4). Based on a national database of Dutch workers, subjects scoring above the 75th percentile (scores between 2.69 and 3.20 suggest highly workaholic; scores of 3.21 or more indicated that the respondent is a workaholic to a very high extent) on both subscales can be classified as workaholics (Schaufeli, van Wijhe, Peeters, & Taris, 2011). Different versions of DUWAS exist (17-item and 10-item scale). DUWAS has shown good psychometric properties in several studies (del Libano, Llorens, Salanova, & Schaufeli, 2010; Schaufeli et al., 2009).

Bergen Work Addiction Scale (BWAS)

Although different measures of workaholism have been developed, most of them lack a firm theoretical anchoring, and show poor convergent validity with each other (Andreassen et al., 2014). Against this backdrop, Andreassen et al. (2012) recently developed a new scale, the Bergen Work Addiction Scale (BWAS) based on data from a sample of 12,137 Norwegian employees. Since the workaholism concept stems from the addiction field, the authors argued that the operationalization of workaholism should be closely linked to core elements of addiction: (1) Salience (preoccupied with work), (2) Mood modification (work to

Table 4.4 Dutch Work Addiction Scale (DUWAS; Schaufeli et al., 2009)

Item	*Wording*	*Subscale*[a]
1	I seem to be in a hurry and racing against the clock	WE
2	I find myself still working after my co-workers have called it quits	WE
3	I stay busy and keep many irons in the fire	WE
4	I spend more time working than on socializing with friends, on hobbies, or on leisure activities	WE
5	I find myself doing two or three things at one time, such as eating lunch and writing a memo, while talking on the telephone	WE
6	It is important to me to work hard, even when I do not enjoy what I am doing	WC
7	I often feel there is something inside me that drives me to work hard	WC
8	I feel obliged to work hard, even when it is not enjoyable	WC
9	I feel guilty when I take time off work	WC
10	It is hard for me to relax when I am not working	WC

All items are scored along following scale: "(almost) never"=1, "sometimes"=2, "often"=3, "(almost) always"=4; a) WE=Working Excessively, WC=Working Compulsively and divided by the number of items in the scale.

escape or avoid dysphoria), (3) Conflict (work comes in conflict with own and others' needs), (4) Withdrawal (dysphoria when prohibited from working), (5) Tolerance (work ever more to achieve same mental and physiological effect), (6) Relapse (falls back into old pattern after a period of improvement), and (7) Problems (works so much that health, relationships, and well-being are negatively affected). BWAS consequently consists of seven items (see Table 4.5). The wording is in line with diagnostic criteria for addiction (American Psychiatric Association, 1994; World Health Organization, 1992). Scoring "often" or "always" on four out of seven criteria suggest that one is a workaholic. The scale correlates in expected ways with the WART (Robinson, 1999), the WorkBAT (Spence & Robbins, 1992), and the DUWAS (Schaufeli et al., 2009). It does not correlate with the Enjoyment of Work subscale of the WorkBAT, but correlates highly with the Drive subscale. Proposed cut-off values for categorization of workaholism based on the BWAS show good discriminative capability in relation to working hours, manager positions, and subjective health complaints. The BWAS has overall shown good psychometric properties (Andreassen et al., 2012). Several studies about the properties of the BWAS, among others in other languages than Norwegian, are needed.

Table 4.5 Bergen Work Addiction Scale (BWAS; Andreassen et al., 2012)

Item	*Wording* *How often during the last year have you:*	*Addiction Component*
1	Thought of how you could free more time to work?	Salience
2	Spent much more time working than initially intended?	Tolerance
3	Worked in order to reduce feelings of guilt, anxiety, helplessness and/or depression?	Mood modification
4	Experienced that others have told you to cut down on work without listening to them?	Relapse
5	Become stressed if you have been prohibited from working?	Withdrawal
6	Down-prioritized hobbies, leisure activities, and/or exercise because of your work?	Conflict
7	Worked so much that it has negatively influenced your health?	Problems

All items are scored along the following scale: "never"=1, "rarely"=2, "sometimes"=3, "often"=4, "always"=5. Scoring "often" or "always" on at least four of the seven criteria may suggest workaholism. Addication component is not displayed to the respondent. Bergen Work Addication Scale may be freely used for research purposes only. Non-scientific or commercial use requires granted permission by authors.

Schedule for Nonadaptive and Adaptive Personality–Workaholism (SNAP-Work)

As part of her doctoral thesis, Clark developed a psychological test to measure unidimensional personality traits across the adaptive–dysfunctional spectrum, including SNAP-Work (Clark, 1993, 1996; Clark, Livesley, Schroeder, & Irish, 1996). The SNAP was constructed based on a literature review of personality disorders symptoms and other mental disorders with traitlike manifestations. The symptoms were then subjected to a conceptual sorting task, items were written to these, and the scales were finalized following data collection and psychometric testing in multiple samples (Clark et al., 1996). The SNAP consists of 375 factor-analytically derived items; 12 trait scales assessing maladaptive personality; three temperament scales assessing higher-order domains of normal range personality; 13 personality disorders; and six validity scales. Median Cronbach's alphas ranging from 0.71 to 0.92 ($M = 0.81$) in both normal and clinical samples were found (Clark, 1996); median one-week test-retest reliability for the test scores was 0.81 in the patient sample (Clark, 1996). Two-month retest stabilities ranged from 0.70 to 0.85 (Clark, 1993). SNAP has shown to overlap substantially with other established personality measures (Clark, 1996; Livesley & Jackson, 2002; Tellegen & Waller, 2008). The workaholism subscale consists of

18 items answered on a binary true/false-format. High scores indicate high levels of workaholism. The item-pool covers work issues (13 items, such as "People say I neglect other important parts of my life because I work so hard") and obsessive-compulsive traits (five items) such as perfectionism and rigidity (e.g., "I don't consider a task finished until it's perfect"). A high correlation between the SNAP-Work and the WorkBAT-Drive subscale (Spence & Robbins, 1992) and good split-half reliability (0.82) has been found in later studies (McMillan et al., 2002), although the SNAP-Work needs further psychometric evaluation, as it has received little empirical attention so far. A second edition of SNAP (SNAP-2) (Calabrese, Rudick, Simms, & Clark, 2012; Clark, 2009) and an adolescent edition (SNAP-Youth) (Linde, Stringer, Simms, & Clark, 2013) have recently been developed.

Non-Required Work Scale and Control of Others Scale

Mudrack and Naughton (2001) developed two scales, one reflecting workaholic cognitions and behavior of performing non-required work, and one assessing the cognitive and behavioral attempt to control the work of others. The scales was based on a theoretical assumption that workaholism is manifested as behavioral tendencies relevant to work activities that are not obligatory and that involve free choice. Another theoretical assumption was that workaholism has both an interpersonal as well as an intrapersonal dimension. Thus, the theoretical underpinning was based on Scott et al.'s (1997) definition of workaholism: (1) spending discretionary time in work activities; (2) thinking about work when not at work; and (3) working beyond organizational or economic requirements. Each scale consists of four items answered on a five-point Likert scale ranging from 1 ("none/not applicable") to 5 ("very large amount of time and energy are spent"). The four Non-Required Work items specifically ask how much time and energy is spent on: (1) "Thinking of ways to improve the quality of work provided to customers and/or co-workers," (2) "Thinking of ways to improve the quantity of work provided to customers and/or co-workers," (3) "Thinking of ways to be more productive," and (4) "Taking responsibility for initiating assignments and projects." The Control of Others Scale items ask how much time and energy is spent on: (1) "Fixing problems created by other people," (2) "Checking the accuracy of other people's work," (3) "Taking responsibility for the work of other people," and (4) "Dealing with crisis situations." The initial study demonstrated evidence for good psychometric properties (Mudrack & Naughton, 2001). However, these scales have been used to little extent; thus, more studies on these are needed.

Shorter PROMIS Questionnaire–Work (SPQ-Work)

The PROMIS Questionnaire was originally designed to reflect key characteristics of addictive behaviors (preoccupation, using alone, using for effect, using as a medicine, protection of supply, using more than planned, and tolerance) (Stephenson, Maggi, Lefever, & Morojele, 1995). The Shorter PROMIS Questionnaire (SPQ) is a self-report scale developed by Christo and co-workers (Christo, Jones, Haylett, Stephenson, Lefever, & Lefever, 2003) that measures 16 chemical and non-chemical addictive behaviors, including addiction to work. It was based upon samples involving 497 inpatients from the PROMIS Recovery Centre and 508 participants from a non-clinical community sample. Each of the 16 scales consists of ten items (160 items in total; originally 480 items) answered on a six-point Likert scale ranging from 0 ("strongly disagree") to 5 ("strongly agree"), thus yielding an overall score from 0 to 50. Scores of 90th percentile indicate addiction in the nonclinical (normative) group. The SPQ-Work items are thus based on a comprehensive conceptual model of addiction (i.e., "Once I start work in any day I find it difficult to get out of the swing of it and relax," "Others have expressed repeated serious concern over the amount of time I spend working," "I have taken on a piece of work that I actively disliked not so much out of necessity but more simply to keep myself occupied"). So far, further psychometric validation is needed, particularly concerning the SPQ-Work scale and the appropriateness of the suggested cut-off values.

Workaholic Adjective Checklist (WAC)

As part of her doctoral thesis, Haymon (1992) developed the Workaholic Adjective Checklist. The WAC consists of 72 items answered in a Likert rating format. The scale was created based on an item pool of attributes reported in the literature. Five subscales were identified through exploratory factor analysis: Anxiety (e.g., "I forget where I put things"), Obsessive-compulsiveness (e.g., "I self-impose unrealistic deadlines for completing projects"), Mania (e.g., "I keep lists of things I do"), Intolerance (e.g., "I get bored easily"), and Self-doubt (e.g., "I often think my work is not as good as it could be"). High scores on the checklist indicate workaholism. Respondents with high WAC scores also scored higher on depression, anxiety, and anger. Although Senholzi (2005) re-evaluated the questionnaire in her doctoral thesis, further validation of the WAC is warranted.

Children of Workaholic Parents Screening Test (CWST)

The CWST is a self-report instrument particularly designed to measure the perceptual processes of workaholics' adult children, and how they perceive and experience their parents' work behavior. The test items were formulated from experiences and behavior patterns reported by clinically diagnosed children of workaholics, from case studies, and from the behavior patterns reported in the clinical and empirical literature (e.g., "Have you ever thought that one of your parents worked too much?"; "Have you ever lost sleep because of a parent's working too much?"; "Have you ever heard your parents fight because one of them was working too much?"). It was constructed by Robinson and Carroll (1999) and comprises 30 items answered on a forced-choice scale ("yes" = 1/"no" = 0). The CWST has been considered as a one-dimensional scale. High sum scores indicate parental workaholism. Robinson and Carroll (1999) found support for good psychometric properties. However, the scale has rarely been used in studies—although it has been incorporated in a few recent publications (Chamberlin & Zhang, 2009; Ng et al., 2007).

Work Attitudes Questionnaire (WAQ)

Doty and Betz (1981) constructed the Work Attitudes Questionnaire (WAQ) to assess attitudes and behaviors towards work, and the degree to which these are healthy or unhealthy. The questionnaire consists of two subscales, one "Commitment to Work"-scale (23 items, e.g., "I would rather stay at work and finish a task than leave something half-done and rush to get home") and one "Psychological Health"-scale (22 items, e.g., "I get restless and irritable during a long weekend"). All 45 questions are answered along a five-point scale ranging from 1 ("strongly disagree") to 5 ("strongly agree"), yielding a score range from 45 to 225. Scores greater than 69 on the Commitment subscale indicate highly committed individuals. Highly committed individuals with scores greater than 66 on the Health subscale indicate workaholism, whereas highly committed individuals with scores lower than 66 on the Health subscale indicate balanced work commitment (healthy attitudes and lifestyles). The item-pool was generated based on available descriptions of work commitment, Type-A behavior, and workaholism, as well as discussions with highly work committed or self-identified workaholic workers. The authors concluded that the WAQ showed good psychometric properties, although it has never been used since—thus needing more psychometric evaluations.

Overall Comment

Together, the ten specific measures emphasize somewhat different aspects of workaholism (see Table 4.1). Some operationalize workaholism first and foremost as an attitude (e.g., WorkBAT; Spence & Robbins, 1992), a behavior (e.g., Non-Required Work and Control of Others Scales; Mudrack & Naughton, 2001), or a trait (e.g., SNAP-Work; Clark et al., 1996), others as a compulsion and/or obsession (e.g., DUWAS; Schaufeli et al., 2009), whereas still others assess it as an addiction (e.g., BWAS; Andreassen et al., 2012). Some of them are brief (e.g., BWAS and DUWAS), which makes them suitable for epidemiological studies. Most of them measure workaholism as a multidimensional phenomenon (e.g., WorkBAT, WART, DUWAS), whereas other instruments primarily tap into one dimension (e.g., BWAS). Obviously, some of the scales are more popular among researchers than others. A recent meta-analysis shows, for example, that WorkBAT (Spence & Robbins, 1992) has been used in approximately 500 studies (Patel, Bowler, Bowler, & Methe, 2012), whereas WART (Robinson, 1999) has been used in roughly 150 studies (Patel et al., 2012).

Practical Implications

Knowledge about workaholism may be of practical interest to clinicians, organizational consultants, human resource management, as well as to employees and employers. Some possibly practical implications of this review will thus be highlighted in the following.

First, an efficient assessment may be warranted among practitioners to measure workaholism in working life or in a clinical setting. How do they choose from the array of instruments available if they want to assess workaholism? Psychometric evaluations justify practical use of several assessments at this point. The BWAS (Andreassen et al., 2012) and DUWAS (Schaufeli et al., 2009) are particularly applicable in a clinical setting due to their brevity, as well as for use in epidemiological studies or organizational surveys. The BWAS is also one of few instruments that are anchored within a theoretical well-founded frame—namely addiction theory. The items are worded in line with addiction in DSM (APA, 1994, 2013). These instruments efficiently deliver practitioners useful information related to status quo and intervention planning as well as providing scholars measures for investigating the structure and heterogeneity of workaholism. However, relying merely on scores from these assessments is not recommended. Assessment should always be accompanied with broader discussions about the individual's work behavior, and, if possible, collateral reports.

Second, what can be done with individuals exhibiting workaholism? No randomized controlled studies on treatment of workaholism have yet been published, but several recommendations for treatment approaches have been proposed—such as cognitive-behavioral therapy (e.g., Rational Emotive Behavioral Therapy) (Chen, 2006; Ellis, 1957), family therapy (Robinson, 2013), Motivational Interviewing (Miller & Rollnick, 2012), positive psychology (e.g., self-caring, develop life vision) (Burnwell & Chen, 2008), and Anonymous Workaholics (e.g., 12-step program) (Fry, Matherly, & Vitucci, 2006). Recommended organizational interventions involve establishing norms that promote work engagement rather than workaholism, creating a job situation that satisfies basic work needs (e.g., autonomy, relatedness, competency), focusing on management behavior (e.g., promoting healthy attitude towards work), and life–work balance programs (e.g., stress reduction techniques) (Andreassen, 2014).

Theoretical Implications and Future Research Directions

At the present time research in this field lags behind. One weakness relates to the definition, operationalization, and vagueness of the workaholism concept. Most of the measurement methods are poorly anchored within stringent theoretical frameworks. Moreover, they have rarely been tested (cross-validated) against each other and against instruments that reflect similar and potentially overlapping constructs, such as for example work overinvolvement (Lehr et al., 2010) and obsessive job passion (Vallerand et al., 2010). A broader consensus in terms of operationalization will facilitate comparison of results across studies. Such a consensus will also make it easier to develop norms and useful cut-off values for categorization of workaholism. This will also aid effect measurement of treatment. Moreover, by establishing useful and validated cut-offs, accurate estimates of the prevalence of workaholism in the general population will become possible.

Another weakness regards the frequent use of cross-sectional studies as well as studies lacking objective data of behavior and health. Studies building upon collateral information (e.g. partner, colleagues) are also lacking in this field.

Thus, future research efforts in this field should prioritize longitudinal designs, including objective and collateral data of behavior and health based on stringent theoretical frameworks.

Conclusion

This chapter provides a narrative overview of workaholism in terms of its definitions and assessments. Although the workaholism concept has been difficult to define, several measurements have been developed since the late 1980s. These have been validated to a small extent against each other or against already existing, potentially overlapping constructs. Only when validation is properly done will it be possible to establish accurate classifications (by using valid and reliable instruments) and thus to facilitate effective treatment of affected individuals in the long run. This field is in great need of longitudinal studies including objective measures of behavior and health.

Acknowledgement

Valuable comments provided by reviewers, and permissions to reprint items from particular workaholism scales by key authors, were greatly appreciated.

References

American Psychiatric Association (1994). *Diagnostic and Statistical Manual for Mental Disorders* (4th ed.). Washington, DC: American Psychiatric Association.

American Psychiatric Association (2013). *Diagnostic and Statistical Manual for Mental Disorders* (5th ed.). Arlington, VA: American Psychiatric Publishing.

Andreassen, C. S. (2013). Work addiction. In P. Miller (ed.). *Principles of addiction: Comprehensive addictive behaviors and disorders* (pp. 837–845). San Diego, CA: Elsevier.

Andreassen, C. S. (2014). Workaholism: An overview and current status of the research. *Journal of Behavioral Addictions, 3*, 1–11.

Andreassen, C. S., Griffiths, M. D., Hetland, J., & Pallesen, S. (2012). Development of a work addiction scale. *Scandinavian Journal of Psychology, 53*, 265–272.

Andreassen, C. S., Hetland, J., & Pallesen, S. (2014). Psychometric assessment of workaholism measures. *Journal of Managerial Psychology, 29*, 7–24.

Bonebright, C. A., Clay, D. L., & Ankenmann, R. D. (2000). The relationship of workaholism with work–life conflict, life satisfaction, and purpose in life. *Journal of Counseling Psychology, 47*, 469–477.

Brown, R. I. F. (1993). Some contributors of the study of gambling to the study of other addications. In W. R. Eadington & J. A. Cornelius (eds.), *Gambling behaviour and problem gambling* (pp. 241–272). Reno: University of Nevada Press.

Buelens, M., & Poelmans, S. A. Y. (2004). Enriching the Spence and Robbins' typology of workaholism. Demographic, motivational and organizational correlates. *Journal of Organizational Change Management, 17*, 440–458.

Burnwell, R., & Chen, C. P. (2008). Positive psychology for work–life balance: A new approach in treating workaholism. In R. J. Burke & C. L. Cooper (eds.), *The long work hours culture. Causes, consequences and choices* (pp. 295–313). Bingley: Emerald.

Caudroit, J., Boiché, J., Stephan, Y., Le Scanff, C., & Trouilloud, D. (2011). Predictors of work/family interference and leisure-time physical activity among teachers: The role of passion towards work. *European Journal of Work and Organizational Psychology, 20*, 326–344.

Calabrese, W. R., Rudick, M. M., Simms, L. J., & Clark, L. A. (2012). Development and validation of Big-Four scales for the Schedule for Nonadaptive and Adaptive Personality 2nd Edition (SNAP-2). *Psychological Assessment, 24*, 751–763.

Chamberlin, C. M., & Zhang, N. J. (2009). Workaholism, health, and self-acceptance *Journal of Counseling and Development, 87*, 159–169.

Chen, C. P. (2006). Improving work–life balance: REBT for workaholic treatment. In R. J. Burke (ed.), *Research companion to working time and work addiction* (pp. 310–329). Cheltenham: Edward Elgar.

Christo, G., Jones, S. L., Haylett, S., Stephenson, G. M., Lefever, R. M., & Lefever, R. (2003). The shorter PROMIS questionnaire: further validation of a tool for simultaneous assessment of multiple addictive behaviors. *Addictive Behavior, 28*, 225–248.

Clark, L. A. (1993). *Schedule for Nonadaptive and Adaptive Personality (SNAP): Manual for administration, scoring, and interpretation.* Minneapolis, MN: University of Minnesota Press.

Clark, L. A. (1996). *Schedule for Nonadaptive and Adaptive Personality: Manual for administration, scoring, and interpretation.* Minneapolis, MN: University of Minnesota Press.

Clark, L. A. (2009). *Schedule for Nonadaptive and Adaptive Personality: Second edition (SNAP-2).* (2nd ed). Minneapolis, MN: University of Minnesota Press.

Clark, L. A., Livesley, W. J, Schroeder, M. L., & Irish, S. L. (1996). Convergence of two systems for assessing specific traits of personality disorder. *Psychological Assessment, 8*, 294–303.

del Libano, M., Llorens, S., Salanova, M., & Schaufeli, W. (2010). Validity of a brief workaholism scale. *Psicothema, 22*, 143–150.

Doty, M. S., & Betz, N. E. (1981). *Manual for the Work Attitude Questionnaire.* Columbus: Marathon Consulting and Press.

Ellis, A. (1957). Rational psychotherapy and individual psychology. *Journal of Individual Psychology, 13*, 38–44.

Flowers, C. P., & Robinson, B. (2002). A structural and discriminant analysis of the work addiction risk test. *Educational and Psychological Measurement, 62*, 517–526.

Fry, L. W., Matherly, L. L., & Vitucci, S. (2006). Spiritual leadership theory as a source for future theory, research, and recovery from workaholism. In R. J. Burke (ed.), *Research companion to working time and work addiction* (pp. 330–352). Cheltenham: Edward Elgar.

Griffiths, M. D. (2005). A components model of addiction within a biopsychological framework. *Journal of Substance Use, 10*, 191–197.

Griffiths, M. D. (2011). Workaholism: A 21st century addiction. *The Psychologist: Bulletin of the British Psychological Society, 24*, 740–744.

Haymon, S. (1992). *The relationship of work addiction and depression, anxiety, and anger in college males.* Unpublished Doctoral dissertation. Florida State University.

Huang, J. C., Hu, C., & Wu, T. C. (2010). Psychometric properties of the Chinese version of the Workaholism Battery. *Journal of Psychology, 44*, 163–183.

Kanai, A., Wakabayashi, M., & Fling, S. (1996). Workaholism among employees in Japanese corporations: An examination based on the Japanese version of the workaholism scales. *Japanese Psychological Research, 38*, 192–203.

Lehr, D., Koch, S., & Hillert, A. (2010). Where is (im)balance? Necessity and construction of evaluated cut-off points for effort-reward imbalance and over-commitment. *Journal of Occupational and Organizational Psychology, 83*, 251–261.

Linde, J. A., Stringer, D., Simms, L. J., & Clark, L. A. (2013). The Schedule for Nonadaptive and Adaptive Personality for Youth (SNAP-Y): A new measure for assessing adolescent personality and personality pathology. *Assessment, 20*, 387–404.

Machlowitz, M. (1980). *Workaholics: Living with them, working with them.* Reading, MA: Addison-Wesley.

McMillan, L. H. W., O'Driscoll, M. P., Marsh, N. V., & Brady, E. C. (2001). Understanding workaholism: Data synthesis, theoretical critique, and future design strategies. *International Journal of Stress Management, 8*, 69–91.

McMillan, L. H. W., Brady, E. C., O'Driscoll, M. P., & Marsh, N. V. (2002). A multifaceted validation study of Spence and Robbins' (1992) Workaholism Battery. *Journal of Occupational and Organizational Psychology, 75*, 357–368.

Miller, W. R., & Rollnick, S. (2012). *Motivational Interviewing: Preparing people to change* (3rd ed.). New York: Guildford Press.

Mosier, S. K. (1983). *Workaholics: An analysis of their stress, success, and priorities.* Unpublished master's thesis, University of Texas, Austin, USA.

Mudrack, P. E. (2006). Understanding workaholism: The case for behavioral tendencies. In R. J. Burke (ed.), *Research companion to working time and work addiction* (pp. 108–128). Northampton, MA: Edward Elgar Publishing.

Mudrack, P. E., & Naughton, T. J. (2001). The assessment of workaholism as behavioral tendencies: Scale development and preliminary empirical testing. *International Journal of Stress Management, 8*, 93–111.

Ng, T. W. H., Sorensen, K. L., & Feldman, D. C. (2007). Dimensions, antecedents, and consequences of workaholism: A conceptual integration and extension. *Journal of Organizational Behavior, 28*, 111–136.

Oates, W. (1971). *Confessions of a workaholic: The facts about work addiction.* New York: World.

Patel, A. S., Bowler, M. C., Bowler, J. L., & Methe, S. A. (2012). A meta-analysis of workaholism. *International Journal of Business and Management, 7*, 2–17.

Robinson, B. E. (1989). *Workaholism: Hidden legacies of adult children.* Deerfield Beach, FL: Health Communications.

Robinson, B. E. (1998). *Chained to the desk: A guidebook for workaholics, their partners and children and the clinicians who treat them.* New York: New York University Press.

Robinson, B. E. (1999). The work addiction risk test: Development of a tentative measure of workaholism. *Perceptual and Motor Skills, 88*, 199–210.

Robinson, B. E. (2013). *Chained to the desk: A guidebook for workaholics, their partners and children, and the clinicians who treat them* (3rd ed.). New York: New York University Press.
Robinson, B. E., & Carroll, J. (1999). Assessing the offspring of workaholic parents: The Children of Workaholics Screening Test. *Perceptual and Motor Skills, 88*, 1127–1134.
Robinson, B. E., & Phillips, B. (1995). Measuring workaholism: Content validity of the Work Addiction Risk Test. *Psychological Reports, 77*, 657–658.
Robinson, B. E., & Post, P. (1995). Split-half reliability of the Work Addiction Risk Test: Development of a measure of workaholism. *Psychological Reports, 3*, 200–206.
Robinson, B. E., Post, P., & Khakee, J. F. (1992). Test–retest reliability of the Work Addiction Risk Test. *Perceptual and Motor Skills, 74*, 926.
Schaufeli, W. B., Shimazu, A., & Taris, T. W. (2009). Being driven to work excessively hard. The evaluation of a two-factor measure of workaholism in the Netherlands and Japan. *Cross-Cultural Research, 43*, 320–348.
Schaufeli, W. B., Taris, T. W., & Van Rhenen, W. (2008). Workaholism, burnout, and work engagement: Three of a kind or three different kinds of employee well-being? *Applied Psychology: An International Review, 57*, 173–203.
Schaufeli, W. B., van Wijhe, C. I., Peeters, M. C. W, & Taris, T. (2011), Reek's psychological instruments. Work addiction, a concept measured. *Gedrag & Organisatie, 24*, 43–63.
Scott, K. S., Moore, K. S., & Miceli, M. P. (1997). An exploration of the meaning and consequences of workaholism. *Human Relations, 50*, 287–314.
Senholzi, M. (2005). The validation and generalization of the Work Attitudes and Behaviors Inventory (WABI). *Dissertation Abstracts International.*
Snir, R., & Harpaz, I. (2012). Beyond workaholism: Towards a general model of heavy work investment. *Human Resource Management Review, 22*, 232–243.
Spence, J. T., & Robbins, A. S. (1992). Workaholism: definition, measurement, and preliminary results. *Journal of Personality Assessment, 58*, 160–178.
Stephenson, G. M., Maggi, P., Lefever, R. M. H., & Morojele, N. K. (1995). Excessive behaviours: An archival study of behavioural tendencies reported by 471 patients admitted to an addiction treatment centre. *Addiction Research, 3*, 245–265.
Sussman, S. (2012). Workaholism: A review. *Journal of Addiction Research and Theory, S6*. doi:10.4172/2155–6105.S6–001
Taris, T. W., Schaufeli, W. B., & Shimazu, A. (2010). The push and pull of work: The difference between workaholism and work engagement. In A. B. Bakker & M. P. Leiter (eds.), *Work engagement. A handbook of essential theory and research* (pp. 39–53). Hove: Psychological Press.
Vallerand, R. J., Blanchard, C., Magneau, G. A., Koestner, R., Ratelle, C., Leonard, M., Gagne, M., & Marsolais, J. (2003). Les passions de l'Ame: On obsessive and harmonious passion. *Journal of Personality and Social Psychology, 85*, 756–767.
Vallerand, R. J., Paquet, Y., Philippe, F. L., & Charest, J. (2010). On the role of passion for work in burnout: A process model. *Journal of Personality, 78*, 289–312.

van Beek, I., Taris, T. W., & Schaufeli, W. B. (2011). Workaholic and work engaged employees: Dead ringers or worlds apart? *Journal of Occupational Health Psychology, 16*, 468–482.

van Vegchel, N., de Jonge, J., Bosma, H., & Schaufeli, W. (2005). Reviewing the effort–reward imbalance model: Drawing up the balance of 45 empirical studies. *Social Sciences & Medicine, 60*, 1117–1131.

World Health Organization (1992). *The ICD-10 Classification of Mental and Behavioural Disorders. Clinical and descriptions and diagnostic guidelines.* Geneva: World Health Organization.

5

DISPOSITIONAL HEAVY WORK INVESTMENT

A Review of Assessments Designed to Measure Addiction to and Passion for Work

Kim Nimon and Mariya Gavrilova Aguilar

Snir and Harpaz (2012) developed a model of heavy work investment (HWI) to help advance research on workaholism. Building on McMillan and O'Driscoll's (2004) work, they considered *both* time and effort as requisite dimensions of HWI, such that only individuals investing both considerable time and effort at work are considered heavily invested in their work. They further separated HWI into two major subtypes (i.e., situational and dispositional) based on theoretical predictors of such an investment in work. Situational HWI is theorized to stem from *external predictors* such as basic financial needs and labor-market conditions, whereas dispositional HWI is theorized to stem from *internal predictors* such as addiction to and passion for work. The HWI model further delineates situational work investors into two types based on the source of external influence: (a) personal needs (e.g., employees who need to pay debts) and (b) employer-directed influences (e.g., high-tech workers); and dispositional work investors into four types based on the source of internal influence: (a) workaholics, (b) work-devoted, (c) intimacy-avoiders, and (d) leisure-low-interested. This chapter focuses on the two types of dispositional HWI that revolve around work (i.e., workaholics and work-devoted) and reviews assessments purported to measure constructs that predict such HWI (i.e., addiction to and passion for work). Identifying assessments consistent with the HWI model and that yield reliable and valid data is critical to advancing research on HWI. With appropriate assessments that do not confuse the predictors of HWI with the act of HWI, not only can the model of HWI be empirically tested, but research may reveal similarities and differences between individuals that are addicted to and those that are passionate about their work.

In distinguishing between workaholism and work devotion, Snir and Harpaz (2012) indicated that workaholism was based on an addiction to work that is an internal, uncontrollable, and stable predictor of HWI (e.g., addiction to work, fear of intimacy, obsessive-compulsive personality) and that work devotion was an expression of passion to work that is an internal, controllable, and stable predictor of HWI (e.g., work ethic, work centrality, organizational commitment) (p. 236). Note that a theoretical differentiation between the two constructs is the concept of control, where addiction to work is considered *uncontrollable* and passion for work is considered *controllable*. This distinction is important as we consider relevant assessments. The landscape of existing assessments that are conceptually similar to the constructs of workaholism and work devotion is also important.

Workaholism

Snir and Harpaz (2012) identified three major assessments that measure constructs related to workaholism. These assessments are the (a) Work Addiction Risk Test (WART; Robinson, 1989, 1999), (b) Workaholism Battery (WorkBAT, Spence & Robbins, 1992), and (c) Dutch Workaholism Scale (DUWAS; Schaufeli, Shimazu, & Taris, 2009).

Work Addiction Risk Test

The WART was originally conceived as a five-scale instrument with each scale containing five items to measure the following symptoms of workaholism: overdoing, self-worth, control-perfectionism, intimacy, and future reference/mental preoccupation. However, in subsequent analyses of the dimensionality of WART scores, Flowers and Robinson (2002) found a different factor structure with an unbalanced number of items/scale as follows: compulsive tendencies (items 3, 5, 6, 7, 8, 15, 18, 19, 20), control (2, 4, 11, 12, 16, 17, 22), impaired communication/self-absorption (13, 21, 23, 24, 25), inability to delegate (1), and self-worth (9, 10). They further found that only three of the constructs discriminated between workaholics and non-workaholics (i.e., compulsive tendencies, control, and impaired communication/self-absorption). In addition to containing only a few items, the remaining scales (i.e., inability to delegate, self-worth) demonstrated minimal concurrent validity.

Workaholism Battery

The WorkBAT (Spence & Robbins, 1992) is a 25-item scale originally conceived to measure three attitudinal aspects of work: involvement, drive, and enjoyment. In addition to work involvement scale scores demonstrating poor psychometric properties (Andreassen, Hetland, & Pallesen, 2010; Andreassen, Hetland, Molde, & Pallesen, 2011; Kanai, Wakabayashi, & Fling, 1996), subsequent factor analyses failed to confirm the three-factor WorkBAT structure causing McMillan, Brady, O'Driscoll, and Marsh (2002) to investigate its dimensionality. Results from McMillan et al. (2002) yielded a two-factor structure of the data with revised item alignment to two of the originally conceived factors: enjoyment (2, 4, 7, 9, 10, 11, 17) and drive (3, 14, 18, 20, 21, 22, 25). Still, others (e.g., Russo & Waters, 2006) have found that the original set of drive and enjoyment items has demonstrated accepted levels of reliability and factor loadings. Kanai et al. (1996) developed the Japanese version of the WorkBAT scale that yielded a two-factor structure of the data with revised item alignment to two of the originally conceived factors: enjoyment (2, 4, 7, 9, 10, 11, 16, 17, 22, 23) and drive (3, 5, 12, 14, 18, 20, 21, 24, 25). Other versions of the WorkBAT also appear in the literature; however, evidence of construct validity and identification of item to factor alignment appears to be lacking in many instances.

Dutch Workaholism Scale

Supporting the definition of workaholism "as the tendency to work excessively hard in a compulsive fashion" (Schaufeli et al., 2009, p. 338), the DUWAS contains two scales with five items each to measure working excessively (WE) and working compulsively (WC). The WE scale contains five of the nine items from the compulsive tendencies scale of the WART (Robinson, 1989, 1999; Flowers & Robinson, 2002). The WC scale contains four of the eight items from the drive scale of the WorkBAT (Spence & Robbins, 1992) and one item from the compulsive tendencies scale of the WART (Robinson, 1989, 1999; Flowers & Robinson, 2002). Scale scores demonstrated convergent validity with measures of excess working time and discriminant validity with measures of burnout and work engagement.

Work Devotion

Zigarmi, Nimon, Houson, Witt, and Diehl (2009) considered the construct of employee engagement as theoretically related to the construct of work devotion. According to Shuck, Nimon, and Zigarmi (2013), four major instruments measure constructs related to employee engagement: (a) Utrecht Work Engagement Scales (UWES-17, Schaufeli, Salanova, Gonzalez-Roma, & Bakker, 2002; UWES-9; Schaufeli, Bakker, & Salanova, 2006), (b) Psychological Engagement Scale (May, Gilson, & Harter, 2004), (c) Job Engagement Scale (Rich, Lepine, & Crawford, 2010), and (d) Passion Scale (Vallerand et al., 2003).

Utrecht Work Engagement Scales

The Utrecht Work Engagement Scale with 17 items (UWES-17) and nine items (UWES-9) operationalizes engagement as a "positive, fulfilling, work-related state of mind that is characterized by vigor, dedication, and absorption" (Schaufeli et al., 2002, p. 17). The UWES scales attempt to measure the constructs of vigor (high levels of energy), dedication (a sense of significance), and absorption (the perception of being fully engrossed in one's work). Both the UWES-17 and the UWES-9 have proven construct validity as well as confirmation of the three-factor structure, discriminant and convergent validity (Schaufeli et al., 2002; Schaufeli et al., 2006).

Psychological Engagement

The 13-item scale published by May et al. (2004) builds on Kahn's (1990) concept of psychological engagement characterized by three distinct dimensions (cognitive, emotional, and physical engagement). However, May et al. (2004) offered the scale as a means to assess an overall measure of psychological engagement since three distinct constructs did not emerge from the data.

Job Engagement

Rich et al. (2010) developed the 18-item job engagement scale that measures physical, emotional, and cognitive engagement with three six-item scales. Rich et al. provided evidence that data from the job engagement scales fit a higher-order factor structure with the three first-order factors loading on a second-order factor.

The Passion Scale

Vallerand et al. (2003, p. 757) defined passion as a "strong inclination toward an activity that people like, that they find important, and in which they invest time, and energy." The long and short form of the Passion Scale, which respectively contain 14 and 10 items (items 6, 7, 10, and 14 are omitted from the short version), include separate scales for the constructs of harmonious passion and obsessive passion. Harmonious passion stems from an autonomous internalization of the activity into one's identity whereas obsessive passion results from a controlled internalization. Passion Scale scores have demonstrated evidence of construct validity including confirmation of the two-factor structure for the long version and concurrent validity for the short and long versions. There are other versions of the Passion Scale featured in the literature. However, a 12-item version of the Passion Scale referencing Vallerand et al., as well as a 12-item version by Bélanger, Lafrenière, Vallerand,

and Kruglanski (2013) presented little evidence of construct validity. Note that although Zigarmi et al. (2008) identified employee engagement as being theoretically related to the construct of work devotion and Shuck et al. (2013) seemed to consider obsessive passion as a measure of employee engagement, it appears in our analyses that obsessive passion is more characteristic of what Snir and Harpaz (2012) refer to as workaholism.

Analysis of Assessments

In our review of assessments related to workaholism and employee engagement previously presented, two scales appear to be consistent with the HWI model in measuring predictors of the two types of dispositional HWIs that revolve around work (i.e., workaholics, the work-devoted). These are the 14-item version of the Passion Scale (Vallerand et al., 2003) and various versions of the drive and enjoyment scales of the WorkBAT (Ersoy-Kart, 2005; Kanai et al., 1996; McMillan et al., 2002; Spence & Robbins, 1992). Not only did these scales appear to measure internal predictors of HWI consistent with addiction to and passion for work, but also they uniquely contain items that distinguish the predictors as being uncontrollable and controllable (see Table 5.1). Note that we did not

Table 5.1 Assessments Consistent with Internal Predictors of Workaholic and Work-Devoted HWIs

Instrument Scale[a]	*Sample Item*	*Related HWI Subtype*
Passion Scale Harmonious passion	For me it is a passion that I still manage to control	Work-devoted
WorkBAT Enjoyment Enjoyment-R[b,c,d]	I do more work than is expected of me strictly for the fun of it	Work-devoted
Passion Scale Obsessive passion	The urge is so strong. I can't help myself from doing this activity	Workaholic
Work BAT Drive Drive-R[e,f]	I seem to have an inner compulsion to work hard	Workaholic

Note: [a]Unless otherwise noted, original set of items listed. [b]Revised by McMillan et al. (2002) containing 7 items (2, 4, 7, 9, 10, 11, 17). [c]Revised by Kanai et al. (1996) containing 10 items (2, 4, 7, 9, 10, 11, 16, 17, 22, 23). [d]Revised by Ersoy-Kart (2005) containing 9 items (2, 4, 7, 8, 9, 10, 11, 17, 19). [e]Revised by McMillan et al. (2002) containing 7 items (3, 14, 18, 20, 21, 22, 25). [f]Revised by Kanai et al. (1996) containing 9 items (3, 5, 12, 14, 18, 20, 21, 24, 25).

include the 12-item or the 10-item version of the Passion Scale because it omitted item 6, which we consider a key item as it specifically considers control ("For me it is a passion that I still manage to control").

Our analysis is congruent with the work of Snir and Harpaz (2012) who associated harmonious passion with passion for work and obsessive passion with addiction to work. We agree with Snir and Harpaz that these scales should only be considered as predictors of HWI as they do not specifically measure the key components of HWI (i.e., time and effort at work). As indicated by Kanungo (1979) and others, it is important for scales to be focused on specific constructs and not confuse a construct with its antecedents. In this case, it is important to separate predictors of HWI from the act of HWI to avoid blurring. If such blurring occurs, responses may not be used to distinguish between the reason for and the act of HWI. It is important to acknowledge that some of the items in the WorkBAT drive scale make reference to working hard (e.g., item 25, see Table 5.1), which suggests an investment of energy in work. However, the items do not appear to specifically measure how much energy one invests. It is also important to note that although some authors (e.g., Mudrack, 2006) do not consider work enjoyment as a defining characteristic of workaholism, we find the WorkBAT enjoyment scale useful when assessing the predictors of HWI.

To develop an understanding of the similarities and differences in the magnitude of relationships between work related measures and addiction to and devotion for work, we reviewed key studies that incorporated the 14-item version of the Passion Scale and appropriate versions of the drive and enjoyment scales of the WorkBAT (Ersoy-Kart, 2005; Kanai et al., 1996; McMillan et al., 2002; Spence & Robbins, 1992). We selected peer-reviewed articles that reported correlations between appropriate WorkBAT and Passion Scale scores and scores from work related constructs (e.g., well-being, self-esteem, burnout, conflict) for populations represented by "working individuals." We excluded studies that used the Passion Scale to assess passion in the context of sports (e.g., Donahue, Rip, & Vallerand, 2009; Lafrenière, Jowett, Vallerand, & Carbonneau, 2011), online gaming (e.g., Lafrenière, Vallerand, Donahue, & Lavigne, 2009; Utz, Jonas, & Tonkens, 2012), and interpersonal relationships (e.g., Seguin-Levesque, Lyne, Lalibertea, Pelletier, Blanchard, & Vallerand, 2003). We also excluded studies that used WorkBAT scales to assess workaholism and its influence on personal relationships (e.g., McMillan, O'Driscoll, & Brady, 2004) and studies that proposed a modified version of the instrument with lack of clarity on which items were included (e.g., Andreassen, Ursin, & Eriksen, 2007).

While there does not appear to be a consistent set of correlates examined (see Tables 5.2 and 5.3), comparisons can be made within the scales of the two assessments. When comparing the magnitude of the

Table 5.2 Key Empirical Studies Reporting on Correlations (r) with Obsessive Passion (OP) and Harmonious Passion (HP) Scores

Study	*Measure (α)*	*Sample*	*Correlate*	r_{OP}	r_{HP}
Carpentier, Mageau, & Vallerand (2011)	OP (0.89) HP (0.70)	172 Canadian college students	Harmonious passion (Vallerand et al., 2003)	0.41	1.00
			Ruminations during studies (Conway et al., 2000)	0.45	0.18
			Flow experiences during studies (Jackson & Marsh, 1996)	0.00	0.13
			Flow experiences during activity (Jackson & Marsh, 1996)	0.32	0.64
			Subjective well-being (Blais et al., 1989; Diener et al., 1985; Watson et al., 1988)	–0.16	0.18
Ho, Wong, & Lee (2011)	OP (0.85) HP (0.90)	509 insurance employees	Harmonious passion (Vallerand et al., 2003)	0.30	1.00
			Job satisfaction (Quinn & Shepard, 1974)	0.31	0.66
			Organizational commitment (Meyer & Allen, 1997)	0.46	0.61
			Job identification (Leiter, 1992)	0.29	0.59
			Attention (Rothbard, 2001)	0.16	0.38
			Absorption (Rothbard, 2001)	0.25	0.33
			Work performance (organization's records)	–0.05	0.12
			Education (Ho et al., 2011)	–0.20	–.07
			Gender (Ho et al., 2011)	0.06	0.04
			Tenure (Ho et al., 2011)	0.12	0.09
			Rank (Ho et al., 2011)	–0.09	0.09
Klaukien, Shepherd, & Patzelt (2013)	OP (0.87) HP (0.69)	90 German entrepreneurs	Harmonious passion (Vallerand et al., 2003)	0.33	1.00
			Age (Klaukien et al., 2013)	–0.14	0.16
			Work experience (Klaukien et al., 2013)	0.01	–0.05
Vallerand et al. (2003)	OP (0.89) HP (0.79)	520 college students	Activity as a passion (Vallerand et al., 2003)	0.46[a]	0.43[a]
			Activity valuation (Vallerand et al., 2003)	0.57[a]	0.37[a]
			Time and energy investment (Vallerand et al., 2003)	0.20[a]	0.35[a]
			Inclusion in the self (Aron et al., 1992)	0.49[a]	0.16[a]
			Conflict with other activities (Vallerand et al., 2003)	0.50[a]	0.11[a]
			Flow challenge (Jackson & Marsh, 1996)	–0.01[a]	0.38[a]

			Flow absence of self-consciousness (Jackson & Marsh, 1996)	–0.04[a]	0.16[a]
			Flow control (Jackson & Marsh, 1996)	–.01[a]	0.24[a]
			Positive emotions during activity (Vallerand et al., 1993)	–0.02[a]	0.46[a]
			Concentration (Vallerand et al.,1989; Vallerand et al., 1993)	–0.01[a]	0.33[a]
			Anxiety (Vallerand et al., 1989; Vallerand et al., 1993)	0.12[a]	–0.01[a]
			Shame (Vallerand et al., 1989; Vallerand et al., 1993)	0.25[a]	–0.24[a]
			Positive emotions after engagement in activity (Vallerand et al., 2003)	–0.09[a]	0.43[a]
			Negative emotions after engagement in activity (Vallerand et al., 2003)	0.21[a]	–0.23[a]
			Negative cognition when prevented from activity (Vallerand et al., 2003)	0.54[a]	0.06[a]
			Negative affect when prevented from activity (Vallerand et al., 2003)	0.55[a]	–0.04[a]
Vallerand, Paquet, Philippe, & Charest (2010)	OP (0.72) HP (0.72)	97 French nurses	Harmonious passion (Vallerand et al., 2003)	0.35	1.00
			Satisfaction with work (Diener et al., 1985)	0.14	0.50
			Conflict (Vallerand et al., 2010)	0.44	0.07
			Burnout (Maslach et al., 1996)	0.02	–0.31
Vallerand, Paquet, Philippe, & Charest (2010)	OP (0.71) HP (0.86)	258 French-Canadian nurses	Harmonious passion – T1 (Vallerand et al., 2003)	0.19	1.00
			Satisfaction at work – T1 (Diener et al., 1985)	0.05	0.61
			Conflict – T1 (Vallerand et al., 2010)	0.35	–0.17
			Burnout – T1 (Maslach et al., 1996)	0.11	–0.43
			Satisfaction at work – T2 (Diener et al., 1985)	0.08	0.58
			Conflict – T2 (Vallerand et al., 2010)	0.29	–0.18
			Burnout – T2 (Maslach et al., 1996)	0.13	–0.41

Note: [a]Partial correlations reported between outcome and one type of passion while controlling for the other ($r_{HP.OP} = 0.46$).

Table 5.3 Key Empirical Studies Reporting on Correlations (r) with WorkBAT Drive (D) and WorkBAT Enjoyment (E) Scores

Study	*Measure*[a] *α*	*Sample*	*Correlate*	r_D	r_E
Andreassen, Hetland, Molde, & Pallesen (2011)	WorkBAT-D (0.82) WorkBAT-E (0.77)	661 Norwegian cross-occupational employees	Enjoyment of work (Spence & Robbins, 1992)	0.03	1.00
			Drive (Spence & Robbins, 1992)	1.00	0.03
			Work involvement (Spence & Robbins, 1992)	0.30	0.14
			Job satisfaction (Brayfield & Rothe, 1951)	–0.33	0.52
			Life satisfaction (MSLSS: Huebner, 2001)	–0.27	0.35
			Insomnia (BIS: Pallesen et al., 2008)	0.30	–0.13
			Subjective health complaints (Eriksen et al., 1999)	0.31	–0.12
			Work hours (Andreassen et al., 2011)	0.21	0.21
Andreassen, Hetland, & Pallesen (2010)	WorkBAT-D (0.82) WorkBAT-E (0.77)	661 Norwegian cross-occupational employees	Enjoyment of work (Spence & Robbins, 1992)	0.03	1.00
			Drive (Spence & Robbins, 1992)	1.00	0.03
			Work involvement (Spence & Robbins, 1992)	0.30	0.14
			Autonomy (Deci et al., 2001)	0.33	0.35
			Competence (Deci et al., 2001)	0.20	0.42
			Relatedness (Deci et al., 2001)	0.13	0.23
			Neuroticism (Costa & McCrae, 1992)	0.34	0.20
			Extraversion (Costa & McCrae, 1992)	0.02	0.26
			Openness to experience (Costa & McCrae, 1992)	0.05	0.16
			Agreeableness (Costa & McCrae, 1992)	0.13	0.01
			Conscientiousness (Costa & McCrae, 1992)	0.11	0.15
Bonebright, Clay, & Ankenmann (2000)	WorkBAT-D (0.73) WorkBAT-E (0.85)	171 salaried high-tech US Midwest employees	Enjoyment of work (Spence & Robbins, 1992)	0.00	1.00
			Drive (Spence & Robbins, 1992)	1.00	0.00
			Work involvement (Spence & Robbins, 1992)	0.24	0.08
			Work–life conflict (Gutek et al., 1991)	0.42	–0.14
			Life Satisfaction (Diener et al., 1985)	–0.20	0.37
			Purpose in Life, Part A (Crumbaugh & Maholick, 1964)	–0.08	0.42

Burke (1999)	WorkBAT-D (0.80) WorkBAT-E (0.88)	530 Canadian MBA graduates working full-time	Enjoyment of work (Spence & Robbins, 1992)	0.09	1.00
			Drive (Spence & Robbins, 1992)	1.00	0.09
			Work involvement (Spence & Robbins, 1992)	0.25	0.22
			Job involvement (Spence & Robbins, 1992)	0.34	0.53
			Time to work (Spence & Robbins, 1992)	0.51	0.27
			Perfectionism (Spence & Robbins, 1992)	0.42	0.16
			Nondelegation (Spence & Robbins, 1992)	0.20	–0.15
			Extra hours worked (Burke, 1999)	0.26	–0.26
			Hours worked (Burke, 1999)	0.30	0.22
Burke (2000)	WorkBAT-D (0.80) WorkBAT-E (0.88)	530 Canadian MBA graduates working full-time	Enjoyment of work (Spence & Robbins, 1992)	0.09	1.00
			Drive (Spence & Robbins, 1992)	1.00	0.09
			Work involvement (Spence & Robbins, 1992)	0.25	0.22
			Striving against others (Lee et al., 1996)	0.16	–0.14
			No moral principles (Lee et al., 1996)	0.30	–0.21
			Prove oneself (Lee et al., 1996)	0.40	–0.14
			Beliefs (Lee et al., 1996)	0.37	–0.20
Burke & Koksal (2002)	WorkBAT-D (0.46) WorkBAT-E (0.79)	60 Turkish managers and professionals	Work involvement (Spence & Robbins, 1992)	NR	0.56
			Job involvement (Spence & Robbins, 1992)	0.27	0.71
			Job stress (Spence & Robbins, 1992)	0.43	–0.55
			Perfectionism (Spence & Robbins, 1992)	NR	0.32
			Time on the job (Spence & Robbins, 1992)	NR	0.48
			Emotional satisfaction (Kofodimos, 1993)	–0.35	0.26
			Community satisfaction (Kofodimos, 1993)	–0.31	0.31
			Relationship satisfaction (Kofodimos, 1993)	NR	0.23
			Family satisfaction (Kofodimos, 1993)	–0.29	0.33
			Job satisfaction (Kofodimos, 1993)	0.23	0.47
			Career satisfaction, (Greenhaus et al., 1990)	NR	0.27
			Org. values work–personal life balance (Kofodimos, 1993)	NR	–0.24
			Future career prospects (Greenhaus et al., 1990)	0.22	NR
			Beliefs (Lee et al., 1996)	0.46	NR

(*Continued*)

Table 5.3 Continued

Study	*Measure*[a] *(α)*	*Sample*	*Correlate*	r_D	r_E
Ersoy-Kart (2005)	WorkBAT-E Revised[b] (0.81)	175 Turkish employees	Drive (Spence & Robbins, 1992)		0.47
			Type A behavior (Jenkins et al., 1979)		0.22
Graves, Ruderman, Ohlott, & Weber (2012)	WorkBAT-D Revised[c] (0.69) WorkBAT-E Revised[c] (0.80)	346 managers in the United States	Enjoyment of work (McMillan et al., 2002)	–0.07	1.00
			Drive (McMillan et al., 2002)	1.00	–0.07
			Self-esteem (Rosenberg, 1965)	–0.19	0.21
			Psychological strain (Caplan et al., 1980)	0.15	–0.51
			Career satisfaction (Greenhaus et al., 1990)	0.01	0.25
			Performance 1– skills (Graves et al., 2012)	–0.02	0.22
			Performance 2– reversed derailment factors (Graves et al., 2012)	–0.04	0.19
			Performance 3– global rating (Graves et al., 2012)	0.05	0.23
			Marital status (Graves et al., 2012)	0.06	0.01
			Parental status (Graves et al., 2012)	0.02	0.11
			Gender (Graves et al., 2012)	–0.02	0.02
			Age (Graves et al., 2012)	–0.14	0.07
			Tenure (Graves et al., 2012)	–0.04	0.13
Johnstone & Johnston (2005)	WorkBAT-D Revised[c] (0.71) WorkBAT-E Revised[c] (.85)	151 New Zealand employees	Enjoyment of work (McMillan et al., 2002)	0.13	1.00
			Drive (McMillan et al., 2002)	1.00	0.13
			Work pressure (Moos, 1994)	0.21	NR
			Age (Johnstone & Johnston, 2005)	–0.30	NR
			Hours worked (Johnstone & Johnston, 2005)	0.20	NR
			Involvement (Moos, 1994)	NR	0.25
			Coworker cohesion (Moos, 1994)	NR	0.32
			Supervisor support (Moos, 1994)	NR	0.30
			Work pressure (Moos, 1994)	0.21	–0.17

Kanai, Wakabayashi, & Fling (1996)	WorkBAT-D Revised[d] (0.72) WorkBAT-E Revised[d] (0.85)	962 Japanese male employees	Enjoyment of work (Spence & Robbins, 1992)	0.32	1.00
			Drive (Spence & Robbins, 1992)	1.00	0.32
			Time commitment (Spence & Robbins, 1992)	0.67	0.36
			Job involvement (Spence & Robbins, 1992)	0.40	0.70
			Job stress (Rizzo et al., 1970; Watanabe et al., 1990)	0.57	–0.01
			Perfectionism (Spence & Robbins, 1992)	0.58	0.30
			Non delegation of responsibility (Spence & Robbins, 1992)	0.38	0.07
			Health complaints (Spence et al., 1987)	0.31	–0.06
			Work overload (Watanabe et al., 1990)	0.31[e]	0.00[e]
Kanai, Wakabayashi, & Fling (1996)	WorkBAT-D Revised[d] (0.51) WorkBAT-E Revised[d] (0.86)	110 Japanese female employees	Work overload (Watanabe et al., 1990)	0.09[e]	–0.04[e]
McMillan, Brady, O'Driscoll & Marsh (2002)	WorkBAT-D (0.74) WorkBAT-E (0.85)	320 New Zealand employees	Enjoyment of work (Spence & Robbins, 1992)	0.29	1.00
			Drive (Spence & Robbins, 1992)	1.00	0.29
			Work Involvement (Spence & Robbins, 1992)	0.40	0.25
			Intrinsic job motivation (Warr et al., 1979)	0.40	NR
			Job satisfaction (Warr et al., 1979)	NR	0.46
			SNAP-Work (Clark, 1993)	0.59	0.36
McMillan, Brady, O'Driscoll & Marsh (2002)	WorkBAT-D Revised[c] (0.75) WorkBAT-E Revised[c] (0.85)	320 New Zealand employees	Enjoyment of work (McMillan et al., 2002)	0.22	1.00
			Drive (McMillan et al., 2002)	1.00	0.22
			Intrinsic job motivation (Warr et al., 1979)	0.39	0.28
			Job satisfaction (Warr et al., 1979)	0.09	0.48
			Work involvement (Warr et al., 1979)	0.35	0.36
			SNAP-Work (Clark, 1993)	0.61	0.27
			Hours worked (McMillan et al., 2002)	0.22	0.16

(*Continued*)

Table 5.3 Continued

Study	*Measure*[a] *(α)*	*Sample*	*Correlate*	r_D	r_E
Russo & Waters (2006)	WorkBAT-D (0.85) WorkBAT-E (0.88)	169 Australian legal employees	Enjoyment of work (Spence & Robbins, 1992)	0.25	1.00
			Drive (Spence & Robbins, 1992)	1.00	0.25
			Work–family conflict (Bohen & Viveros-Long, 1981)	0.46	–0.07
			Supervisor support (Shinn et al., 1989)	0.01	0.18
			Job flexibility (Russo & Waters, 2006)	–0.12	0.09
			Gender (Russo & Waters, 2006)	0.04	–0.02
			Number of dependent children (Russo & Waters, 2006)	–0.03	0.07
			Age (Russo & Waters, 2006)	–0.05	–0.09
			Young Children (Russo & Waters, 2006)	–0.12	0.13
			Relationship Type (Russo & Waters, 2006)	–0.02	–0.13
			Professional status (Russo & Waters, 2006)	0.10	0.03
			Employment status (Russo & Waters, 2006)	0.24	0.12
Snir (2011)	WorkBAT-E Revised[c] (0.83)	238 full-time workers	Desired weekly hours after a hypothetical lottery win (Snir, 2011)	NR	0.48
Snir (2011)	WorkBAT-E Revised[c] (0.86)	251 full-time workers	Expected relative work centrality (Snir, 2011)	NR	0.34
Spence & Robbins (1992)	WorkBAT-D (0.81) WorkBAT-E (0.86)	134 male social workers	Enjoyment of work (Spence & Robbins, 1992)	0.07	1.00
			Drive (Spence & Robbins, 1992)	1.00	0.07
			Work involvement (Spence & Robbins, 1992)	0.46	0.22
			Health complaints (Spence et al., 1987)	0.36	–0.22
			Time commitment (Spence & Robbins, 1992)	0.47	0.33
			Job involvement (Spence & Robbins, 1992)	0.21	0.62
			Job stress (Spence & Robbins, 1992)	0.66	–0.11
			Perfectionism (Spence & Robbins, 1992)	0.65	0.09
			Non delegation of responsibility (Spence & Robbins, 1992)	0.55	–0.19

Spence & Robbins (1992)	WorkBAT-D (.067) WorkBAT-E (0.86)	157 female social workers	Enjoyment of work (Spence & Robbins, 1992)	–0.06	1.00
			Drive (Spence & Robbins, 1992)	1.00	–0.06
			Work involvement (Spence & Robbins, 1992)	0.50	0.24
			Time commitment (Spence & Robbins, 1992)	0.45	0.28
			Job involvement (Spence & Robbins, 1992)	0.35	0.56
			Job stress (Spence & Robbins, 1992)	0.64	–0.10
			Perfectionism (Spence & Robbins, 1992)	0.61	0.05
			Non-delegation of responsibility (Spence & Robbins, 1992)	0.45	–0.00
			Health complaints (Spence et al., 1987)	0.38	–0.22

Note: [a]Unless otherwise noted, original set of items used. [b]Revised by Ersoy-Kart (2005) containing 9 items (2, 4, 7, 8, 9, 10, 11, 17, 19). [c]Revised by McMillan et al. (2002) containing 7 items for Drive (3, 14, 18, 20, 21, 22, 25) and 7 items for Enjoyment (2, 4, 7, 9, 10, 11, 17). [d]Revised by Kanai et al. (1996) containing 9 items for Drive (3, 5, 12, 14, 18, 20, 21, 24, 25) and 10 items for Enjoyment (2, 4, 7, 9, 10, 11, 16, 17, 22, 23). [e]Reported by Kanai & Wakabayashi (2004). NR=not reported correlations among the correlates to harmonious and obsessive passion scores from the Passion Scale (Vallerand et al., 2003), it appears that the work-devoted may (a) invest more time and energy at work, and (b) have more satisfaction with life and positive affect at work than workaholics. Similarly, workaholics may (a) experience more burnout, conflict, and anxiety at work and (b) feel more negative affect when they are unable to work than the work-devoted.

When comparing the magnitude of the correlations among the correlates to enjoyment and drive scores from variations of the WorkBAT (Ersoy-Kart, 2005; Kanai et al., 1996; McMillan et al., 2002; Spence & Robbins, 1992), it appears that the work-devoted and workaholics may both (a) be intrinsically motivated and (b) invest time and energy at work, with the work-devoted investing more energy and the workaholics investing more time. Similarly, workaholics may experience more stress, conflict, exhaustion, overload, cynicism, and health issues than the work-devoted and the work-devoted may be more absorbed, dedicated, and satisfied with work and life than workaholics.

Future Research

Based on our analysis of published literature related to the measure of addiction to and passion for work, we offer three recommendations for future research. We recommend that future research (a) examine and compare the nomological and concurrent validity of the harmonious and obsessive passion scales (Vallerand et al., 2003) and various versions of the WorkBAT drive and enjoyment scales (Ersoy-Kart, 2005; Kanai et al., 1996; McMillan et al., 2002; Spence & Robbins, 1992), (b) investigate if and how the work-devoted control their passion for work, and (c) test the propositions set forth in this chapter.

It would add to the body of knowledge on HWI to use the Passion Scale (Vallerand et al., 2003) and appropriate versions of the WorkBAT drive and enjoyment scales (e.g., Spence & Robbins, 1992) to see how the scales work either separately or in conjunction with each other in identifying HWIs who are workaholics or work-devoted. It is possible that concurrent validity deficiencies in one set of scales might be overcome with items from the other set of scales. For example, the harmonious passion, obsessive passion, work drive, and enjoyment items could be factor analyzed to determine if a two-factor structure results and how such factors might predict types of HWI in relation to the original scales themselves. It would also be interesting to examine the nomological net of the Passion Scale, the WorkBAT drive and enjoyment scales, and combined versions of the scales. As seen in Tables 5.2 and 5.3, there appears to be only a minimal amount of congruence in the correlates to work addiction and work devotion across the two sets of assessments analyzed in this chapter. Specifically testing the nomological net of the Passion Scale and appropriate versions of the WorkBAT drive and enjoyment scales would help future researchers, who wish to test the HWI model, understand how each scale relates to work-related measures such as job satisfaction, job involvement, and organizational commitment.

A key consideration in the HWI model is the idea that addiction to work is an *uncontrollable* predictor of HWI and that passion to work is a *controllable* predictor of HWI. However, literature reveals that there appears to be a substantive amount of shared variance between, for example, harmonious and obsessive passion. It is likely that the shared variance is what might be considered passion. The question remains how some individuals appear to control their passion for work. If such a question can be answered empirically, the results might be helpful to those who are addicted to work as it appears that the outcomes associated with work devotion appear to be more favorable than the outcomes associated with workaholism.

The propositions set forth in this chapter suggest more positive outcomes for the work-devoted than for the workaholics. However, our analysis is based only on relevant correlations reported in the literature. Future research should test such propositions and determine the population groups in which they appear in order to be supported or refuted. It might also be useful to merge the propositions set forth in this chapter with the propositions set forth in Snir and Harpaz (2012) in order to develop and examine a more holistic model of the dispositional HWI subtypes that revolve around work.

Conclusion

Based on our analysis of assessments related to workaholism and work devotion, we conclude that two instruments appear to have scales that may be useful in distinguishing between addiction to and passion for work. They are the 14-item version of the Passion Scale (Vallerand et al., 2003) and appropriate versions of the drive and enjoyment scales of the WorkBAT (Ersoy-Kart, 2005; Kanai et al., 1996; McMillan et al., 2002; Spence & Robbins, 1992). Data from these scales have demonstrated accepted levels of construct and concurrent validity and contain items that appear to distinguish work devotion as being a controllable predictor and workaholism as being an uncontrollable predictor of HWI. It is important to note that other versions of these instruments exist. However, not all versions appear to be supported by evidence of construct validity or concurrent validity. Nor do all variants of the assessments contain items that consider aspects of internal control.

Based on our analysis of correlates related to data from these two assessments, it appears the outcomes associated with the work-devoted (e.g., satisfaction with life, positive affect at work) appear to be more positive than the outcomes associated with workaholics (e.g., conflict, burnout, anxiety at work). More research is needed to test such propositions, compare the concurrent validity and nomological validity of the Passion Scale and WorkBAT drive and enjoyment scales, and evaluate how the work-devoted control their passion for work.

References

Andreassen, C. S., Hetland, J., Molde, H., & Pallesen, S. (2011). Workaholism and potential outcomes in well-being and health in a cross-occupational sample. *Stress & Health, 27*, e209–e214.

Andreassen, C. S., Hetland, J., & Pallesen, S. (2010). The relationship between workaholism, basic needs satisfaction at work and personality. *European Journal of Personality, 24*, 3–17.

Andreassen, C. S., Ursin, H., & Eriksen, H. R. (2007). The relationship between strong motivation to work, "workaholism," and health. *Psychology and Health, 22*, 615–629.

Aron, A., Aron, E. N., & Smollan, D. (1992). Inclusion of other in the Self Scale and the structure of interpersonal closeness. *Journal of Personality and Social Psychology, 63*, 596–612.

Bélanger, J. J., Lafrenière, M. K., Vallerand, R. J., & Kruglanski, A. W. (2013). Driven by fear: The effect of success and failure information on passionate individuals' performance. *Journal of Personality and Social Psychology, 104*, 180–195.

Blais, M. R., Vallerand, R. J., Pelletier, L. G., & Brie're, N. M. (1989). L'e´chelle de satisfaction de vie: Validation canadienne-francaise du "Satisfaction With Life Scale" [French-Canadian Validation of the Satisfaction With Life Scale]. *Canadian Journal of Behavioural Sciences, 21*, 210–223.

Bohen, H. H., & Viveros-Long, A. (1981). *Balancing jobs and family life: Do flexible work schedules really help?* Philadelphia, PA: Temple University Press.

Bonebright, C. A., Clay, D. L., & Ankenmann, R. D. (2000). The relationship of workaholism with work–life conflict, life satisfaction, and purpose in life. *Journal of Counseling Psychology, 47*, 469–477.

Brayfield, A. H., & Rothe, H. F. (1951). An index of job satisfaction. *Journal of Applied Psychology, 35*, 307–311.

Burke, R. J. (1999). Workaholism in organizations: Measurement validation and replication. *International Journal of Stress Management, 6*, 45–55.

Burke, R. J. (2000). Workaholism in organizations: The role of personal beliefs and fears. *Anxiety, Stress and Coping, 13*, 53–64.

Burke, R. J., & Koksal, H. (2002). Workaholism among a sample of Turkish managers and professionals: An exploratory study. *Psychological Reports, 91*, 60–68.

Caplan, R. D., Cobb, S., French, J. R. P., Jr., Harrison, R. V., & Pinneau, S. R., Jr. (1980). *Job demands and worker health: Main effects and occupational differences.* Ann Arbor, MI: Institute for Social Research.

Carpentier, J., Mageau, G. A., & Vallerand, R. J. (2011). Ruminations and flow: Why do people with a more harmonious passion experience higher well-being? *Journal of Happiness Studies, 13*, 501–518.

Clark, L. A. (1993). *Manual for the Schedule for Nonadaptive and Adaptive Personality*. Minneapolis, MN: University of Minnesota Press.

Conway, M., Csank, P. A. R., Holm, S. L., & Blake, C. K. (2000). On assessing individual differences in rumination on sadness. *Journal of Personality Assessment, 75*, 404–425.

Costa, P. T., & McCrae, R. R. (1992). *NEO PI-R professional manual*. Odessa, FL: Psychological Assessment Resources.

Crumbaugh, J. C., & Maholick, L. T. (1964). An experimental study in existentialism: The psychometric approach to Frankl's concept of noogenic neurosis. *Journal of Clinical Psychology, 20*, 200–207.

Deci, E. L., Ryan, R. M., Gagné, M., Leone, D. R., Usunov, J., & Kornazheva, B. P. (2001). Need satisfaction, motivation, and well-being in the work organizations of a former Eastern Bloc country: A cross-cultural study of self-determination. *Personality and Social Psychology Bulletin, 27*, 930–942.

Diener, E., Emmons, R. A., Larsen, R. J., & Griffin, S. (1985). The Satisfaction With Life Scale. *Journal of Personality Assessment, 49*, 71–76.

Donahue, E. G., Rip, B., & Vallerand, R. J. (2009). When winning is everything: On passion, identity, and aggression in sport. *Psychology of Sport and Exercise, 10*, 526–534.

Eriksen, H. R., Ihlebæk, C., & Ursin, H. (1999). A scoring system for subjective health complaints (SHC). *Scandinavian Journal of Public Health, 27*, 63–72.

Ersoy-Kart, M. (2005). Reliability and validity of the Workaholism Battery (Work-BAT): Turkish form. *Social Behavior and Personality: An International Journal, 33*, 609–618.

Flowers, C. P., & Robinson, B. (2002). A structural and discriminant analysis of the Work Addiction Risk Test. *Educational and Psychological Measurement, 62*, 517–526.

Graves, L. M., Ruderman, M. N., Ohlott, P. J., & Weber, T. J. (2012). Driven to work and enjoyment of work: Effects on managers' outcomes. *Journal of Management, 38*, 1655–1680.

Greenhaus, J. H., Parasuraman, S., & Wormley, W. (1990). Organizational experiences and career success among black and white managers. *Academy of Management Journal, 33*, 64–86.

Gutek, B. A., Searle, S., & Klepa, L. (1991). Rational versus gender role explanations for work–family conflict. *Journal of Applied Psychology*, 76, 560–568.

Ho, V. T., Wong, S., & Lee, C. H. (2011). A tale of passion: Linking job passion and cognitive engagement to employee work performance. *Journal of Management Studies, 48*, 26–47.

Huebner, S. (2001). *Manual for the Multidimensional Students' Life Satisfaction Scale*. Retrieved from the University of South Carolina website http://src6.cas.sc.edu/psyc11/sites/default/files/huebslssmanual.pdf (accessed March 24, 2014).

Jackson, S. A., & Marsh, H. W. (1996). Development and validation of a scale to measure optimal experience: The Flow Scale. *Journal of Sport & Exercise Psychology, 18*, 17– 35.

Jenkins, C. D., Zyzanski, S. J., & Rosenman, R. H. (1979). *Jenkins Activity Survey manual.* New York: Psychological.

Johnstone, A., & Johnston, L. (2005). The relationship between organizational climate, occupational type and workaholism. *New Zealand Journal of Psychology, 34*, 181–188.

Kahn, W. (1990). Psychological conditions of personal engagement and disengagement at work. *Academy of Management Journal, 33*, 692–724.

Kanai, A., & Wakabayashi, M. (2004). Effects of economic environmental changes on job demands and workaholism in Japan. *Journal of Organizational Change Management, 17*, 537–548.

Kanai, A., Wakabayashi, M., & Fling, S. (1996). Workaholism among employees in Japanese corporations: An examination based on the Japanese version of the workaholism scales. *Japanese Psychological Research, 38*, 192–203.

Kanungo, R. N. (1979). The concept of alienation and involvement revisited. *Psychological Bulletin, 86*, 119–138.

Klaukien, A., Shepherd, D. A., & Patzelt, H. (2013). Passion for work, nonwork-related excitement, and innovation managers' decision to exploit new product opportunities. *Journal of Product Innovation Management, 3*, 574–588.

Kofodimos, J. (1993). *Balancing Act.* San Francisco, CA: Jossey-Bass.

Lafrenière, M. K., Jowett, S., Vallerand, R. J., & Carbonneau, N. (2011). Passion for coaching and the quality of the coach–athlete relationship: The mediating role of coaching behaviors. *Psychology of Sport and Exercise, 12*, 144–152.

Lafrenière, M. K., Vallerand, R. J., Donahue, E. G., & Lavigne, G. L. (2009). On the costs and benefits of gaming: The role of passion. *Cyber Psychology & Behavior, 12*, 285–290.

Lee, C., Jamieson, L. F., & Earley, P. C. (1996) Beliefs and fears and Type A behavior: Implications for academic performance and psychiatric health disorder symptoms. *Journal of Organizational Behavior, 17*, 151–178.

Leiter, M. P. (1992). Burnout as a crisis in professional role structures: Measurement and conceptual issues. *Anxiety, Stress, and Coping, 5*, 79–93.

Maslach, C., Jackson, S. E., & Leiter, M. P. (1996). *Maslach Burnout Inventory* (3rd ed.). Palo Alto, CA: Consulting Psychologists Press.

May, D. R., Gilson, R. L., & Harter, L. M. (2004). The psychological conditions of meaningfulness, safety and availability and the engagement of the human spirit at work. *Journal of Occupational & Organizational Psychology, 77*, 11–37.

McMillan, L. H., & O'Driscoll, M. P. (2004). Workaholism and health: Implications for organizations. *Journal of Organizational Change Management, 17*, 509–519.

McMillan, L. H., O'Driscoll, M. P., & Brady, E. C. (2004). The impact of workaholism on personal relationships. *British Journal of Guidance & Counselling, 32*, 171–186.

McMillan, L. H., Brady, E. C., O'Driscoll, M. P., & Marsh, N. V. (2002). A multifaceted validation study of Spence and Robbins' (1992) Workaholism Battery. *Journal of Occupational and Organizational Psychology, 75*, 357–368.

Meyer, J. P., & Allen, N. J. (1997). *Commitment in the workplace: Theory, research, and application.* Thousand Oaks, CA: Sage.

Moos, R. H. (1994). *Work Environment Scale Manual: Development, applications, research* (3rd ed.). Palo Alto, CA: Consulting Psychologists Press.
Mudrack, P. E. (2006). Understanding workaholism: The case of behavioral tendencies. In R. Burke (Ed.), *Research companion to working time and work addiction* (pp. 108–128). Cheltenham, UK: Edward Elgar.
Pallesen, S., Bjorvatn, B., Nordhus, I. H., Sivertsen, B., Hjørnevik, M., & Morin, C. M. (2008). A new scale for measuring insomnia: The Bergen Insomnia Scale. *Perceptual and Motor Skills, 107*, 691–706.
Quinn, R. P., & Shepard, L. J. (1974). *Quality of employment survey*. Ann Arbor, MI: University of Michigan, Institute for Social Research.
Rich, B. L., Lepine, J. A., & Crawford, E. R. (2010). Job engagement: Antecedents and effects on job performance. *Academy of Management Journal, 53*, 617–635.
Rizzo, J. R., House, R. J., & Lirtzman, S. I. (1970). Role conflict and ambiguity in complex organizations. *Administrative Science Quarterly, 15*, 150–163.
Robinson, B. E. (1989). *Work addiction*. Deerfield Beach, FL: Health Communications.
Robinson, B. E. (1999). The Work Addiction Risk Test: Development of a tentative measure of workaholism. *Perceptual and Motor Skills, 88*, 199–210.
Rosenberg, M. (1965). *Society and the adolescent self-image*. Princeton, NJ: Princeton University Press.
Rothbard, N. P. (2001). Enriching or depleting? The dynamics of engagement in work and family roles. *Administrative Science Quarterly, 46*, 655–84.
Russo, J. A., & Waters, L. E. (2006). Workaholic worker type differences in work–family conflict: The moderating role of supervisor support and flexible work scheduling. *Career Development International, 11*, 418–439.
Schaufeli, W. B., Bakker, A. B., & Salanova, M. (2006). The measurement of work engagement with a short questionnaire: A cross-national study. *Educational and Psychological Measurement, 66*, 701–716.
Schaufeli, W. B., Salanova, M., González-Romá, V., & Bakker, A. B. (2002). The measurement of engagement and burnout: A confirmative analytic approach. *Journal of Happiness Studies, 3*, 71–92.
Schaufeli, W. B., Shimazu, A., & Taris, T. W. (2009). Being driven to work excessively hard: The evaluation of a two-factor measure of workaholism in the Netherlands and Japan. *Cross-Cultural Research, 43*, 320–348.
Seguin-Levesque, C., Lyne, M., Lalibertea, N., Pelletier, L. G., Blanchard, C., & Vallerand, R. J. (2003). Harmonious and obsessive passion for the internet: Their associations with the couple's relationship. *Journal of Applied Social Psychology, 33*, 197–221.
Shinn, M., Wong, N. W., Simko, P., & Ortiz-Torres, B. (1989). Promoting the well-being of working parents: Coping, social support, and flexible job schedules. *American Journal of Community Psychology, 17*, 31–55.
Shuck, B., Nimon, K., & Zigarmi, D. (2013). Employee engagement and HRD: Philosophical underpinning, measurement, and interventions. In D. Chapman & K. P. Desiderio (Eds.), *Proceedings of the Academy of Human Resource Development 2013 International Research Conference in the Americas*. Arlington, VA: AHRD.

Snir, R. (2011). To work or not to work: The measurement of non-financial employment commitment. *International Journal of Business and Social Science, 2*, 271–278.

Snir, R., & Harpaz, I. (2012). Beyond workaholism: Towards a general model of heavy work investment. *Human Resource Management Review, 22*, 232–243.

Spence, J. T., Helmreich, R. L., & Pred, R. S. (1987). Impatience versus achievement strivings in the Type A pattern: Differential effects on students' health and academic achievement. *Journal of Applied Psychology, 72*, 522–528.

Spence, T. J., & Robbins, A. S. (1992). Workaholism, measurement and preliminary results. *Journal of Personality Assessment, 58*, 160–78.

Utz, S., Jonas, K. J., & Tonkens, E. (2012). Effects of passion for massively multiplayer online role-playing games on interpersonal relationships. *Journal of Media Psychology: Theories, Methods, and Applications, 24*, 77–86.

Vallerand, R. J., Blais, M. R., Brière, N. M., & Pelletier, L. G. (1989). Construction et validation de l'Échelle de motivation en éducation (EME) [Construction and validation of the Academic Motivation Scale in French (EME)]. *Canadian Journal of Behavioral Science, 21*, 323– 349.

Vallerand, R. J., Blanchard, C., Mageau, G. A., Koestner, R., Ratelle, C., Leonard, M., Gagne, M., & Marsolais, J. (2003). Les Passions de l'Ame: On obsessive and harmonious passion. *Journal of Personality and Social Psychology, 86*, 756–767.

Vallerand, R. J., Paquet, Y., Philippe, F. L., & Charest, J. (2010). On the role of passion for work in burnout: A process model. *Journal of Personality, 78*, 289–312.

Vallerand, R. J., Pelletier, L. G., Blais, M. R., Brière, N. M., Senécal, C. B., & Vallières, E. F. (1993). On the assessment of intrinsic, extrinsic, and amotivation in education: Evidence on the concurrent and construct validity of the Academic Motivation Scale. *Educational and Psychological Measurement, 53*, 159– 172.

Warr, P., Cook, J., & Wall, T. (1979). Scales for the measurement of some work attitudes and aspects of psychological well-being. *Journal of Occupational Psychology, 52*, 129–148.

Watanabe, N., Mizui, M., & Nozaki, T. (1990). Work stress, organizational commitment, and career plans among contingent workers. *Japanese Journal of Administrative Behavior, 5*, 75–83 (in Japanese with English summary).

Watson, D., Clark, L. A., & Tellegen, A. (1988). Development and validation of brief measures of positive and negative affect: The PANAS Scales. *Journal of Personality and Social Psychology, 54*, 1063–1070.

Zigarmi, D., Nimon, K., Houson, D., Witt, D., & Diehl, J. (2009). Beyond engagement: Toward a framework and operational definition for employee work passion. *Human Resource Development Review, 8*, 300–326.

Part 2

HEAVY WORK INVESTMENT (HWI) SUBTYPES AND OUTCOMES

6

THE BEAUTY VERSUS THE BEAST

On the Motives of Engaged and Workaholic Employees

Toon Taris, Ilona van Beek, and Wilmar Schaufeli

Introduction

The present chapter focuses on two types of heavy work investment: work engagement and workaholism. A body of research has addressed the conceptualization and consequences of these concepts (e.g., Schaufeli, Taris, & Van Rhenen, 2008; Taris, Schaufeli, & Verhoeven, 2005; van Beek, Taris, & Schaufeli, 2011). From this research, we know that both work engaged and workaholic employees work hard and harder than others. We also know that work engagement and workaholism are two relatively independent concepts, and tend to show different patterns of correlations with work outcomes (Schaufeli, Taris, & Bakker, 2006; Schaufeli, Taris, & Van Rhenen, 2008; Shimazu, Schaufeli, Kubota, & Kawakami, 2012). Whereas work engaged employees mainly report positive consequences, workaholic employees mainly experience adverse consequences. Therefore, it has been suggested that work engagement and workaholism are "good" and "bad" forms of heavy work investment, respectively (van Beek et al., 2011). However, to date, the motives of work engaged and workaholic employees to work hard have received little attention. So, two questions remain to be answered: what are the motivational drivers underlying work engagement and workaholism, and do these motivational drivers differ for these two forms of heavy work investment? The present chapter addresses this issue from two different perspectives, namely (1) a *personality-based perspective*, based on Higgins's (1998) regulatory focus theory, and (2) a *situational-based perspective*, using Deci and Ryan's (2000) self-determination theory.

Heavy Work Investment: Workaholism Versus Work Engagement

The term "workaholic" was coined in 1971 by the American minister and psychologist Wayne E. Oates. Oates (the author of 57 books, mostly expressing Christian views on societal issues) worked with alcoholics and realized that his own attitude toward work was much like his clients' attitude toward alcohol. In his book *Confessions of a workaholic*, Oates (1971) defined workaholism as "the compulsion or the uncontrollable need to work incessantly" (p. 11). This compulsion or uncontrollable need is so strong that it could be harmful for one's health, could diminish one's happiness, and could negatively affect the quality of one's interpersonal relations and social functioning (Schaufeli et al., 2006). In line with this reasoning, scholars have tended to consider workaholism as a phenomenon that is inherently bad (e.g., Cherrington, 1980; Robinson, 2007). However, this view is not universally shared. For instance, based on a qualitative interview study, Machlowitz (1980) reported that workaholic employees were productive and satisfied. Similarly, Korn, Pratt, and Lambrou (1987) considered workaholism as a positive phenomenon, calling workaholics "hyper-performers." Furthermore, Peiperl and Jones (2001) stated that workaholic employees are hard workers who find their work enjoyable and get a lot out of it. More recently, Baruch (2011) argued that not only is workaholism linked to high productivity, but also that workaholic employees may function as role models to other employees in competitive environments.

Yet, other scholars acknowledge that workaholism may have *both* positive and negative aspects. They distinguish among different types of workaholism, some of which are "good," whereas others are "bad." The most influential scholars sharing this view have been Janet Spence and Ann Robbins (1992), who proposed the so-called *workaholic triad*. Basically, they argue that workaholism should be conceived as a three-dimensional concept, involving work involvement (referring to the degree to which employees are highly committed to their work and spend much time on it), drive (referring to the degree to which employees feel forced to work due to inner pressures), and work enjoyment (referring to the degree to which employees experience their work as pleasant and fulfilling). The combination of these three dimensions yields eight different types of employees, three of which are termed "workaholic": (a) non-enthusiastic workaholics, who are high in involvement and drive, but low in enjoyment; (b) enthusiastic workaholics, who are high in involvement, drive, and enjoyment; and (c) work enthusiasts who are high in involvement and enjoyment, but low in drive. Buelens and Poelmans (2004) refer to the latter group as the "happy hard workers," because they are "enthusiastic, meet interesting people, love their jobs, and avoid conflict at home and in the workplace, possibly owing to their resulting positive attitude and a high level of social intelligence" (p. 454).

Interestingly, the description of the typical work enthusiast (apparently the "good" type of workaholism) strongly resembles that of the work engaged employee (cf. Snir & Harpaz, 2012). In comparison with workaholism, work engagement is a relatively new concept that emerged in the wake of the positive turn that occupational health psychology took at the end of the last century (Schaufeli & Bakker, 2013). Work engagement refers to "a positive, fulfilling, work-related state of mind that is characterized by vigor, dedication, and absorption" (Schaufeli, Salanova, González-Romá, & Bakker, 2002, p. 74). Vigor is characterized by high levels of energy and mental resilience while working, the willingness to invest effort in one's work, and persistence also in the face of difficulties. Dedication refers to being strongly involved in one's work, and experiencing a sense of significance, enthusiasm, inspiration, pride, and challenge. Finally, absorption is characterized in terms of being fully concentrated on and happily engrossed in one's work, whereby time passes quickly and one has difficulties with detaching oneself from work. Work engaged employees work hard (vigor), are involved in their work (dedication), and are happily engrossed (absorption) in their work, and in this sense they are similar to workaholic employees (i.e., Spence & Robbins', 1992, work enthusiasts). However, work engaged employees lack the strong compulsion to work hard (drive) that is typical for workaholism (i.e., Spence & Robbins', 1992, enthusiastic and non-enthusiastic workaholics). Work engaged employees work hard because they enjoy their work (cf. Schaufeli, Taris, Le Blanc, Peeters, Bakker, & De Jonge, 2001). Instead of distinguishing between "good" and "bad" forms of workaholism, it seems better to distinguish between workaholism as an overall bad type of heavy work investment and work engagement as an overall good type of heavy work investment (cf. Schaufeli et al., 2006; van Beek et al., 2011). Such a distinction will certainly contribute to conceptual clarity, because it excludes perspectives that consider at least some forms of workaholism as a potentially "good" phenomenon (e.g., Korn et al., 1987; Peiperl & Jones, 2001). In addition, it agrees with Porter's (1996) recommendation to "return to the origin of the term [i.e., workaholism as an addiction to work] as a starting point for future research" (p. 71).

In defining workaholism, we follow the lead of Scott, Moore, and Miceli (1997). Based on an extensive literature review, they identified three core features of workaholism. First, workaholic employees spend an excessive amount of time on their work activities when given the discretion to do so. That is, they work *excessively hard*. Second, workaholic employees are unwilling to disengage from their work activities and persistently think about their work. They even think about their work when they are not at work. In other words, they work *obsessively* and *compulsively*. Third, workaholic employees work beyond what is reasonably expected from them in order to meet organizational or economic requirements. In a sense, the third feature is a specification of the first two features and deals with the *motivation* for spending excessive time on work: workaholic employees work harder than is required out of an inner compulsion and not because of external factors such as financial rewards or an overtime-promoting organizational culture. Hence, the two main aspects of workaholism are working excessively and working compulsively (Schaufeli, Taris, & Van Rhenen, 2008).

Previous research on the correlates of workaholism and work engagement has shown that these two forms of heavy work investment retain different patterns of correlations with employee health and well-being (such as distress and depression), work characteristics (e.g., job demands and job control), and work outcomes (such as job satisfaction; e.g., Salanova, del Libano, Llorens, & Schaufeli, 2014; Schaufeli, Taris, & Bakker, 2008; Schaufeli, Taris, & Van Rhenen, 2008). Generally speaking, comparisons have shown that high levels of work engagement tend to be associated with positive outcomes (such as good health, and high levels of satisfaction and autonomy) and that high levels of workaholism tend to be associated with negative outcomes (such as bad health, and low levels of satisfaction and autonomy), lending credit to the notion that work engagement and workaholism are "good" and "bad" forms of heavy work investment, respectively. However, this research did not touch upon the issue of the motivational origins of these two forms of heavy work investment: *why* do work engaged and workaholic employees work so hard? In the past decade, these issues have been addressed from two different major points of view: a personality-based perspective and a situational-based perspective.

A Personality-Based Perspective on Heavy Work Investment

One obvious way to answer the question of why work engaged and workaholic employees work so hard—to psychologists, at least—is to look at the role of personal dispositions or traits. It is conceivable that workaholic and work engaged employees can be distinguished from other employees and from each other on the basis of their personality. A straightforward starting point for research in this tradition is to relate workaholism and work engagement to the Big Five personality dimensions: openness to experience, conscientiousness, extraversion, agreeableness, and neuroticism (e.g., Digman, 1990; Ng, Sorensen, & Feldman, 2007). Studies from this perspective provided converging evidence that conscientiousness, extraversion, and neuroticism are positively related to workaholism (Andreassen, Hetland, & Pallesen, 2010; Aziz & Tronzo,

2011; Burke, Matthiesen, & Pallesen, 2006; Clark, Lelchook, & Taylor, 2010), whereas agreeableness is negatively related to workaholism (Andreassen et al., 2010; Aziz & Tronzo, 2011). In other words, employees who tend to have high aspirations and to focus on the goals they have set (McCrae & Costa, 2003), to be gregarious, to experience distress and negative affect, and to be less caring, collaborative, and sympathetic toward others (Costa & McCrae, 1992), are more likely to be workaholic. Other research in this area has focused on more specific personality traits, finding that especially high levels of narcissism (Andreassen, Ursin, Eriksen, & Pallesen, 2012; Clark et al., 2010) and perfectionism (Clark et al., 2010) are related to high levels of workaholism. Taris, van Beek, and Schaufeli (2010) showed that workaholism is especially positively related to socially prescribed perfectionism, that is, people's belief that significant others hold high standards for them and that they will be accepted only if they meet these standards (Hewitt & Flett, 1991). However, recently, Stroeber, Davis, and Townley (2013) found that workaholism is positively associated with *self*-prescribed perfectionism (i.e. setting exceedingly high standards for oneself and striving for perfection), rather than with *socially* prescribed perfectionism.

Similar research on the personality correlates of work engagement showed that of the Big Five personality factors, conscientiousness and emotional stability (i.e., low levels of neuroticism) independently account for most of the variance in work engagement (Kim, Shin, & Swanger, 2009). In addition, research showed that the more "active" sub-factors within extraversion and conscientiousness are important (Inceoglu & Warr, 2011). In other words, employees who tend in dispositional terms to be emotionally stable, socially proactive, and achievement oriented are likely to be work engaged. Furthermore, there is also some evidence that high levels of narcissism (Andreassen et al., 2012), agreeableness (Rossier, Zecca, Stauffer, Maggiori, & Dauwalder, 2012), proactivity (Bakker, Tims, & Derks, 2012), and Type-A behavior (i.e., low levels of irritability and high levels of achievement striving, Hallberg, Johansson, & Schaufeli, 2007) are associated with high levels of work engagement.

Comparing the findings for work engagement to those obtained for workaholism shows that high levels of narcissism, conscientiousness, and extraversion are related to higher levels of work engagement as well as workaholism. Furthermore, whereas work engagement relates positively to agreeableness and negatively to neuroticism, workaholism relates negatively to the former and positively to the latter personality dimension. Apparently, there are some differences in the way work engagement and workaholism relate to various personality dimensions. Nevertheless, overall the similarities seem at least as strong as these differences. At least as far as narcissism, neuroticism, and agreeableness are concerned, these findings support the conceptualization of workaholism as a "bad" form of heavy work investment and work engagement as a "good" form of heavy work investment.

However, note that this comparison of the associations between personality aspects on the one hand and the two forms of heavy work investment on the other suffers from two critical limitations. First, much research on the relation between personality and workaholism has employed Spence and Robbins' (1992) three-dimensional conceptualization of workaholism as a combination of drive, work involvement, and work enjoyment. Since these dimensions were usually studied *separately* (among others, Aziz & Tronzo, 2011; Burke et al., 2006), this research did not distinguish among specific types of workaholism. This is a major issue, since Spence and Robbins (1992) distinguished among three types of workaholism, with two of these being "bad" and one very closely resembling our notion of work engagement (i.e., the "good" type of workaholism). Indeed, according to Spence and Robbins, high *as well as* low scores on drive and enjoyment can be typical for workaholism, depending on the specific type of workaholism that is considered. In effect, it is extremely difficult to interpret the associations between "workaholism" (drive and enjoyment) and personality, because both positive and negative associations between these concepts would provide support for the idea that personality and workaholism are related. In the presence of this conceptual ambiguity, it comes as no surprise that the findings for "workaholism" and work engagement can be similar.

Second, research directly comparing the effects of personality on workaholism versus work engagement is largely absent (with the exception of Andreassen et al., 2012). In conjunction, both limitations mean that the available evidence does not allow for drawing strong conclusions (or even *any* conclusion) on the patterns of correlations between personality traits, workaholism, and work engagement.

Regulatory Focus Theory and Heavy Work Investment

In an attempt to address this issue, van Beek, Schaufeli, Taris, and Brenninkmeijer (2014) examined the associations between personality (prevention vs. promotion focus: Higgins, 1997, 1998) on the one hand, and workaholism and work engagement on the other. Higgins' regulatory focus theory (RFT) assumes that individuals approach pleasure and avoid pain, and that individuals use different strategies to achieve this. More specifically, RFT distinguishes between two motivational systems that mirror these individual differences: the *promotion system* and the *prevention system*. These systems differ in terms of the needs that are attempted to be satisfied, the goals that are pursued, and the psychological situations that are deemed salient by an individual (Brockner & Higgins, 2001). Basically, RFT assumes that promotion-focused individuals seek to satisfy the need for growth and development, and are sensitive to the pleasurable presence or painful absence of positive outcomes, that is, advancement and gains (hopes, wishes, and aspirations). They are likely to *approach* matches to desired goals, that is, to strive actively to achieve these goals and to take advantage of any opportunity to bring achievement of these goals closer. When desired goals are obtained, promotion-focused individuals experience cheerfulness-related emotions (e.g., enthusiasm and joy), whereas failing to obtain these goals leads to dejection-related emotions (such as disappointment and dissatisfaction). Conversely, prevention-focused individuals seek to satisfy the need for security. They are sensitive to the pleasurable absence or painful presence of negative outcomes and are likely to *avoid* mismatches to desired goals, that is, safety and non-losses (duties, obligations, and responsibilities). Prevention-focused individuals associate obtaining desired goals with quiescence-related emotions (e.g., contentment and calmness), and failing to obtain these goals with agitation-related emotions (such as feeling uneasy and upset). Thus, RFT proposes that promotion-focused individuals are inclined to *approach matches* to desired goals, whereas prevention-focused individuals tend to *avoid mismatches* to desired goals (van Beek et al., 2013).

Since the promotion and prevention systems are differentially linked to the way individuals pursue different goals, RFT offers a handle in examining the personality-related and motivational correlates of workaholism and work engagement. Based on the views of Mudrack (2006), van Beek et al. (2014) argued that workaholism develops in response to feelings of low self-worth and insecurity. As individuals with a negative self-view tend to pursue avoidance/prevention goals, that is, to avoid negative outcomes (Judge, Bono, Erez, & Locke, 2005), they expected that workaholic employees would be primarily driven by avoidance motivation. Conversely, work engagement is positively related to personal resources such as self-esteem, self-efficacy, and optimism (Xanthopoulou, Bakker, Demerouti, & Schaufeli, 2007), meaning that work engaged employees will usually be confident about their capabilities and optimistic about the future. Since individuals with a positive self-view tend to pursue self-concordant goals (Elliot & Sheldon, 1998), they are likely to pursue approach goals, that is, positive outcomes such as learning and development, or accomplishment through the achievement of aspirations. Therefore, van Beek and colleagues (2014) expected that work engaged employees would be driven by approach motivation that is characteristic of a promotion focus. Drawing on cross-sectional data from 680 bank employees, van Beek and colleagues (2014) confirmed these expectations, showing that workaholism is moderately positively related to having a prevention focus, and that work engagement is moderately positively related to having a promotion focus. Hence, this study provides strong evidence that the motivational drivers of the "good" (work engagement) and the "bad" (workaholism) forms of heavy work investment differ. Since personality reflects a set of psychological traits and mechanisms within the individual that are relatively enduring (Higgins, 1998; Larsen & Buss, 2002), this study is consistent with the idea that workaholism and work engagement are differentially related to personality factors.

A Situational-Based Perspective on Heavy Work Investment

The second perspective on the motivational antecedents of work engagement and workaholism draws on the idea that specific characteristics of the work environment can satisfy particular psychological needs, that the extent to which these needs are satisfied determines the type of employee motivation, and that employee motivation results in different types of heavy work investment. Central to this idea is Deci and Ryan's (2000) self-determination theory (SDT).

SDT proposes that human beings are active, growth-oriented organisms that are predisposed to engage in interesting and enjoyable activities, to use their capacities fully, to search for connectedness with others, and to integrate their experiences (both intrapersonal and interpersonal; Deci & Ryan, 2000). This growth-oriented tendency requires fulfilment of three innate psychological needs: the needs for autonomy (i.e., the need for experiencing freedom of choice and initiating behavior), competence (i.e., the need for accomplishing challenging tasks successfully), and relatedness (i.e., the need for experiencing positive relationships with others). SDT posits that motivation, optimal functioning, and psychological well-being are affected by the extent to which the social environment allows satisfaction of and individuals can find or create the conditions necessary to satisfy these needs (Deci & Ryan, 2000).

Types of Motivation

SDT makes a primary distinction between intrinsic and extrinsic motivation. Individuals who are intrinsically motivated for an activity perform that activity because they consider it as interesting, enjoyable, and satisfying. They engage in that activity for its own sake and act with a full sense of volition (Gagné & Deci, 2005; Ryan & Deci, 2000a). Therefore, intrinsically motivated behavior is considered *self-determined.* To foster intrinsic motivation, need satisfaction is required. Conversely, individuals can be externally motivated for an activity. In this case, an activity is performed because of its instrumental value (Gagné & Deci, 2005; Ryan & Deci, 2000b), meaning that externally motivated individuals engage in an activity because of the outcome (e.g., monetary reward, social prestige, and promotion prospects). For most employees, their activities at work will be at least partly externally motivated because work is usually not exclusively interesting, enjoyable, and satisfying.

Furthermore, SDT distinguishes between four different types of extrinsic motivation: external regulation, introjected regulation, identified regulation, and integrated regulation. Dependent on the degree to which the three innate psychological needs are fulfilled, both the type of extrinsic motivation and the extent to which behavior is self-determined vary (Deci & Ryan, 2000). *Externally regulated behavior* is motivated by external contingencies involving threats of punishments, and material or social rewards. This type of behavior is regulated by the social environment and is, thus, fully non-self-determined. *Introjected regulation* is a product of an internalization process, in which individuals adopt external standards of self-worth and social approval without fully identifying with them. Thus, individuals must comply with partially internalized external standards that may conflict with their personal preferences (Ryan & Deci, 2000a). Therefore, introjected regulation is experienced as relatively non-self-determined. Identified regulation and integrated regulation are the product not only of an internalization process in which individuals adopt external standards, but also of an integration process in which individuals transform these standards to become an integral part of the self. When individuals accept and identify with the underlying value of a particular activity, their motivational regulation is *identified*. Since some ownership of behavior is experienced, identified regulation is considered as relatively self-determined. When the underlying value of a particular behavior is experienced as consistent with other important values and constitutes an integral part of the self, its regulation is *integrated* (Ryan & Deci, 2000a). Individuals experience their behavior totally as their own and, thus, as self-determined. Basically, these four types of external motivation and intrinsic motivation can be located on a continuum that ranges from (fully) externally regulated behavior, via introjected regulation, identified and integrated regulation, to (fully) intrinsically motivated behavior.

Work Characteristics and Need Satisfaction

As outlined above, one central assumption in the SDT approach is that characteristics of the social environment (in this case, the work environment) affect the degree to which the needs for autonomy, competence, and relatedness are satisfied, and, hence, what type of motivation will occur. Drawing on Demerouti, Bakker, Nachreiner, and Schaufeli (2001), and Schaufeli and Bakker (2004), Van den Broeck, Vansteenkiste, De Witte, and Lens (2008) proposed that job resources (defined as the physical, psychological, social, or organizational aspects of the job that can reduce job demands and their health-impairing impact, are functional in achieving work goals, or stimulate personal growth) would allow for satisfaction of the needs for autonomy, competence, and relatedness. Conversely, they argued that high job demands (i.e., those aspects of the job that tax employees' personal capacities and are, therefore, associated with certain psychological and/or physiological costs) would thwart satisfaction of these needs. Drawing on cross-sectional data from 740 Flemish employees, Van den Broeck and colleagues (2008) confirmed these expectations, showing that job demands are negatively associated with need satisfaction, whereas job resources are positively related to need satisfaction. Similarly, Fernet, Austin, Trépanier, and Dussault (2013) found that high levels of job resources were related to high levels of perceived autonomy, competence, and relatedness, whereas negative associations were found for high levels of job demands. In conjunction, this research shows that work characteristics are indeed associated with the satisfaction of the basic needs specified in SDT.

Motivation and Heavy Work Investment

As indicated earlier on, workaholism has little to do with true love of one's work or with a genuine desire to contribute to organizational goals. Rather, workaholic employees work hard because they *must* do so: they are compelled to work, and not working evokes intolerable distress and negative emotions, such as irritability, anxiety, shame, and guilt. It has been suggested that workaholism develops in response to feelings of low self-worth and insecurity (Mudrack, 2006), and Ryan (1982) has argued that performing an activity in order to enhance or maintain self-esteem and self-worth, is prototypical for introjected regulation (one of the four types of extrinsic motivation). Furthermore, we have seen that workaholism is positively linked to socially prescribed perfectionism (Taris et al., 2010), which is another way of saying that workaholic employees' work investment is externally regulated (i.e., by their social environment). In addition, recent findings confirmed the idea that satisfaction of the three innate psychological needs is negatively linked to working compulsively (Andreassen et al., 2010), suggesting that for workaholic employees the possibility to be intrinsically motivated is curtailed. Based on this reasoning, it appears likely that workaholism is positively associated with the more non-self-determined types of motivation (i.e., external regulation and introjected regulation).

Conversely, work engaged employees work hard because they genuinely *want* to (Schaufeli et al., 2006). Since work engaged employees experience high self-esteem, self-efficacy, and optimism, they are confident about their capabilities and optimistic about their future (Xanthopoulou et al., 2007). Individuals who evaluate themselves positively are less strongly affected by the social environment and by feedback (Brockner, 1988), and are more likely to pursue goals that fit their own ideals, interests, and values (Judge et al., 2005). Therefore, it is likely that engaged employees are driven by self-concordant goals and engage in their work activities for intrinsic rather than extrinsic reasons. Thus, work engagement will be positively associated with the more self-determined types of motivation (i.e., identified regulation and intrinsic motivation).

van Beek and colleagues (van Beek, Hu, Schaufeli, Taris, & Scheurs, 2012; Nijhuis, van Beek, Taris, & Schaufeli, 2012) tested the idea that workaholism should be associated with the more non-self-determined types of motivation (external regulation and introjected regulation) and work engagement with the more self-determined types of motivation (identified regulation and intrinsic motivation). Drawing on data from 760 Chinese employees (544 nurses and 216 physicians), van Beek and colleagues (2012) found that workaholism is positively associated with introjected regulation and identified regulation, but negatively with intrinsic motivation. Indeed, workaholic employees personally value their work activities, which may explain why they continue working hard despite the adverse consequences for themselves and the organization. Conversely, they found that work engagement is strongly and positively associated with intrinsic motivation and—to a considerably lesser degree—introjected regulation and identified regulation. Since many jobs also consist of mundane, repetitive, and unpleasant tasks, it makes sense that engaged employees are to some degree extrinsically motivated as well. Using data from 680 Dutch bank employees, Nijhuis and colleagues (2012) largely replicated van Beek and colleagues' findings. Thus, these two studies provide converging evidence that the two types of heavy work investment studied here (workaholism and work engagement) are differentially related to various forms of motivation. Work engagement is primarily associated with high scores on intrinsic motivation, whereas workaholism is primarily linked to high scores on introjected regulation and identified regulation. Again, this underlines the conceptualization of workaholism as being a "bad" form of heavy work investment, whereas engagement is a "good" form of heavy work investment.

Personality–Situation Interaction

As outlined previously, both differences in personality (e.g., the Big Five personality traits and having a promotion vs. a prevention focus) and the work environment (job characteristics) seem to determine which type of heavy work investment will occur. Clearly, the issue of the motivational antecedents of workaholism and work engagement goes beyond the simplistic nature versus nurture division. It is likely that the *combination* of both matters in determining the type of heavy work investment that will occur. Although personality is thought to have a biological basis and, therefore, to be stable over time, how it manifests itself in actual behavior may depend on the situation and vary considerably (Larsen & Buss, 2002). Personality will affect behavior the strongest when situations are weak or ambiguous, and the least when situations are strong. In the latter case, nearly all individuals will react in the same way. Furthermore, personality affects the situations individuals opt to place themselves in. When given the choice, individuals usually choose situations that match their personality. Personality may also evoke responses from the environment (i.e., from others), indicating that individuals may create their own environment. In other words, reality seems to be far more complicated than a simplistic nature versus nurture division: it is likely that the Big Five personality traits and having a promotion or prevention focus, and the extent to which the work environment satisfies the three psychological needs and determines motivation, interact in producing workaholism and/or work engagement.

More specifically, it is conceivable that the Big Five personality dimensions relate differently to need satisfaction and motivation. Individuals high in openness to experience, that is, who show a strong intellectual curiosity, might be more likely to engage in their (work) activities for self-determined reasons than others (Komarraju, Karau, & Schmeck, 2009). Individuals high in conscientiousness are disciplined and achievement-oriented, and, therefore, their need for competence might be easily satisfied (Ingledew, Markland, & Sheppard, 2004) and they might engage in their (work) activities for self-determined reasons (Komarraju et al., 2009). Extraverted individuals have the tendency to be warm and sociable. On the one hand, it can be speculated that it is relatively easy for them to satisfy their need for relatedness and that they are led by a self-determined type of motivation (Ingledew et al., 2004). On the other hand, extraverted individuals might be strongly focused on their social context and externally regulated (a non-self-determined form of motivation; Komarraju et al., 2009). Because agreeable individuals are cooperative and likely to follow (work) requirements, it can be argued that they will engage in their work activities for non-self-determined reasons. Finally, individuals high in neuroticism tend to experience distress and negative affect, and, therefore, they might be motivated by introjected regulation (a non-self-determined form of motivation). Clearly, more research on this issue is badly needed.

The prevention vs. promotion, or the avoidance vs. approach distinction, cannot encompass the non-self-determined vs. self-determined distinction (Deci & Ryan, 2000). For instance, pursuing tangible rewards (i.e., an approach orientation) reduces autonomy and self-determined motivation because rewards shift individuals from a more internal to external perceived locus of causality (Ryan & Deci, 2000b). Also, it is possible to identify self-determined avoidance behaviors: an individual can completely endorse and follow a physician's advice to stop smoking in order to avoid health risks (Deci & Ryan, 2000). Hence, there are instances of non-self-determined approach and avoidance goals, and of self-determined approach and avoidance goals. It is conceivable that having a prevention focus or having a promotion focus influences the type of goals that are pursued within every regulatory style, varying from non-self-determined (external regulation) to self-determined (intrinsic motivation). However, the relation between personality and situations is probably far more complicated, meaning that more comprehensive research is needed to address this issue.

Concluding Remarks

The present chapter sought to explore the motivational antecedents of heavy work investment: workaholism and work engagement, respectively. Although both types of work investment have amply been examined, as yet little is known about the motivational bases underlying workaholism and work engagement. In this chapter we have discussed theory and research on this issue from two perspectives: a personality-based perspective, in which the motivational bases for heavy work investment were sought in stable individual differences in personality, and a situational-based perspective, in which the motivation for heavy work investment was examined as a function of differences in the work context. The second aim of this chapter was to examine the degree to which the motivational bases for work engagement and workaholism differed.

Workaholism Versus Work Engagement

One important issue in research on heavy work investment concerns the definition of this concept. It is intuitively clear to what type of behaviors heavy work investment refers: namely, heavy investment in work in terms of both time and effort (Snir & Harpaz, 2012). However, the fact that there is agreement as to what type of behavior the term refers to does not preclude the possibility that different types of heavy work investment exist. For example, previous research on workaholism—a type of heavy work investment—has typically started from the three-dimensional conceptualization proposed in the seminal work of Spence and Robbins (1992). However, these authors distinguished among no less than three types of workaholism, with some having clear positive connotations and others having primarily negative characteristics. Clearly it is undesirable to refer to very different phenomena using the same label. In the present chapter we therefore distinguished between workaholism (conceptualized as a phenomenon consisting of working excessively and compulsively) and work engagement (referring to high levels of vigor, dedication, and absorption). The fact that both workaholism and work engagement can be considered subtypes of heavy work investment raises the question of whether these concepts are really different. Previous comparative research (Salanova et al., 2014; Schaufeli, Taris, & Bakker, 2008; Schaufeli, Taris, & Van Rhenen, 2008) has shown that the work-related outcomes of these concepts are indeed different, with workaholism being related to high scores on "negative" work outcomes (e.g., high levels of distress and low job satisfaction) and work engagement being related to high scores on "positive" work outcomes. The focal question in this chapter is, do these conceptual and empirical differences generalize to the motivational bases underlying these two types of heavy work investment? To address this question, we focused on two motivational frameworks that could be relevant in explaining heavy work investment; that is, differences in employees' personalities, and differences in their work environment.

A Personality-Based Perspective on Heavy Work Investment

This chapter revealed that a small body of research has related workaholism and work engagement to the Big Five personality dimensions. Assuming that personality affects employees' motivation and attitudes, such research could be relevant in examining the motivational differences between workaholic and work engaged employees. Although the available research showed some minor differences in the personality-related antecedents of these two forms of heavy work investment, it was concluded that little could be said on these differences, because the conceptualization of workaholism was weak; most of the research in this area examined the associations between various personality dimensions and the three separate dimensions of Spence and Robbins' (1992) conceptualization of workaholism. Conversely, research on the relations between personality and work engagement is scarce. In a study that was based on regulatory focus theory (Higgins, 1997, 1998), van Beek and colleagues (2014) showed that workaholics are driven by the motivation to satisfy the need for security and to avoid negative outcomes, whereas work engaged employees are driven by the motivation to pursue approach goals (i.e., positive outcomes, such as learning, development, and the achievement of aspirations). This research thus provided evidence that the motives of workaholic and work engaged employees differ strongly.

A Situation-Based Perspective on Heavy Work Investment

The second perspective here started from the assumptions that specific characteristics of the work environment can satisfy particular innate psychological needs, and that these needs trigger different types of motivation (Deci & Ryan, 2000; Van den Broeck et al., 2008). Drawing on Deci and Ryan's (2000) self-determination theory, Van den Broeck and colleagues (2008) showed that job resources such as high autonomy satisfy the needs for autonomy, competence, and relatedness, and that job demands such as high workload thwart satisfaction of these needs. A higher degree of satisfaction of these needs triggers self-determined (as opposed to non-self-determined) motivation for a particular work activity. Since work engaged employees work hard because they genuinely want to and are likely to pursue goals that fit their own values, ideals, and needs, van Beek and colleagues (2012) expected that work engaged employees would report high levels of self-determined motivation. Conversely, since workaholics work hard because of a compulsion, workaholics were expected to report relatively high levels of non-self-determined motivation. This reasoning was for the greater part confirmed in three independent samples (Nijhuis et al., 2012; van Beek et al., 2012), again underlining the differences in the motivational make-up of workaholic and work engaged employees.

Motivation and Heavy Work Investment

Based on the material in this chapter, four conclusions on the differences in the motivational drivers of two types of heavy work investment can be drawn. First and foremost, few studies have addressed the motivational correlates of heavy work investment, and even fewer of these have explicitly compared these correlates for different types of heavy work investment. Moreover, the quality of much of this research is questionable, mainly because it is unclear what type of workaholism was involved. Thus, there is a need for more (high-quality) research on the motivational correlates of heavy work investment.

Second, although at present little research addresses the motivational drivers of different types of heavy work investment, the material presented in this chapter suggests that conducting such research could be interesting and worthwhile. Research on the motivational correlates of different types of workaholism and work engagement shows interesting and theoretically interpretable differences. Clearly, the currently available evidence suggests that further research on the motivational bases of heavy work investment is promising and warrants further attention.

Third, this chapter showed that there are different types of heavy work investment. We have focused here on work engagement (the "good" type of heavy work investment) versus workaholism (the "bad" type of heavy work investment). In this chapter we have shown that the motivational correlates of these two concepts differ quite strongly, and in a theoretically interpretable manner: workaholism is primarily associated with an extrinsic motivation and a prevention focus, whereas work engagement is mainly linked to intrinsic motivation and a promotion focus. It is likely that these motivational differences translate into different behaviors at work: although both workaholic and work engaged employees invest much effort in their jobs, their specific behaviors and the goals they pursue seem to differ strongly. Finally, the present chapter suggested that differences in both personality (Big Five personality dimensions; promotion versus prevention focus) and environment (job characteristics) may determine which type of heavy work investment will occur. Despite these advances, a comprehensive framework containing both factors is lacking and needs to be addressed in future research.

References

Andreassen, C.S., Hetland, J., & Pallesen, S. (2010). The relationship between workaholism, basic needs satisfaction at work and personality. *European Journal of Personality, 24,* 3–17.

Andreassen, C.S., Ursin, H., Eriksen, H.R., & Pallesen, S. (2012). The relationship of narcissism with workaholism, work engagement, and professional position. *Social Behavior and Personality, 40,* 881–890.

Aziz, S. & Tronzo, C.L. (2011). Exploring the relationship between workaholism facets and personality traits: A replication in American workers. *The Psychological Record, 61,* 269–286.

Bakker, A.B., Tims, M., & Derks, D. (2012). Proactive personality and job performance: The role of job crafting and work engagement. *Human Relations, 65,* 1359–1378.

Baruch, Y. (2011). The positive wellbeing aspects of workaholism in cross cultural perspective. *Career Development International, 16,* 572–591.

Brockner, J. (1988). The effects of work layoffs on survivors: Research, theory, and practice. In B.M. Staw and L.L. Cummings (Eds.), *Research in organizational behavior* (Vol. 10, pp. 213–255). Greenwich, CT: JAI Press.

Brockner, J. & Higgins, E.T. (2001). Regulatory focus theory: Implications for the study of emotions at work. *Organizational Behavior and Human Decision Processes, 86,* 35–66.

Buelens, M. & Poelmans, S.A.Y. (2004). Enriching the Spence and Robbins' typology of workaholism: Demographic, motivational and organizational correlates. *Journal of Organizational Change Management, 17,* 440–458.

Burke, R.J., Matthiesen, S.B., & Pallesen, S. (2006). Personality correlates of workaholism. *Personality and Individual Differences, 40,* 1223–1233.

Cherrington, D.J. (1980). *The work ethic.* New York: American Management Association.

Clark, M.A., Lelchook, A.M., & Taylor, M.L. (2010). Beyond the Big Five: How narcissism, perfectionism and dispositional affect relate to workaholism. *Personality and Individual Differences, 48,* 786–791.

Costa, P.T. & McCrae, R.R. (1992). Normal personality assessment in clinical practice: The NEO Personality Inventory. *Psychological Assessment, 4,* 5–13.

Deci, E.L. & Ryan, R.M. (2000). The "what" and "why" of goal pursuits: Human needs and the self-determination of behavior. *Psychological Inquiry, 11*, 227–268.

Demerouti, E., Bakker, A.B., Nachreiner, F., & Schaufeli, W.B. (2001). The job demands-resources model of burnout. *Journal of Applied Psychology, 86*, 499–512.

Digman, J.M. (1990). Personality structure: Emergence of the five-factor model. *Annual Review of Psychology, 41*, 417–440.

Elliot, A.J. & Sheldon, K.M. (1998). Avoidance personal goals and the personality-illness relationships. *Journal of Personality and Social Psychology, 75*, 1282–1299.

Fernet, C., Austin, S., Trépanier, S.G., & Dussault, M. (2013). How do job characteristics contribute to burnout? Exploring the distinct mediating roles of perceived autonomy, competence, and relatedness. *European Journal of Work and Organizational Psychology, 22*, 123–137.

Gagné, M. & Deci, E. (2005). Self-determination theory and work motivation. *Journal of Organizational Behavior, 26*, 331–362.

Hallberg, U.E., Johansson, G., & Schaufeli, W.B. (2007). Type A behavior and work situation: Associations with burnout and work engagement. *Scandinavian Journal of Psychology, 48*, 135–142.

Hewitt, P.L. & Flett, G.L. (1991). Perfectionism in the self and social contexts: Conceptualization, assessment, and association with psychopathology. *Journal of Personality and Social Psychology, 60*, 456–470.

Higgins, E.T. (1997). Beyond pleasure and pain. *American Psychologist, 52*, 1280–1300.

Higgins, E.T. (1998). Promotion and prevention: Regulatory focus as a motivational principle. *Advances in Experimental Social Psychology, 30*, 1–46.

Inceoglu, I. & Warr, P. (2011). Personality and job engagement. *Journal of Personnel Psychology, 10*, 177–181.

Ingledew, D.K., Markland, D., & Sheppard, K.E. (2004). Personality and self-determination of exercise behavior. *Personality and Individual Differences, 36*, 1921–1932.

Judge, T.A., Bono, J.E., Erez, A., & Locke, E.A. (2005). Core self-evaluations and job and life satisfaction: The role of self-concordance and goal attainment. *Journal of Applied Psychology, 90*, 257–268.

Kim, H.J., Shin, K.H., & Swanger, N. (2009). Burnout and engagement: A comparative analysis using the Big Five personality dimensions. *International Journal of Hospitality Management, 28*, 96–104.

Komarraju, M., Karau, S.J., & Schmeck, R.R. (2009). Role of the Big Five personality traits in predicting college students' academic motivation and achievement. *Learning and Individual Differences, 19*, 47–52.

Korn, E.R., Pratt, G.J., & Lambrou, P.T. (1987). *Hyper-performance: The A.I.M. strategy for releasing your business potential*. New York: John Wiley.

Larsen, R.J. & Buss, D.M. (2002). *Personality psychology: Domains of knowledge about human nature*. New York: McGraw-Hill.

Machlowitz, M. (1980). *Workaholics: Living with them, working with them*. New York: Simon and Schuster.

McCrae, R.R. & Costa, P.T., Jr. (2003). *Personality in adulthood. A five factor theory perspective.* New York: The Guildford Press.

Mudrack, P.E. (2006). Understanding workaholism: The case of behavioral tendencies. In R.J. Burke (Ed.), *Research companion to working time and work addiction* (pp. 108–128). Cheltenham, MA: Elgar.

Ng, T.W.H., Sorensen, K.L., & Feldman, D.C. (2007). Dimensions, antecedents, and consequences of workaholism: A conceptual integration and extension. *Journal of Organizational Behavior, 28,* 111–136.

Nijhuis, N., van Beek, I., Taris, T.W., & Schaufeli, W.B. (2012). Motivation and performance of workaholic, engaged and burned-out workers [in Dutch]. *Gedrag & Organisatie, 25,* 325–346.

Oates, W.E. (1971). *Confessions of a workaholic.* New York: World Publishers.

Peiperl, M. & Jones, B. (2001). Workaholics and overworkers: Productivity or pathology? *Group and Organization Management, 26,* 369–393.

Porter, G. (1996). Organizational impact of workaholism: Suggestions for researching the negative outcomes of excessive work. *Journal of Occupational Health Psychology, 1,* 70–84.

Robinson, B.E. (2007). *Chained to the desk: A guidebook for workaholics, their partners and children, and the clinicians who treat them* (2nd ed.). New York: New York University Press.

Rossier, J., Zecca, G., Stauffer, S.D., Maggiori, C., & Dauwalder, J.P. (2012). Career Adaptabilities Scale in a French-speaking Swiss sample: Psychometric properties and relationships to personality and work engagement. *Journal of Vocational Behavior, 80,* 734–743.

Ryan, R.M. (1982). Control and information in the intrapersonal sphere: An extension of cognitive evaluation theory. *Journal of Personality and Social Psychology, 43,* 450–461.

Ryan, R.M. & Deci, E.L. (2000a). Self-determination theory and the facilitation of intrinsic motivation, social development, and well-being. *American Psychologist, 55,* 68–78.

Ryan, R.M. & Deci, E.L. (2000b). Intrinsic and extrinsic motivation: Classic definitions and new directions. *Contemporary Educational Psychology, 25,* 54–67.

Salanova, M., del Libano, M., Llorens, S., & Schaufeli, W.B. (2014). Engaged, workaholic, burned-out or just 9-to-5? Toward a typology of employee well-being. *Stress & Health, 30,* 71–81.

Schaufeli, W.B. & Bakker, A.B. (2004). Job demands, job resources, and their relationship with burnout and engagement: A multi-sample study. *Journal of Organizational Behavior, 25,* 293–315.

Schaufeli, W.B. & Bakker, A.B. (2013). Burnout and work engagement [in Dutch]. In W.B. Schaufeli and A.B. Bakker (Eds.), *De psychologie van arbeid en gezondheid* (pp. 305–322). Houten: Bohn Stafleu van Loghum.

Schaufeli, W.B., Salanova, M., González-Romá, V., & Bakker, A.B. (2002). The measurement of engagement and burnout: A confirmatory factor-analytic approach. *Journal of Happiness Studies, 3,* 71–92.

Schaufeli, W.B., Taris, T.W., & Bakker, A.B. (2006). Dr Jekyll or Mr Hyde? On the differences between work engagement and workaholism. In R.J. Burke

(Ed.), *Research companion to working time and work addiction* (pp. 193–217). Cheltenham: Edward Elgar.

Schaufeli, W.B., Taris, T.W., & Bakker, A.B. (2008). It takes two to tango. Workaholism is working excessively and working compulsively. In R.J. Burke and C.L. Cooper (Eds.), *The long work hours culture: Causes, consequences and choices* (pp. 203–226). Bingley: Emerald.

Schaufeli, W.B., Taris, T.W., & Van Rhenen, W. (2008). Workaholism, burnout, and work engagement: Three of a kind or three different kinds of employee well-being? *Applied Psychology: An International Review, 57,* 173–203.

Schaufeli, W.B., Taris, T., Le Blanc, P., Peeters, M., Bakker, A.B., & De Jonge, J. (2001). Does work make one healthy? The quest for the engaged worker [in Dutch]. *De Psycholoog, 36,* 422–428.

Scott, K.S., Moore, K.S., & Miceli, M.P. (1997). An exploration of the meaning and consequences of workaholism. *Human Relations, 50,* 287–314.

Shimazu, A., Schaufeli, W.B., Kubota, K., & Kawakami, N. (2012). Do workaholism and work engagement predict employee well-being and performance in opposite directions? *Industrial Health, 50,* 316–321.

Snir, R. & Harpaz, I. (2012). Beyond workaholism: Towards a general model of heavy work investment. *Human Resource Management Review, 22,* 232–243.

Spence, J.T. & Robbins, A.S. (1992). Workaholism: Definition, measurement, and preliminary results. *Journal of Personality Assessment, 58,* 160–178.

Stroeber, J., Davis, C.R., & Townley, J. (2013). Perfectionism and workaholism in employees: The role of work motivation. *Personality and Individual Differences, 55,* 733–738.

Taris, T.W., Schaufeli, W.B., & Verhoeven, L.C. (2005). Workaholism in the Netherlands: Measurement and implications for job strain and work–nonwork conflict. *Applied Psychology: An International Review, 54,* 37–60.

Taris, T.W., van Beek, I., & Schaufeli, W.B. (2010). Why do perfectionists have a higher burnout risk than others? The mediational effect of workaholism. *Romanian Journal of Applied Psychology, 12,* 1–7.

van Beek, I., Taris, T.W., & Schaufeli, W.B. (2011). Workaholic and work engaged employees: Dead ringers or worlds apart? *Journal of Occupational Health Psychology, 16,* 468–482.

van Beek, I., Taris, T.W., Schaufeli, W.B., & Brenninkmeijer, V. (2014). Heavy work investment: Its motivational make-up and outcomes. *Journal of Managerial Psychology, 49,* 46–62.

van Beek, I., Hu, Q., Schaufeli, W.B., Taris, T.W., & Schreurs, B.H.J. (2012). For fun, love, or money: What drives workaholic, engaged, and burned-out employees at work? *Applied Psychology: An International Review, 61,* 30–55.

Van den Broeck, A., Vansteenkiste, M., De Witte H., & Lens, W. (2008). Explaining the relationships between job characteristics, burnout and engagement: The role of basic psychological need satisfaction. *Work & Stress, 22,* 277–294.

Xanthopoulou, D., Bakker, A.B., Demerouti, E., & Schaufeli, W.B. (2007). The role of personal resources in the Job Demands–Resources model. *International Journal of Stress Management, 14,* 121–141.

7

DISTINCTIONS BETWEEN OVEREMPLOYMENT, OVERWORK, WORKAHOLISM, AND HEAVY INVESTMENTS IN WORK TIME

Lonnie Golden

Adam Smith once observed, "the innate human desire to improve one's lot is strong enough to make workmen apt to overwork themselves and ruin their health and constitution in a few years" (1776, Wealth of Nations, Book One, Chapter VIII, paragraph 44). Contemporary labor economics has focused far more on that first part, the "desire," i.e., preferred labor supply, and much less on whether workers are able to get the hours they truly desire; or on the second part, that even when one's labor supply could be considered voluntarily provided time and effort, it could lead to unanticipated adverse consequences on their own well-being. Industrial–organizational and occupational health psychology has focused on this latter issue of negative well-being consequences, but less so on the difference in the extent to which situational labor supply is entirely voluntary versus at least partly involuntary. The emerging issue of "heavy work investment" re-frames the issue of the motivations behind labor supply preferences as having short-term costs but often with potential longer term payoffs (Snir & Harpaz, 2012). It could benefit from finer detail regarding the characteristics of workers who work the hours they prefer vs. those who work longer hours than they personally prefer.

The purpose of this chapter is to consider why at least some people are driven to work longer hours beyond their initially preferred time commitment, defined as "overemployment," and perhaps beyond their own capacity that is sustainable in terms of physical or mental health or well-being, referred to as "overwork." The first aim is to display a comprehensive model of work hours determination. This employs recent behavioral economics' emphases on relative status, aspirations, preference adaptation, and process benefits. It emphasizes how work hours may be a forward-looking (and also a backward-looking) form of investment for a potential return in future well-being, in the form of income or perhaps non-income amenities at work. This chapter explores the role of incentives, explicit and implicit, in determining a worker's preferred number of hours. The former refers to extrinsic motivation, such as a monetary bonus for extra production. The latter involves intrinsic motivation, such as public recognition or title with status, for performing extra work. This chapter then goes on to focus on overemployment, the inability to reduce one's work hours toward preferred shorter hours (and not just a shift in daily timing of a given duration of hours), despite a willingness to sacrifice some pay. For example, 18 percent of polled workers in the US answered "yes" that they would take advantage of an "opportunity to work one less day each week and receive 20 percent less pay," while another 15 percent were "not sure." It makes subtle but important distinctions between being overemployed and being overworked or workaholic. The first is "situational," whereas the second may be either situational or dispositional and the latter largely dispositional. It also contrasts the possible intrinsic, extrinsic, and institutional motivations for working longer hours, sometimes to the point of becoming overworked or even addicted to work. It then provides empirical estimation of the incidence and distribution of worker overemployment—the most crucial type for models in labor economics, largely because of its involuntary property. Workers who maintain a preference for reduced hours of work even if accompanied by reduced earnings are contrasted with those who express satisfaction with their number of work hours, by their demographic, work hours, and occupation type status. Finally, this chapter explores potential returns on investment in time not only in work time but in "non-work" time. It distinguishes several separate types of non-work time uses, at least two of which are work-related and may have investment-type properties, such as "productive leisure." The chapter closes by exploring implications of the overemployment findings and types of excessive work hours and non-work time uses for future research, both empirical and theoretical.

What are the forces and counterforces that ultimately determine the length of individuals' time commitment toward paid work hours—economic, social–psychological–cultural, organizational, and institutional? To what extent are patterns or trends in work hours attributable to workers' internal preferences, external incentives to alter those initial preferences, and employers' constraints? Even if initially motivated by an apparently voluntary choice by an individual to increase their own work hours, at what point does such an unforced addiction to incessant work activity become detrimental to one's own well-being or spill over negatively to others—risking harm to other workers, families, co-workers, or performance of an organization or even a national economy? To answer such fundamental questions requires development of a comprehensive, multidisciplinary model, to identify the myriad of motivations behind working or desiring longer work hours.

An Eclectic Model of Working Hours Determination

A natural starting point for explaining individuals' supply of paid labor time is the conventional economic model of labor supply. It portrays the determination of working time as the result of optimizing agents of supply (i.e., applicants for positions/employees) interacting with agents demanding labor services (i.e., hiring managers). Workers' preferred hours of labor supply are assumed to reflect a combination of innate "preferences" reflecting their unique, inherent taste or distaste for work or leisure, and voluntary responses to external, monetary incentives, such as their available wage rate and income from non-labor sources. Preferences for work are associated inversely and unambiguously with the presence of non-wage income and positively with education levels, household production, and technological advances. It tends to be an inverse U-shaped relationship with age over the life cycle. The net effect of changes in workers' wage rate is ambiguous—whether workers wish to increase or decrease their preferred hours of labor supply, on balance, reveals their relative preference for income versus non-work time. However, the conventional model's focus on rational individual or even household choice provides no more than a starting point. Conventional labor supply studies have paid scant attention to the influence of social, cultural, and workplace conditions over preference formation (Altman, 2001; Philp et al., 2005; Spencer, 2011).

A comprehensive model of individuals' time devoted to work (H^*) would incorporate the economic, psychological, physiological, social, and cultural sources of workers' constraints and preferences (Golden, 2009). Individuals' desired work hours, and adaption of their preferences, may be depicted as a weighted contribution from seven potential sources in a linear model, where: H^* = desired hours of work (per week, year); (1) W = current wage rate, deflated by the price P level; (2) NY = non-wage and net asset income; (3) W^e = expected future upward wage adjustment; (4) S = relative status gained among reference groups; (5) I = intrinsic rewards, process benefits, or amenities acquired through work; (6) H^d = hours demanded by employer (e.g., workload for salaried workers, required overtime for hourly workers); (7) α = reflecting the heterogeneous, physiological capacity of a given individual for working, including their general physical or mental health. Thus, a model of the individual's desired hours of labor supply is:

$$H^* = \alpha + \left[h_1 \left(\frac{w}{p} \right)_t + h_2 NY + h_3 \Delta w^e{}_{t+1} + h_4 I + h_5 S + h_6 H_t{}^d \right]$$

$$(weights : h_1 + h_2 + \cdots + h_6 = 1)$$

Where:

$$-\infty \leq h_1, \alpha \leq \infty; \quad h_3, h_4, h_5, h_6 \geq 0; \quad h_2 \leq 0$$

Such a comprehensive model allows individuals to be motivated to work by the extrinsic rewards, as well as intrinsic rewards (Ellingsen & Johannesson, 2007; Kelloway et al., 2004), job perks (Douglas & Morris, 2006), and the more subtle underlying cultural characteristics of the workplace or economy that exert influence on preference formation regarding the value of work, material goods, services, and uses of time. Specifying six separate arguments is not meant to suggest there is no endogeneity or interdependence among them, nor is this model meant to be directly, empirically tractable. Rather, the purpose here is to present the potential contributing factors, derived from emphases of separate research literatures, each entering in with its own weight, depending on how an individual responds to external incentives.

To the extent that such preferences are adaptable, the key component, for the focus of this book, is motivation (3), the forward-looking, potential reward of higher wage trajectories. The most strictly economic model that explains forward-looking reasons to "invest" in longer work hours is the development of human capital (Booth et al., 2003). For example, employees might choose to undertake overtime, even unpaid, to more quickly acquire specific human capital (i.e., knowledge, skills, abilities), which in turn increase their chances for promotion, wage increases or non-wage benefits, or desired career trajectory (Michelacci & Pijoan-Mas, 2007; Van Echtelt et al., 2007). As an example, there is a spirited debate regarding whether regulatory limits on medical interns' and residents duty hours limits the extent of their skills development (e.g., Axelrod, Shah, & Jena, 2013).

Another motivation to work harder, through long hours, may stem from economic incentives in one's workplace, occupation, or industry that reward increases in productivity improvement. Particularly where individual worker output is difficult to measure, employers may evaluate performance, in absolute and/or relative terms, with the potential reward offered of raises, bonuses, or promotions. Since these are promised in the future, they are considered forward-looking incentives (Bell & Freeman, 2001). As they are also subject to some uncertainty and risk, they may be considered a form of "heavy work investment." The relatively longer work hours in the US may be explained by workers' responses to differences in wage inequality—the greater the disparity in earnings in one's occupation, or even their country, the longer the average hours of work (Bell, 2000). Compensation practices that have heightened variation in earnings within each occupational classification have raised the incentive to supply work beyond the standard 40 hours per week (Kuhn & Lozano, 2006). The wider gap among pay grades in occupations leads more workers to attempt to exceed the hours worked by their co-workers or the tacit norm in the workplace (Bowles & Park, 2005; Drago et al., 2009). Indeed, occupations with longer workweeks have higher hourly earnings in the US (Hecker, 1998). Thus, if future wage trajectories in more jobs are getting steeper (or short hours' penalty more severe), worker concern for long-term relative status lengthens average hours.

A similar but subtly different motivation can be derived from models of reciprocal employment relationships. Workers who feel they are treated kindly or fairly (for example, paid well) are more inclined to work more or better to demonstrate their commitment to their employer. This has been referred to as a backward-looking incentive. A forward-looking incentive for working longer hours is signaling behavior of the employee (DeRiviere, 2008; Montinari, 2010; Sousa-Poza & Ziegler, 2003). When the cost of monitoring employee productivity is prohibitively high, employers may use long hours as one readily observed mechanism to rank the estimated productivity of workers. Indeed, employers may create few shorter-hour jobs purposely, as a way to screen out potentially less productive workers or applicants (Rebitzer & Taylor, 1995). Thus, the highly productive workers might rationally choose to work inefficiently long hours (Sousa-Poza & Ziegler, 2003), performing extra work, with face-time (a form of presenteeism) beyond the standard or norm of a job or workplace, as a way to signal future promotability. Over time, there may be more and more jobs that valorize long hours, where requesting shorter hours would be seen as detrimental to long-term career success in the organization (Landers et al., 1996; Yakura, 2001). Indeed, employees' present wages, via raises or promotions, are positively associated with their past amount of unpaid overtime work, especially among managers (Campbell & Green, 2002; Pannenberg, 2005). However, research has so far found no difference between the effects of paid and unpaid overtime work on such wage gains or promotion (Booth et al., 2003; Bratti & Staffolani, 2007). The most direct study, with US longitudinal data, found a positive but nonlinear relationship between weekly hours and hourly wage growth. As long as a worker put in over 47 hours per week, five extra hours are associated with a 1 percent increase in annual wage growth. The effect is stronger for younger professionals (Gicheva, 2013). Another more direct estimate found a wage growth of 2 percent return for a sustained increase in one hour of unpaid overtime per week, during a 10-year period, among workers who had stayed with their employer (Pannenberg, 2005). Moreover, reciprocity can be horizontal, not just vertical, and it can be either positive or negative reciprocal behavior. Workers naturally make comparisons to reference groups they regard as having similar status in the workplace, regarding how much s/he earns and works versus others. When an employer promises a high monetary payment to the worker that undertakes overtime when other colleagues refuse to do so, the worker choosing to undertake overtime prevents the colleague(s) from gaining the higher monetary compensation. This induces the colleague(s) to have a negative orientation toward him/her, motivating that worker to undertake additional work hours as part of a negative reciprocity (Montinari, 2010).

Motivation (4) the relative social status gained by working longer suggests that there is a relative positioning at the workplace, beyond that angling for future promotion, much like the status gained by households in consumption vis-à-vis its social reference groups. Individuals may try to compete for higher relative social status by accumulating status-conferring goods and services (Schor, 1999). To the extent that individuals seek a higher relative position in consumption, they may wish for more paid market work (Altman, 2001). In the context of growing income inequality, this requires that relatively less well-off individuals work more hours in order to sustain their relative position in consumption levels, to emulate consumption patterns of the already wealthy (Bowles & Park, 2005; Schor, 1992). The cumulative effects of intensifying advertising and promotional efforts eventually lead workers to develop a taste for an array of products or services that were once considered luxuries, now converted into necessities (Cowling et al., 2011; Fraser & Paton, 2003; George, 1997). This process is solidified by bandwagon effects, if individuals derive satisfaction from consuming goods and services others are consuming (Altman, 2001). Whereas income serves a positional function, leisure time provides virtually no gain in relative rank (Carlsson et al., 2007). Such consumerism is a primary force behind a rising proportion of workers engaged in very long hours of work (Drago et al., 2009). One potential counter force is if respect is accorded those who work few hours yet produce much value per hour (Haight, 1997), perhaps in lieu of pay (Ellingsen & Johannesson, 2007). However, the term *S* will be unambiguously positive if more respect is granted just for being busy (Gershuny, 2005).

Motivation (5) suggests that if work or a job is intrinsically rewarding, safer, discretionary, and autonomous, rather than stress or anxiety-producing, hazardous, onerous, routinized, and alienating, this either induces longer hours or reduces worker resistance to them. Some jobs or tasks have "process benefits"—outcomes that actually might improve worker well-being (Juster & Stafford, 1985) or provide social interactions and self-growth, so that their incumbents feel more exalted than exploited (Feldman, 2002). In addition, amenities and perks of the workplace may be more available to those workers willing to work additional hours (Douglas & Morris, 2006), even to the point of allocating time away from the household (Hochschild, 2005). Indeed, greater autonomy in work scheduling tends to be associated positively with the number of hours workers are willing to put in (Drago et al., 2009; Golden, 2009; Kelliher & Anderson, 2010). The extension of hours has been facilitated by electronic connectivity devices and network-based telecommunications, by promoting more teleworking (Porter, 2010; Noonan & Glass, 2010).

Finally, motivation (6) reflects the often crucial role for the demand side—employers' demand for hours and minimum hours constraints in jobs. This leads to the two potential sources of overemployment—one element is involuntary overtime or extra work that cannot be refused and the other involuntary full-time employment—downwardly rigid hours in the face of a preference to adjust hours shorter (Golden & Gebreselassie, 2007; Yamguchi, 2008). In the conventional labor market model, the demand side is considered a passive force, accommodating workers' preferences, at least in the long run. However, working time may be arranged less according to employee preferences and more as part of rigorous market competition (Hart, 2004; Rebitzer & Taylor, 1995; Rubery et al., 2005), often in shifts of fixed lengths. In addition, there are "fixed costs" of adding employees, such as the costs of hiring and training new employees and costs of contributions to employee benefits that are affixed to the number of employees rather than hours. This incents firms to lengthen hours of existing employees rather than hire new employees in upturns, and keep hours long while offering part-time jobs rather than shorten hours of full-time employees during downturns. Moreover, a worker who is employed beyond their desired number of hours, willing but unable to sacrifice pay for reduced hours, may quite rationally settle for a longer than optimal workweek, because compensation losses associated with part-time status are more than proportional to the hours reduction.

Overemployment, Overwork, and Workaholism: Definitions, Distinctions, and Interactions

There is a lack of theoretical development on the question of why people work long hours or overtime and the nature of "workaholism" (Douglas & Morris, 2006). At this point, the aim is to disentangle working long hours from overemployment, overwork, and workaholism. Overemployment is considered here to exist when there are workers who are willing but unable to reduce their hours of paid work at their current (or comparable) job even if they are prepared to accept proportionately lower current or future income. Estimates of the aggregate overemployment rate range widely between countries and also even within the US. Estimates range from as little as 6 percent to as much as 50 percent (Bell & Freeman, 2001; Campbell & van Wanrooy, 2013; Feather & Shaw, 2000; Golden & Gebreselassie, 2007; Reynolds, 2004; Schor, 1999; Stier & Lewin-Epstein, 2003). The estimate is quite sensitive to the type of sample, instrument, wording, and context of the question from which it can be derived—in large part because the question posed regarding the willingness to trade income for time varies so much. When presented simultaneously with the alluring "more money" option, choosing fewer hours may lose its relative appeal, even if such hours are not available at their current job. In contrast, if workers are presented only with various hours and pay reduction options, proportions indicating overemployment are higher. One survey found that 17 percent would accept a 20 percent pay cut to get a four-day workweek while over 50 percent would accept a 10 percent cut in their pay to get it (Schor, 2001). Another survey found that as much as 27 percent of the unionized and 39 percent of nonunion employees were willing to reduce their incomes (by either 10 or 20 percent) in order to get proportionately shorter weekly hours (Work in America Institute, 2003). Second, the rate of overemployment varies inversely with the extent to which respondents inherently believe they are unable in practice to change their own hours toward their truly preferred hours. Workers may perceive that reduction of hours is infeasible (e.g., under established organizational and job norms and rigidities regarding their working hours), penalized, or impermissible. Moreover, because survey questions do not address the intensity of work, respondents may well be interpreting the "work less" question as implying not only less pay but also greater work effort or pace. Questions with hours preferences are challenging not only because they are trickier to measure than actual working hours (Tijdens, 2003), but because it is often left unclear whether and how workers would get their "preferred" number of hours and whether they implicitly assume they would receive a more (or less) than proportional reduction in compensation, such as access to employee benefit coverage or premium pay (see Simic, 2002). A willingness to forgo future income, such as a coming year's raise, in contrast, might be greeted with greater favor (see Hart, 2003). In sum, survey estimates of overemployment may be biased downward if a survey provokes certain implicit assumptions among respondents about the current income foregone, and the amount and dimensions of hours reduced involved.

Overemployment at the macroeconomic level can be treated as analogous to classifying the sources of unemployment and the time-related sources of underemployment (see Wilkins & Wooden, 2011). There are three distinct types: structural, cyclical, and frictional. Structural overemployment occurs because of the presence of structural incentives inherent in labor market-related institutions or work organizations that lengthen hours demanded per worker. This includes the growing use of mandatory (forced) overtime practices (Golden & Wiens-Tuers, 2003), underused available state subsidies for adopting work-sharing systems, the escalating cost of premiums for employee health benefit coverage (Cutler and Madrian, 1998), and the weakening of labor unions, a traditional brake on overtime (Trejo, 1993). Cyclical factors alter the extent of overemployment. When aggregate demand (orders, customers) is surging, cyclical overemployment is created when employers' demand for hours per worker is rising faster than workers' desired hours (the latter induced by rising wages if the substitution effect on labor supply is dominant).

Conversely, cyclical overemployment would diminish when a weak macroeconomic climate leads employers to scale back (overtime) hours, leading to underemployment (including involuntary part-time). Finally, frictional overemployment stems from the bundling of wages and hours in most employment contracts and from incomplete markets and information. Frictions in the workplace and labor market exist when there are barriers to full, perfect information among employers about their employees' preferences and among worker applicants about job requirements and alternative jobs. Lags and asymmetries in the transmission of information about individuals' changing preferences and typical (when not explicitly stipulated in contracts) jobs lead to greater incidence of mismatches.

Workers are overemployed if their actual hours (h) exceed desired hours (h^*) given the current wage and job:

$$h^* < h$$

This gap may occur so long as some employers are not induced to adjust h downward toward h^*:

$$\lambda (h - h^*)^{\theta} \quad \textit{given } \lambda > 0; \ \theta > 1$$

Overemployment occurs at the microeconomic level when a worker's actual hours (h) exceed their desired hours (h^*) given the current wage and job: this gap may occur so long as some employers are not induced to adjust h downward toward h^*; when there are non-trivial administrative costs associated with discovering each employee's h^* and facilitating a constant adjustment of h toward each employee's h^*; when the long-term cost consequences for the organization associated with overemployment are small or discounted (θ is not much greater than one); employees lack bargaining leverage to impose adverse unit labor cost consequences (e.g., absences, tardiness, turnover, reduced average hourly labor productivity) on employers; it is relatively less costly for firms to induce employees to adjust upward their h^*, by internalizing the pressures from their social reference groups in the workplace or in consumption targets.

Dynamics of Overemployment, Adaptive Preferences for Hours, and Interactions

Survey and experimental evidence suggest that preferences adapt to market outcomes, a phenomenon referred to as "preference endogeneity" (Schor, 2005). Many workers who put in long hours may be considered "volunteers" who prefer such additional work hours, but some, at least initially, are "conscripts." The latter are those who conform themselves to the "ideal worker" norm and/or carry high levels of consumer debt

(Drago, Wooden, & Black, 2009). A state of overemployment first creates a feeling of time scarcity in the household. This in turn may lead a household to alter its preferences from self-produced goods and services to those that are market-produced. The household may also then shift from time-using goods and services to the more time-saving type. In addition, households are likely to shift preferences from time-intensive to income intensive leisure activities. All three such shifts may ratchet upward individuals' targeted income levels, and ultimately begin to dissipate the initial desire for shorter work hours (Rothschild, 1982). Persistence occurs in the sense that workers who usually work 50 or more hours per week continue working such long hours indefinitely into the future (Drago et al., 2009). Thus, workers may tend to adjust their preferences toward existing hours, an application of observational equivalence (Schor, 1995).

The length of hours per worker not only is a consequence, but may be a cause of workaholism. *Workaholism* is at least slightly positively associated with work hours (McMillan & O'Driscoll, 2006). Working long hours may often reflect an individual's personality-based, positive relationship to work effort or striving for improved equity (Peiperl & Jones, 2001; Porter, 2005). Workaholism becomes problematic when long hours go beyond an enthusiastic work ethic or signaling of commitment, and become an addiction or compulsion, particularly as the life cycle progresses. Workaholism occurs when there is an excessive, sustained allocation of time devoted toward work-related activities that is not derived from necessity or other external pressures (Snir et al., 2006). It is characterized by a tendency to over-commit time at work, in excess of that expected either organizationally or financially or at the expense of one's own health or family and social time (Buelens & Poelmans, 2004; Scott et al., 1997). When work involvement is manifest through long work hours, especially organizationally based, it may yield detrimental types of workaholism (Burke, 1999). Estimates suggest that about 30 percent of workers in North America self-identify as workaholic (Kemeny, 2002). The rate is 53 percent among those who report working an average of 60 or more weekly hours.

Overwork is defined as working beyond one's endurance and recuperative capacities, which may be a hazard particularly for those engaged in open-ended occupations that do not have a finite workday, and for personality types that ignore the commonplace signs that inform one of the need for rest or recreation. They may at times exceed their bodies' ability to recover or make provision for one's physical and emotional needs (Rhoads, 1977). The point at which working hours begin to entail escalating risks or cause harm beyond those associated with normal, standard, agreed-upon hours is considered here to constitute overwork. Overwork refers specifically to the cumulative consequences of operating at "overcapacity." Additional hours spent at work eventually create fatigue or stress so that the worker's physical or mental health, well-being, or quality of life is not sustainable in the longer run. Adverse effects of excess work on various indicators of workers' well-being from individuals and families to employers and the (national or global) economy have been fairly well established empirically. Individuals who work to excess are considered overworkers not because of perceived returns but rather despite a perceived lack of such returns from the organization (Peiperl & Jones, 2001).

Figure 7.1 illustrates that overemployment is fundamentally distinct from the notion of overwork and merely working long hours. However, there is overlap, reflecting interactions between them. Many who are working long hours are overworked and/or overemployed, but not all. Many, but not all, workers with overwork symptoms work long hours. Overwork may occur even if the excess work hours are partly or even wholly voluntary. Many but not all overworked workers prefer reduced hours. Finally, many who prefer reduced work hours work overtime.

Overemployment creates four separate types of potential spillover costs: accident risks that result in injury, illness or adverse public health and safety; time squeeze on family, relationships, children, and social capital development; underemployment and negative employment effects; and negative effects on average productivity per hour at the organizational and/or national levels. Feeling driven to work longer is generally more likely to be associated with negative well-being at work outcomes,

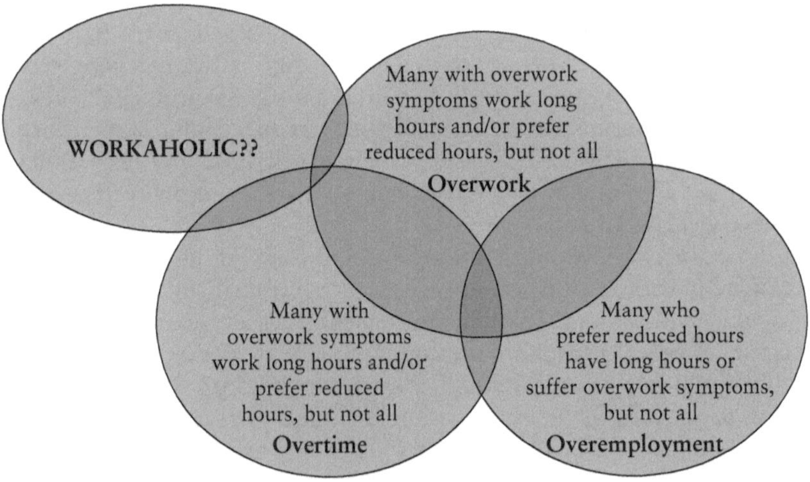

Figure 7.1 Overemployment, overwork, and workaholism—definitions, distinctions, and interactions

in contrast to work enjoyment as the prime motivation (Burke, 1999). Workers who work longer hours or more days than they prefer, for reasons such as employer expectations, tend to feel more overworked than others (Galinsky et al., 2005). However, working more hours for personal motivation or financial reasons—such as "to advance at my job" or "to buy things I need"—are not associated with feeling overworked. About 44 percent of those who work more hours than they prefer indicate feeling overworked, markedly more than the 26 percent that express no preference for shorter hours. Similarly, 45 percent of those who are not permitted at their job to change their own work schedules toward their preferred hours experience significantly higher levels of feeling overworked.

Worker Characteristics Associated with Overemployment

Which workers are more likely to be satisfied with their current working hours and which are more likely to be overemployed? This can be answered empirically with available data for the US work force, the May 2001 Current Population Survey's (CPS) Work Schedule Supplement, with a sample of over 57,000 participants. The key question asks heads of households if, "given the choice, [would you] opt for more income and more hours, less income and fewer hours or the same income and hours?" "More income and hours" signifies overemployment, and "same income and hours" is considered to be "hours satisfied." Overemployment is hypothesized to be more prevalent among workers with personal characteristics that are associated with relatively shorter hours preferences because of more caregiving responsibilities, such as parents with children present in the household or married with spouses working; those at the point in their life cycle approaching retirement; and non-minorities, who are less apt to be underemployed (Moen & Clarkberg, 2001; Reynolds, 2004); also, those whose actual work hours are relatively longer and/or earnings per hour relatively higher, and in occupations that might face more structural constraints on reducing hours or lack job autonomy to exert control over hours (Reynolds, 2004).

The descriptive cross-tabulation statistics of the key variables used appear in Table 7.1. Equation 1 is the estimation equation of the likelihood of an individual responding affirmatively to the option of (i) reducing both hours and income, i.e., being overemployed, or (ii) same hours and income, thus satisfied with their current hours. It is determined by a worker's personal (β) as well as job (δ) characteristics, including work hours and occupation, and the respective vectors of estimated coefficients, X and Y:

Equation 1: $OVER_i = \alpha + X_i\,\beta + Y_i\,\delta + \varepsilon$

Table 7.1 Hours Preference by Workers' Characteristics, 2001 CPS

	Same Hours	*Fewer Hours*	*More Hours*	*Number of Cases*
Total	65.8	7.0	27.25	42,956
Usually full time	67.0	7.4	25.6	25,098
Male—usually full time	67.7	5.6	26.8	14,050
Female—usually full time	69.6	10.0	20.3	11,048
Actual weekly hours				
1 to 14	62.1	5.1	32.9	
15 to 29	60.3	6.0	33.7	
30 to 34	58.9	8.1	33.1	
35 to 39	64.0	7.7	28.3	
40	69.8	5.6	24.5	
41 to 48	66.6	8.1	25.3	
49 to 59	69.7	9.6	20.6	
60+	66.1	13.3	20.7	
Major Occupations				
Executive, admin. and managerial occs	72.8	10.4	16.9	
Professional specialty occs	73.0	9.5	17.5	
Technicians and related support occs	69.9	8.2	22.0	
Sales occs	63.1	6.8	30.1	
Admin support occs, incl. clerical	67.5	7.7	24.9	
Private household occs	54.6	4.7	40.7	
Protective services occs	65.4	4.2	30.4	
Service occs, executive protective and household	56.1	4.2	39.7	
Precision production, craft and repair occs	64.3	4.3	31.4	
Machine operators, assemblers, and inspectors	60.8	3.9	35.4	
Transportation and material moving occs	64.5	5.3	30.2	
Handlers, equipment cleaners, helpers, laborers	54.8	3.7	41.5	
Farming, forestry and fishing occs	54.0	4.5	41.5	

The model is estimated using probit analysis. The dependent variable is bi-variate, taking on a value of one if the employed worker reports having a preference for fewer hours and less income, and then if the preference is for same hours and income. The coefficients are derivatives of the probit estimates, representing the marginal probabilities that an individual possessing a given characteristic prefers fewer hours and less income. Table 7.2

Table 7.2 Preference for Fewer Hours and Reduced Income, by Detailed Occupational Classification Groupings, All Workers

	dF/dx	*z*	*dF/dx*	*z*	*dF/dx*	*z*
Age	0.001**	2.870	0.001	2.870	0.001*	2.450
Age squared	–0.00001*	–2.200	–0.00001	–2.200	0.00001+	–1.790
Female	0.038**	17.240	0.038	17.240	0.034**	15.170
African American	–0.018**	–5.670	–0.018	–5.670	–0.016**	–5.310
Married	0.016**	5.090	0.016	5.090	0.015**	5.050
Divorced/separated/widowed	–0.006	–1.650	–0.006	–1.650	–0.005	–1.450
Child 0–2	0.016**	2.990	0.016	2.990	0.015**	2.870
Child 3–5	0.008+	1.750	0.008	1.750	0.008	1.730
Child 6–13	–0.005+	–1.790	–0.005	–1.790	–0.005+	–1.660
Child 14–17	–0.010**	–3.320	–0.010	–3.320	–0.009**	–3.120
Work hours 20/week	–0.020**	–4.610	–0.020	–4.610	–0.019**	–4.690
21–34	–0.001	–0.180	–0.001	–0.180	–0.001	–0.260
40	0.006+	1.960	0.006	1.960	0.005	1.570
41–49	0.037**	7.040	0.037	7.040	0.032**	6.260
50+	0.051**	11.200	0.051	11.200	0.045**	10.190
Day shift	0.012**	2.820	0.012	2.820	0.010*	2.430
Night shift	0.010	1.280	0.010	1.280	0.011	1.440
Other shift	0.005	0.860	0.005	0.860	0.004	0.660
Self-employment	0.019**	4.350	0.019	4.350	0.015**	3.560
Union coverage	0.009	1.370	0.009	1.370	0.012	1.870
Federal government	0.000	–0.040	0.000	–0.040	–0.003	–0.440

(*Continued*)

Table 7.2 Continued

	dF/dx	*z*	*dF/dx*	*z*	*dF/dx*	*z*
State and local government	–0.001	–0.200	–0.001	–0.200	–0.004	–1.220
Informal flexible schedule	–0.005*	–2.170	–0.005	–2.170	–0.006**	–2.640
Formal flexible schedule	0.021**	6.510	0.021	6.510	0.017**	5.700
Work home	0.010**	3.760	0.010	3.760	0.006*	2.330
Occupation: group 1						
Officials and administrators, public admin.	–0.001	–0.120				
Other executive, admin, and managerial	0.017**	5.240				
Management related occs	0.016**	3.040				
Engineers	0.041**	4.830				
Mathematical and computer scientists	0.021**	2.650				
Natural scientists	0.042**	2.600				
Health diagnosing occs	0.042**	3.590				
Health assessment and treatment occs	0.033**	5.050				
Teachers, college, and university	0.018	1.490				
Teachers, except college and university	–0.001	–0.240				
Lawyers and judges	0.019+	1.660				
Other professional specialty occs	0.002	0.450				
Occupation: group 2						
Health technologists and technicians			0.019	2.160		
Engineering and science technicians			0.011	1.030		
Technicians, engineers, and science			0.019	1.860		
			–0.002	–0.370		

Supervisors and proprietors, sales occs	0.001	0.080		
Sales reps, finance and business services	0.000	0.040		
Sales reps, commodities, excl. retail	–0.001	–0.200		
Sales workers, retail, and personal services	0.016	1.200		
Supervisors and proprietors, sales occ.	0.032	1.630		
Computer equipment operators	0.005	0.760		
Secretaries, stenographers, and typists	–0.004	–0.550		
Financial records processing	0.013	0.980		
Mail and message distributing	0.007	1.970		
Other admin support, incl. clerical	0.004+	0.049		
Occupation: group 3				
Private household service occs			–0.026*	–2.290
Protective service			–0.012	–1.610
Food service			–0.018**	–3.600
Health service			–0.020**	–3.300
Cleaning and building service			–0.011+	–1.670
Personal service			–0.024**	–4.120
Mechanics and repairers			–0.013*	–2.470
Construction trades			–0.031**	–6.540
Other precision production, craft, and repair			–0.008	–1.390
Machine operators and tenders, excl. precis.			–0.019**	–3.560
Fabricators, assemblers, inspectors, samplers			–0.021**	–3.200
Motor vehicle operators			–0.006	–1.100

(Continued)

Table 7.2 Continued

	dF/dx	*z*	*dF/dx*	*z*	*dF/dx*	*z*
Other transport and material moving occs					–0.009	–0.880
Construction laborers					–0.026*	–2.110
Freight, stock, and materials handlers					–0.002	–0.280
Other handlers, equipment cleaners, helpers, laborers					–0.014+	–1.800
Farm operators and managers					–0.050**	–4.150
Farm workers and related occupations					–0.015*	–2.060
Forestry and fishing occs					–0.040	–1.380
log likelihood	–10,910.2		–10,944.3		–10,875.1	
Pseudo R^2	0.048		0.043		0.049	

Note: ** denotes statistical significance of t at the 0.01 level, * at the 0.05 level, + at the 0.10 level of significance.

contains the probit estimation results, displaying the distribution of overemployment by personal, work, and occupation characteristics (46 detailed occupational classifications, grouped into three, like types).

Demographic and Worker Characteristics

Female workers appear to be significantly more at risk of being overemployed than their male counterparts, on the order of about 4 percent greater likelihood (which is reduced only negligibly by inclusion of job characteristics as controls). Conversely, African-American workers are significantly less likely to be overemployed than others. This probably owes to their significantly greater likelihood (not reported here) of being underemployed. The effect of age is actually linear when controlling for workers' work hours and shift characteristics. This suggests that the risk of overemployment increases through the life cycle. Being married raises the likelihood of overemployment, on the order of about 2 percent, relative to the (omitted) reference group of single workers. Being divorced, separated, or widowed, however, does not. Having children in the household (relative to having either no or fully grown children) is important, but with nuances. When the youngest child in the household is younger than three years old, this raises the likelihood of feeling overemployed, by an additional 2 percent. Having children aged three through five, preschool age, has a significant but weaker effect, about half the magnitude of the youngest children. Interestingly, when the youngest child present in the household reaches the age of 14, this reverses the effect of having children on the likelihood of overemployment. Thus, it is apparent that when children first appear, there is a significantly greater demand for time. However, as they age, parents gradually shift their preference toward income, to the point where they actually prefer more income relative to time when children are teenagers.

Work Hours and Job Status Characteristics

A clear pattern is evident as a worker's average work week lengthens. The longer their usual hours, the progressively higher likelihood full-time workers have of being overemployed, relative to those working 35 to 39 hours per week (the reference group). Even working a standard work week of exactly 40 hours creates a significant although small additional likelihood of being overemployed. Working from 41 to 49 hours raises the probability of overemployment considerably. Working 50 or more raises it still further, on the order of about 5 percent when including a control for having variable weekly hours (which, perhaps surprisingly, exhibits a reduced tendency to be overemployed). However, this may be attributable to the disproportionate share of workers in this category who are part-time workers (working 34 or fewer usual hours per week), which tends to reduce the probability of overemployment. Thus, part-time work hours provide workers with a good deal of (but not complete) relief from the risk of overemployment.

Compared to those working the evening shift (the reference group), those on a regular daytime shift, the vast majority of workers, have a slightly raised likelihood of being overemployed. Those on an irregular shift time have the highest probability of being overemployed. Being a union member neither significantly increases nor decreases the chances of overemployment. Being self-employed quite surprisingly heightens rather than lessens the willingness to trade income for more time, given the presumption that self-employed workers would have more discretion over their hours and schedules than payroll employees. Finally, workers who have some ability to vary their starting and ending times of work have a somewhat reduced likelihood of overemployment, but exclusively those who have informal arrangements in the workplace to arrive later or leave work earlier. In contrast, workers with formal flexitime scheduling actually have a higher probability of being overemployed. Thus, formal flexibility in daily work scheduling does not appear to be a solution to overemployment. The dual face of flexibility lends support to the notion that work hours' interference with work and family is rather independent of flexibility of schedule (Major et al., 2002). Moreover, having to do some work at home exacerbates rather than alleviates overemployment. Work-at-home appears to be a source of working longer than preferred hours rather than a vehicle to attain preferred hours.

Job Characteristics: Occupations

There are several occupations that heighten the likelihood of desired fewer hours, and many that reduce it, relative to dissimilar occupations. The major occupational classifications that exhibit the greatest overemployment fall in the managerial and professional groups. Specifically, by magnitude, these are engineers, health diagnosing occupations, natural scientists, math/computer scientists, health assessment and treatment, private (but not public) sector managers and administrators, lawyers/judges, and management-related occupations. There are two technicians jobs, health and those other than health, science or engineering, and other administrative support (computer equipment operators is borderline) where overemployment is significantly higher. In general, it appears that the higher the general pay (skill or preparation) level of the job, the greater is the tendency toward overemployment. Several blue collar occupations, notably construction trades and laborers, farm operators, and fabricators/assemblers, and service jobs such as personal, health, or food service occupations, are less likely to experience overemployment (indeed, these workers are more likely to experience underemployment).

When controlling for occupation types, the effect of all other variables remains the same in terms of their size and significance. The only exceptions are that union coverage seems to somewhat raise the probability of overemployment. The positive effect of long hours and formal flexitime scheduling appears somewhat more attenuated in managerial and professional jobs. Finally, when controlling for a blue-collar occupation, the positive effect of age is linear rather than diminishing. This suggests that in these occupations, overemployment is more common for its relatively older work force.

Table 7.3 displays the results of probit estimations on those workers who are satisfied with their current duration of work hours, neither overemployed nor underemployed. Because the third alternative of underemployment is not presented here, a significantly positive variable might promote satisfaction by its prevention of being underemployed. Indeed, being female, having a greater degree of education, and working longer than 40 hours per week (in the non-profit sector) all are associated with feeling satisfied with current hours. Individuals with managerial, health profession, and certain supervisor, tech, and secretarial jobs are more satisfied with their hours than others.

Expanded Taxonomy of "Leisure" Time: T = H + L

Rather than the typical three categories applied in Becker type economic models of the household—work, household production, and leisure time—the latter two will be subdivided further. In addition to the first type of time allocation, paid work hours (H), there are an additional six classifications, all of which involve non-work time: (1) productive leisure; (2) recuperative leisure; (3) social reproductive leisure; (4) consumptive leisure; (5) nonproductive work-related leisure; and (6) nonproductive "pure" leisure. This subdivision is necessary because uses of non-work time may indirectly be an "investment" if time is devoted to activities that affect the future returns to work, not just their current but future work productivity and well-being. Indeed, each subcategory of non-market time use not only affects an individual's utility and productivity, but also has a unique economic and social impact.

Equation 2: Given $T = H + L; \quad (L) = L\,(L_1 + L_2 + L_3 + L_4 + L_5 + L_6)$

L_1, productive leisure, is when non-work time enhances human capital development, such as studying time in formal education or informal learning, such as career-relevant reading. L_2, recuperative leisure, includes rest and recreation and other health and energy-restorative type

Table 7.3 Preference for Same Hours, by Detailed Occupation, All Workers

Hours Satisfied	*dF/dx*	*z*	*dF/dx*	*z*	*dF/dx*	*z*
Age	0.00	–0.44	0.00	–0.61	0.00	–0.20
Age squared	0.00	3.86	0.00	3.98	0.00	3.58
Female	0.04	7.43	0.04	7.21	0.03	5.78
African American	–0.06	–8.40	–0.06	–8.42	–0.06	–8.22
Married	0.05	6.98	0.05	7.10	0.05	6.71
Divorced/separated/widowed	–0.01	–0.90	–0.01	–0.90	–0.01	–1.03
Child 0–2	0.02	1.34	0.02	1.35	0.02	1.36
Child 3–5	–0.01	–0.62	–0.01	–0.75	–0.01	–0.81
Child 6–13	0.00	0.66	0.00	0.56	0.00	0.60
Child 14–17	0.01	1.45	0.01	1.40	0.01	1.43
Less than HS	–0.10	–10.62	–0.10	–11.10	–0.08	–8.22
HS	–0.03	–5.46	–0.04	–6.09	–0.03	–4.65
College degree (BA, BSc etc.)	0.02	2.38	0.03	4.98	0.03	3.61
Post graduate (MA, PhD, MD etc.)	0.01	0.54	0.03	3.26	0.02	1.86
Work hours 20/week	–0.03	–2.23	–0.03	–2.10	–0.02	–1.91
21–34	–0.05	–3.74	–0.05	–3.73	–0.05	–3.54
40	0.05	5.24	0.05	5.16	0.05	5.22
41–49	0.04	3.34	0.04	3.46	0.04	3.29
50+	0.05	4.42	0.05	4.69	0.05	4.38
Variable hours – FT	0.02	1.45	0.02	1.49	0.02	1.53
Variable hours – PT	–0.14	–6.62	–0.14	–6.62	–0.13	–6.27

Day shift	0.01	0.88	0.01	0.80	0.00	0.08
Night shift	0.01	0.52	0.01	0.43	0.01	0.53
Other shift	0.03	2.33	0.03	2.20	0.02	1.82
Flexible schedule	–0.02	–3.00	–0.01	–2.25	–0.02	–2.91
Federal government	0.01	0.99	0.04	2.33	0.01	0.83
State government	0.02	1.77	0.03	2.42	0.03	2.25
Local government	0.01	0.62	0.01	0.75	0.01	0.68
Private non-profit	0.03	2.70	0.03	3.46	0.03	3.43
Occupations	0.09	3.08				
Officials and administrators, public admin	0.05	5.60				
Other executive, admin, and managerial	0.04	3.07				
Management related occupations	0.06	3.26				
Engineers	0.07	3.97				
Mathematical and computer scientists	0.02	0.54				
Natural scientists	0.00	0.08				
Health diagnosing occs	0.06	3.94				
Health assessment and treatment occs	0.07	2.72				
Teachers, college, and university	0.03	1.97				
Teachers, except college and university	0.01	0.29				
Lawyers and judges	0.06	4.74				
Other professional specialty occs						
Health technologists and technicians			0.02	1.04		
Engineering and science technicians			–0.01	–0.44		

(*Continued*)

Table 7.3 Continued

Hours Satisfied	*dF/dx*	*z*	*dF/dx*	*z*	*dF/dx*	*z*
Technicians, engineers, and science			0.07	3.03		
Supervisors and proprietors, sales occs			0.04	2.81		
Sales reps, finance and business services			–0.02	–1.34		
Sales reps, commodities, excl. retail			0.04	2.07		
Sales workers, retail, and personal services			–0.04	–3.84		
Sales related occs			0.05	0.53		
Supervisors, administrative support occs			–0.01	–0.43		
Computer equipment operators			0.10	2.51		
Secretaries, stenographers, and typists			0.05	3.44		
Financial records processing			0.02	0.89		
Mail and message distributing			–0.08	–2.55		
Other admin support, incl. clerical			0.00	0.33		
Private household service occs					–0.08	–2.34
Protective service					–0.04	–2.07
Food service					–0.07	–5.96
Health service					–0.04	–2.50
Cleaning and building service					–0.08	–4.85
Personal service					–0.06	–3.51
Mechanics and repairers					0.00	–0.37
Construction trades					–0.03	–2.46
Other precision production, craft, and repair					–0.05	–3.34

Machine operators and tenders, excl. precis					–0.05	–3.49
Fabricators, assemblers, inspectors, samplers					–0.08	–4.62
Motor vehicle operators					–0.01	–0.71
Other transport and material moving occs					–0.04	–1.69
Construction laborers					–0.09	–3.20
Freight, stock, and materials handlers					–0.06	–3.30
Other handlers, equipment cleaners, helpers, laborers					–0.06	–3.33
Farm operators and managers					0.21	2.12
Farm workers and related occupations					–0.10	–4.97
Forestry and fishing occupations					0.02	0.29
n	42,956		42,956		42,956	
log likelihood	–26,673.3		–26,679		–26,653	
Pseudo R^2	0.033		0.033		0.034	

activities. As with productive leisure, such time spent can indirectly facilitate achievement of one's productive potential, both in the short and long run. Third, there is time toward "social reproduction" including professional networking, investment in the human capital of one's children (e.g., Guryan, et al. 2008) and time spent beyond one's own family, such as volunteer work and civic participation, and unpaid activities that build future human and "social capital" formation (Heymann & Earle, 2001). In addition, a fourth type is "consumptive leisure," which encompasses activities such as shopping. Finally, there are two types of "nonproductive work-related leisure" that reflects inactivity. The first is work-related, such as commuting time. The second is nonproductive "pure" leisure. This includes personal care or activities that disengage the mind and body.

Too rarely do models of time use or time allocation consider the choice to pursue time investments in educational-type activities, such as an investigation of the demand for informal education (Fahr, 2005). On the one hand, time spent in "productive leisure" may be considered a spillover of work into non-work time and space, which leads to symptoms of "overwork" or even a work addiction. On the other hand, discretionary time spent this way also represents an investment in time today that will lead to either higher earnings or production efficiency in the future, which in turn might reduce commitment in work hours sometime in the future. In addition, non-work time spent in human capital formation, such as unpaid internship or a long commute to a job that provides a stepping stone to a better, future match with one's preferences, can lead to both overwork symptoms and constitute a form of heavy work investment. Similarly, a time commitment to fitness activities can lead to either greater productivity per hour worked, if it is mentally restorative, or conversely, symptoms of overwork, if it produces physical fatigue or injury. Finally, if we let C be total consumption spending, a rate of "consumptivity" (C/L) can be constructed (Gershuny, 1992). Thus, when individuals, households, or even countries reduce their work hours, total consumption spending may not fall proportionately if C/L rises proportionally to offset it—making reduced work time a rational choice that could reduce the risk of both overwork and overemployment. Of course, the future of combining work with work-related and non-work-related activities lies in investigating the issue of multi-tasking (Kalenkoski & Foster, 2012), as either a coping mechanism for overemployment or source of overwork or workaholism, but this is a matter for future research.

Conclusions and Future Directions

This chapter has contributed to the discussion regarding major HWI subtypes by distinguishing the concepts of overemployment, overwork, and workaholism from each other and from overtime or long work hours—each with similar and dissimilar consequences on current worker well-being. The latter emanates mainly from the individual, the first from the employer or labor market conditions, while the second may be a mix of both. The chapter also briefly distinguishes between various non-work time activities that may feed back into returns from work. Focusing on overemployment, it primarily explores its sources and its distribution among workers, finding it most prevalent among certain occupations and longer workweeks. Future research should endeavor to establish the extent to which the net returns from extra work hours depend on the extent of its involuntariness. A more macro investigation could explore the extent to which underemployment is a complement rather than a substitute of overemployment, in the same workplace or occupation, and if so, how might alleviating one curb the other, for a net gain in welfare for all workers? Future work should also deploy time use data to view the potential future returns of non-work time uses, such as educational activities, into future earnings.

Acknowledgments

The author would like to thank Tesfayi Gebreselassie and Arthur Delaney.

References

Altman, Morris. 2001. Preferences and Labor Supply: Casting Some Light Into the Black Box of Income-Leisure Choice. *Journal of Socio-Economics*, 30(3): 199–219.

Altman, Morris and Golden, Lonnie. 2004. Alternative Economic Approaches to Analyzing Hours of Work Regulation and Reform. In Margaret Oppenheimer and Nicholas Mercuro, eds., *Law and Economics: Alternative Economic Approaches to Legal and Regulatory Issues*. Armonk, NY: Sharpe, pp. 286–307.

Axelrod, L., Shah, D.J., and Jena, A.B. 2013. The European Working Time Directive: An Uncontrolled Experiment in Medical Care and Education. *JAMA*, 309(5): 447–448.

Başlevent, Cem and Kirmanoğlu, Hasan. 2013. The Impact of Deviations from Desired Hours of Work on the Life Satisfaction of Employees, *Social Indicators Research*, September 2013.

Bell, L. 2000. The Incentive to Work Hard: Differences in Black and White Workers' Hours and Preferences. In L. Golden and D. Figart, eds., *Working Time: International Trends, Theory and Policy Perspectives*. New York: Routledge, pp. 106–126.

Bell, L. and Freeman, R.B. 2001. The Incentive for Working Hard: Explaining Hours Worked Differences in the U.S. and Germany. *Labour Economics*, 8(2): 181–202.

Booth, Alison L., Francesconi, Marco, and Frank, Jeff. 2003. A Sticky Floors Model of Promotion, Pay, and Gender. *European Economic Review*, 47(2): 295–322.

Carlsson, Fredrik, Johansson-Stenman, Olof, and Martinsson, Peter. 2007. Do You Enjoy Having More Than Others? Survey Evidence of Positional Goods. *Economica*, 74(296): 586–598.

Bowles, Samuel and Park, Yongjin. 2005. Emulation, Inequality, and Work Hours: Was Thorsten Veblen Right? *The Economic Journal*, 115(507): F397–F412.

Bratti, Massimiliano and Staffolani, Stefano. 2007. Effort-Based Career Opportunities and Working Time. *International Journal of Manpower*, 2(6): 489–512.

Buelens, M. and Poelmans, S. 2004. Enriching the Spence and Robbins' Typology of Workaholism: Demographic, Motivational and Organizational Correlates. *Journal of Organizational Change Management*, 17(5): 440–58.

Burke, R. (1999). It's Not How Hard You Work but How You Work Hard: Evaluating Workaholism. *International Journal of Stress Management*, 6(4): 225–239.

Campbell, Iain and van Wanrooy, Brigid. 2013. Long Working Hours and Working-Time Preferences: Between Desirability and Feasibility. *Human Relations*, August (66): 1131–1155.

Clarkberg, Marin and Moen, Phyllis. 2001. Understanding the Time-Squeeze: Married Couples' Preferred and Actual Work-Hour Strategies. *The American Behavioral Scientist*, 44(7): 1115–1136.

Cowling, Keith, Poolsombat, Rattanasuda, and Tomlinson, Philip R. 2011. Advertising and Labour Supply: Why Do Americans Work Such Long Hours? *International Review of Applied Economics*, 25(3): 283–301.

Cutler, D.M. and Madrian, B.C. 1998. Labor Market Responses to Rising Health Insurance Costs: Evidence on Hours Worked. *RAND Journal of Economics*, 29(3): 509–530.

DeRiviere, Linda. 2008. Lower Monetary Returns for That Many Overtime Hours? Forget It! *Journal of Socio-Economics*, 37(2): 613–626.

Dollard, M. and Winefield, A. 2002. Mental Health: Overemployment, Underemployment, Unemployment and Healthy Jobs. *Australian e-Journal for the Advancement of Mental Health*, 1(3): 1446–7984.

Douglas, Evan J. and Morris, Robyn J. 2006. Workaholic, or Just Hard Worker? *Career Development International*, 11(5): 394–417.

Drago, Robert, Wooden, Mark, and Black, David. 2009. Long Work Hours: Volunteers and Conscripts. *British Journal of Industrial Relations*, 47(3): 571–600.

Ellingsen, T. and Johannesson, M. 2007. Paying Respect. *Journal of Economic Perspectives*, 21(4): 135–149.

Fahr, R. 2005. Loafing or Learning? The Demand for Informal Education. *European Economic Review*, 49(1): 75–98.

Feather, Peter and Shaw, Douglass. 2000. The Demand for Leisure Time in the Presence of Constrained Work Hours. *Economic Inquiry*, 38(4): 651–662.

Feldman, D. 2002. Managers' Propensity to Work Longer Hours: A Multilevel Analysis. *Human Resource Management Review*, 12(3): 339–357.

Feldman, Daniel C. 1996. The Nature, Antecedents and Consequences of Underemployment. *Journal of Management*, 22(3): 385–407.

Fenwick, R. and M. Tausig. 2001. Scheduling Stress: Family and Health Outcomes of Shift Work and Schedule Control. *American Behavioral Scientist*, 44(7): 1179–1198.

Fraser, S. and Paton, D. 2003. Does Advertising Increase Labour Supply? Time Series Evidence from the UK. *Applied Economics*, 35(11): 1357–1368.

Friedman, Will. and Casner-Lotto, J. 2003. *Time is of the Essence: New Scheduling Options for Unionized Employees*. Work in America Institute and Labor Project for Working Families.

Galinsky, E., Bond, J.T., Kim, S., Backon, L., Brownfield, E., and Sakai, K. 2005. *Overwork in America: When the Way We Work Becomes Too Much*. New York: Families and Work Institute.

George, D. 1997. Working Longer Hours: Pressure from the Boss or from Marketers? *Review of Social Economy*, 55(1): 33–65.

Gershuny, J. 1992. Are We Running Out of Time? *Futures*, 24(1): 3–22.

Gershuny, J. 2005. Busyness as the Badge of Honor for the New Superordinate Working Class. *Social Research*, 72(2): 287–314.

Gicheva, Dora. 2013. Working Long Hours and Early Career Outcomes in the High-End Labor Market. *Journal of Labor Economics*, 31(4) (October): 785–824.

Golden, Lonnie. 2006. How Long? The Historical, Economic and Cultural Factors Behind Overwork. In R. Burke, *Work Hours and Work Addiction: Research Companion to Workaholism in Organizations, New Horizons in Management*. Edward Elgar, pp. 36–57.

Golden, Lonnie. 2009. A Brief History of Long Work Time and the Contemporary Sources of Overwork. *Journal of Business Ethics*, 84(2): 217–227.

Golden, Lonnie and Wiens-Tuers, Barbara. 2006. To Your Happiness? Overtime Work, Worker Happiness and Satisfaction. *Journal of Socio-Economics*, 35(2): 382–397.

Golden, Lonnie and Gebreselassie, Tesfayi. 2007. Overemployment and Underemployment Mismatches in the US Work Force. *Monthly Labor Review*, April.

Green, Francis. 2004. Work Intensification, Discretion and the Decline in Well-Being at Work. *Eastern Economic Journal*, 30(4): 615–25.

Guryan, Jonathan, Hurst, Erik, and Kearney, Melissa. 2008. Parental Education and Parental Time with Children. *Journal of Economic Perspectives*, 22(3): 23–46.

Haight, A.D. 1997. Padded Prowess: A Veblenian Interpretation of the Long Hours of Salaried Workers. *Journal of Economic Issues*, 31(1): 29–38.

Hamermesh, Daniel S. and Slemrod, Joel B. 2008. The Economics of Workaholism: We Should Not Have Worked on This Paper. *The BE Journal of Economic Analysis & Policy*, 8(1). 1793.

Harpaz, I. and Snir, R. 2003. Workaholism: Its Definition and Nature. *Human Relations*, 56(3): 291–319.

Hart, P. 2003. *Imagining the Future of Work*. New York: Alfred P. Sloan.

Hart, R. 2004. *The Economics of Overtime Working*. Cambridge: Cambridge University.

Hecker, Daniel. 1998. How Hours of Work Affect Occupational Earnings. *Monthly Labor Review, 121*(1998): 8.
Heymann, S. Jody and Earle, Alison. 2001. The Impact of Parental Working Conditions on School-Age Children: The Case of Evening Work. *Community, Work & Family*, 4(3): 305–325.
Hill, E.J., Hawkins, A., Ferris, M., and Weitzman, M. 2001. Finding an Extra Day a Week: Positive Influence of Perceived Job Flexibility on Work and Family Life Balance. *Family Relations*, 50(1): 49–58.
Hochschild, A. (2005). On the Edge of the Time Bind: Time and Market Culture. *Social Research*, 72(2): 339–354.
Juster, Francis Thomas and Stafford, Frank P., eds. 1985. *Time, Goods, and Well-Being*. Ann Arbor, MI: Survey Research Center, Institute for Social Research, University of Michigan.
Kalenkoski, Charlene and Foster, Gigi. 2010. The Multitasking of Household Production, Discussion paper series/Forschungsinstitut zur Zukunft der Arbeit, No. 4845.
Kelliher, Clare and Anderson, Deirdre. 2010. Doing More with Less? Flexible Working Practices and the Intensification of Work. *Human Relations*, 63(1): 83–106.
Kelloway, K., Gallagher, D., and Barling, J. 2004. Work, Employment and the Individual. In B. Kaufman, *Theoretical Perspectives on Work and the Employment Relationship*. Urbana, IL: Industrial Relations Research Association Series, pp. 105–132.
Kemeny, A. 2002. Driven to Excel: Canada's Workaholics. *Canadian Social Trends*. No. 2. Statistics Canada Catalogue no. 11–008-XIE, pp. 2–7.
Krueger, A. 2007. Are We Having More Fun Yet? Categorizing and Evaluating Changes in Time Allocation. *Brookings Papers in Economic Activity*, 38(2), 193–218.
Kuhn, P. and Lozano, F. 2008. The Expanding Workweek? Understanding Trends in Long Work Hours among U.S. Men, 1979–2006. *Journal of Labor Economics*, 26(2): 311–343.
Landers, R., Rebitzer, J., and Taylor, L. 1996. Rat Race Redux: Adverse Selection in the Determination of Work Hours in Law Firms. *American Economic Review*, 86(June): 3229–3248.
Layard, R. 2006. Happiness and Public Policy: A Challenge to the Profession. *The Economic Journal*, 116(510): C24–C33.
Major, Virginia, Klein, K., and Ehrhart, M. 2002. Work Time, Work Interference with Family and Psychological Distress. *Journal of Applied Psychology*, 87(3): 427–436.
Maume, D.J. and Jr Bellas, M.L. 2001. The Overworked American or the Time Bind? *American Behavioral Scientist*, 44(7): 1137–1156.
McMillan, L.H.W. and O'Driscoll, M.P. 2004. Workaholism and Health: Implications for Organizations. *Journal of Organizational Change Management*, 17(5): 509–519.
Michelacci, Claudio, and Pijoan-Mas, Josep. 2007. The Effects of Labor Market Conditions on Working Time: the US-EU Experience. CEMFI Working Paper 0705, June.

Montinari, Natalia. 2010. Reciprocity in Teams: A Behavioral Explanation for Unpaid Overtime. No. 0114, "Marco Fanno" Working Papers, Dipartimento di Scienze Economiche.

Noonan, Mary C. and Glass, Jennifer L. 2012. The Hard Truth about Telecommuting. *Monthly Labor Review*, June, 38–46.

Pannenberg, Markus. 2005. Long-Term Effects of Unpaid Overtime: Evidence from West Germany. *Scottish Journal of Political Economy*, 52(2):177–193.

Peiperl, M. and Jones, B. 2001. Workaholics and Overworkers: Productivity or Pathology? *Group & Organization Management*, 26(3): 369–94.

Philp, B., Slater, G., and Harvie, D. 2005. Preferences, Power, and the Determination of Working Hours. *Journal of Economic Issues*, 39(1): 75–91.

Porter, Gayle. 2005. Workaholism Sloan Work and Family Encyclopedia Entry, Sloan Work and Family Research Network. Retrieved from http://wfnetwork.bc.edu/encyclopedia_entry.php?id=1191 (accessed March 21, 2014).

Porter, Gayle. 2010. Work Ethic and Ethical Work: Distortions in the American Dream. *Journal of Business Ethics*, 96(4): 535–550.

Rebitzer, James and Taylor, Lowell. 1995. Do Labor Markets Provide Enough Short-Hour Jobs? An Analysis of Work Hours and Work Incentives. *Economic Inquiry*, 33: 257–273.

Reynolds, Jeremy. 2004. When Too Much Is Not Enough: Overwork and Underwork in the U.S. and Abroad. *Sociological Forum*, 19(1): 89–120.

Rhoads, J.M. 1977. Workaholism and Health. *Journal of the American Medical Association*, 237(24): 2615–2618.

Rothschild, K.W. 1982. A Note on Some Economic and Welfare Aspects of Working-Time Regulation. *Australian Economic Papers*, 21(38): 1982: 214–218.

Rubery, J., Ward, K., Grimshaw, D., and Beynon, H. 2005. Working Time, Industrial Relations and the Employment Relationship. *Time & Society*, 14(1): 89–111.

Russo, J. and Waters, L. 2006. Workaholic Worker Type Differences in Work–Family Conflict: The Moderating Role of Supervisor Support and Flexible Work Scheduling. *Career Development International*, 11(5): 418–439.

Schor, J. 1992. *The Overworked American*. New York: Basic Books.

Schor, J. 1999. *The Overspent American: Upscaling Downshifting and the New Consumer*. New York: Basic Books.

Schor, J. 2005. Sustainable Consumption and Worktime Reduction. *Journal of Industrial Ecology*, 9(1–2): 37–50 .

Scott, K.S., Moore, K., and Miceli, P.M. 1997. An Exploration of the Meaning and Consequences of Workaholism. *Human Relations*, 50(3): 287–314.

Simic, M. 2002. Volume of Underemployment and Overemployment in the UK. *Labour Market Trends*, (October): 511–521.

Snir, R., Harpaz, I., and Burke, R. 2006. Workaholism in Organizations New Research Directions. *Career Development International*, 11(5): 369–373.

Snir, Raphael and Harpaz, Itzhak. 2012. Beyond Workaholism: Towards a General Model of Heavy Work Investment. *Human Resource Management Review*, 22(3) (September): 232–243.

Sousa-Poza, A. and Henneberger, Fred. 2002. An Empirical Analysis of Working Hours Constraints in Twenty-One Countries. *Review of Social Economy*, 60(2): 1470–1162.

Sousa-Poza, A. and Ziegler, A. 2003. Asymmetric Information about Workers' Productivity as a Cause for Inefficient Long Working Hours. *Labour Economics*, 10(6): 727–747.

Spence, J. and Robbins, A. 1992. Workaholism: Definition, Measurement and Preliminary Results. *Journal of Personality Assessment*, 58(1): 160–178.

Spencer, David A. 2011. Work Is a Four-Letter Word: The Economics of Work in Historical and Critical Perspectives. *American Journal of Economics and Sociology*, 78(7): 563–586.

Stier, Haya and Lewin-Epstein, Noah. 2003. Time to Work: A Comparative Analysis of Preferences for Working Hours. *Work and Occupations*, 30(3) (August): 302–326.

Thomas, W., Ng, H., Sorensen, K. L., and Feldman, D. 2007. Dimensions, Antecedents and Consequences of Workaholism: A Conceptual Integration and Extension. *Journal of Organizational Behavior*, 28(1): 111–136.

Trejo, Stephen. 1993. Overtime Pay, Overtime Hours, and Labor Unions. *Journal of Labor Economics*, 11(2): 253–278.

Van Emmerik, I.J.H. and Sanders, Karin. 2005. Mismatch in Working Hours and Effective Commitment. *Journal of Managerial Psychology*, 20(8): 712–726.

Virtanen, Marianna, Singh-Manoux, Archana, Ferrie, Jane, Gimeno, David, Marmot, Michael, Elovainio, Marko, Jokela, Markus, Vahtera, Jussi, and Kivimäki, Mika. 2009. Long Working Hours and Cognitive Function: The Whitehall II Study. *American Journal of Epidemiology*, 169(5): 596–605.

Wunder, Christoph and Heineck, Guido. 2013. Working Time Preferences, Hours Mismatch and Well-Being of Couples: Are There Spillovers? *Labour Economics*, 24(September): 244–252.

Wilkins, Roger and Wooden, Mark. 2001. Economic Approaches to Studying Underemployment. In D.C. Maynard and D.C. Feldman, eds., *Underemployment: Psychological, Economic, and Social Challenges*. New York: Springer, pp. 13–35.

Yakura, E. 2001. Billables: The Valorization of Time in Consulting. *American Behavioral Scientist*, 44(7): 1076–1096.

Yamaguchi, Kazuo. 2008. *Overemployment: The Structure, Determinants, and Countermeasures of Involuntarily Long Work Hours*. RIETI Research Institute of Economy, Trade and Industry, Incorporated Administrative Agency, September 2008. 08-J-051.

YouGov, Omnibus Poll, July 19–20, 2013. Huffington Post. Retrieved from www.huffingtonpost.com/2013/08/02/extra-hour-a-day_n_3697387.html (accessed March 21, 2014).

8

HOW WORKAHOLISM AFFECTS EMPLOYEES AND THEIR FAMILIES

Akihito Shimazu, Kazumi Kubota, and Arnold B. Bakker

Since the term "workaholism" was coined in the late 1960s (Oates, 1968), both laymen and academics have heavily debated the meaning, antecedents, and consequences of workaholism. Although there is accumulating empirical research on workaholism, much is unclear particularly about the underlying psychological mechanisms that are involved in the (negative) consequences of workaholism. The aim of this chapter is to clarify the impact workaholism has on individual well-being and family life.

In the first part of the chapter, we define the concept of workaholism, and describe several characteristics of workaholic employees. Then, we move to a general overview of the consequences of workaholism. In the second part, we go into further detail about the psychological mechanisms that are involved in the relationship between workaholism and individual well-being. In the third part, we discuss the underlying psychological mechanisms that are involved in the relationship between workaholism and family members' (especially partners') well-being. Finally, we refer to possible strategies to reduce the adverse effects of workaholism, and we discuss directions for future research.

Concept of Workaholism

What is Workaholism?

The term workaholism originates from Oates, who described it as "the compulsion or the uncontrollable need to work excessively" (Oates, 1971). The term quickly gained its popularity, and nowadays it generates 274,000 Google hits (October 2013). However, the studies investigating workaholism are still limited in number, with only 131 scholarly publications identified in the scientific business literature (Ng, Sorensen, & Feldman, 2007). Our own literature search using PubMed (July 2013) revealed 54 publications with the keyword workaholism, of which only 34 used this term in the title. In addition, our literature survey of PsycINFO resulted in 297 publications, of which only 147 used workaholism in the title (July 2013). One of the main reasons for this large discrepancy between public and scientific interest in workaholism is that no agreement exists regarding the conceptualization and measurement of workaholism (McMillan & O'Driscoll, 2006).

In spite of this disagreement, Scott and her colleagues (Scott, Moore, & Miceli, 1997) found three common characteristics of workaholism present in various definitions. First, workaholics spend a great deal of time on work activities when given the discretion to do so. Second, workaholics are reluctant to disengage from work and they persistently and frequently think about it when they are not at work. Third, workaholics work beyond what is reasonably expected from them to meet organizational or economic requirements. The third common feature is a specification of the first and the second features because it deals with a particular manifestation of working hard and compulsively. Indeed, in seven of the nine workaholism definitions that are listed by McMillan and O'Driscoll (2006), working excessively hard and being propelled by an obsessive inner drive are mentioned as core characteristics. More recently, based on a conceptual analysis, Schaufeli, Taris, and Van Rhenen (2008) defined workaholism as the tendency to work excessively hard (the behavioral dimension) and be obsessed with work (the cognitive dimension), which manifests itself in working compulsively. Their definition agrees with that of the founding father, who described workaholism as "the compulsion or the uncontrollable need to work incessantly" (Oates, 1971, p. 11). It also agrees with a recent analysis of scholarly definitions that concludes that hard work at the expense of other important life roles and a strong internal drive to work are two key aspects of workaholism (Ng et al., 2007). On this basis, Schaufeli et al. constructed the Dutch Workaholism Scale (DUWAS), reflecting these two dimensions: working excessively and working compulsively. From a clinical addictive perspective, Andreassen and her colleagues (Andreassen, Griggiths, Hetland, & Pallesen, 2012) defined workaholism as being overly concerned about work, being driven by an uncontrollable motivation, and spending so much energy and effort on work that it impairs private relationships, spare-time activities, and/or health. On this basis, they developed the Bergen Work Addiction Scale (BWAS), reflecting seven core elements of addiction (i.e., salience, mood modification, tolerance, withdrawal, conflict, relapse, and problems).

Causes of Workaholism

Three theoretical perspectives on addiction, i.e., individual dispositions, socio-cultural experiences, and behavioral reinforcements in the environment, can help shed light on the causes of workaholism (Ng et al., 2007). These perspectives suggest that people become workaholics because (1) they possess certain personality traits (Scott et al., 1997), (2) their social or cultural experiences facilitate workaholism (Oates, 1971; Robinson & Post, 1995; Schaufeli, Bakker, Van der Heijden, & Prins, 2009), and/or (3) their workaholic behaviors are reinforced repeatedly (Ng et al., 2007).

In terms of personality traits, people scoring high on Type A personality, extraversion, and neuroticism as well as need for achievement are considered vulnerable to becoming addicted to their work (Burke, Matthiesen, & Pallesen, 2006; Ng et al., 2007). In this perspective, workaholism is considered as a stable pattern of behavior that is dispositional in nature though it may be heightened in particular situations (Burke et al., 2006).

In terms of socio-cultural experiences, stressful or dysfunctional childhood/family experiences, competitive work environments, and role modeling are supposed to trigger workaholism. On the family side, various negative experiences at home can lead to workaholism because work can be seen as a socially acceptable way of avoiding the stressful family (Ng et al., 2006). Workaholism is also seen as a learned addictive response to a dysfunctional family of origin system. Similar to other addictive behaviors, workaholism is intergenerational and passed on to future generations through family processes and dynamics (Burke, 2000a). On the work side, work environments that reward excessive work, place emphasis on work input rather than work output, and sustain a "winner-takes-all" culture are thought to stimulate workaholism (Ng et al., 2007). In addition, the organizational culture in which employees who work long hours are the "heroes" who are displayed as role models can lead to workaholism (Shimazu & Schaufeli, 2009).

Finally, in terms of behavioral reinforcement of workaholism, learning theory can explain the development of workaholism. Learning theory generally encompasses three models: classical conditioning, social learning theory, and operant learning. Research on addiction based on operant learning suggests that the initiation of workaholism is a result of positive reinforcement of workaholic behaviors or the lack of punishment of such behaviors (Ng et al., 2006). Because operant conditioning implies that workaholism will develop only where working leads to desired outcomes, workaholism would be expected to be more prevalent in higher earning and higher status jobs, and more prevalent where home and leisure are not particularly satisfying (McMillan, O'Driscoll, Marsh, & Brady, 2001).

Consequences of Workaholism

Previous studies have shown that workaholism is associated with poor health. By definition, workaholic people spend an excessive amount of time on their work. This suggests that they have insufficient opportunity to recover from their excessive efforts (Bakker, Demerouti, Oerlemans, & Sonnentag, 2013; Schaufeli, Shimazu, & Taris, 2009), leaving them emotionally or cognitively exhausted over time (Taris, Schaufeli, & Verhoeven, 2005). In addition, they persistently and frequently think about work when they are not at work (Taris et al., 2005), which may result in sympathetic arousal and emotional distress. Consequently, workaholism is associated with poor physical health, such as psychosomatic complaints and disabling back pain (e.g., Burke, 2000b; Kanai, Wakabayashi, & Fling, 1996; Matsudaira, Shimazu, Fujii, Kubota, Sawada, Kikuchi, & Takahashi, 2013; Schaufeli et al., 2008, 2009; Shimazu, Demerouti, Bakker, Shimada, & Kawakami, 2011; Shimazu & Schaufeli, 2009; Shimazu, Schaufeli, Kubota, & Kawakami, 2012) and diminished sleep quality such as longer sleep latency, impaired awakening, workplace sleepiness, and higher levels of daytime dysfunction (Kubota, Shimazu, Kawakami, Takahashi, Nakata, & Schaufeli, 2010, 2012; Kubota, Shimazu, Kawakami, & Takahashi, in press). Workaholism is also associated with impaired psychological health such as psychological distress, depression, and burnout (e.g., Bartczak & Ogińska-Bulik, 2012; McMillan & O'Driscoll, 2006; Porter, 1996; Schaufeli et al., 2008, 2009; Shimazu & Schaufeli, 2009; Shimazu et al., 2009, 2011, 2012) and sickness absence (e.g., Matsudaira et al., 2013).

Another type of outcome concerns satisfaction—including job and family satisfaction. Because workaholics work hard, not because they like their job but because of an obsessive inner drive, they tend to report low levels of job satisfaction (Burke, 1999a; Taris, Schaufeli, & Shimazu, 2010; Shimazu & Schaufeli, 2009; Shimazu et al., 2012). In addition, their tendency to invest much time and effort in their work at the expense of other important life roles (Ng et al., 2007) is likely to lead to impaired family functioning. In line with this notion, previous studies revealed that workaholics reported low family satisfaction (Burke, 1999b; Taris et al., 2010).

Further, workaholism is related to poor job performance. Since workaholics spend more time on their work, they may become emotionally or cognitively exhausted over time (Taris et al., 2005). In addition, workaholics work hard rather than smart, create difficulties for themselves and their coworkers, suffer from perfectionism, are rigid and inflexible, and do not delegate tasks to others. These characteristics can lead to poor performance. Furthermore, since workaholics are so deeply involved in their work, they have unreasonably high performance standards (Porter, 1996), which can lead to more negative perceptions of one's own abilities and performance (Ng et al., 2007).

These findings suggest that workaholism is a negative phenomenon. However, the underlying mechanisms of why workaholism leads to poor well-being have not fully been examined empirically.

Psychological Mechanisms Involved in Individual Well-Being

In the second part of this chapter, we go into further detail about the underlying psychological mechanisms that are involved for individual well-being. In doing so, we focus on coping and work–family conflict as potential mediators between workaholism and well-being.

Coping

Coping is defined as ongoing cognitive and behavioral efforts to manage specific external and/or internal demands that are appraised as taxing or exceeding the resources of the person (Lazarus, 1993, 1999). The coping resource model (Pierce, Sarason, & Sarason, 1996) can provide an explanation regarding why coping should play a mediating role between workaholism and well-being. Accordingly, workaholism affects the choice of coping strategies in stressful situations and, depending on the way of coping, workaholism may have a positive or negative impact on employee well-being.

Shimazu, Schaufeli, and Taris (2010) conceptualized coping as a mediator in the relationship between workaholism on the one hand and ill-health and performance on the other hand (Figure 8.1). They focused on active coping and emotional discharge among a wide range of coping strategies, because these two forms of coping conceptually reflect the behavioral and/or cognitive efforts to manage stressful situations among workaholics. Active coping refers to attempts to get to grips with problems at work by cognitively analyzing the situation and/or by taking concrete actions

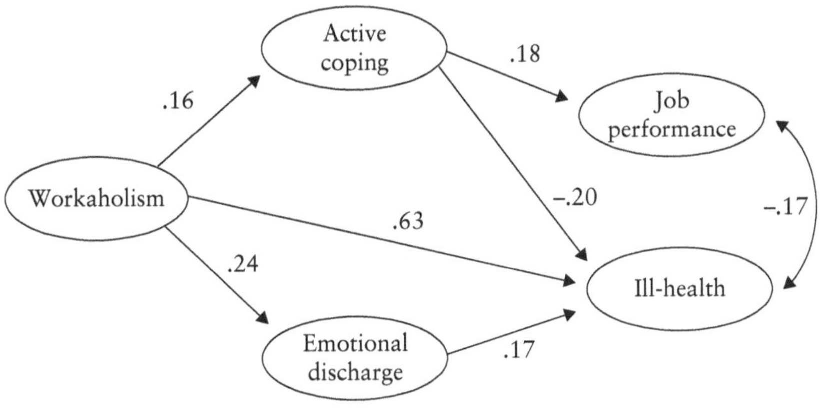

Figure 8.1 Relationship between workaholism, coping, and outcomes: standardized solution (maximum likelihood estimates) of the hypothesized model. N=757

Note: Only significant paths are shown in the figure. Error terms were omitted for clarity.

to solve or overcome these problems (de Rijk, Le Blanc, Schaufeli, & De Jonge, 1998). Emotional discharge refers to openly venting one's negative emotions to others (Carver, Scheier, & Weintraub, 1989).

Shimazu and his colleagues (2010) expected that workaholic people would cope more actively than others (which could lead to better health and performance) in stressful situations at work because they would invest more effort in solving the problems experienced in the workplace. They also expected that workaholic people would more easily disclose their negative emotions than others (which could lead to poor health and performance due to lack of social support), because (1) the primary purpose of their hard work is the avoidance and reduction of negative emotions when not working, and (2) they perceive their coworkers as being less valuable to the organization than themselves (Porter, 2001). Further, Shimazu et al. expected direct relationships between workaholism on the one hand and ill-health and performance on the other hand; working excessively in a compulsive manner could lead to excessive fatigue, leading to ill-health (and, possibly, poor performance).

Results of structural equation modeling among 757 Japanese employees showed that workaholism is both directly and indirectly (through active coping and emotional discharge) associated with ill-health. Specifically, (1) workaholism coincides with ill-health, (2) workaholism is associated with better health through active coping, and (3) workaholism is associated with poor health through emotional discharge. Since the adverse effects of workaholism (i.e., its direct effect and its indirect effect through emotional discharge) are much stronger than its favorable effect (i.e., the indirect effect through active coping), the strong adverse effects on health are not compensated for by workaholics' higher use of active coping strategies. Therefore, workaholic people will on average be less healthy than others.

Shimazu et al. (2010) also showed that workaholism and performance are only weakly and indirectly connected through active coping. Although workaholic people may perform slightly better than others through their use of active coping strategies, this indirect effect is relatively small. Given that workaholic people will on average be less healthy than others, the costs for the workaholic people themselves (in terms of ill-health) are high. Therefore, workaholics will on average perform more poorly than others (e.g., Gorgievski, Bakker, & Schaufeli, 2010).

Work–Family Conflict

Work–family conflict is defined as "a form of inter-role conflict in which the role pressures from the work and family domains are mutually incompatible in some respect" (Greenhaus & Beutell, 1985, p. 77). This definition of work–family conflict implies a bidirectional relationship between work and family life in such a way that work can interfere with family life (i.e., work-to-family conflict: WFC), and family life can interfere with work (i.e., family-to-work conflict: FWC) (Frone, 2000). The scarcity hypothesis (Edwards & Rothbard, 2000) can provide an explanation regarding why workaholism should be related to WFC. Accordingly, people possess limited and fixed amounts of resources (e.g., time and energy). Managing multiple roles, such as those of employee and spouse, is problematic as it draws on the same scarce resources (e.g., limited time and energy). Because workaholic people tend to invest more resources in their work at the cost of non-work activities (Ng et al., 2007), they are likely to experience interference from their work with their family lives (i.e., WFC) due to fewer resources left to devote to their family (e.g., Bonebright, Clay, & Ankenmann, 2000; Brady, Vodanovich, & Rotunda, 2008; Russo & Waters, 2006). For example, workaholic people may experience a time-based WFC because they spend an excessive amount of time on their work at the expense of leisure time (Schaufeli, Shimazu et al., 2009). Similarly, workaholics may experience a strain-based WFC because they persistently and frequently think about work when they are not at work (Taris et al., 2005).

Shimazu and his colleagues (2011) examined the impact of workaholism on employees' WFC and psychological distress among 994 Japanese dual-earner workers. Results of logistic regression analyses showed that workaholics (i.e., employees scoring high on both working excessively and working compulsively) were more likely to experience WFC (odds ratio = 10.20 for men and 7.70 for women) and psychological distress (odds ratio = 5.89 for men and 4.23 for women) compared to relaxed workers (i.e., low on both working excessively and working compulsively). Although they did not examine the mediating role of WFC in their analysis, workaholism is assumed to have an indirect effect on psychological distress through WFC because of positive correlations between WFC and psychological distress (r = 0.36 for men and 0.38 for women).

Another empirical study by Bakker and his colleagues (Bakker, Shimazu, Demerouti, Shimada, & Kawakami, 2014) examined the mediating role of WFC in the relationship between workaholism and family satisfaction. The unique feature of this study was that it also included work engagement, which is defined as a positive, fulfilling, work-related state of mind that is characterized by vigor, dedication, and absorption (Schaufeli, Salanova, Gonzalez-Roma, & Bakker, 2002, p. 74). Bakker et al. examined how the two different types of heavy work investment (Beal, Weiss, Barros, & MacDermid, 2005; Demerouti & Cropanzano, 2010)—work engagement and workaholism—are related to family satisfaction. They hypothesized that workaholism has a negative relationship with family satisfaction through WFC, whereas work engagement has a positive relationship with family satisfaction through work-to-family facilitation (WFF), "the extent to which participation at work is made easier by virtue of the experiences, skills, and opportunities gained or developed at home (or work)" (Frone, 2003, p.145). Results of structural equation modeling among 389 Japanese dual-earner parents showed that workaholism was positively related to WFC, which, in turn, predicted lower family satisfaction, one year later. In contrast, work engagement was positively related to WFF, which predicted higher family satisfaction, also one year later. This study suggests the differences between two important work experiences—workaholism and work engagement—and sheds a new light on the process through which employee workaholism and work engagement influence one's family satisfaction.

Psychological Mechanisms Involved in Family Members' Well-Being

In the previous section, we referred to psychological mechanisms involved for individual well-being. However, what are the mechanisms involved when it comes to family members' well-being? In this section, we use the spillover–crossover model (Bakker & Demerouti, 2013; Bakker, Demerouti, & Burke, 2009; Bakker, Demerouti, & Dollard, 2008) to explain how workaholism may influence one's partner's well-being.

According to the spillover–crossover model, there are two different ways in which experiences are carried over from the work to the family domain. Spillover, or work–family conflict, is a within-person across-domains transmission of demands and consequent strain from one area of life to another. (Please note that although research has clearly indicated that positive spillover is also possible, the focus in previous work–family studies has primarily been on negative spillover.) For example, an employee may experience a time-based conflict between work and private life when work overload results in overwork at the expense of leisure time. Similarly, a worker may experience a strain-based work–family conflict when confronted with something unfair during the day at work, about which he or she continues worrying during the evening at home (Bakker & Demerouti, 2013). In contrast, crossover involves transmission across individuals, whereby demands and their consequent strain cross over between closely related persons (Westman, 2001). Thus, in crossover, stress experienced in the workplace by an individual may lead to stress being experienced by the individual's partner at home. The spillover–crossover model integrates both approaches.

In recent spillover–crossover studies that incorporated partner dyads (e.g., Bakker et al., 2008, 2009; Shimazu et al., 2009), job and family demands were found to be the common antecedents of the crossover process. For instance, Bakker et al. (2008), in a sample of 168 dual-earner couples, showed that one's WFC led to increased social undermining (i.e., negative behaviors directed toward the target person) and higher home demands for the partner, which resulted in greater FWC and exhaustion for the partner. These findings clearly suggest that the demands employees face at work have an unfavorable impact on their partner. In a similar vein, in their study among 99 Japanese dual-earner parents, Shimazu et al. (2009) found that job demands had a positive impact on self- and partner-ratings of WFC, which, in turn, had a negative impact on partners' reports of relationship quality (i.e., increased social undermining and reduced social support) and physical and psychological health. Several other studies have provided evidence for the spillover–crossover model by showing that work-related strain first spills over to the home domain, and then affects the partner (Bakker et al., 2008; Shimazu et al., 2011). These findings suggest that workaholism may be associated with one's partner's well-being through one's WFC and relationship quality. However, there have been few empirical studies that directly examined the relationship between one's workaholism and one's partner's well-being and its underlying mechanisms.

One exception is the study of Bakker and his colleagues (2009) among 168 Dutch dual-earner couples. They found that workaholism was positively related to WFC (spillover), and consequently impacted on own and partner's relationship satisfaction (crossover) through reduced levels of social support. These findings indicate that workaholic employees were more likely to bring their work home, which resulted in lower efforts to help their partner. This reduced social support had a negative impact on their partner's relationship satisfaction. Another exception is the study of Bakker et al. (2014) among 389 Japanese dual-earner couples. They found that workaholism showed a positive relationship with WFC (spillover), and had an indirect negative effect on own and partner's family satisfaction (crossover), also one year later. In contrast, work engagement was positively related to WFF (spillover), and had an indirect positive effect on own and partner's family satisfaction, also one year later.

These findings clarify the mechanisms connecting workaholism and family functioning (e.g., relationship satisfaction and family satisfaction). Future research needs to examine other possible mechanisms in the relationship between one's workaholism and one's partner's well-being. For instance, we can assume that workaholics are so involved in their work that they neglect their relationship with their partner, which may lead to withdrawal and reduced love by the intimate partner. Also, theories about social modeling (Bandura, 1977) and equity (Adams, 1965) would suggest that the partner may start to imitate the workaholic's behavior, and also focus more time on work than on the family and the relationship. Finally, when workaholics are constantly working at home, this may influence the recovery opportunities of their partner, because the partner will need to take care of the family, have less time for relaxation, and cannot invite mutual friends home to socialize.

Future Directions

In this chapter, we referred to the underlying psychological mechanisms that explain the impact of workaholism on individual well-being and on family life. There are several implications for future research. First, although we clarified possible psychological mechanisms (i.e., coping and work–family conflict) that connect between workaholism and subjective health, future research needs to clarify biological mechanisms, such as autonomic nerve system, immune system, and endocrine system, which connect between workaholism and objective health. Studies on Type A personality, a similar concept of workaholism (McMillan et al., 2001), suggested that people with Type A personality operate on the fight-or-flight response, which leads to resistance to central catecholamine depletion, increased peripheral catecholamine availability, increased beta-receptor sensitivity, and suppression of cortisol responses (e.g., Richard, 1989; Weiss, Glazer, Pohorecky, Brick, & Miller, 1975). Given that workaholics also operate on the fight-or-flight response, the similar biological mechanisms can lead to heart disease and heart attacks, diabetes, compromised immune systems, and gastro-intestinal problems.

Second, although this chapter focused on the crossover between one's own workaholism and one's partner's well-being, crossover may also be found between one's workaholism and well-being of the other members of the family, such as any child(ren) and parent(s). For instance, Breevaart and Bakker (2012) showed that employees' psychological distress can lead to poor involvement with their children, less modeling opportunities, and less secure attachment, which, in turn, has a negative impact on adaptive child development. In addition, due to demographic changes, a growing number of employees provide in-home care to an elderly family member (e.g., Major & Germano, 2006, p. 17; Neal & Hammer, 2007, p. 59). Hence, the focus of crossover research should be extended in the family from the spouse to also include children and parents. Workaholism could influence the care for children and parents in several ways. For instance, workaholic people may experience a time-based WFC because they spend an excessive amount of time on their work at the expense of their private life. This can lead to less involvement in care for their children and parents. Furthermore, they may experience a strain-based WFC because they persistently and frequently think about work when they are not at work (Taris et al., 2005). The experience of strain-based WFC and its accompanying frustration, tension, or psychological distress can lead them to initiate or exacerbate a negative interaction sequence with their children and parents (Westman, 2001, 2006).

Finally, it would be interesting and highly relevant to clarify the relationship between one's workaholism and one's colleagues' and subordinates' well-being. Workaholism can spread by vicarious learning and role modeling of supervisors and mentors (Ng et al., 2007). In addition, workaholic people feel that others do not work hard because they themselves work beyond what is reasonably expected from them to meet organizational or economic requirements; they perceive their coworkers as being less valuable to the organization than themselves, and their coworkers' work to be of lower quality than their own (Porter, 2001). As a result, workaholic people may more easily disclose negative emotions to others in stressful situations at work, which may lead to impaired well-being of their colleagues. Therefore, to understand the relationship between one's workaholism and one's colleagues' and subordinates' well-being and its underlying mechanisms would contribute to building a healthy work place.

Practical Implication

There are no clear indications that workaholism, the tendency to work excessively hard in a compulsive manner, involves any advantages to the individual worker or his/her family. In contrast, workaholism is consistently associated with one's own and one partner's unwell-being. Since workaholism is directly and indirectly associated with unwell-being, decreasing the tendency of workaholism is a possible first step to improve one's own and one's partner's well-being. There are several ways in which workaholism may be addressed.

First, the organizational culture in which employees who work long hours are the "heroes" who are displayed as role models should be replaced by a culture that stimulates working smart rather than hard and that values a healthy work–life balance. This is not an easy thing to accomplish, though, because those who are in charge of that culture change are often work addicts themselves (Shimazu & Schaufeli, 2009).

Second, for employees who are at risk for workaholism, training programs that focus on prioritization, time management, and problem solving skills might be helpful, because workaholics take on more work than they can handle and accept new tasks before completing previous ones (Van Wijhe et al., 2010).

Third, employees should be encouraged to detach and recover from a hard day's work. A demanding work situation increases the need for recovery because it draws on an individual's resources (Zijlstra, 1996). Successive depletion of resources will result in negative effects, such as fatigue and, eventually, when no recovery occurs, exhaustion. Distraction as a coping strategy may help employees detach and recover from their work (Shimazu & Schaufeli, 2008). Recently, Bakker and his colleagues (2013) showed that several activities during off-job time (e.g., exercise/sport, and social activities) can particularly help workaholics to recover and feel well during the evening. Additionally, recent work of Hahn and colleagues (Hahn, Binnewies, Sonnentag, & Mojza, 2011) showed that recovery can be trained.

Fourth, workaholics must be encouraged to decrease the tendency towards perfectionism and to seek the support of others. Because workaholics are heavily concerned with their work, they have unreasonably high performance standards (i.e., perfectionism) and, therefore, find it difficult to trust their colleagues to perform up to their standards (Porter, 1996). Rational Emotive Behavioral Therapy (REBT; Ellis, 1993, 2000) to challenge their own irrational beliefs, and social skills training to acquire support-seeking skills may be helpful for workaholic people.

Finally, training programs that focus on regulating (negative) emotions might also be helpful, because workaholics are more likely to use emotional discharge as a coping strategy in a stressful situation (Shimazu et al., 2010). Programs focusing on assertiveness might be helpful in order to deal adequately with employees' (negative) emotions experienced in the workplace (Schabracq, 2005).

Conclusion

Workaholism has a negative impact on employee well-being through inadequate coping and work–family conflict (WFC). Workaholism also has a negative impact on one's partner's well-being, through WFC and impaired relationship quality. We hope that the present chapter encourages a richer understanding of how and why workaholism has negative impacts on one's own and one's partner's well-being. Individuals with workaholic tendencies should become aware of the detrimental effects of their behavior for work–family balance, personal health, and job performance. By adjusting their way of coping with job demands, perhaps with professional help, they can prevent work–family conflict and improve their own life satisfaction.

References

Adams, J. S. (1965). Inequity in social exchange. In L. Berkowitz (Ed.), *Advances in experimental social psychology Vol. 2* (pp. 267–299). New York, NY: Academic Press.

Andreassen, C. S., Griffiths, M. D., Hetland, J., & Pallesen, S. (2012). Development of a work addiction scale. *Scandinavian Journal of Psychology*, 53, 265–272.

Bakker, A. B., & Demerouti, E. (2013). The spillover–crossover model. In J. Grzywacz & E. Demerouti (Eds.), *New frontiers in work and family research*. Hove, Sussex: Psychology Press.

Bakker, A. B., Demerouti, E., & Burke, R. (2009). Workaholism and relationship quality: A spillover–crossover perspective. *Journal of Occupational Health Psychology*, 14, 23–33.

Bakker, A. B., Demerouti, E., & Dollard, M. (2008). How job demands influence partners' experience of exhaustion: Integrating work–family conflict and crossover theory. *Journal of Applied Psychology*, 93, 901–911.

Bakker, A. B., Demerouti, E., Oerlemans, W., & Sonnentag, S. (2013) Workaholism and daily recovery: A day reconstruction study of leisure activities. *Journal of Organizational Behavior*, 34, 87–107.

Bakker, A. B., Shimazu, A., Demerouti, E., Shimada, K., & Kawakami, N. (2014). Work engagement versus workaholism: A test of the spillover–crossover model. *Journal of Managerial Psychology, 29*, 63–80.

Bandura, A. (1977). *Social learning theory*. New York: General Learning Press.

Bartczak, M. & Ogi ska-Bulik, N. (2012) Workaholism and mental health among Polish academic workers. *International Journal of Occupational Safety and Ergonomics*, 18, 3–13.

Beal, D. J., Weiss, H. M., Barros, E., & MacDermid, S. M. (2005). An episodic process model of affective influences on performance. *Journal of Applied Psychology*, 90, 1054–1068.

Bonebright, C. A., Clay, D. L., & Ankenmann, R. D. (2000). The relationship of workaholism with work–life conflict, life satisfaction, and purpose in life. *Journal of Counseling Psychology*, 47, 469–477.

Brady, B. R., Vodanovich, S. J., & Rotunda, R. (2008). The impact of workaholism on work–family conflict, job satisfaction, and perception of leisure activities. *The Psychologist-Manager Journal*, 11, 241–163.

Breevaart, K. & Bakker, A. B. (2012). The influence of job and parental strain on typically and atypically developing children: A vicious circle? *Community, Work & Family*, 15, 173–188.

Burke, R. J. (1999a). Are workaholics job satisfied and successful in their careers? *Career Development International*, 4, 277–282.

Burke, R. J. (1999b). Workaholism and extra-work satisfaction. *International Journal of Organizational Analysis,* 7, 352–64.

Burke, R. J. (2000a). Workaholism in organizations: Concepts, results and future research directions. *International Journal of Management Reviews*, 2, 1–16.

Burke, R. J. (2000b). Workaholism in organizations: Psychological and physical wellbeing consequences. *Stress and Health*, 16, 11–16.

Burke, R. J., Matthiesen, S. B., & Pallesen, S. (2006). Personality correlates of workaholism. *Personality and Individual Differences*, 40, 1223–1233.

Carver, C. S., Scheier, M. F., & Weintraub, J. K. (1989). Assessing coping strategies: A theoretically based approach. *Journal of Personality and Social Psychology*, 56, 267–283.

Demerouti, E. & Cropanzano, R. (2010). From thought to action: Employee work engagement and job performance. In A. B. Bakker & M. P. Leiter (Eds.), *Work engagement: A handbook of essential theory and research* (pp. 147–163). New York: Psychology Press.

Edwards, J. R., & Rothbard, N. P. (2000). Mechanisms linking work and family: Clarifying the relationship between work and family constructs. *Academy of Management Review*, 25, 178–199.

Ellis, A. (1993). Changing Rational–Emotive Therapy (RET) to Rational Emotive Behavior Therapy (REBT). *The Behavior Therapist*, 16, 257–258.

Ellis, A. (2000). Rational Emotive Therapy. In R. J. Corsini & D. Wedding (Eds.), *Current psychotherapies* (pp. 168–204). Itasca, IL: F.E. Peacock Publishers.

Frone, M. R. (2000). Work–family conflict and employee psychiatric disorders: The national comorbidity survey. *Journal of Applied Psychology*, 85, 888–895.

Frone, M. R. (2003). Work–family balance. In J. C. Quick & L. E. Tetrick (Eds.), *Handbook of occupational health psychology* (pp. 143–162). Washington, DC: American Psychological Association.

Gorgievski, M., Bakker, A. B., & Schaufeli, W. B. (2010). Work engagement and workaholism: Comparing the self-employed and salaried employees. *Journal of Positive Psychology*, 5, 83–96.

Greenhaus, J. H., & Beutell, N. J. (1985). Sources of conflict between work and family roles. *Academy of Management Review*, 10, 76–88.

Hahn, V. C., Binnewies, C., Sonnentag, S., & Mojza, E. J. (2011). Learning how to recover from job stress: Effects of a recovery training program on recovery, recovery-related self-efficacy, and well-being. *Journal of Occupational Health Psychology*, 16, 202–216.

Kanai, A., Wakabayashi, M., & Fling, S. (1996). Workaholism among employees in Japanese corporations: An examination based on the Japanese version of the Workaholism scales. *Japanese Psychological Research*, 38, 192–203.

Kubota, K., Shimazu, A., Kawakami, N., & Takahashi, M. (in press). Workaholism and sleep quality among Japanese employees: A prospective cohort study. *International Journal of Behavioral Medicine*.

Kubota, K., Shimazu, A., Kawakami, N., Takahashi, M., Nakata, A., & Schaufeli, W. B. (2010) Association between workaholism and sleep problems among hospital nurses. *Industrial Health*, 48, 864–871.

Kubota, K., Shimazu, A., Kawakami, N., Takahashi, M., Nakata, A., & Schaufeli, W. B. (2012). The empirical distinctiveness of workaholism and work engagement among hospital nurses in Japan: The effect on sleep quality and job performance. *Ciencia & Trabajo*, 14, 31–36.

Lazarus, R. S. (1993). Coping theory and research: Past, present, and future. *Psychosomatic Medicine*, 55, 234–247.

Lazarus, R. S. (1999). *Stress and emotion*. New York: Springer.

Major, D. A., & Germano, L. M. (2006). The changing nature of work and its impact on the work–home interface. In F. Jones, R. J. Burke, & M. Westman (Eds.), *Work–life balance: A psychological perspective* (pp. 13–38). East Sussex: Psychology Press.

Matsudaira, K., Shimazu, A., Fujii, T., Kubota, K., Sawada, T., Kikuchi, N., & Takahashi, M. (2013). Workaholism as a risk factor for depression, disabling back pain, and sickness absence among Japanese workers. *PLoS ONE*, 8, e75140. doi:10.1371/journal.pone.0075140.

McMillan, L. H. W. & O'Driscoll, M. P. (2006). Exploring new frontiers to generate an integrated definition of workaholism. In R. J. Burke (Ed.), *Research companion to working time and work addiction* (pp. 89–107). Cheltenham: Edward Elgar.

McMillan, L. H. W., O'Driscoll, M. P., Marsh, N. V., & Brady, E. C. (2001). Understanding workaholism: Data synthesis, theoretical critique, and future design strategies. *International Journal of Stress Management*, 8, 69–91.

Neal, M. B. & Hammer, L. B. (2007). *Working couples caring for children and aging parents: Effects on work and well-being.* Mahwah, NJ: Lawrence Erlbaum.

Ng, T. W. H., Sorensen, K. L., & Feldman, D.C. (2007). Dimensions, antecedents, and consequences of workaholism: A conceptual integration and extension. *Journal of Organizational Behavior*, 28, 111–136.

Oates, W. E. (1968). On being a "workaholic" (A serious jest). *Pastoral Psychology*, 19, 16–20.

Oates, W. (1971). *Confessions of a workaholic: The facts about work addiction.* New York: World Publishing.

Pierce, G. R., Sarason, I. G., & Sarason, B. R. (1996). Coping and social support. In M. Zeidner and N. Endler (Eds.), *Handbook of coping: Theory, research, applications* (pp. 434–451). New York: Wiley.

Porter, G. (1996). Organizational impact of workaholism: Suggestions for researching the negative outcomes of excessive work. *Journal of Occupational Health Psychology*, 1, 70–84.

Porter, G. (2001). Workaholic tendencies and the high potential for stress among co-workers. *International Journal of Stress Management*, 8, 147–164.

Richard, A. (1989). Arousal and physiological toughness: Implications for mental and physical health. *Psychological Review*, 96, 84–100.

de Rijk, A. E., Le Blanc, P. M., Schaufeli, W. B., & de Jonge, J. (1998). Active coping and need for control as moderators of the job demand–control model: Effects on burnout. *Journal of Occupational and Organizational Psychology*, 71, 1–18.

Robinson, B. E. & Post, P. (1995). Work addiction as a function of family of origin and its influence on current family functioning. *The Family Journal*, 3, 200–206.

Russo, J. A. & Waters, L. E. (2006). Workaholic worker type differences in work–family conflict: The moderating role of supervisor support and flexible work scheduling. *Career Development International*, 11, 418–439.

Schabracq, M. J. (2005). Well-being and health. What HRM can do about it. In R. J. Burke & C. L. Cooper (Eds.), *Reinventing HRM* (pp. 187–206). London: Routledge.

Schaufeli, W. B., Bakker, A. B., Van der Heijden, F. M. M. A., & Prins, J. T. (2009) Workaholism among medical residents: It is the combination of working excessively and working compulsively that counts. *International Journal of Stress Management,* 16, 249–272.

Schaufeli, W. B., Salanova, M., González-Romá, V., & Bakker, A. B. (2002). The measurement of engagement and burnout: A two-sample confirmatory factor analytic approach. *Journal of Happiness Studies*, 3, 71–92.

Schaufeli, W. B., Shimazu, A., & Taris, T. W. (2009). Being driven to work excessively hard: The evaluation of a two-factor measure of workaholism in the Netherlands and Japan. *Cross-Cultural Research*, 43, 320–348.

Schaufeli, W. B., Taris, T. W., & Van Rhenen, W. (2008). Workaholism, burnout and engagement: Three of a kind or three different kinds of employee well-being? *Applied Psychology: An International Review*, 57, 173–203.

Scott, K. S., Moore, K. S., & Miceli, M. P. (1997). An exploration of the meaning and consequences of workaholism. *Human Relations*, 50, 287–314.

Shimazu, A., Bakker, A. B., & Demerouti , E. (2009). How job demands affect the intimate partner: A test of the spillover–crossover model in Japan. *Journal of Occupational Health*, 51, 239–248.

Shimazu, A., Demerouti, E., Bakker, A. B., Shimada, K., & Kawakami, N. (2011). Workaholism and well-being among Japanese dual-earner couples: A spillover–crossover perspective. *Journal of Occupational Health Psychology*, 73, 345–360.

Shimazu, A. & Schaufeli, W. B. (2008). Does distraction facilitate problem-focused coping with job stress? A 1-year longitudinal study. *Journal of Behavioral Medicine*, 30, 423–434.

Shimazu, A. & Schaufeli, W. B. (2009). Is workaholism good or bad for employee well-being? The distinctiveness of workaholism and work engagement among Japanese employees. *Industrial Health*, 47, 495–502.

Shimazu, A., Schaufeli, W. B., Kubota, K., & Kawakami, N. (2012). Do workaholism and work engagement predict employee well-being and performance in opposite directions? *Industrial Health*, 50, 316–321.

Shimazu, A., Schaufeli, W. B., & Taris, T. W. (2010). How does workaholism affect worker health and performance? The mediating role of coping. *International Journal of Behavioral Medicine*, 17, 154–160.

Taris, T. W., Schaufeli, W. B., & Shimazu, A. (2010). The push and pull of work: About the difference between workaholism and work engagement. In A. B. Bakker & M. P. Leiter (Eds.), *Work engagement: A handbook of essential theory and research* (pp. 39–53). New York: Psychology Press.

Taris, T. W., Schaufeli, W. B., & Verhoeven, L. C. (2005). Internal and external validation of the Dutch work addiction risk test: Implications for jobs and nonwork conflict. *Applied Psychology: An International Review*, 54, 37–60.

Van Wijhe, C., Schaufeli, W. B., & Peeters, M. C. W. (2010). Understanding and treating workaholism: Setting the stage for successful interventions. In R. J. Burke & C. L. Cooper (Eds.), *Risky business: Psychological, physical and financial costs of high risk behavior in organizations* (pp. 107–134). Farnham: Gower.

Weiss, J. M., Glazer, H. I., Pohorecky, L. A., Brick, J., & Miller, N. E. (1975). Effects of chronic exposure to stressors on avoidance–escape behavior and on brain norepinephrine. *Psychosomatic Medicine*, 37, 522–534.

Westman, M. (2001). Stress and strain crossover. *Human Relations*, 54, 557–591.

Westman, M. (2006). Crossover of stress and strain in the work–family context. In F. Jones, R. J. Burke, & M. Westman (Eds.), *Work–life balance: A psychological perspective* (pp. 163–184). East Sussex: Psychology Press.

Zijlstra, F. R. H. (1996). Effort as energy regulation. In W. Battmann & S. Dutke (Eds.), *Processes of the molar regulation of behavior* (pp. 219–235). Berlin: Pabst.

9

AFFECTIVE REACTIONS AND SUBSEQUENT CONSEQUENCES OF HEAVY WORK INVESTMENTS

Malissa A. Clark, Jesse S. Michel, and Gregory W. Stevens

John is wholly devoted to his job, spending more time, energy, and effort on his work projects than many of his colleagues. His supervisors consider John a "star" employee that others should strive to model.

As the example above illustrates, organizations may certainly value employees who devote a good deal of their time and energy towards work. But what does it really *mean* to be heavily invested in one's work? Is it always a good thing? What motivates an individual to be so invested? What are the affective, attitudinal, and behavioral outcomes of such investment? The present chapter will explore all of these questions related to being heavily invested in work, with a particular focus on two types of heavy work investment (HWI): workaholism and work engagement. We propose that workaholism and work engagement are distinct types of HWI with very different work and nonwork behaviors and consequences. A model of these types of HWI is presented, which specifies the mechanisms through which these differences are manifested.

This chapter consists of four primary sections. First, we introduce and review the literature on workaholism and work engagement. We introduce an affect-based theoretical model that proposes these types of HWI possess unique negative and positive characteristics. Second, we describe the motivations behind these types of HWI and how these motivations toward work are related to very different state-based affective reactions, as well as how trait affect moderates the relationship between HWI and affective reactions. Third, we describe how state-based affective reactions to HWI influence work and nonwork behaviors and consequences, and how these relationships may be partially mediated by job attitudes and work perceptions (cf. Judge, Scott, & Ilies, 2006). Finally, we provide suggestions for future research and practice.

Two Types of Heavy Work Investment: Workaholism and Work Engagement

Snir and Harpaz (2012) distinguish between situational heavy work investors (e.g., individuals who need to work to support a large family) and dispositional heavy work investors (i.e., those who are heavily invested in their work because of internal motives). Although Snir and Harpaz discuss several types of dispositional heavy work investors, in the present chapter we focus on two dispositional investors in particular: workaholics and engaged workers. These individuals do not spend long hours at work because of various situational drivers (e.g., need for money, demanding job). Rather, both workaholics and engaged workers are driven to work because of some internal motivating factor. The main premise of this chapter is that workaholics and engaged workers are driven to work because of very different motivations. As a result, workaholics and engaged workers experience very dissimilar state-based affective reactions to their heavy investment in work. Our conceptual model linking these dispositional types of HWI to work and nonwork behaviors and consequences, as mediated through state-based affective reactions and attitudes, is presented in Figure 9.1. Before we describe our proposed model, we first briefly introduce the constructs of workaholism and work engagement.

The term workaholic was first coined by Wayne Oates in 1971. He defined workaholism as "addiction to work, the compulsion or the uncontrollable need to work incessantly" (p. 3). Also encompassed in Oates' definition is the idea that one's need for work has become so extreme that it interferes with other important aspects of one's life (e.g., health, happiness, interpersonal relations). Many researchers have adopted similar perspectives as Oates; that workaholism is an addiction to work with negative outcomes (e.g., Porter, 2006; Robinson, 2007; Schaufeli, Taris, & van Rhenen, 2008; Scott, Moore, & Miceli, 1997). However, there are some researchers who propose workaholism may be in fact a positive phenomenon (e.g., Baruch, 2011). Baruch proposed that workaholics may experience eustress, or a positive form of stress, which can lead to positive individual and organizational outcomes. Striking somewhat of a balance between these two perspectives, some researchers have proposed that there are some negative and some positive types of workaholics (e.g., Bonebright, Clay, & Ankenmann, 2000; Machlowitz, 1980; Scott et al., 1997). For example, Scott et al. (1997) differentiated between compulsive-dependent, perfectionist, and achievement-oriented workaholics; achievement-oriented workaholics are defined as being driven to work by achievement motivation and Type A personality, and are proposed to experience positive outcomes such as low stress, high job and life satisfaction, and high job performance. However, most of these typologies have not been empirically tested in the literature.

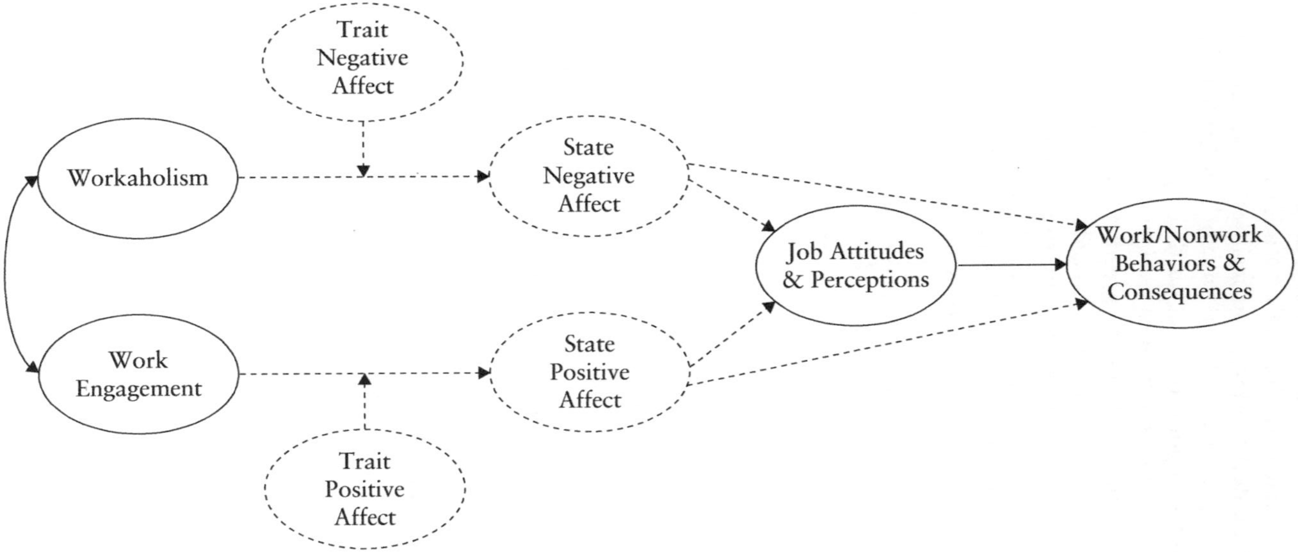

Figure 9.1 An affect-based theoretical model explaining work perceptions and work and nonwork behaviors in response to HWI

Snir and Harpaz (2012) point out that these positive conceptualizations of workaholism do not take into account one of the core features of workaholism: that it is ultimately an addiction to work, comprised of an inability to stop working and feelings of withdrawal when one is engaging in any activity other than work. Schaufeli, Shimazu, and Taris (2009) take this point one step further by stating that this idea of "positive workaholism" is actually a distinct psychological phenomenon called work engagement. We are in agreement with these latter researchers that workaholism should not be considered a "positive addiction to work," nor do we think that it is fruitful to distinguish between positive and negative "types" of workaholics, as these conceptualizations stray away from the origin of the term workaholism and confuse the construct of workaholism with the construct of work engagement, which we turn to next.

The concept of work engagement emerged somewhat later than workaholism. Kahn (1990) was said to be the first to discuss the concept of work engagement, speaking of engaged employees as being fully connected (in terms of physically, cognitively, and emotionally) with their work roles (Bakker, 2011). Work engagement can be defined as a "persistent, positive affective-motivational state of fulfillment in employees that is characterized by vigor, dedication, and absorption" (Maslach, Schaufeli, & Leiter, 2001, p. 417). Vigor can be defined as having high levels of energy and resilience, and high willingness to invest effort and persevere in one's work; dedication refers to being heavily involved and feeling enthusiastic and inspired by one's work; and absorption can be defined as being in a pleasant state of total immersion in one's work (Schaufeli, Salanova, Gonzalez-Roma, & Bakker, 2002). The construct of work engagement has been conceptualized as the "positive antithesis of burnout" (Maslach et al., 2001, p. 417).

With few exceptions (e.g., Halbesleben, Harvey, & Bolino, 2009), research has consistently shown that workaholism is related to negative personal, social, and organizational outcomes, and work engagement is related to positive personal, social, and organizational outcomes (e.g., Aziz & Zickar, 2006; Christian, Garza, & Slaughter, 2011; Harter, Schmidt, & Hayes, 2002; Schaufeli et al., 2008). In line with this research, we propose that workaholism is generally related to negative affective, attitudinal, and behavioral consequences, while work engagement is generally related to positive affective, attitudinal, and behavioral consequences. In the following sections, we discuss how these relationships may be mediated by state-based affective reactions, and job attitudes and perceptions. First, however, we turn to a discussion of the motivations behind workaholism and work engagement, and how these motivational forces are associated with very different state-based affective reactions to these two types of heavy work investment.

Motivations Behind and Affective Reactions to Heavy Work Investment

The first part of our conceptual model specifies that these types of HWI engender different state-based affective reactions. We propose that workaholism is related to the experience of state negative affect, while work engagement is related to the experience of state positive affect. These affective reactions, we argue, stem largely from the motivations behind these two types of HWI. Using self-determination theory (Deci & Ryan, 2000) as a framework, researchers have recently proposed that different motives underlie work engagement and workaholism (Graves, Ruderman, Ohlott, & Weber, 2012; Schaufeli et al., 2009). According to these researchers, whereas engaged workers are primarily motivated by intrinsic motivation (i.e., they work because to them, work is fun), workaholics are primarily motivated by introjected motivation (i.e., they work because of an internal compulsion to work). According to self-determination theory, true enjoyment of one's work (and hence, the experience of positive affect) only comes from freely pursuing activities that are self-integrated (i.e., aligned with deep values, goals, and interests; Deci & Ryan, 2000; Judge, Bono, Erez, & Locke, 2005). Individuals motivated to work by intrinsic motivation (as in the case of engaged workers), who are freely choosing to work because they find it fun, are likely to experience joy and happiness from work. Individuals motivated to work by introjected motivation (as in the case of workaholics), who are driven to work because of an inner compulsion or to resolve an ego depletion, are likely to feel "forced" to work, and are not likely to experience true joy in working. These individuals are likely to experience negative affect as a result of this constant feeling of pressure to be working.

Prior research has acknowledged the important role of affect with both of these types of HWI (Bakker, 2009; Ng et al., 2007). While there appears to be a general consensus that work engagement is related to positive affect and emotions (Bakker, 2011), there is not necessarily a consensus over the link between workaholism and (trait or state) affect. Part of the lack of consensus regarding the affective experiences of workaholics stems from the debate over whether there can be positive types of workaholism (e.g., perhaps certain kinds of workaholics experience positive affect and others negative affect; see Scott et al., 1997). However, there is also disagreement over whether workaholics actually experience enjoyment (a discrete emotion related to positive affect) while working (although most scholars agree that workaholics experience negative emotions/mood while not working). On the one hand, based on interviews with 100 working adults, Machlowitz (1980) concluded that "workaholics are surprisingly happy. They are doing exactly what they love—work—and they can't seem to get enough of it" (p. 16). Ng, Sorensen, and

Feldman (2007) distinguish between joy in one's work (i.e., a more stable assessment of the nature of one's work), and joy in work*ing* (i.e., the momentary experience of joy while one is in the act of working). Ng et al. claim that it is the physical act of working that is pleasurable to workaholics, and as a result they propose a positive relationship between workaholism and state positive affect. On the other hand, others claim that "true" workaholics experience low joy in work (Spence & Robbins, 1992). Consistent with self-determination theory, Gorgievski and Bakker (2010, p. 265) stated, "the crucial difference between workaholism and work engagement is that workaholism lacks the positive affective (fun) component of work engagement." Empirical evidence supports the idea that workaholism is related to negative affective states and work engagement is related to positive affective states. For example, Clark, Michel, Stevens, Howell, and Scruggs (2013) found that workaholism was positively related to guilt, anxiety, anger, and disappointment at work and negatively related to joviality and self-assurance at work, while work engagement was negatively related to guilt, anxiety, anger, and disappointment at work, and positively related to joviality, attentiveness, and self-assurance at work. Other studies have also shown links between workaholism and general negative affect (e.g., Clark, Lelchook, & Taylor, 2010; Van Wijhe, Peeters, & Schaufeli, 2011). Only one known study (Snir & Zohar, 2008) has found a link between workaholism and positive affect during work-related activity; however, workaholism was operationalized as discretionary investment of considerable time at work, so it is unclear what type of HWI that particular measure was assessing.

Research has shown that moods and emotions are transient states that can fluctuate dramatically throughout the day (Weiss, Nicholas, & Daus, 1999), and these emotion episodes have both immediate and delayed effects on attentional processing and performance (Beal, Weiss, Barros, & MacDermid, 2005). Recall that self-determination theory (e.g., Deci & Ryan, 2000) suggests that true positive affect is engendered by intrinsic motivation, rather than introjected motivation. Thus, it is unlikely that workaholics experience true positive emotions while working, and if they do occur they may be more in the form of relief, than of true joy. We argue that even if employees may experience momentary episodes of joy, this is just one instance of many emotion episodes the typical worker experiences during a given work day. Other examples of emotion episodes are when that worker arrives at work, leaves work, switches from one task to another, takes a break for lunch, or is interrupted by a client or co-worker. These other emotion episodes may not be as positive (e.g., the employee may be irritated or anxious if a co-worker interrupts them from their work), and these negative emotional experiences are likely to be more influential when considering the entire work day as an aggregate than any potential fleeting positive emotional experiences. Indeed, research has consistently found that negative events have a larger influence on moods than positive events (Taylor, 1991). Furthermore, using an experience sampling study, Miner, Glomb, and Hulin (2005) found that even though positive events were much more likely to be reported during the work day than negative events, negative events had approximately five times the effect on mood state than positive events. Based on this information, we argue that for workaholics, momentary experiences of joy or happiness are unlikely, and if they occur they are fleeting, and quickly overwhelmed by negative emotions and negative affect (cf. Baumeister, Bratslavsky, Finkenauer, & Vohs, 2001).

Finally, we propose that trait levels of positive and negative affect are likely to exacerbate the experience of momentary affective states that occur as a result of HWI. Trait positive affect is characterized by a general tendency to be energetic, excited, and joyful, whereas trait negative affect is characterized by a general tendency to be anxious, afraid, and angry (Cropanzano, James, & Konovsky, 1993). When engaged workers, who are motivated by intrinsic motivation, are heavily involved with work, trait positive affect is proposed to prime positively toned appraisals and optimism regarding that HWI (Carver, Scheier, & Weintraub, 1989; Lazarus, 1991), which enhances the experience of state positive affect. On the other hand, when workaholics, who are motivated by introjected motivation, are heavily invested in their work, trait negative affect is proposed to prime negatively toned appraisals and decreased coping resources (Carver et al., 1989), which will enhance the experience of state negative affect. In line with this idea, Miner et al. (2005) found that trait hedonic tone (someone's typical level of mood state in terms of pleasantness–unpleasantness) moderated the relationship between positive events and mood following those events. Specifically, these individuals experienced stronger positive moods following positive events if they were higher in trait hedonic tone (i.e., had a generally pleasant mood disposition). Next, we turn to a discussion of the positive and negative effects of these state-based affective reactions to HWI.

Consequences of Heavy Work Investment

Our model suggests that state-based affective reactions to workaholism and work engagement will subsequently influence work and nonwork behaviors and consequences. This indirect mediation effect is supported by the belief that state negative and positive affect are related to different motivational systems (Watson, Wiese, Vidya, & Tellegen, 1999), where state negative affect facilitates withdrawal motivation (e.g., apprehensiveness and cautiousness) and state positive affect facilitates approach motivation (e.g., goal-directed behavior). Additionally, this is consistent with Affective Events Theory (AET; Weiss & Cropanzano, 1996), which suggests that the occurrence of workplace events (e.g., heavy work investment) leads to specific emotional states (i.e., state-based affective reactions), which in turn shape job attitudes and behaviors. Further, AET proposes a cognitive process model in which employees determine whether workplace events threaten their well-being, and then evaluate the importance of that event (Weiss & Cropanzano, 1996). Consequently, workplace events have been defined in cognitive and affective terms as appraisal of and emotional reaction to ongoing job-related events (Basch & Fisher, 2000). The type, intensity, and duration of affective responses differ on the basis of this processing, and these affective responses lead to subsequent work and nonwork behaviors (Gray & Watson, 2001). In the case of workaholism and work engagement, and as outlined in the previous section, it is expected that employees will appraise and react to HWI differently, such that workaholics experience state negative affect and engaged workers experience state positive affect, and these state-based affective reactions subsequently and differentially influence work and nonwork behaviors and consequences.

Returning to our overarching motivational framework, and the notion of different motivational systems, research suggests the facilitation of withdrawal motivation when people consistently feel negative emotions (Watson et al., 1999). Indeed, individuals who experience high state-based negative affect have been found to use ineffective coping strategies, are prone to anxiety, experience poor emotional adjustment, have greater emotional exhaustion and depersonalization, and report fewer perceived accomplishments (Watson & Pennebaker, 1989; Zellars & Perrewé, 2001). Interestingly, this is consistent with Conservation of Resources (COR) theory, which suggests that people acquire and manage personal and social resources wisely, and any threat to those resources results in increased stress (Hobfoll, 1989). COR theory serves to explain how people respond to stressors in their environment (e.g., heavy work investment), and how managing those stressors influences well-being and behaviors (Hobfoll, 2002; Ten Brummelhuis, & Bakker, 2012). Individuals who display withdrawal motives and behaviors will have fewer opportunities and solutions to help manage workplace demands, reducing psychological and physical resources, and thought-action repertoires, and triggering withdrawal behaviors aimed at the conservation of resources. Thus, individuals who experience high state negative affect are likely to retreat and get discouraged, and as a result, they are less likely to build up and expend resources.

According to the broaden-and-build theory of positive emotions (Fredrickson, 1998, 2001, 2003), when people consistently feel positive state-based emotions their momentary thought-action repertoire is expanded, which promotes the discovery of novel and creative actions, ideas, and relationships and increases resources. With an expanded repertoire of personal resources and an inclination to constructively react to domain stressors (e.g., heavy work investment), people high in state positive affect are likely to use personal and workplace resources to improve functioning. Thus, those who consistently experience high state positive affect are likely to seek out solutions to help facilitate functioning and performance.

Taken together, we propose that state-based affective reactions to HWI influence work and nonwork behaviors and consequences, where state negative affective responses to workaholism will result in undesirable relationships with work and nonwork outcomes, such as reduced task performance and organizational citizenship behavior, increased counterproductive work behaviors, increased experiences of work–nonwork conflict, and decreased experiences of work–nonwork enrichment. This is because workaholics who experience greater state negative affect operate with greater withdrawal motivation and use ineffective coping strategies, and have fewer opportunities and solutions to help manage workplace demands, reducing psychological and physical resources. Meanwhile, we propose that state-based affective reactions to HWI influence work and nonwork behaviors and consequences, where state positive affective responses to work engagement will result in desirable relationships with work and nonwork outcomes, such as increased task performance and organizational citizenship behavior, decreased counterproductive work behaviors, decreased experiences of work–nonwork conflict, and increased experiences of work–nonwork enrichment. This is because engaged workers who experience greater state positive affect operate with greater approach motivation, use effective coping strategies, and have more opportunities and solutions to help manage workplace demands, increasing psychological and physical resources.

There is evidence that state affect leads to various work and nonwork behaviors and consequences. For example, meta-analytic results suggest that trait negative and positive affect are differentially related to task performance and contextual performance (including organizational citizenship behaviors and counterproductive work behaviors; Kaplan, Bradley, Luchman, & Haynes, 2009), as well as perceptions of work–nonwork conflict and enrichment (Michel, Clark, & Jaramillo, 2011). Though state and trait affect are conceptually and empirically distinct constructs, where state affect represents temporary affective reactions and trait affect represents general dispositional tendencies, they share similar affective content. More specifically, state and trait negative and positive affect both represent similar psychological and behavioral tendencies: where negative affect is characterized by being anxious, afraid, and angry; and positive affect is characterized by being energetic, excited, and joyful (Cropanzano et al., 1993). Therefore, we believe state affect should exhibit similar patterns of relationships as previous trait-based research, which is consistent with the limited literature examining state affect and various work and nonwork behaviors and consequences. For example, a recent longitudinal examination exploring the influence of workload and affect at work on work–family conflict utilizing an experience sampling methodology found that negative state-based affect at work was significantly predictive of work–family conflict (Ilies, Schwind, Wagner, Johnson, DeRue, & Ilgen, 2007), which is consistent with meta-analytic results linking trait negative affect and work–family conflict (Michel et al., 2011).

Additionally, we propose that the relationship between state-based affective reactions to HWI and work and nonwork behaviors and consequences is partially mediated by job attitudes and perceptions. This is consistent with previous research examining job attitudes and perceptions as a mediator between various stressors and workplace behaviors, which typically pull from the social exchange and emotional labor literatures for theoretical support (e.g., Crede, Chernyshenko, Stark, Dalal, & Bashshur, 2007; Judge et al., 2006). This partial indirect mediation effect is also consistent with patterns of covariance found in previous research. For example, a meta-analysis by Thoresen, Kaplan, Barsky, Warren, and de Chermont (2003) found that state-based negative and positive affect are related to job attitudes and perceptions, including job satisfaction, organizational commitment, and emotional exhaustion. Similarly, job attitudes and perceptions, such as job satisfaction, have been shown meta-analytically to be related to job performance, subjective well-being, and work–family conflict and enrichment (Bowling, Eschleman, & Wang, 2010; Judge, Thoresen, Bono, & Patton, 2001; McNall, Nicklin, & Masuda, 2010; Michel & Hargis, 2008; Michel, Mitchelson, Kotrba, LeBreton, & Baltes, 2009).

Suggestions for Future Research and Practice

In the remaining section of this chapter, we turn our attention to future research directions and implications for practice that stem from the proposed integrative model. First, we focus on the measurement and methodological implications of our model, followed by more substantive and content-oriented contributions to the literature, working towards a better understanding of the processes that underlie these types of relationships. Finally, we address several practical implications.

Methodological and Measurement Recommendations

As we noted earlier in this chapter, a crucial aspect of our theoretical model is the acknowledgement that affect plays both relatively stable (via trait positive and negative affect as moderators) and dynamic (via state positive and negative affect as mediators) roles in the relationships between work engagement and workaholism and relevant outcomes. Furthermore, one may also expect dynamic fluctuations in many of the observed consequences of heavy work investment, including job attitudes and perceptions, work–nonwork conflict and enrichment, and contextual performance (including organizational citizenship behaviors and counterproductive work behaviors). In order to capture these fluctuations and move beyond cross-sectional designs that only account for between-person variability, we recommend that future research adopt an experience sampling methodology (ESM) to capture the multilevel relationships illustrated in our model.

ESM (Beal & Weiss, 2003) is uniquely situated to capture the experiences of individuals as they occur in a natural context. Broadly, this approach involves the repeated measurement of the variables of interest over an appropriate interval (e.g., hourly, daily, weekly) dictated by the substantive research question and the phenomenon of interest, and through any of a variety of methods that capture everyday experiences "in situ" (e.g., completing paper diaries or other logs, smartphone or e-mail reminders and assessment delivery technologies, methods of capturing physiological data). This approach allows researchers to explicitly model relationships at the within-person level of analysis (e.g., daily fluctuations), the between-person level of analysis (e.g., traits or other stable attributes), as well as cross-level effects such as the moderation that we propose. These are important aspects to capture as prior research has typically found that over half of the variability in affect–outcome relationships is attributable to the within-person level of analysis (e.g., Judge et al., 2006; Miner et al., 2005), despite a preponderance of empirical studies that have focused solely at the between level of analysis, primarily through cross-sectional designs.

Furthermore, ESM allows one to examine different aspects of these relationships with regard to the function of time. Specifically, substantive questions of interest surrounding the model might involve potential daily, weekly, or other cyclical patterns, speaking to the importance of specifying an appropriate interval between measurements. It is possible, for instance, that different patterns may be observed upon arrival at work versus departing from work, particularly as a result of the difficulty that those who are heavily invested have from detaching from work tasks; similarly, one may need to account for different patterns at the beginning of a work week versus the end (Sonnentag, Mojza, Binnewies, & Scholl, 2008).

Directions for Future Research

Prior research has consistently linked workaholism with negative outcomes and work engagement with positive outcomes (Christian et al., 2011; Ng et al., 2007). Our model proposes that these differential effects may be due in part to the different emotions experienced by workaholics and engaged workers. As we noted earlier, both workaholism and work engagement share a core feature of becoming absorbed in work (also see Schaufeli et al., 2008), yet differ on the motivations underlying that work pattern: a compulsion-based drive for workaholics, intrinsic value for engaged employees. Acknowledging these complex relationships between the two types of heavy work investment, and, subsequently, how those relationships drive the downstream implications, both affectively and in terms of important work and nonwork outcomes, should be an important goal for future research. Furthermore, future research would be well served to refine the proposed relationships through various conceptualizations of state affect (in terms of discrete emotions, themselves representing motivational constructs) and a range of attitudes and outcomes that take into account subjective and objective forms of well-being and performance. Finally, although not directly depicted in Figure 9.1, we recommend the inclusion of relevant contextual and environmental factors that could influence the proposed relationships. Some examples may include the role of objective job demands or resources (e.g., working hours, job strain; Schaufeli et al., 2008), policies or organizational structures that either support or weaken the proposed relationships (e.g., flexible working hours, supervisory support), or subjective perceptions of either the work or home environment (e.g., permeability and/or flexibility of boundaries between work and home domains; Matthews & Barnes-Farrell, 2010). The end result should be a nomological network that helps researchers and practitioners to better understand the processes that are involved among heavily invested employees.

Practical Implications

Perhaps the primary dilemma for practitioners returns to the opening epigraph for this chapter: how to motivate and sustain those who are heavily invested in work in a positive fashion, while avoiding the more negative aspects and consequences of workaholic patterns. Through the theoretical model that we have proposed, we hope to offer practitioners a better understanding of the dual forces of workaholism and work engagement, as well as insight into the pathways through which those types of heavy work investment lead to more positive or more negative outcomes and consequences. Specifically, it is incumbent upon practitioners to understand the motivations of their employees who work excessively, in light of their stable tendencies to exhibit positive versus negative affect, how those factors combine with the immediate work environment to lend to the experience of state-based affective reactions, and how those brief states contribute to attitudes and outcomes that are either beneficial or not. Practitioners may benefit from developing self-regulation interventions that help workaholic employees to understand the source of their negative emotions and behaviors towards work and to develop more reasonable self-expectations (Porath & Bateman, 2006). Overall, our model suggests that effective strategies will be those that seek to enhance the pathways through which work engagement leads to positive outcomes, while ameliorating or diminishing the pathways through which workaholism leads to negative outcomes. This is particularly important given that prior research has shown that work engagement is likely to be sustained only in work contexts that are enriching or intrinsically motivating, while workaholics tend to expend the same effort regardless of how enriching the context is, reinforcing potentially negative outcomes (Schaufeli et al., 2008).

In conclusion, we propose that both workaholics and engaged workers are heavily invested in their work, but because of different internal motives. This chapter outlines a theoretical framework that details different work and nonwork behaviors and consequences for each of these types of HWI. Central to our model is the idea that workaholics are driven to work by introjected motivation (i.e., an inner compulsion to work), while engaged workers are driven to work by intrinsic motivation (i.e., they find it fun). Because of these different motivational factors, workaholics and engaged workers are likely to experience very different state-based affective reactions, which differentially influence job attitudes and perceptions and, in turn, different work and nonwork behaviors and consequences.

References

Aziz, S., & Zickar, M. J. (2006). A cluster analysis investigation of workaholism as a syndrome. *Journal of Occupational Health Psychology, 11,* 52–62.

Bakker, A. B. (2009). Building engagement in the workplace. In R. Burke & C. Cooper (Eds.), *The Peak Performing Organization* (pp. 50–72). New York: Routledge.

Bakker, A. B. (2011). An evidence-based model of work engagement. *Current Directions in Psychological Science, 20,* 265–269.

Baruch, Y. (2011). The positive wellbeing aspects of workaholism in cross cultural perspective: The chocoholism metaphor. *Career Development International, 16,* 572–591.

Basch, J., & Fisher, C. D. (2000). Affective events–emotions matrix: A classification of work events and associated emotions. In N. Ashkanasy, C. Hartel, & W. Zerbe (Eds.), *Emotions in the workplace: Research, theory, and practice* (pp. 36–48). Westport, CT: Quorum.

Baumeister, R. F., Bratslavsky, E., Finkenauer, C., & Vohs, K. D. (2001). Bad is stronger than good. *Review of General Psychology, 5,* 323–370.

Beal, D. J., & Weiss, H. M. (2003). Methods of ecological momentary assessment in organizational research. *Organizational Research Methods, 6,* 440–464.

Beal, D. J., Weiss, H. M., Barros, E., & MacDermid, S. M. (2005). An episodic process model of affective influences on performance. *Journal of Applied Psychology, 90,* 1054–1068.

Bonebright, C. A., Clay, D. L., & Ankenmann, R. D. (2000). The relationship of workaholism with work–life conflict, life satisfaction, and purpose in life. *Journal of Counseling Psychology, 47,* 469–477.

Bowling, N. A., Eschleman, K. J., & Wang, Q. (2010). A meta-analytic examination of the relationship between job satisfaction and subjective well-being. *Journal of Occupational and Organizational Psychology, 83,* 915–934.

Carver, C. S., Scheier, M. F., & Weintraub, J. K. (1989). Assessing coping strategies: A theoretically based approach. *Journal of Personality and Social Psychology, 56,* 267–283.

Christian, M. S., Garza, A. S., & Slaughter, J. E. (2011). Work engagement: A quantitative review and test of its relations with task and contextual performance. *Personnel Psychology, 64,* 89–136.

Clark, M. A., Lelchook, A. M., & Taylor, M. L. (2010). Beyond the big five: How narcissism, perfectionism, and dispositional affect relate to workaholism. *Personality and Individual Differences, 48,* 786–791.

Clark, M. A., Michel, J. S., Stevens, G. W., Howell, J. W., & Scruggs, R. S. (2013). Workaholism, work engagement, and work–home outcomes: Exploring the mediating role of positive and negative emotions. *Stress & Health.* Advance online publication. doi: 10.1002/smi.2511

Crede, M., Chernyshenko, O. S., Stark, S., Dalal, R. S., & Bashshur, M. (2007). Job satisfaction as mediator: An assessment of job satisfaction's position within the nomological network. *Journal of Occupational and Organizational Psychology, 80,* 515–538.

Cropanzano, R., James, K., & Konovsky, M. A. (1993). Dispositional affectivity as a predictor of work attitudes and job performance. *Journal of Organizational Behavior, 14,* 595–606.

Deci, E. L., & Ryan, R. M. (2000). The "what" and "why" of goal pursuits: Human needs and the self-determination of behavior. *Psychological Inquiry, 11,* 227–268.

Fredrickson, B. L. (1998). What good are positive emotions? *Review of General Psychology, 2,* 300–319.

Fredrickson, B. L. (2001). The role of positive emotions in positive psychology. *American Psychologist, 56,* 218–226.

Fredrickson, B. L. (2003). The value of positive emotions. *American Scientist, 91,* 330–335.

Gorgievski, M. J., & Bakker, A. B. (2010). Passion for work: Work engagement versus workaholism. In S. L. Albrechi (Ed.), *Handbook of employee engagement: Perspectives, issues, research and practice* (pp. 264–271). Gloucestershire: Edward Elgar.

Graves, L. M., Ruderman, M. N., Ohlott, P. J., & Weber, T. J. (2012). Driven to work and enjoyment of work: Effects on managers' outcomes. *Journal of Management, 38,* 1655–1680.

Gray, E. K., & Watson, D. (2001). Emotion, mood, and temperament: Similarities, differences, and a synthesis. In R. Payne & C. Cooper (Eds.), *Emotions at Work* (pp. 21–43). New York: Wiley.

Halbesleben, J. R. B., Harvey, J., & Bolino, M. C. (2009). Too engaged? A conservation of resources view of the relationship between work engagement and work interference with family. *Journal of Applied Psychology, 94,* 1452–1465.

Harter, J. K., Schmidt, F. L., & Hayes, T. L. (2002). Business-unit-level relationships between employee satisfaction, employee engagement, and business outcomes: A meta-analysis. *Journal of Applied Psychology, 87,* 268–279.

Hobfoll, S. E. (1989). Conservation of resources: A new attempt at conceptualizing stress. *American Psychologist, 44,* 513–524.

Hobfoll, S. E. (2002). Social and psychological resources and adaptation. *Review of General Psychology, 6,* 307–324.

Ilies, R., Schwind, K. M., Wagner, D. T., Johnson, M. D., DeRue, D. S., & Ilgen, D. R. (2007). When can employees have a family life? The effects of daily workload and affect on work–family conflict and social behaviors at home. *Journal of Applied Psychology, 92,* 1368–1379.

Judge, T. A., Scott, B. A., & Ilies, R. (2006). Hostility, job attitudes, and workplace deviance: Test of a multilevel model. *Journal of Applied Psychology, 91,* 126–138.

Judge, T. A., Bono, J. E., Erez, A., & Locke, E. A. (2005). Core self-evaluations and job and life satisfaction: The role of self-concordance and goal attainment. *Journal of Applied Psychology, 90,* 257–268.

Judge, T. A., Thoresen, C. J., Bono, J. E., & Patton, G. K. (2001). The job satisfaction–job performance relationship: A qualitative and quantitative review. *Psychological Bulletin, 127,* 376–407.

Kahn, W. A. (1990). Psychological conditions of personal engagement and disengagement at work. *Academy of Management Journal, 33,* 692–724.

Kaplan, S., Bradley, J. C., Luchman, J. N., & Haynes, D. (2009). On the role of positive and negative affectivity in job performance: A meta-analytic investigation. *Journal of Applied Psychology, 94,* 162–176.

Lazarus, R. S. (1991). Progress on a cognitive–motivational–relational theory of emotion. *American Psychologist, 46,* 819–834.

Machlowitz, M. (1980). *Workaholics: Living with them, working with them.* Reading, MA: Addison-Wesley.

Maslach, C., Schaufeli, W. B., & Leiter, M. P. (2001). Job burnout. *Annual Review of Psychology, 52,* 397–422.

Matthews, R. A., & Barnes-Farrell, J. L. (2010). Development and initial evaluation of an enhanced measure of boundary flexibility for the work and family domains. *Journal of Occupational Health Psychology, 15,* 330–346.

McNall, L. A., Nicklin, J. M., & Masuda, A. D. (2010). A meta-analytic review of the consequences associated with work–family enrichment. *Journal of Business and Psychology, 25,* 381–396.

Michel, J. S., & Hargis, M. B. (2008). Linking mechanisms of work–family conflict and segmentation. *Journal of Vocational Behavior, 73,* 509–522.

Michel, J. S., Mitchelson, J. K., Kotrba, L. M., LeBreton, J. M., & Baltes, B. B. (2009). A comparative test of work–family conflict models and critical examination of work–family linkages. *Journal of Vocational Behavior, 74,* 199–218.

Miner, A. G., Glomb, T. M., & Hulin, C. (2005). Experience sampling mood and its correlates at work. *Journal of Occupational and Organizational Psychology, 78,* 171–193.

Ng, T. W. H., Sorensen, K. L., & Feldman, D.C. (2007). Dimensions, antecedents, and consequences of workaholism: A conceptual integration and extension. *Journal of Organizational Behavior, 28,* 111–136.

Oates, W. E. (1971). *Confessions of a workaholic: The facts about work addiction*. New York: World Publishing.

Porath, C. L., & Bateman, T. S. (2006). Self-regulation: From goal orientation to job performance. *Journal of Applied Psychology, 91,* 185–192.

Porter, G. (2006). Profiles of workaholism among high-tech managers. *Career Development International, 11,* 440–462.

Robinson, B. E. (2007). *Chained to the desk: A guidebook for workaholics, their partners and children, and the clinicians who treat them* (2nd ed.). New York: New York University Press.

Schaufeli, W. B., Salanova, M., Gonzalez-Roma, V., & Bakker, A. B. (2002). The measurement of engagement and burnout: A two sample confirmatory factor analytic approach. *Journal of Happiness Studies, 3,* 71–92.

Schaufeli, W. B., Shimazu, A., & Taris, T. W. (2009). Being driven to work excessively hard: The evaluation of a two-factor measure of workaholism in the Netherlands and Japan. *Cross-Cultural Research, 43,* 320–348.

Schaufeli, W. B., Taris, T. W., & van Rhenen, W. (2008). Workaholism, burnout, and work engagement: Three of a kind or three different kinds of employee well-being? *Applied psychology: An International Review, 57,* 173–203.

Scott, K. S., Moore, K. S., & Miceli, M. P. (1997). An exploration of the meaning and consequences of workaholism. *Human Relations, 50,* 287–314.

Snir, R., & Harpaz, I. (2012). Beyond workaholism: Towards a general model of heavy work investment. *Human Resource Management Review, 22,* 232–243.

Snir, R., & Zohar, D. (2008). Workaholism as discretionary time investment at work: An experience-sampling study. *Applied Psychology: An International Review, 57,* 109–127.

Sonnentag, S., Mojza, E. J., Binnewies, C., & Scholl, A. (2008). Being engaged at work and detached at home: A week-level study on work engagement, psychological detachment, and affect. *Work and Stress, 22,* 257–276.

Spence, J. T., & Robbins, A. S. (1992). Workaholics: Definition, measurement, and preliminary results. *Journal of Personality Assessment, 58,* 160–178.

Taylor, S. E. (1991). Asymmetrical effects of positive and negative events: The mobilization–minimization hypothesis. *Psychological Bulletin, 110,* 67–85.

Ten Brummelhuis, L. L., & Bakker, A. B. (2012). A resource perspective on the work–home interface. *American Psychologist, 67,* 545–556.

Thoresen, C. J., Kaplan, S. A., Barsky, A. P., Warren, C. R., & de Chermont, K. (2003). The affective underpinnings of job perceptions and attitudes: A meta-analytic review and integration. *Psychological Bulletin, 129,* 914–945.

Van Wijhe, C. I., Peeters, M. C. W., & Schaufeli, W. B. (2011). To stop or not to stop, that's the question: About persistence and mood of workaholics and work engaged employees. *International Journal of Behavioral Medicine, 18,* 361–372.

Watson, D., & Pennebaker, J. W. (1989). Health complaints, stress, and distress: Exploring the central role of negative affectivity. *Psychological Review, 96,* 234–254.

Watson, D., Wiese, D., Vidya, J., & Tellegen, A. (1999). The two general activation systems of affect: Structural findings, evolutionary considerations, and psychobiological evidence. *Journal of Personality and Social Psychology, 76,* 820–838.

Weiss, H. M., & Cropanzano, R. (1996). Affective events theory: A theoretical discussion of the structure, causes and consequences of affective experiences at work. In B. M. Staw & L. L. Cummings (Eds.), *Research in organizational behavior* (pp. 1–74). Greenwich, CT: JAI Press.

Weiss, H. M., Nicholas, J. P., & Daus, C. S. (1999). An examination of the joint effects of affective experiences and job beliefs on job satisfaction and variations in affective experiences over time. *Organizational Behavior and Human Decision Processes, 78,* 1–24.

Zellars, K. L., & Perrewé, P. L. (2001). Affective personality and the content of emotional social support: Coping in organizations. *Journal of Applied Psychology, 86,* 459–467.

10

THE RELATIONSHIP BETWEEN HEAVY WORK INVESTMENT AND EMPLOYEES' HAPPINESS

Orit Shamai

Introduction

Modern life has made the workplace one of the most meaningful domains in people's lives. Harpaz and Meshoulam (2004) note that people deem work more important than leisure, community, and religion. In several studies, work was ranked second only to family (Harding & Hikspoors, 1995; Harpaz, 1990; MOW—International Research Team, 1987; Harpaz & Meshoulam, 2009). The workplace also plays a crucial role in helping individuals achieve and maintain their self-esteem, status, and sense of accomplishment (Harpaz, 1990; Snir & Harpaz, 2002b; Snir & Harpaz, 2004). Organizational scholars have found that work can be a source of happiness (Judge & Kammeyer-Mueller, 2011). The great importance of the work domain, combined with opportunities for actualization in the workplace, has caused many individuals to work excessively and invest long hours in their jobs. The term "workaholism," coined by Oates (1971), is now commonplace in daily language to express employees' heavy work investment in their jobs (Harpaz & Snir, 2003; McMillan, Brady, O'Driscoll, & Marsh, 2002; Snir & Harpaz, 2012). Burke (2000a) notes the ongoing debate on the association between heavy work investment and personal well-being, and the lack of consensus as to whether the relationship between these two variables is positive or negative.

The central issue of this chapter is to lay the foundation for the relationship between Heavy Work Investment (HWI) and employees' happiness, defined as Subjective Well-Being (SWB). Most research on HWI has concentrated on other types of well-being (e.g., emotional and physical health) (Burke, Koyuncu, & Fiksenbaum, 2007; Vodanovich, Piotrowski, & Wallace, 2007). Our discussion is based on the HWI model proposed by Snir and Harpaz (2012), which relies on established scientific theories and is supported by relevant empirical data demonstrating HWI predictors, dimensions, types, and outcomes. According to this model, the dimensions of happiness are referred to as implications of heavy work investment. After introducing the conceptual–theoretical background for each of the constructs, heavy work investment and global happiness, we address the relationship between these two concepts. Finally, the implications of happiness on organizational behavior are discussed.

Conceptual–Theoretical Background

Heavy Work Investment

The discourse on heavy work investment in most academic frameworks refers to the phenomenon of workaholism and enjoys considerable attention in the popular press (Burke, 2000a) and the research community (Douglas & Morris, 2006). The past decade has witnessed increased empirical research on the topic (Burke & Matthiesen, 2004). It has focused on types of heavy work investors (Buelens & Poelmans, 2004; Oates, 1971; Naughton, 1987; Scott, Moore, & Miceli, 1997; Spence & Robbins, 1992); how HWI relates to health (Burke, 2000d; McMillan & O'Driscoll, 2004; Vodanovich et al., 2007), to personality (Burke, Matthiesen, & Pallesen, 2006; Mudrack, 2004), to personal relations (Burke, 2000c; McMillan, O'Driscoll, & Brady, 2004; Robinson, Flowers, & Carroll, 2001), to demographic criteria (Snir & Harpaz, 2004), to women in various countries (Burke, 1999; Burke & Matthiesen, 2004; Burke, Oberklaid, & Burgess, 2004; Burke et al., 2007), to organizational values (Burke, 2000b); and the consequences of HWI (Scott et al., 1997).

Nevertheless, researchers emphasize the need to refine our understanding of heavy work investment (Ng, Sorensen, & Feldman, 2007; Snir, Harpaz, & Burke, 2006). Many criticize the absence of an acceptable definition of the term and the lack of standardized measures for it (Burke, 2000a; Harpaz & Snir, 2003; Mudrack, 2004; Scott et al., 1997; Snir & Harpaz, 2012). Others note the absence of theoretical development concerning the nature of HWI (Douglas & Morris, 2006). Consequently, it may be regarded as a construct at a crossroads or still in its infancy (Zohar, 2006).

The literature provides a variety of definitions for HWI, or workaholism as it is frequently called—a term first coined by Oates (1971). By his definition, a workaholic is "a person whose need for work has become so excessive that it creates noticeable disturbance or interference with his bodily health, personal happiness, and interpersonal relationships, and with his smooth social functioning" (Oates, 1971, p. 4).

Many other researchers have since offered a variety of definitions, which somewhat complicates research on the subject. Some view workaholism as a neutral phenomenon; for example, Mosier (1983 in Harpaz & Snir, 2003) defines workaholics as those who work at least 50 hours a week. Scott et al. (1997) conceptualize workaholics as those who spend a great deal of time on work activities beyond organizational requirements or economic needs. McMillan, O'Driscoll, Marsh, and Brady (2001) and McMillan et al. (2002) also define workaholism as personal reluctance to disengage from work demonstrated by the tendency to work (or to think about work) anytime and anywhere.

Some definitions take a negative view of HWI, seeing it as an addiction like any other. For Porter (1996), workaholism is "excessive involvement with work evidenced by neglect in other areas of life and based on internal motives of behavior maintenance rather than requirements of the job or organization" (p. 71). In greater detail, Ng, Sorensen, and Feldman (2007) see HWI as an addiction with three dimensions: affect, cognition, and behavior. They define workaholics as those whose emotions, thoughts, and behaviors are strongly dominated by their work. They enjoy the act of working, are obsessed with working, and devote long hours and personal time to work.

The empirical perspective of HWI is demonstrated by the "workaholic triad" of Spence and Robbins (1992). Their model distinguishes types of workers and has three dimensions: work involvement, feeling driven to work, and work enjoyment. According to their triad, workaholics score high on work involvement and drive, and low on work enjoyment. However, the factor structure of these three dimensions has not been fully replicated in empirical studies (e.g., McMillan et al., 2002; Kanai et al., 1996 in Ng et al., 2007). Testing this workaholic triad, Buelens and Poelmans (2004) identified a new type: the reluctant hard worker. This type of workaholic reported relatively long working hours, at a relatively low hierarchical level, with a strong perception of external pressure.

Snir and Zohar (2008) view workaholism as a heavy time investment in work that does not stem from external demands (e.g., financial needs) but from internal patterns that cause employees to work excessively.

Recently Snir and Harpaz (2012) extended this definition with a more holistic approach. Referring to HWI in general, they state that it involves time commitment, but also investment of effort, mental or physical. With this new observation, Snir and Harpaz (2012) present a general model of the nature of HWI, demonstrating its predictors, dimensions, types, and outcomes. In this model, workaholism is one of four HWI subtypes and incorporates two core elements: time and effort. This model serves as the theoretical foundation of the current discussion as depicted in Figure 10.1.

The model differentiates common full-time workers from heavy work investors according to input of time or effort. Time investment refers to average weekly working hours. In most modern countries, the average working hours per week is between 30 and 40 hours (Sparks, Cooper, Fried, & Shirom, 1997), while heavy work investors work about 50 hours per week (Halevi, 2006; Schaufeli, Taris, & Bakker, 2006; Wharton &

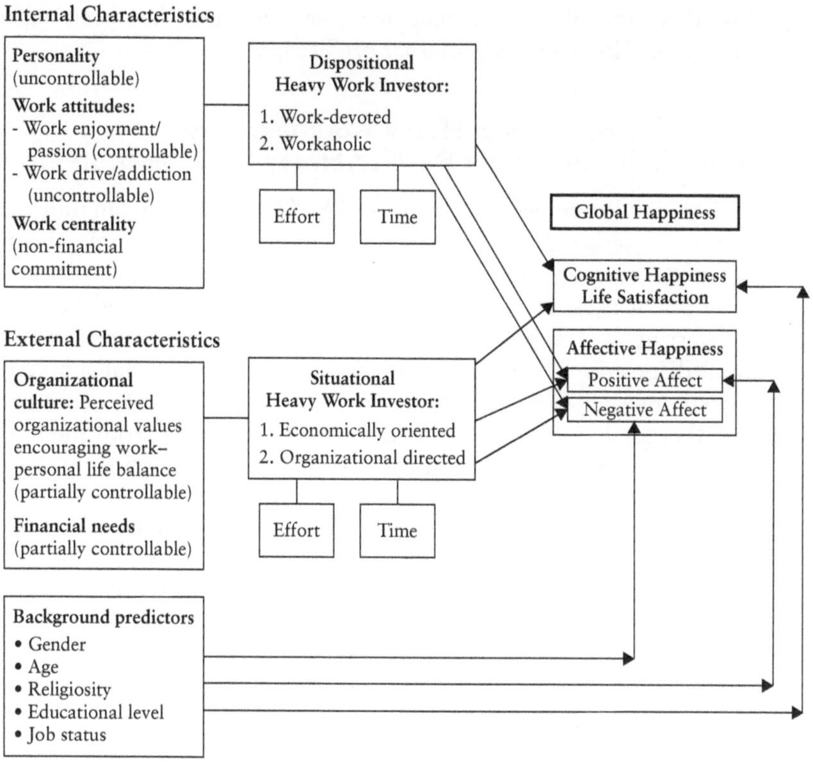

Figure 10.1 The relationship of Heavy Work Investment (HWI) and employees' happiness

Blair-Loy, 2006). Hence, common workers are full-time employees who work fewer than 50 hours a week, while heavy work investors work more than 50 hours a week. Effort is defined as the quantity and the quality of strenuous physical activities or complex cognitive tasks required for the job (Gorman & Kmec, 2007; Dwyer & Ganster, 1991), so heavy work investors are required to invest more effort in their work. According to Snir and Harpaz (2012), time and effort investments in work correlate positively. On these grounds, we first differentiate heavy work investors from common workers according to investment of time or effort.

Based on Attribution Theory (Weiner, 1985), Snir and Harpaz (2012) specified a classification of possible HWI predictors according to the three categories presented in the theory: causal locus (whether the cause of HWI is internal or external to the person), controllability (whether the cause is under volitional control or not), and stability (whether the cause is constant or varies over time). These authors also distinguish positive (e.g., love of work, job involvement) from negative (e.g., low preference for leisure, addiction to work) internal predictors.

Dispositional Heavy Work Investors: Workaholics and Work Devoted Heavy Work Investors

The HWI model distinguishes dispositional HWI, stemming from internal predictors (e.g., personality traits), from situational HWI, stemming from external predictors (e.g., organizational demands). Each type of heavy work investment presented in the model has subtypes. Snir and Harpaz (2012), referring to Attribution Theory, recognize internal characteristics as relevant dispositional predictors of HWI, so the dispositional subtypes derive from internal characteristics: workaholism and work devotion. Based on this logic, workaholism is a subtype that arises from internal predictors and is observed as a negative and uncontrollable phenomenon. This observation supports Porter's (1996) position that like alcoholism, workaholism is an addiction characterized by excessive work behavior. Thombs (1994 in Ng et al., 2007) and Fassel (1990) treat HWI as a pathology. Fassel suggests that workaholism is a progressive, fatal disease—an addiction to working. More importantly, she also suggests that the workaholic's personal life becomes unmanageable in relation to work.

Work devotion, by contrast, is an expression of a passion for work and is observed as an internal positive and controllable predictor (Snir & Harpaz, 2012). Recent research found that both passion and work engagement correlated with measures of job and work investments (Burke & Fiksenbaum, 2009; Schaufeli, Taris, & van Rhenen, 2008).

With the internal characteristics, Snir and Harpaz (2012) include personality traits and work attitudes, namely drive and enjoyment, on which the subtypes of dispositional heavy work investors differ. Referring to these same characteristics, Douglas and Morris (2006) suggest that drive is activated when a person is motivated by the work effort per se, while work enjoyment is the level of pleasure derived from work and it correlates with job satisfaction (McMillan et al., 2002). McMillan et al. (2001) suggest that drive is a harmful element while enjoyment is a protective factor that buffers the influence of drive. Spence and Robbins (1992) propose that work enthusiasm involves enjoyment.

Trait theory is a well-known explanatory framework for workaholic behaviors (McMillan et al., 2002). Surprisingly, there is no canonical definition in current use. Personality is defined as a set of attributes characterizing an individual or as the underlying system that generates the attributes. We adopt Funder's (1997 in Saucier, 2008) approach, which combines these two descriptions and defines personality as the individual's pattern of thought, emotion, and behavior together with the psychological mechanism, hidden or not, behind those patterns.

Only a few studies have probed the relationship between personality traits and HWI (Burke et al., 2006; Clark, McEwen, Collard, & Hickok, 1993; Lodi-Smith & Roberts, 2007; McMillan et al., 2001; Mudrack, 2004; Naughton, 1987). Moreover, in investigating the various types of heavy work investors, only a few scholars refer to compulsion (Burke, 2000b; Mudrack, 2004; Naughton, 1987; Schwartz, 1982; Scott et al., 1997); others refer to Type A personality.

Haynes, Legine, Scotch, Feinleib, and Kannel (1978) characterize Type A by ambitiousness, competitiveness, time urgency, impatience, and aggressiveness or hostility. Individuals who are relatively free of these characteristics are identified as Type B (Haynes et al., 1978). Friedman and Rosenman (1971) noted that the Type A behavior pattern emerges only when certain challenges or conditions of the milieu (or job) arise, which elicit a particular complex of responses. Jenkins, Zyzanski, and Rosenman (1971, in Spence, Helmreich, & Pred, 1987) state that individuals with the Type A pattern are usually conscientiously committed to their occupation and often achieve success in it. Mudrack (2004) found a significant relation between Type A and involvement and tendencies to engage in non-required work. Empirical evidence exists that the Type A behavior pattern is a potent personality predictor of workaholism (Robinson, 1999). Therefore, workaholics are distinguished from other subgroups of HWI partly by the Type A personality trait.

The literature also refers to work centrality as a basic significant predictor variable of investment in work and workaholism (Harpaz & Snir, 2003; Heller, Judge, & Watson, 2002; Snir, Harpaz, & Ben-Baruch, 2009; Snir & Zohar, 2000). Work centrality is identified through the concept of non-financial employment commitment, which is a wish to continue working—not necessarily in one's current job but in general (England & Harpaz, 1983; Snir & Harpaz, 2002a). One way to measure work centrality by inference is by the so-called lottery question (Arvey, Harpaz, & Liao, 2004; England & Harpaz, 1983; Harpaz & Fu, 2002); in it the economic rationale or necessity for working is removed, so a person's non-financial or psychological commitment to work can be assessed. Though hypothetical, the situation reflects reality. Confirmation for this postulation can be found in a study with American lottery winners: 85 percent of them continued to work after winning. It was also shown that winners were less likely to quit work if they had relatively greater degrees of work centrality (Arvey et al., 2004). Work centrality was significantly related to HWI (Harpaz & Snir, 2003; Snir & Zohar, 2000) and a comparison of employees in the private and the public sector showed the former were more likely to be heavy work investors (Harpaz & Snir, 2003).

As for occupation types, Harpaz and Meshoulam (2004) observed that workers in the high-tech industry had higher work centrality and a more expressive orientation than workers in traditional industries. Among high-tech workers, fathers reported higher work centrality, and investment of more weekly hours in paid work, than childless men. Mothers reported lower work centrality and investment of fewer weekly hours in paid work than women without children (Snir et al., 2009).

Situational Heavy Work Investors: Organizational-Directed and Economically-Oriented Heavy Work Investors

Workaholism (addiction to work) and work devotion (passion for work) are both dispositional subtypes deriving from internal characteristics. Two further HWI subtypes are organizational-directed heavy work investors and economically-oriented heavy work investors, which are both situational subtypes (Snir & Harpaz, 2012).

Person–Situation Interaction Theory may explain the interaction between individuals and their work environments, which dominates the variance between people in the time and effort they invest in the workplace. In the organizational context the environment is represented by the situational setting, characterized by external characteristics: organizational culture and an individual's financial orientation. The amount of physical or mental demands in the workplace is associated with time spent at work (Pleck, Staines, & Lang, 1980) and with the length of the workweek (Maume & Bellas, 2001).

Following Maume and Bellas (2001), we address organizational culture in the form of employees' perceptions of their employers' and supervisors' demands and expectations regarding family commitment and, more specifically, their perceptions of their organization's values regarding the work–personal life balance. As organizational culture addresses the employee body, rather than the separate individuals, it reflects the work environment focusing on responsiveness to employees' family and personal needs. Organizational family support is a global construct encompassing all the work–family policies and practices offered by an organization. The interest of organizations lies in helping employees achieve a viable balance between work and family life (Jahn, Thompson, & Kopelman, 2003). Relying on important research frameworks, Jahn et al. (2003) present two theoretical family support dimensions, which were empirically demonstrated. One of the dimensions is tangible support while the other is intangible. Tangible support consists of instrumental practices (adequate leave programs, financial assistance for childcare, and flexible scheduling) and informational practices (resource and referral programs, and actual communications about family-friendly policies and programs); intangible support consists of emotionally supportive practices for employees' lives outside the workplace (acknowledgement and acceptance of their family-related needs). Perceived organizational family support (POFS) is thus conceptualized as the employee's perception of instrumental, informational, and emotional support available to him or her from the organization (Jahn et al., 2003). Nowadays, many organizations try to apply these family support dimensions in environmental strategies and programs to reduce work–family conflict and maintain their balance (Jahn et al., 2003). However, in doing so, the organizational culture seems to create higher expectations of organizational commitment and of more time and effort being invested in work.

The individual's basic economic needs may affect HWI as well. Like Harpaz and Snir (2003), we refer to perceived financial needs. These researchers found that employees reported greater financial need when they had to support more people financially. Thus, economically-oriented heavy work investors are distinguished from other situational heavy work investors according to employees' perception of their own financial circumstances.

A comparative cross-cultural study by Snir and Harpaz (2009) on HWI and the subtypes of heavy work investors showed that HWI was more common in societies where survival and mastery values were important. Situational HWI was found to be more common in societies where survival values were important, while the work-devoted type was more common in societies where self-expression values were important. However, dispositional HWI was more common in societies where mastery values were high. The implications of heavy work investment for workers' happiness are highly intriguing; to date no study has examined the relationship between these two important domains.

Happiness as Subjective Well-Being

The desire to be happy is a ubiquitous aspiration among people and being happy is the mode of life individuals prefer in the modern and competitive world (Diener, Suh, Smith, & Shao, 1995). This is attested in a recent survey conducted in 47 countries, where happiness was overwhelmingly ranked as the most important of all personal values, that is, above wealth, health, love, and more (Kim-Prieto, Diener, Tamir, Scollon, & Diener, 2005 in Warr, 2007). The concept of happiness has fascinated thinkers for millennia, but only in the last decade or so has it been measured and studied systematically by positive psychologists (Diener, Suh, & Oishi, 1997).

The shift of psychological research to the positive aspects of human existence, including the pursuit of happiness, have contributed to the development of a new, lively research discipline termed Subjective Well-Being Studies or Happiness Studies (Bilski, 2004, p. 46). Subjective Well-Being (SWB), the phrase prevalent in academic research, emerged in the late 1950s in the search for useful indicators of quality of life to monitor social change and improve social policy (Land, 1975 in Keyes, Shmotkin, & Ryff, 2002).

Since then, happiness has been researched in a large number of domains and personal aspects: the national sphere and public policy (Ashkanasy, 2011; Veenhoven, 2000, 2005a, 2005b); economy and financial state (Kahneman, Krueger, Schkade, Schwarz, & Stone, 2006); a social network (Fowler & Christakis, 2008); health (Barak, 2006; Pressman & Cohen, 2005); cultural setting (Ahuvia, 2002; Lu & Shih, 1997); extreme life circumstances (Brickman, Coates, & Janoff-Bulman, 1978); activities' quality (Csikszentmihalyi, 1975 in Diener et al., 1997; Csikszentmihalyi & LeFevre, 1989); personality (Hills & Argyle, 2001); emotional intelligence (Furnham & Petrides, 2003); individual values (Cohen & Shamai, 2010; Sagiv & Schwartz, 2000); and virtue and altruism (Martin, 2007; Seligman, 2002).

The Construct of Happiness

Seligman (2002) proposes a psychologist's standard definition of happiness as Subjective Well-Being (SWB) (hereinafter "happiness") in the form of overall satisfaction with life or high average levels of enjoyment and other desired emotions. Hence, the field of happiness as a subfield of positive psychology comprises the scientific analysis of how people evaluate their lives. These evaluations may be primarily cognitive (e.g., life satisfaction) or may consist of the frequency at which people experience pleasant emotions (e.g., joy) and unpleasant emotions (e.g., depression) (Diener et al., 1997; Diener, Oishi, & Lucas, 2003; Keyes et al., 2002). Evaluations of life can be at a given moment or over longer periods, such as the previous year. Hence, the construct of happiness consists of three components: life satisfaction, positive affect, and negative affect. This construct has been consistently confirmed in numerous studies (Diener, Suh, Lucas, & Smith, 1999; Diener et al., 2003; Keyes et al., 2002; Lucas, Diener, & Suh, 1996). Warr (2007) proposes a comprehensive model with three "scopes" of happiness as well-being based on breadth. Each scope has a cognitive and an affective aspect. The broad scope is context-free well-being, which consists of global affect (with more affective emphasis) and life satisfaction (with more cognitive emphasis). The second scope is moderate, referring to domain-specific well-being (e.g., job domain). The third, according to Warr, is a narrow scope of happiness, entitled "facet-specific well-being," referring to one specific facet in one specific domain (e.g., feelings about colleagues, satisfaction with pay).

Following Warr's terminology (2007), we deal with the broad scope of happiness, applying to context-free well-being. Like other researchers (Diener et al., 1997; Glenn & Weaver, 1979, 1981; Kahneman et al., 2006) we call Warr's broad scope of context-free happiness "global happiness." According to Diener and colleagues (Diener et al.,1997; Diener et al., 1999; Eid & Diener, 1998), global happiness or global SWB refers to the two global aspects of happiness: the affective (referring to positive and negative affect) and the cognitive.

The Cognitive Aspect of Happiness

The cognitive aspect of happiness refers to life satisfaction, which reflects people's global judgments and evaluations of their lives (Warr, 2007; Kahneman et al., 2006; Diener et al., 2003).

The Affective Aspect of Happiness

The affective aspect of happiness is defined by Lyubomirsky, King, and Diener (2005) as a frequent experience of positive emotions over time such as joy, interest, and pride, and infrequent (though not absent) negative emotions, such as sadness, anxiety, and anger. This definition follows Bradburn's (1969 in Lucas et al., 1996) classic work that states that happiness results from a balance between positive and negative affect (Lucas et al., 1996). The work of Diener and Emmons (1984) was the first to show the independence of positive and negative affect. Later studies repeated this separation (Keyes et al., 2002).

The Relationship between Heavy Work Investment and Employees' Happiness

Diener and Seligman (2002) assert that attaining high happiness seems contingent on several preconditions. These preconditions presumably involve not only personal characteristics, but also the environmental setting, which requires investment of time and effort at the workplace.

Affective Events Theory proposes that affective experiences at work elevate work events as proximal causes of affective reactions (Weiss & Cropanzano, 1996). Activity Theory and Flow Theory provide an explanation for the relationship between work activities and affect. The former posits that interesting activities at work provide enjoyment that is achieved through people's emotions and physical comforts (Diener et al., 1997). The latter posits that interesting activities, in which there is a balance between challenge and skill (Csikszentmihalyi, 1975, in Diener et al., 1997) and absolute concentration (Robbins, 2001), are observed as flow experiences (Csikszentmihalyi, 1975; 1982 in Csikszentmihalyi & LeFevre, 1989). According to Flow Theory, affect depends on being involved in such experiences. Assuming that the job matches employees' skills, it can provide challenge and experiences of flow. Interestingly, Csikszentmihalyi and LeFevre (1989) found that people report most flow experiences not in their leisure time but at work; the accompanying feelings are more active, alert, concentrated, happy, satisfied, and creative. Investigating experiences of positive feelings in heavy investment workers, Snir and Zohar (2008) found that in contrast to common workers, heavy work investors experienced more positive affect during work than during leisure activities. On the basis of Activity Theory and the Flow Theory, heavy work investors, who spend more hours at the workplace than common workers, presumably will experience more flow than the latter, and hence are expected to report greater levels of positive affect.

Proposition 1: *Heavy work investors exhibit higher levels of positive affect (as one component of the affective aspect of happiness) than common workers.*

Diener (1984) claims that the more a person feels positive affect, the less that person will feel negative affect. Diener and Emmons (1984) have offered extensive evidence for the independence of negative and positive affect. However, they showed that people rarely experience strong negative and positive affect at the same time, which suggests that the two vary inversely in frequency. Following these assumptions, not only do we expect heavy work investors to reveal higher levels of positive affect than common workers, but we also expect lower levels of negative affect than the latter. Therefore:

Proposition 2: *Heavy work investors exhibit lower levels of negative affect (as the other component of the affective aspect of happiness) than common workers.*

As mentioned before, we posit that heavy work investors, who spend more hours at the workplace than common workers, experience more flow than the latter. Bottom-up Theory maintains that happiness is simply the sum of many small pleasures. According to this view, an individual's life satisfaction is a mental calculation of the sum of the momentary pleasures and pains (Diener, 1984). Hence, we may conclude that heavy work investors who experience more positive affect at work than common workers are expected to report greater levels of life satisfaction than the latter.

Proposition 3: *Heavy work investors exhibit higher levels of life satisfaction (the cognitive aspect of happiness) than common workers.*

Dispositional heavy work investors are differentiated by attitude toward work. Snir and Harpaz (2012) point to high enjoyment and attachment to work underlying work-devoted employees, and high drive and Type A personality underlying workaholics' addiction to their work. Snir and Harpaz (2012) anticipate possible differences between levels of affective aspect of happiness according to investment at work and expect affective reactions, whether positive (e.g., pleasure) or negative (e.g., frustration), to work-related events to be stronger in "dispositional investors" than in other workers. In reference to the cognitive aspect of happiness, Diener, Sapyta, and Suh (1998) maintain that life satisfaction is estimated based on people's individual values, goals, and life circumstances. Unlike common workers dispositional heavy work investors prefer to spend more hours at the workplace. Their voluntary choice of dispositional heavy work investors presumably involves interesting and pleasurable activities at work, positive social relationships, and feelings of making progress towards their goals as well. Therefore, dispositional heavy work investors are expected to exhibit higher levels of life satisfaction than common workers. This estimation is also presented by Snir and Harpaz (2012).

Situational heavy work investors, namely organizational-directed and economically-oriented heavy work investors, invest long hours and effort at work due to external needs: organizational culture and financial needs. Self-determination theory is concerned with the psychological processes that promote optimal functioning and health (Deci & Ryan, 2000). According to this theory, a goal-directed behavior, that is autonomous rather than controlled, is in a better quality and has a positive affect on health and well-being. Unlike common workers, situational heavy work investors are goal-directed (whether financially or organizationally) and their heavy investment at work is autonomous. Therefore, situational heavy work investors are expected to report higher levels of life satisfaction than common workers. In addition, the affective element of happiness may also be higher among heavy work investors, as "people tend to be happier when they are in settings that meet their particular needs" (Diener, Larsen, & Emmons, 1984, p. 582).

As mentioned before, global happiness refers to both affective and cognitive global aspects of happiness (Warr, 2007). Since dispositional and situational heavy work investors are expected to be higher in the affective and cognitive aspect of happiness than common workers, they are expected to report higher levels of global happiness as well. The next proposition expresses this logic.

Proposition 4: *Dispositional and situational heavy work investors exhibit higher levels of global happiness than common workers.*

Contributions

Our discussion involves the relationship between happiness and heavy work investment. We addressed global happiness as well as its cognitive and affective aspects in reference to different types of workers.

The contributions of this discussion concern the positive organizational behavior (POB) movement, which is defined as the study of positively oriented human resource strengths and psychological capacities that can be effectively managed to improve performance in today's workplace (Luthans, 2002 in Fry & Matherly, 2006). Many studies have shown that happy individuals are also successful, in part because they exhibit numerous adaptive characteristics, resources, and skills that help them to thrive and succeed (Lyubomirsky, King, & Diener, 2005). Furthermore, organizational researchers have shown a significant positive relationship between employees' happiness and positive performance (Brief & Wiess, 2002; Wright & Bonett, 1997; Wright, Bonett, & Sweeney, 1993; Wright & Cropanzano, 2000).

The World Health Organization maintains that happiness is a component of health (Fowler & Christakis, 2008) having potential implications for employees' health status. Organizational theorists have long been aware of the great human and financial costs of employees' dysfunctional well-being (George, 1992 in Wright & Cropanzano, 2000; Quick, Quick, Nelson, & Hurrell, 1997 in Wright & Cropanzano, 2000). Hence, it seems that organizations would benefit from attempting to elevate happiness in the workplace. Since it has been demonstrated that autonomous regulation leads to greater happiness (Deci & Ryan, 2000), formulating work guidelines that enable employees to control long work hours that they invest can be very effective. A cognitive-behavioral training program to adopt an optimistic attribution style has proven to be another effective option for elevating employees' well-being and enhancing performance (Proudfoot, Corr, Guest, & Dunn, 2009).

Finally, we recommend future studies to validate Snir and Harpaz's (2012) HWI model and the proposed relationship between heavy work investment and individuals' happiness.

References

Ahuvia, A.C. (2002). Individualism–collectivism and cultures of happiness: A theoretical conjecture on the relationship between consumption, culture and subjective well-being at the national level. *Journal of Happiness Studies, 3*, 23–36.

Arvey, R.D., Harpaz, I., & Liao, H. (2004). Work centrality and post-award work behavior of lottery winners. *The Journal of Psychology, 138*, 404–420.

Ashkanasy, N.M. (2011). International happiness: A multilevel perspective. *Academy of Management Perspectives, 25*, 6–22.

Barak, Y. (2006). The immune system and happiness. *Autoimmunity Review, 5*, 523–527.

Bilski, R. (2004). *Maximizing Happiness*. Carmel: Jerusalem Publishing [Hebrew].

Brickman, P., Coates, D., & Janoff-Bulman, R. (1978). Lottery winners and accident victims. Is happiness relative? *Journal of Personality and Social Psychology, 36*, 917–297.

Brief, A.P., & Wiess, H.M. (2002). Organizational behavior: Affect in the workplace. *Annual Reviews Psychology, 53*, 279–307.

Buelens, M., & Poelmans, S.A.Y. (2004). Enriching the Spence and Robbins' typology of workaholism: Demographic, motivational and organizational correlates. *Journal of Organizational Change Management, 17*, 440–458.

Burke, R.J. (1999). Workaholism among women managers: Work and life satisfactions and psychological well-being. *Equal Opportunities International, 18*, 25–35.

Burke, R.J. (2000a). Workaholism in organizations: Concepts, results and future research directions. *International Journal of Management Reviews, 2*, 1–16.

Burke, R.J. (2000b). Workaholism in organizations: The role of organizational values. *Personnel Review, 30*, 637–645.

Burke, R.J. (2000c). Workaholism and divorce. *Psychological Reports, 86*, 219–220.

Burke, R.J. (2000d). Workaholism in organizations: Psychological and physical well-being consequences. *Stress Medicine, 16*, 11–16.

Burke, R.J., & Fiksenbaum, L. (2009). Work motivations, work outcomes, and health: Passion versus addiction. *Journal of Business Ethics, 84*, 257–263.

Burke, R.J., & Matthiesen, S. (2004). Short communication: Workaholism among Norwegian journalists—antecedents and consequences. *Stress and Health, 20*, 301–308.

Burke, R.J., Koyuncu, M., & Fiksenbaum, L. (2007). Career priority patterns among managerial and professional women in Turkey: Benefits of putting career first? *Women in Management, 22*, 405–417.

Burke, R.J., Matthiesen, S.B., & Pallesen, S. (2006). Workaholism, organizational life and well-being of Norwegian nursing staff. *Career Development International, 11*, 463–477.

Burke, R.J., Oberklaid, F., & Burgess, Z. (2004). Workaholism among Australian women psychologists: Antecedents and consequences. *International Journal of Management, 21*, 263–277.

Clark, L.A., McEwen, J.L., Collard, L.M., & Hickok, L.G. (1993). Symptoms and traits of personality disorder: Two new methods for their assessment. *Psychological Assessment, 5*, 81–91.

Cohen, A., & Shamai, O. (2010). The relationship between individual values, psychological well-being, and organizational commitment among Israeli police officers. *Policing: An International Journal of Police Strategies & Management, 33*, 30–51.

Csikszentmihalyi, M., & LeFevre, J. (1989). Optimal experience in work and leisure. *Journal of Personality and Social Psychology, 56*, 815–822.

Deci, E.L., & Ryan, R.M. (2000). The "What" and "Why" of goal pursuits: Human needs and the self-determination of behavior. *Psychological Inquiry, 11*, 227–268.

Diener, E. (1984). Subjective well-being. *Psychological Bulletin, 95*, 542–575.

Diener, E., & Emmons, R.A. (1984). The independence of positive and negative affect. *Journal of Personality and Social Psychology, 47*, 1105–1117.

Diener, E., & Seligman, M. (2002). Very happy people. *Psychological science, 13*, 81–84.

Diener, E., Larsen, R., & Emmons, R. (1984). Person X situation interactions: Choice of situations and congruence response models. *Journal of Personality and Social Psychology, 47*, 580–592.

Diener, E., Oishi, S., & Lucas, R.E. (2003). Personality, culture, and subjective well-being: Emotional and cognitive evaluations of life. *Annual Review of Psychology, 54*, 403–425.

Diener, E., Suh, E.M., & Oishi, S. (1997). Recent findings on subjective well-being. *Indian Journal of Clinical Psychology, 24*, 25–41.

Diener, E., Suh, E.M., Lucas, R.E., & Smith, H.L. (1999). Subjective well-being: Three decades of progress. *Psychological Bulletin, 125*, 276–302.

Diener, E., Suh, E.M., Smith, H., & Shao, L. (1995). National differences in reported subjective well-being: Why do they occur? *Social Indicators Research, 34*, 7–32.

Douglas, E.J., & Morris, R.J. (2006). Workaholic, or just hard worker? *Career Development International, 11*, 394–417.

Dwyer, D.J., & Ganster, D.C. (1991). The effects of job demands and control on employee attendance and satisfaction. *Journal of Organizational Behavior, 12*, 595–608.

Eid, M., & Diener, E. (1998). *Global judgments of subjective well-being: Situational variability and long-term stability.* Unpublished manuscript, University of Illinois at Urbana–Champaign.

England, G.W., & Harpaz, I. (1983). Some methodological and analytic considerations in cross-national comparative research. *Journal of International Business Studies, 14*, 49–59.

Fassel, D. (1990). *Working Ourselves to Death: The High Costs of Workaholism, the Rewards of Recovery*. San Francisco, CA: Harper Collins.

Fowler, J.H., & Christakis, N.A. (2008). Dynamic spread of happiness in a large social network: Longitudinal analysis over 20 years in the Framingham Heart Study. *British Medical Journal, 337*, 338–347.

Friedman, M., & Rosenman, R.H. (1971). Type A behavior pattern: Its association with coronary heart disease. *Annual Clinical Research, 3*, 300–312.

Fry, L.W., & Matherly, L.L. (2006). *Spiritual Leadership as an Integrating Paradigm for Positive Leadership Development.* Paper presented at the 2006 Gallup Leadership Summit, Washington DC.

Furnham, A., & Petrides, K.V. (2003). Trait emotional intelligence and happiness. *Social Behavior and Personality, 31*, 815–824.

Glenn, N.D., & Weaver, C.N. (1979). A note on family situation and global happiness. *Social Forces, 57*, 960–967.

Glenn, N.D., & Weaver, C.N. (1981). The contributions of marital happiness to global happiness. *Journal of Marriage and the Family, 43*, 161–168.

Gorman, E.H., & Kmec, J.A. (2007). We (have to) try harder: Gender and required work effort in Britain and the United States. *Gender and Society, 21*, 828–856.

Halevi, K. (2006). *Who are the People Who Work 50 Hours and More in a Week?* (CBS Working Paper No. 23). Jerusalem, Israel: Central Bureau of Statistics [Hebrew].

Harding, S.D., & Hikspoors, F.J. (1995). New work values: In theory and in practice. *International Social Science Journal, 47*, 441–455.

Harpaz, I. (1990). *The Meaning of Work in Israel: Its Nature and Consequences*. New York: Praeger.

Harpaz, I., & Fu, X. (2002). The structure of the meaning of work: A relative stability amidst change. *Human Relations, 55*, 639–668.

Harpaz, I., & Meshoulam, I. (2004). Differences in the meaning of work in Israel: Workers in high-tech vs. traditional work industries. *The Journal of High Technology Management Research, 15,* 163–182.

Harpaz, I., & Meshoulam, I. (2009). The meaning of work, employment relations, and strategic human resources management in Israel. *Human Resource Management Review, 3,* 1–30.

Harpaz, I., & Snir, R. (2003). Workaholism, its definition and nature. *Human Relations, 56,* 291–320.

Haynes, S.G., Legine, S., Scotch, N., Feinleib, M., & Kannel, W.B. (1978). The relationship of psychological factors to coronary heart disease in the Framingham study: Methods and risk factors. *American Journal of Epidemiology, 107,* 362–383.

Heller, D., Judge, T.A., & Watson, D. (2002). The confounding role of personality and trait affectivity in the relationship between job and life satisfaction. *Journal of Organizational Behavior, 23,* 815–835.

Hills, P., & Argyle, M. (2001). Happiness, introversion–extraversion and happy introverts. *Personality and Individual Differences, 30,* 595–608.

Jahn, E.W., Thompson, C.A., & Kopelman, R.E. (2003). Rationale and construct validity evidence for a measure of perceived organizational family support (POFS): Because purported practices may not reflect reality. *Community, Work & Family, 6,* 123–140.

Judge, T.A., & Kammeyer-Mueller, J.D. (2011). Happiness as a societal value. *The Academy of Management Perspectives, 25,* 30–41.

Kahneman, D., Krueger, A.B., Schkade, D., Schwarz, N., & Stone, A.A. (2006). Would you be happier if you were richer? A focusing illusion. *Science, 312,* 1908–1910.

Keyes, C.L.M., Shmotkin, D., & Ryff, C.D. (2002). Optimizing well-being: The empirical encounter of two traditions. *Journal of Personality and Social Psychology, 82,* 1007–1022.

Lodi-Smith, J., & Roberts, B.W. (2007). Social investment and personality: A meta-analysis of the relationship of personality traits to investment in work, family, religion, and volunteerism. *Personality and Social Psychology, 11,* 68–86.

Lu, L., & Shih, J.B. (1997). Sources of happiness: A qualitative approach. *The Journal of Social Psychology, 137,* 181–182.

Lucas, R.E., Diener, E., & Suh, E. (1996). Discriminant validity of well-being measures. *Journal of Personality and Social Psychology, 71,* 616–628.

Lyubomirsky, S., King, L., & Diener, E. (2005). The benefits of frequent positive affect: Does happiness lead to success? *Psychological Bulletin, 131,* 803–855.

Martin, M.W. (2007). Happiness and virtue in positive psychology. *Journal for the Theory of Social Behavior, 31,* 89–103.

Maume, D., & Bellas, M. (2001). The overworked American or the time bind. *American Behavioral Scientist, 44,* 1137–1156.

McMillan, L.H.W., & O'Driscoll, M.P. (2004). Workaholism and health implications for organizations. *Journal of Organizational Change Management, 17,* 509–519.

McMillan, L.H.W., Brady, E.C., O'Driscoll, M.P. & Marsh, N.V. (2002). A multifaceted study of Spence and Robbins' (1992) workaholism battery. *Journal of Occupational and Organizational Psychology, 75,* 357–368.

McMillan, L.H.W., O'Driscoll, M.P., & Brady, E.C. (2004). The impact of workaholism on personal relationships. *British Journal of Guidance & Counselling, 32*, 171–186.

McMillan, L.H.W., O'Driscoll, M.P., Marsh, N.V., & Brady, E.C. (2001). Understanding workaholism: Data synthesis, theoretical critique, and future design strategies. *International Journal of Stress Management, 8*, 69–91.

MOW—International Research Team (1987). *The Meaning of Work: An International View*. London: Academic Press.

Mudrack, P.E. (2004). Job involvement, obsessive-compulsive personality traits, and workaholic behavioral tendencies. *Journal of Organizational Change Management, 17*, 490–508.

Naughton, T.J. (1987). A conceptual view of workaholism and implications for career counseling and research. *Career Development Quarterly, 6*, 180–187.

Ng, T.W.H., Sorensen, K.L., & Feldman, D.C. (2007). Dimensions, antecedents, and consequences of workaholism: A conceptual integration and extension. *Journal of Organizational Behavior, 28*, 111–136.

Oates, W. (1971). *Confessions of a Workaholic: The Facts About Work Addiction*. New York: World Publishing.

Pleck, J.H., Staines, G.L., & Lang, L. (1980). Conflicts between work and family life. *Monthly Labor Review, 103*, 29–32.

Porter, G. (1996). Organizational impact of workaholism: Suggestions for researching the negative outcomes of excessive work. *Journal of Occupational Health Psychology, 1*, 70–84.

Pressman, S.D., & Cohen, S. (2005). Does positive affect influence health? *Psychological Bulletin, 131*, 925–971.

Proudfoot, J.G., Corr, P.J., Guest, D.E., & Dunn, G. (2009). Cognitive–behavioral training to change attributional style improves employee well-being, job satisfaction, productivity, and turnover. *Personality & Individual Differences, 46*, 147–153.

Robbins, S.P. (2001). *Organizational Behavior* (10th edition). Upper Saddle River, NJ: San Diego State University.

Robinson, B.E. (1999). The work addiction risk test: Development of a tentative measure of workaholism. *Perceptual and Motor Skills, 88*, 199–210.

Robinson, B.E., Flowers, C., & Carroll, J. (2001). Work stress and marriage: A theoretical model examining the relationship between workaholism and marital cohesion. *International Journal of Stress Management, 8*, 165–175.

Sagiv, L., & Schwartz, S.H. (2000). Values, priorities and subjective well-being direct relations and congruity effects. *European Journal of Social Psychology, 30*, 177–198.

Saucier, G. (2008). Measures of the personality factors found recurrently in human lexicons. In G.J. Boyle, G. Matthews, & D. Saklofske (Eds.), *Handbook of Personality Theory and Testing, 2—Personality Measurement and Assessment* (pp. 29–54). London: Sage.

Schaufeli, W.B., Taris, T.W., & Bakker, A.B. (2006). Research companion to working time and work addiction. In R.J. Burke (Ed.), *Research Companion to Working Time and Work Addiction* (pp. 193–217). Northampton, MA: Edward Elgar.

Schaufeli, W.B., Taris, T.W., & van Rhenen, W. (2008). Workaholism, burnout, and work engagement: Three of a kind or three different kinds of employee well-being? *Applied Psychology: An International Review, 57*, 173–203.

Schwartz, H. (1982). Job involvement as obsession-compulsion. *Academy of Management Review, 7*, 429–432.

Scott, K.S., Moore, K.S., & Miceli, M.P. (1997). An exploration of the meaning and consequences of workaholism. *Human Relations, 50*, 287–314.

Seligman, M.E.P. (2002). *Authentic Happiness*. New York: Free Press.

Snir, R., & Harpaz, I. (2002a). To work or not to work: Non-financial employment commitment and the social desirability bias. *The Journal of Social Psychology, 142*, 635–644.

Snir, R., & Harpaz, I. (2002b). The meaning of work for public sector versus private sector employees. In E. Vigoda (Ed.), *Public Administration—The New Generation: An Interdisciplinary Critical Analysis* (pp. 119–138). New York: Marcel Dekker.

Snir, R., & Harpaz, I. (2004). Attitudinal and demographic antecedents of workaholics. *Journal of Organizational Change Management, 17*, 520–536.

Snir, R., & Harpaz, I. (2009). Cross-cultural differences concerning heavy work investment. *Cross-Cultural Research, 43*, 309–319.

Snir, R., & Harpaz, I. (2012). Beyond workaholism: Towards a general model of heavy work investment. *Human Resource Management Review, 22*, 232–343.

Snir, R., & Zohar, D. (2000). *Workaholism: Work Addiction or Workphilia?* International Conference on Psychology "Psychology after The Year 2000," University of Haifa, Haifa, Israel.

Snir, R., & Zohar, D. (2008). Workaholism as discretionary time investment at work: An experience-sampling study. *Applied Psychology: An International Review, 57*, 109–127.

Snir, R., Harpaz, I., & Ben-Baruch, D. (2009). Centrality of and investment in work and family among Israeli high-tech workers: A bicultural perspective. *Cross-Cultural Research, 43*, 366–385.

Snir, R., Harpaz, I., & Burke, R. (2006). Workaholism in organizations: New research directions (Guest editorial). *Career Development International, 11*, 369–373.

Sparks, K., Cooper, C., Fried, Y., & Shirom, A. (1997). The effects of hours of work on health: A meta-analytic review. *Journal of Occupational and Organizational Psychology, 70*, 391–408.

Spence, J.T., & Robbins, A.S. (1992). Workaholism: Definition, measurement, and preliminary results. *Journal of Personality Assessment, 58*, 160–178.

Spence, J.T., Helmreich, R.L., & Pred, R.S. (1987) Impatience versus achievement strivings in the Type A pattern: Differential effects on students' health and academic achievement. *Journal of Applied Psychology, 72*, 522–528.

Veenhoven, R. (2000). Well-being in the welfare state: Level not higher, distribution not more equitable. *Journal of Comparative Policy Analysis, 2*, 91–125.

Veenhoven, R. (2005a). Apparent quality-of-life in nations: How long and happy people live. *Social Indicators Research, 71*, 61–86.

Veenhoven, R. (2005b). Happiness as a public policy aim: The greatest happiness principle. In A. Linley & S. Joseph (Eds.), *Positive Psychology in Practice* (pp. 658–678). Hoboken, NJ: Wiley.

Vodanovich, S.J., Piotrowski, C., & Wallace, J.C. (2007). The relationship between workaholism and health: A report of negative findings. *Organization Development Journal, 25*, 70–75.

Warr, P.B. (2007). *Work, Happiness and Unhappiness*. Mahwah, NJ: Lawrence Erlbaum Associates.

Weiner, B. (1985). An attributional theory of achievement motivation and emotion. *Psychological Review, 92*, 548–573.

Weiss H.M., & Cropanzano, R. (1996). Affective events theory: A theoretical discussion of the structure, causes, and consequences of affective experiences at work. *Research in Organizational Behavior, 18*, 1–74.

Wharton, A., & Blair-Loy, M. (2006). Long work hours and family life: A cross-national study of employees' concerns. *Journal of Family Issues, 27*, 415–436.

Wright, T.A., & Bonett, D.G. (1997). The role of pleasantness and activation-based well-being in performance prediction. *Journal of Occupational Health Psychology, 2*, 212–219.

Wright, T.A., & Cropanzano, R. (2000). Psychological well-being and job satisfaction as predictors of job performance. *American Psychological Association Volume, 5*, 84–94.

Wright, T.A., Bonett, D.G., & Sweeney, D.A. (1993). Mental health and work performance: Results of a longitudinal field study. *Journal of Occupational and Organizational Psychology, 66*, 277–284.

Zohar, D. (2006). On the vicissitudes of the study of workaholism: A construct at a crossroad. *Career Development International, 11*, 478–482.

Part 3

SPECIAL ISSUES IN THE STUDY OF HEAVY WORK INVESTMENT (HWI)

11

WORK–FAMILY BALANCE IN THE ERA OF INTENSIVE WORK

Haya Stier and Avital Sella-Dotan

The last three decades have witnessed important changes in the world of work, which have affected the ways individuals and families organize their time schedules: changes in the organization of work, due to technological changes and the growth of knowledge-based industries; increasing competition, with the development of globalized markets; and economic instability accompanied by an erosion of labor power, which has changed employment contracts and created new sources of stress to individuals and their families. In many labor markets, work schedules have changed from more rigid to non-conventional, flexible, and diverse hours of work (Brannen, 2005; Perrons, Fagan, McDowell, Ray, & Ward, 2005). The postindustrial work schedules offer more opportunities for individual schedules (and, therefore, for combining work and family), but also introduce more tension between the two domains (Jacobs & Gerson, 2004).

At the same time, demographic and behavioral changes have posed new challenges to families. The rate of female labor force participation increased rapidly in all industrialized countries, in many of which women now account for almost half of the workforce. This increase is predominantly attributed to a commitment by married women and mothers to lifelong employment, which is associated with the increased number of dual-earner families. These families are faced with the need to combine paid work and care work, operating in two "greedy institutions"—the labor market and the family—both with high demands on parents' time and energy. In addition to dual-earner families with children, the rate of single-headed families also increased, introducing yet another source of strain to workers with care responsibilities (Bianchi, 2011; Eby, Casper, Lockwood, Bordeaux, & Brinley, 2005; Kossek, 2005; Spain & Bianchi, 1996). Related to these challenges is the complexity employees, especially in their 40s, may face caring for young children as well as elderly parents, during curtailing times in their careers. These new demands are intensified with the increase in life expectancy and the late entrance to parenthood.

Along with the transition from male breadwinner families to dual-earner and single-parent households, a sense of "overwork" may have been created (McNamara, Pitt-Catsouphes, Mata-Costa, Brown, & Valcour, 2013). As a whole, studies consistently demonstrate that dual-earner families are working harder than before (Jacobs & Gerson, 2004). According to recent estimates in the United States, the percentage of professional women working at least 50 hours a week has more than doubled, from 6 percent in the 1970s to 14 percent in the late 2000s; the increase among men is more modest, from 34 to 38 percent during the same time period (Williams & Boushey, 2010). The changing nature of work, especially the increase in working hours among professionals and managers, though not necessarily in other segments of the workforce, has increased levels of stress and created a mismatch between work and other life domains (Brett & Stroh, 2003; Ford & Collinson, 2011; Jacobs & Gerson, 2004) and has brought the issue of balancing work and other areas of life to the forefront of policy as well as academic debates.

However, it is not just the hours worked that contribute to an increased conflict between work and other life domains. Work intensification, which refers to the work effort or pace required in a job (Green, 2001), has increased as well. The combination of increased time and effort invested in work constitutes the two core elements of "heavy work investment" (Snir & Harpaz, 2012). Heavy work investment may reflect a continuous pressure from organizations that demand high productivity and set challenging deadlines. Professional occupations exert more pressure than other occupations, although they often offer high levels of rewards (Blair-Loy, 2003; McGinnity & Calvert, 2008; Moen et al., 2013; Wharton & Blair-Loy, 2006). The pressures may also stem from internal characteristics such as addiction to work or work devotion (Snir & Harpaz, 2012). Another indication for the intensification of work is the constant need to multitask (Offer & Shchnieder, 2011), which is often associated with increased negative affect and stress.

Moreover, not only has work intensified, at least for part of the workforce, but technological advances have also contributed to the blurring of boundaries between work and family life (Burke, 2001), further increasing the pressures to work outside the workplace and at non-conventional hours. Moen, Lam, Ammons, and Kelly (2013), who documented the work patterns of professionals, argue that work has become more flexible and is no longer defined by a particular place or time, but is nevertheless overlaid with traditional expectations of a five-day week, eight-hour day of physical presence at work. This infiltration of work to other life domains increases the difficulties of workers in balancing their lives, especially professionals and those who work long hours, and creates further sources of conflicts. In the remainder of this chapter we focus on the inevitable clash between family and work among workers who work intensively. We focus on the work–family conflict, as this area gained most of the attention at the organizational level with the introduction of specific policies and arrangements to increase the balance between these two central areas in life. We discuss both the sources of tensions and the strategies employed by individual workers and their organizations to enhance the fit between these two areas of life.

The Conflicting Relationships between Work and Family

For the rest of this chapter, we discuss and elaborate on the most prevalent conflict arising from the intensification of work—the work–family clash. We center on this topic because it pertains to all workers, and is currently at the center of policy debates both within organizations and more generally, at the state level. Greenhaus and Beutell (1985) define the work–family conflict as "a form of inter-role conflict in which the role pressures from the work and family domains are mutually incompatible in some respect" (p. 77). This implies bi-directional relations between work and family life, that is, conflict may originate in either domain (Mauno, Kinnunen, & Ruokolainen, 2006). Work to family conflict (WFC) occurs when work interferes with our family life, and family to work conflict (FWC) occurs when family life interferes with work (Frone, Yardley, & Markel, 1997). Consistent with that, the two constructs were found to be distinct, having different antecedents and outcomes (Allen, Herst, Bruck, & Sutton, 2000; Byron, 2005; Frone et al., 1997; Frone, Russell, & Cooper, 1992), with most of the research focusing on how work conflicts with family (Allen et al., 2000; Frone, 2003).

Several theoretical approaches have tried to explain the conflicting relationships between work and family, especially in the era of dual-earner families. The *time availability* approach (Coverman, 1985; Jager, 2002) argues that when attempting to balance work and family demands, the longer hours spent in the labor market are likely to result in a time squeeze. This approach has received considerable attention from policy-makers as well as empirical support (Batt & Valcour, 2003; Dex & Bond, 2005; Grzywacz & Marks, 2000; Major, Klein, & Ehrhart, 2002; Voydanoff, 2004; White, Hill, McGovern, Mills, & Smeaton, 2003). Working time is just one aspect of the pressures that individuals experience in their daily activities. Another important aspect is addressed by the *family demands* approach (Coverman, 1985), which posits that the greater the household demands, the more difficult it is to balance work and family (Ford, Heinen, & Langkamer, 2007; Hill, 2005; Wharton & Blair-Loy, 2006). Household demands vary with family composition and are especially high when young children are present. As women typically bear the major responsibility for childcare, the WFC is more pronounced among employed mothers of young children, as several studies have shown (Dex & Bond, 2005; Kinnunen & Mauno, 1998; Maume & Houston, 2001; Moen et al., 2013; Wharton & Blair-Loy, 2006). However, recent studies emphasize the growing involvement of fathers in childcare, which blurs the boundaries between their separate roles as economic providers and caregivers. Consequently, men too may experience conflict between work and family demands, associated with their role as fathers (Nomaguchi, 2007; Winslow, 2005).

A related construct is work–family balance (WFB). Although other definitions exist, we refer to an "accomplishment of role related expectations that are negotiated and shared between an individual and his or her role related partners in the work family domains" as suggested by Grzywacz and Carlson (2007, p. 458). This definition focuses on the social aspects of the interplay between work and family and emphasizes the ability of an individual to engage with and meet responsibilities in both domains.

While our focus is on work–family balance issues, researchers have elaborated the debate to consider other aspects of "non-work" in addition to family (i.e., leisure, community involvement, education, etc.). However, it seems that the terms work–family balance and work–life balance are sometimes used interchangeably and that the definition of work–life balance is yet to be agreed upon (Lyness & Judiesch, 2013). This is also true regarding related constructs. For example, Kossek, Lewis, and Hammer (2010) define "cultural work life support" as informal workplace social and relational support. This pertains, for example, to support employers receive from supervisors and coworkers that alongside the cultural norms in the organization increase the individual perception of employees that a joint involvement in work and family roles is valued (p. 4). Hence, the discussion on work–life issues is yet to be accomplished. Taking this under consideration, we believe that the discussion below is relevant to other aspects of employees' lives as well.

Working intensively has the potential to undermine the WFB, as there may be less time and energy for caregiving responsibilities (as well as for other non-work activities) (Brown, 2012). Hence, employees today are more likely to experience continued conflict between work and family (and probably other life domains), due to the time and effort devoted to work and the infiltration of work into the home. These conflicting relationships have gained vast support in the research (Byron, 2005; Frone et al., 1997; Geurts, Beckers, Taris, Kompier, & Smulders, 2009; Kelly, Moen, & Tranby, 2011; Major et al., 2002; Schieman, Milkie, & Glavin, 2009; Shockley & Allen, 2007; Valcour, 2007). WFC may also intensify when the job carries authority or involves uncertainty. Ford and Collinson (2011) have demonstrated that for managers, paradoxically, the expectation to balance life might also intensify the pressures they face. Ultimately, these pressures, along with the nature of the job and work schedules, affect the ability to balance work and non-work time. It is therefore important to look at the implications of work pressures for individuals and their families, and how organizations react to the challenge that intensified work poses.

Implications of Work Intensification: Job Performance, Individual Wellbeing, and Family Life

As stated above, working intensively may reflect a constant pressure imposed on workers to achieve high productivity and meet challenging deadlines. This pressure intensifies when workers need to meet demands from other spheres of life, hence resulting in negative consequences to individuals, their families and social lives, and to their employer. From the perspective of the employer, work intensification has been associated with a range of negative outcomes such as lower job satisfaction, heightened stress (and the associated health care costs), involvement in accidents, and workplace injuries. Working long hours was also found to be a major contributor to fatigue, insomnia, and reduced levels of alertness and expected retention (see: Brown, 2012; Burke et al., 2010; Richman, Civian, Shannon, Hill, & Brennan, 2008). Increased WFC resulting from long hours and intensified work as discussed previously has been associated with increased absenteeism (Goff, Mount, & Jamison, 1990) and turnover (Anderson, Coffey, & Byerly, 2002), and with decreased job satisfaction (Kossek & Ozeki, 1998) and organizational commitment (Netemeyer, Boles, & McMurrian, 1996), all of which affect employees' performance.

From the perspective of the employee, WFC has been found to lead to decreased life satisfaction (Eby, 2005; Frye & Breaugh, 2004; Kossek & Ozeki, 1998) and negative physical and psychological health outcomes (Frone et al., 1997; Frone, 2000; Major et al., 2002). Because women still perform the lion's share of housework and childcare, they also tend to leave demanding jobs with long work hours more than men do (Blair-Loy, 2003; Moen et al., 2013) affecting their own career prospects and lifelong income.

Numerous studies have focused on the effect of work–life conflicts on family wellbeing, especially relationships with children and child outcomes, and on the quality of marriage. When people work long hours, the time spent with children may be limited and the type of shared activities may change (Bianchi & Milkie, 2010; Bianchi, Robinson, & Milkie, 2005; Bulanda, 2004; Yeung, Sandbers, Davis-Kean, & Hofferth, 2001). Empirical findings suggest that the lack of time for shared family activities has consequences for children, with more risky behaviors for adolescents in families with fewer shared activities (Crouter, Head, & McHale, 2004), and reduced parental time in developmentally important activities

(Johnson, Li, Kendall, Strazdins, & Jacoby, 2013). Additionally, the combination of long hours and high overload was consistently associated with less positive father–adolescent relationships (Crouter, Bumpus, Head, & McHale, 2001). According to Johnson et al. (2013), boys whose fathers worked 55 hours per week or more had significantly higher levels of externalizing behavior. Mothers' work hours, however, were not found to be related to children's behavioral problems.

Long working hours may also affect marital relationships; men's long work hours were related to less time spent with their wives; intensive workers who were occupied with their work even when at home were found to offer less emotional and instrumental support to their partners (Bakker, Demerouti, & Burke, 2009), or to affect their strain level (Klumb, Hoppmann, & Sttaats, 2006). In a study of 168 dual-career couples, Bakker, Demerouti, and Dollard (2008) showed that higher WFC for one partner led to higher home demands upon the other, which in turn resulted in greater FWC. However, the relationship between long working hours and marital satisfaction is not entirely clear. Coverman (1989), for example, found that working longer hours was positively linked to marital satisfaction for husbands and wives. Other studies found no direct association between individuals' extended time demands and marital tension (Hughes, Galinsky, & Morris, 1992; Pittman, 1994), although long hours and high demand had the potential to influence marital quality indirectly through spouses' overall satisfaction with the fit between work and family. In a recent study, Barnett, Gareis, and Brennan (2009) found that when husbands work long hours, wives experience lower marital quality; when wives work long hours, both experience increased marital quality. Possibly marital relationships are not affected as much because couples adjust their work hours to the needs of the family, and there are other benefits that compensate for time scarcity.

At the same time, given the appropriate context, hard work can be satisfying. Brett and Stroh (2003) found that male managers' long work hours can be explained by intrinsic rewards such as accomplishment and self-esteem, aside from economic compensation. Working long hours may also be associated with the fulfillment of traditional roles, as fathers' intensive work can be regarded as a demonstration of caring for the family (Townsend, 2002; Wharton & Blair-Loy, 2006). It may be associated with higher earnings, rewards, career advancement, enriched work, and greater career satisfaction (Valcour, 2007; Burk, Singh, & Fiksenbaum, 2010; Ng et al., 2005). These resources may help meet family demands and offset the negative effects on overall family satisfaction (Valcour, 2007). Moreover, long hours may, in some cases, reflect the shared goals of married couples, such as promotion and extra income; in such cases married partners may view long hours positively (Crouter et al., 2001). Hence, along with the negative consequences associated with long work hours, they may also serve as a valued recourse for the family unit as well as for individuals (Aryee, Srinivas, & Hoon Tan, 2005). Indeed, it has been suggested that work–family conflict does not tell the whole story and that the interface between work and family is expected to provide individuals with distinct resources for improving the quality of life (Carlson, Kacmar, Wayne, & Grzywacz, 2006). Researchers therefore have also considered the positive effects stemming from engaging in both domains (Greenhaus & Powell, 2006; Grzywacz, Almeida, & McDonald 2002).

Strategies to Overcome Work–Family Conflict

In order to find solutions to the pressures of demanding jobs and the family context, workers employ a variety of strategies. As Becker and Moen (1999) show, complex strategies are undertaken within the family context. In many cases, couples decide on how to handle the involvement in the two demanding life domains, with one, most often the woman, scaling back while the other invests more time and energy in the workplace. In this sense, balancing work and family is a family strategy, not an individual's—when one spouse works long hours, the other looks for a less demanding, short-hour job. Couples can decide who will work how and when, that is, some "take turns" working intensively, while others decide upfront on a "division of labor" whereby one spouse invests in a demanding career while the other settles for a regular job. Because these decisions are often gendered and families prioritize men's careers, such strategies may contribute to increased inequality within households and perpetuate women's economic dependency upon their spouses.

Moen et al. (2013) use the concept of "time work" to describe the strategies employed by workers engaged in intensive, long-hour jobs. This concept is embedded within cultural schemes and structural arrangements that shape the ways workers understand their time pressures and the options they have for solving conflicting demands. In the past, workers used two time work strategies—*setting priorities* and *scaling back* on work and personal obligations. As mentioned earlier, these strategies are gendered, with women more likely to prioritize their families over work, whereas men are more devoted to work (Blair-Loy, 2003; Moen et al., 2013). Therefore, women tend to scale back on job obligations and give up job opportunities (Becker & Moen, 1999; Epstein, Seron, Oglensky, & Sauté, 1999; Whittington, 2011). In their study, however, Moen et al. (2013) found that professionals find difficulty in cutting their hours of work; hence they scale back on family obligations. Although most of the scaling back pertains to household chores, there is also reduced time with children, which introduces another source of strain to (especially) mothers. Because of the long hours and difficulties in fulfilling their work and home duties, some mothers decide to leave their jobs altogether. Higgins,

Duxbury, and Lyons (2010) also found that when overloaded with work, employees tend to sacrifice their own needs and expect their families to accommodate their work demands.

Moen et al. (2013) identified two other strategies of balancing work and non-work demands—*blocking out time* (establishing or protecting boundaries by blocking out time for specific activities) and *time shifting* (moving work to different times that employees prefer to better integrate it with non-work activities)—which workers employ to deal with the blurring of work and time boundaries. These strategies, which were not easy to perform, allowed workers to accept the time demands, on the one hand, but adjust them to fit other domains in their lives, on the other hand. In other words, these workers employ "strategic adaptations that are often more *work*-friendly than *family*-friendly, in that they are private responses that largely do not challenge the temporal organization of paid work and do not eliminate the time strains these employees experience" (Moen et al., 2013, p. 104). This study highlights the primacy of work demands over other, non-work interests and obligations, and emphasizes the difficulties that workers face in contemporary employment.

Border theory, which sees people as "border crossers" who make daily transitions between work and non-work life, contributes to understanding individuals' strategies to manage and negotiate the work and family domains to maintain balance (Clark, 2000) and draws attention to employees' "boundary management" strategies. There are two main strategies: segmentation, which refers to the separation of work and family, and integration, which refers to the overlap of the two domains. Employees vary on their preferences for more or less segmentation or integration (Kossek, Lautsch, & Eaton, 2006; Kreiner, 2006). At the same time, organizations differ in the degree of permeability between work and non-work they can tolerate (Kreiner, Hollensbe, & Sheep, 2009) and are assumed to differentially encourage more or less integration or segmentation of work and family domains (Rothbard, Phillips, & Dumas, 2005).

Hence, individual strategies are pursued within the organizational context. In a way, the organizational context dictates the emergence of specific strategies, their legitimacy, and consequences. For example, strategies such as "time shifting" often require the support of managers who permit employees to take personal time. In the absence of such support, this strategy can be seen as a form of resistance—taking a day off after working intensively, or working from home to compensate for the time invested at work (Moen et al., 2013). Overall, individuals and families, with more control over non-work activities and demands, seem to be accommodating work demands rather than the other way around (Lapierre & Allen, 2006). Attention should therefore be devoted to organizational level supports and their contribution to easing the conflict and enhancing the positive effects between the work and family domains.

Organizational Supports

In response to the greater exposure of employees to continued conflict between work and non-work domains, organizations are increasingly being urged to develop programs to address their workers' needs. These programs are commonly referred to as "family-friendly benefits" (FFBs) (Allen, 2001), including (1) dependent care benefits (e.g., referral services, on- or near-site daycare centers, subsidies); (2) benefits that allow greater work schedule flexibility (e.g., part time work, job sharing, variable starting and quitting times, telecommuting, flextime, compressed work weeks, and work from home); and (3) family leave policies such as parental leave, and paid family and medical leave (Appelbaum, Bailey, Berg, & Kalleberg, 2005; Davis & Kalleberg, 2006; Grover & Crooker, 1995). For the organization, benefits are a means of maintaining a competitive advantage in attracting and retaining a dedicated workforce, and are designed as well to help employees cope better with the conflict inherent in managing multiple roles (Allen, 2001).

Indeed, these policies were found to be related to positive work-related outcomes such as greater organizational commitment and employer loyalty, job motivation, lower absenteeism, and lower turnover intentions (see: Batt & Valcour, 2003; Baltes, Briggs, Huff, & Wright, 1999; Behson, 2005; Casper & Harris, 2008; Grover & Crooker, 1995; Hill, 2005; Hill, Ferris, & Martinson, 2003; Lambert, 2000; Premeaux, Adkins, & Mossholder, 2007; Roehling, Roehling, & Moen, 2001; Thomas & Ganster, 1995; Thompson, Beauvais, & Lyness, 1999), even among those who do not stand to benefit (Thomas & Ganster, 1995). Apparently these practices have the potential to encourage individuals to make more time for family and leisure and live a more balanced life (Ford & Collinson, 2011). At the same time, a significant body of literature argues that these policies are not as effective as they should be. To begin with, the evidence shows that not all workers have equal access to such programs (Mumford & Budd, 2006): Gray and Tudball (2003) found that workers in managerial, professional, and administrative occupations enjoyed better access. In addition, employees are not all equally aware of benefit availability (Mumford & Budd, 2006). Research shows that employers do not always transmit information to all employees accurately and comprehensively (Baird & Reynolds, 2004). For instance, managers may adopt policies but fail to provide information on them or on how to access them (Mumford & Budd, 2006). The 2008 National Study of Employers (NSE) reveals, based on a sample of 1,100 employers, that only 21 percent of them think the organization makes a real effort to inform employees of FFBs available to them (Galinsky, Bond, Sakai, Kim, & Giuntoli, 2008). Prottas, Thompson, Kopelman, and Jahn (2007) concluded that employees' limited or inaccurate knowledge of available benefits may be a major obstacle to program effectiveness. Finally, employees might feel that a policy is inaccessible because of barriers such as job requirements or fear of career consequences (Mumford & Budd, 2006). Nonetheless, the effect of FFBs on the number of hours worked, especially in professional and intensive jobs, is not entirely clear. It is also questionable whether these policies can meet the needs of workers who work intensively, because in such jobs, employees cannot utilize options such as part-time employment or long leaves.

Other policies may be more relevant to intensive heavy work investors. Two such policies are flexible or autonomous time schedules, and work from home. When employees are given more control and flexibility in managing work and family time, they can use the time more effectively to benefit both their families and the organization (Hill et al., 2003). Flexibility may improve the fit between work and family by increasing employees' resources and ability to meet the demands of their roles in each domain (Richman et al., 2008). For instance, employees with a flexible schedule can adjust their work time to their most productive hours of the day, thereby becoming more effective, which in turn is expected to reduce the number of hours worked. Moreover, some research suggests that employees experiencing flexibility can work longer hours without impacting their WFB (Hill et al., 2003; Hill, Erickson, Holems, & Ferris., 2010; Geurts et al., 2009; Valcour, 2007). These studies conclude that having the ability to choose where and when to do the work and being able to respond to family needs may result in reduced WFC and increased satisfaction with WFB though working long hours (Valcour, 2007).

However, flexible work arrangements are not a guarantee of more reasonable work hours or reduced work–family conflict for all workers. Flexibility in time schedules is not related to reduction in work hours. In fact, recent studies suggest that higher flexibility may lead to increased opportunity to work longer hours and the infiltration of work into family and other non-work time activities (Abendroth, van der Lippe, & Mass, 2012; Blair-Loy, 2009). Similarly, it was found that instead of exploiting flexibility to fit in family and recreation time, managers are using the time to work longer hours (Lewis, 2003). As Schieman and colleagues (2009) show, employees who work 50 or more hours per week and have some or full schedule control are more likely to report that their work interferes with family life; they therefore conclude that schedule control may be an indicator of "work that never ends." Major et al. (2002) also found that the more hours a week employees worked, the more WFC they reported no matter how flexible their schedules were. Thus, employees who put in long hours and experience excessive work pressures may find that schedule control increases the permeation of work into family and personal life and therefore creates more WFC instead of minimizing it. Moen et al.

(2013) conclude, though, that since the boundary-less nature of work is given in any event, having flexibility allows a better sense of fit between work and family demands.

Work at home may increase time and emotional resources by avoiding office-based strains and interruptions and reducing commute time making more room for other life roles (Hill et al., 2010; Golden, Veiga, & Simsek, 2006). Accompanied with flexibility options, telecommuters are assumed to adjust their schedules with family activities in a more satisfying way. A meta-analysis of 46 studies indicates that telecommuting is related to increased perceptions of autonomy, job satisfaction, and lower WFC, turnover intentions, and stress (Gajendran & Harrison, 2007). However, this policy does not always work as expected. The blurred boundaries between work and family life lead to performing child and home care during conventional work hours, or continuing working after normal work hours (Gajendran & Harrison, 2007; Kraut, 1989). Noonan & Glass (2012) conclude from their analysis based on two nationally representative data sources "that the most telling problem with telecommuting as a work life solution is its strong relationship to long work hours." They suggest that telecommuting is used by employees to complete work assignments beyond the standard workweek, thereby reallocating overtime hours but not avoiding them. Additionally, the possibility to work from home may raise employers' expectations for greater availability during evenings and weekends encouraging longer workdays and workweeks. It was also suggested that telecommuters' greater accessibility may lead to enhanced pressures and expectations for family role involvement that may result in increased FWC (Golden, Veiga, & Simsek, 2006).

Taken together, the findings seem to indicate that these benefits are insufficient in themselves to alleviate WFCs or to affect employees' work attitudes and behaviors. Moreover, overall benefits utilization remains low, as employees are reluctant to take advantage of them lest their careers suffer (Rogier & Padgett, 2004; Thompson, Andreassi, & Prottas, 2005; Thompson et al., 1999; Smithson, Lewis, Cooper, & Dyer, 2007). Indeed, policy use was found to have a negative effect on women's wage growth promotion (Glass, 2004; Judiesch & Lyness, 1999). It was also found that women who opt for flexible working arrangements are aware that their salary and career prospects are lower because of this (Smithson et al., 2007) and that employers perceive workers using flexible schedules as having less career advancement potential (Rogier & Padgett, 2004). Nonetheless, Konard and Yang's (2012) recent study provides more optimistic results, showing that benefits usage hardly reduced promotion opportunities, and that utilization of flexibility options even increased the probability of subsequent promotion. They suggest that having more flexibility enhanced employees' motivation and performance, overweighing the initial short-term negative stigma that might attach to those who use it.

The use of benefits, as well as their consequences, is largely dependent on employees' perceptions of family support and the general work–family culture in the organization (Thompson, Jahn, Kopelman, & Prottas, 2004). A family-supportive culture has been described as one that openly acknowledges employees' family and personal situations by promoting flexibility, tolerance, and support for family needs and obligations (Lapierre et al., 2008), and is at least partly a function of the availability of FFBs (Wayne, Casper, Matthews, & Allen, 2013). Thompson et al. (1999) have suggested that work–family culture is comprised of three components: (a) *organizational time demands* (norms concerning the number of hours employees are expected to spend at work and their use of time); (b) *career consequences* (perceptions of career consequences associated with using FFBs); and (c) *managerial support* (managers' sensitivity to employees' family responsibilities). A family-supportive environment is such that allows employees to feel that integrating work and family roles is an acceptable part of the work experience, and in which the "ideal" employee is not one that devotes his or her entire waking hours to the work role (Aryee, Chu, Kim, & Ryu, 2013). When employees are exposed to this supportive environment, they are more likely to utilize FFBs (Allen, 2001; Dikkers et al., 2007; Thompson et al., 1999) and usually express higher job satisfaction (Allen, 2001; Mauno, Kinnunen, & Piitulainen, 2005b; Thompson & Prottas, 2006), life satisfaction (Hill, 2005), and organizational commitment (Thompson et al., 2004; Hill, 2005; Thompson & Prottas, 2006). Perceptions of a family-supportive culture have also been shown to decrease negative outcomes such as work-related negative mood (Mauno, Kinnunen, & Pyykko, 2005a), turnover intentions (Allen, 2001; Thompson et al., 1999; Thompson & Prottas, 2006), and WFC (Allen, 2001; Anderson et al., 2002; Thompson & Prottas, 2006; Wayne et al., 2013). According to Klumb et al. (2006), a perception of low WFC by spouses due to the job conditions increases the loyalty of employees to their organization and their willingness to stay in the workplace. Behson (2005) found that informal means of organizational work–family support (e.g., managerial support, career impact concerns) explained considerably more variance in employee outcomes than any formal means of organizational support. These findings confirm the idea that informal support influences employee attitudes and behaviors above and beyond simply offering FFBs.

Studies at the organizational level also acknowledge the key role that supervisors play in enabling employees' better adjustment of work and family roles. A family-supportive supervisor may be regarded as one sympathetic to the employee's desire to seek a balance between work and family, and who engages in efforts to help the employee accommodate work and family responsibilities (Thomas & Ganster, 1995). Supportive behaviors include accommodating employees' flexible schedules; being understanding when an employee occasionally leaves early due to family or personal reasons; and helping employees find solutions that allow better adjustment of work and their family or personal needs. Evidently, an organization may offer numerous FFBs, but if a supervisor does not communicate the information properly to employees or limits the use of such programs, the expected benefits may not occur (Thompson et al., 2004). Evidence from a study of 919 Israeli hi-tech women workers (Frenkel, 2003), wherein 40 percent of the respondents agreed that managers do not approve of employees who use FFBs, confirms this notion. The supervisor therefore has a critical role in the actual enactment of FFBs (Aryee et al., 2013).

Coworkers can also become a source of support. Family-supportive coworkers can be regarded as those more motivated to help their colleagues under personal or family stress and absorb the extra work (Wang & Walumbwa, 2007, p. 399). The support of coworkers in work–family issues is complex, as coworkers may feel that employees who utilize these benefits are less productive and less committed to the organization (Giga & Cooper, 2005). Past findings demonstrate that coworkers' support is related to outcomes of interest, such as WFC (Dikkers et al., 2007; Hill, 2005; Mesmer-Magnus & Viswesvaran, 2006; Thompson & Prottas, 2006), work–family facilitation, organizational commitment, job and life satisfaction, stress (Hill, 2005; Thompson & Prottas, 2006), and intention to quit (Thompson & Prottas, 2006). Other studies have focused on the impact of team members and group level factors (e.g., tenure, gender, family status, children's age) on the use of these arrangements (Blair-Loy & Wharton, 2002). Generally, benefits used by team members affect benefits utilization (Sivatte & Guadamillas, 2013). For example, Kossek, Barber, and Winters (1999) found that managers whose work-group peers used flexible scheduling were more likely to use such benefits than those managers whose peers did not. Representing important entities in the work environment, the three sources of support (organizations, supervisors, and coworkers) were found to be closely related, hence perceptions of support given by any one party are likely to influence perceptions of support given by the others (Ng & Sorensen, 2008).

The interaction between individual-level strategies and the organizational context provides some explanations for the weak effect of FFBs on work hours and the sense of balance. First, the extent to which employees believe they will garner rewards for time spent at work ("face time") or penalties for using FFBs, and the way they perceive the expectations of their supervisors, affect the (extra) time they spend on the job (Major et al., 2002; see also Moen et al., 2013). Second, employees with preferences for boundary management that are not matched by the FFBs provided by the organization may not perceive their organization as supportive and will not experience the expected positive outcomes (Kreiner, 2006; Rothbard, Phillips, & Dumas, 2005; Sutton & Noe, 2005). A specific case is that of "workaholics" who tend to work long hours even when they are not required to do so. These employees perceive the organization as more demanding and stressful and less supportive of a work–family balance, regardless of the real requirements and environment (Burke, 2002). Finally, in line with a social exchange perspective, employees who perceive their organization to be concerned with their wellbeing by providing FFBs may feel more obligated to "repay" the organization (Rhoades & Eisenberger, 2002), with positive attitudes and behaviors, and increasing work effort and hours of work being one way to do that. Also, in an environment where benefits use is not supported by managers and coworkers, individuals may feel pressured to exert more effort in order to compensate for the use of FFBs. Hence, work intensification can also be explained by employees trading additional effort in return for benefits (Kelliher & Anderson, 2010).

Concluding Notes

The intensification of work and the pressures to exert more effort and devote more time to work activities have heightened the debates and concerns surrounding the work–family balance. The negative consequences of long work hours and excessive work to organizations, families, and individuals have emphasized the need to implement policies that allow better adjustment of work and family life. Yet individuals engaged in the management of both spheres still see it as a private problem (Moen et al., 2013) and adopt a variety of coping strategies, depending on their family status, values, and priorities. These strategies highlight the primacy of the workplace in affecting individual lives, as most workers would rather adjust to work demands than try to change them. The consequences, therefore, are mostly negative and exact a price in terms of the worker's psychological and physical wellbeing as well as performance and productivity. Because these strategies are pursued in the family context, one outcome is increasing gender inequality within the family and in the labor market, as women are often those who have to make concessions: those who have care responsibilities often scale back, harming their careers and income; others postpone or forgo altogether family and fertility plans. Another outcome is the (short- and long-term) effects on children, who suffer from reduced parental involvement.

While organizations make efforts to resolve the inevitable conflict over work and non-work time, the implemented policies are not always efficient, especially for workers in demanding positions. Taking long leaves, working part time, or taking time off to meet family needs is not possible and has the potential of sending negative signals to employers, thus harming career prospects. Policies that are considered effective, such as autonomous time schedules and work from home, may operate as a double-edged sword, adding more strain and responsibilities, further blurring the boundaries between work and non-work time, and constraining the possibility of applying certain "work time" strategies. Additionally, providing control within the workplace may provide little benefit for employees who lack planning skills (i.e., working overtime to compensate for not prioritizing and completing important tasks on time) (Lapierre & Allen, 2012). Hence, organizations that truly aspire to provide the conditions for a more balanced life must develop a supportive culture that encourages more balanced priorities (Burke, 2001; Bakker et al., 2009). Providing training to both managers and employees will also help to raise awareness and provide the knowledge and specific solutions. Developing self-awareness is especially important for employees and managers who work long hours, as they are more exposed to the inherent conflict between work and family roles and their potential influence on the development of an environment that encourages long work hours (Porter, 1996)

At the same time, organizations need to examine the effectiveness of policies adopted. Workers with different needs at different times may need different arrangements depending on their values and priorities. It is also important to properly communicate these benefits, to make sure employees are aware of the benefits available to them, and to extend the legitimacy and support for their actual use. Additionally, new innovative arrangements should be examined, in response to individual diverse needs and coping strategies (Moen et al., 2013), such as a day off after a few days of intensive work or a free morning after late work hours. Second-order practices can be considered as well, such as limiting meetings to core work hours; increasing the use of video conferences to reduce commute time; blocking time for work; and allowing employees to complete their assignments without interference. These practices have potential to enable employees to be more productive in fewer hours and thereby have more time for personal life.

Finally, as Rantanen et al. (2011) suggest, a combination of different coping strategies—at the personal, family, and organizational levels—and their flexible use would work best in the work–family conflict situation, especially since FFBs may be more useful in reducing WFC, whereas individual strategies might be more useful in reducing FWC. Hence, balance emerges from an ongoing dialog between organization, managers, and employees; each entity has a unique contribution to promoting a more balanced way of life.

References

Abendroth, A. K., Lippe, T., & Mass, I. (2012). Social support and the working hours of employed mothers in Europe the relevance of the state, the workplace, and the family. *Social Science Research*, *41 (3)*, 581–597.

Allen, T. D. (2001). Family-supportive work environments: The role of organizational perceptions. *Journal of Vocational Behavior*, *58 (3)*, 414–435.

Allen, T. D., Herst, D. E. L., Bruck, C. S., & Sutton, M. (2000). Consequences associated with work to family conflict: A review and agenda for future research. *Journal of Occupational Health Psychology*, *5 (2)*, 278–308.

Anderson, S., Coffey, B., & Byerly, R. (2002). Formal organizational initiatives and informal workplace practices: Links to work–family conflict and job-related outcomes. *Journal of Management*, *28 (6)*, 787–810.

Appelbaum, E., Bailey, T., Berg, P., & Kalleberg, A. (2005). Organizations and the intersection of work and family: A comparative perspective. In: S. Ackroyd, R. Batt, P. Thompson, & P. Tolbert (Eds.), *The oxford handbook on work and organization* (pp. 52–73). New York: Oxford University Press.

Aryee, S., Chu, C. W. L., Kim, T. Y., & Ryu, S. (2013). Family supportive work environment work behaviors: An investigation of mediating mechanisms. *Journal of Management*, *39 (3)*, 792–813.

Aryee, D., Srinivas, E. S., & Hoon Tan, H. (2005). Rhythms of life: Antecedents and outcomes of work life balance in employed parents. *Journal of Applied Psychology*, *90 (1)*, 132–146.

Baird, C. L., & Reynolds, J. R. (2004). Employee awareness of family leave benefits: The effects of family, work, and gender. *The Sociological Quarterly*, *45 (2)*, 325–353.

Bakker, A. B., Demerouti, E., & Burke, R. (2009). Workaholism and relationship quality: a spillover perspective. *Journal of Occupational Psychology*, *14 (1)*, 23–33.

Bakker, A. B., Demerouti, E., & Dollard, M. (2008). How job demands influence partners' experience of exhaustion: Integrating work–family conflict and crossover theory. *Journal of Applied Psychology*, *93*, 901–911.

Baltes, B. B., Briggs, T. E., Huff, J. W., & Wright, J. A. (1999). Flexible and compressed workweek schedules: A meta-analysis of their effects on work-related criteria. *Journal of Applied Psychology*, *84*, 496–513.

Barnett, R. C., Gareis, K. C., & Brennan R. T. (2009). Reconsidering work time: A multivariate longitudinal within-couple analysis. *Community, Work & Family*, *12 (1)*, 105–133

Batt, R., & Valcour, M. P. (2003). Human resource practices as predictors of work family outcomes and employee turnover. *Industrial Relations*, *42 (2)*, 189–220.

Becker, P. E., & Moen, P. (1999). Scaling back: Dual earner couples work–family strategies. *Journal of Marriage and the Family*, *61 (4)*, 995–1007.

Behson, S. J. (2005). The relative contribution of formal and informal organizational work–family support. *Journal of Vocational Behavior*, *66 (3)*, 487–500.

Bianchi, S. M. (2011). Changing families, changing workplaces. *The Future of Children*, *21 (2)*, 15–36.

Bianchi, S. M., & Milkie, M. A. (2010). Work and family research in the first decade of the 21st century. *Journal of Marriage and Family*, *72 (3)*, 705–725.

Bianchi, S. M., Robinson, J. P., & Milkie, M. A. (2005). *Changing the rhythms of American family life.* New York: Russle Sage Foundation.

Bianchi, S. M., & Wight, V. R. (2010). The long reach of the job: Employment and time for family life. In: K. Christensen & B. Schneider (Eds.), *Workplace flexibility: Realigning 20th century jobs to 21st century workers* (pp. 17–42). Ithaca, NY: Cornell University Press.

Blair-Loy, M. (2003). *Competing devotions: Career and family among women executives.* Cambridge, MA: Harvard University Press.

Blair-Loy, M. (2009). Work without end? Scheduling flexibility and work-to-family conflict among stockbrokers. *Work and Occupations, 36 (4)*, 279–317.

Blair-Loy, M., & Wharton, A. S. (2002). Employees' use of work–family policies and the workplace social context. *Social Forces, 80 (3)*, 813–845.

Brannen, J. (2005). Time and the negotiation of work–family boundaries. *Time Society, 14 (1)*, 113–131.

Brett, J. M., & Stroh, L. K. (2003). Working 61 plus hours a week: Why do managers do it? *Journal of Applied Psychology, 88 (1)*, 67–78.

Brown, M. (2012). Responses to work intensification: Does generation matter? *The International Journal of Human Resource Management, 23 (17)*, 3578–3595.

Bulanda, R. E. (2004). Paternal involvement with children: The influence of gender ideologies. *Journal of Marriage and Family, 66 (1)*, 40–45.

Burke, R. J. (2001). Workaholism in organizations: The role of organizational values. *Personnel Review, 30 (6)*, 637–645.

Burke, R. J., Singh, P., & Fiksenbaum, L. (2010). Work intensity: Potential antecedents and consequences. *Personnel Review, 39 (5)*, 347–360.

Byron, K. (2005). A meta-analytic review of work–family conflict and its antecedents. *Journal of Vocational Behavior, 67 (2)*, 169–198.

Carlson, D. S., Kacmar, K. M., Wayne, J. H., & Grzywacz, J. G. (2006). Measuring the positive side of the work–family interface: Development and validation of a work–family enrichment scale. *Journal of Vocational Behavior, 68 (1)*, 131–164.

Casper, W. J., & Harris, C. M. (2008). Work–life benefits and organizational attachment: Self interest utility and signaling theory models. *Journal of Vocational Behavior, 72 (1)*, 95–109.

Clark, S. C. (2000). Work/family border theory: A new theory of work/family balance. *Human Relations, 53 (6)*, 747–770.

Coverman, S. (1985). Explaining husbands' participation in domestic labor. *The Sociological Quarterly, 26 (1)*, 81–97.

Coverman, S. (1989). Role overload, role conflict, and stress: Addressing consequences of multiple role demands. *Social Forces, 67 (4)*, 965–982.

Crouter, A. C., Bumpus, M. F., Head, M. R., & McHale, S. M. (2001). Implications of overwork and overload for the quality of men's and family relationships. *Journal of Marriage and Family, 63 (2)*, 404–416.

Crouter, A. C., Head, M. R., & McHale, S. M. (2004). Family time and the psychosocial adjustment of adolescents and their parents. *Journal of Marriage and Family, 66 (1)*, 147–162.

Davis, A. M., & Kalleberg, A. L. (2006). Family-friendly organizations? Work and programs in the 1990s. *Work and Occupations, 33 (2)*, 191–233.

Dex, S., &, Bond, S. (2005). Measuring WLB and its covariates. *Work, Employment and Society, 19 (3)*, 627–37.

Dikkers, J. S. E., Geurts, S. A. E., Den Dulk, L., Peper, B., Taris, T. W., & Kompier, M. A. J. (2007). Dimensions of work–home culture and their relations with the use of work–home arrangements and work–home interaction. *Work & Stress, 21 (2)*, 155–172.

Eby, L. T., Casper, W., Lockwood, A., Bordeaux, C., & Brinley, A. (2005). A twenty year retrospective on work and family research in IO/OB journals: A review of the literature. *Journal of Vocational Behavior, 66 (1)*, 124–197.

Epstein, C. F., Seron, C., Oglensky, B., & Sauté, R. (1999). *The part-time paradox: Time norms, professional life, family, and gender*. New York: Routledge.

Ford, J., & Collinson, D. (2011). In search of the perfect manager? Work life balance and managerial work. *Work, employment and society, 25 (2)*, 257– 273.

Ford, M. T., Heinen, B. A., & Langkamer, K. L. (2007). Work and family satisfaction and conflict: A meta-analysis of cross-domain relations. *Journal of Applied Psychology, 92 (1), 57–80.*

Frenkel, M. (2003). Women in the hi-tech: Has the "motherhood wall" collapsed? Ramat Gan: Women Israeli Lobby (Hebrew).

Frone, M. R. (2000). Work–family conflict and employee psychiatric disorders: The national comorbidity survey. *Journal of Applied Psychology, 85 (6)*, 888–895.

Frone, M. R. (2003). Work–family balance. In: J. C. Quick & L. E. Tetrick (Eds.), *Handbook of occupational health psychology* (pp. 143–162). Washington, DC: American Psychological Association.

Frone, M. R., Russell, M., & Cooper, M. L. (1992). Antecedents and outcomes of work–family conflict: Testing a model of the work–family interface. *Journal of Applied Psychology, 77*, 65–78.

Frone, M. R., Yardley, J. K., & Markel, K. S. (1997). Developing and testing an integrative model of the work–family interface. *Journal of Vocational Behavior, 50 (2)*, 145–167.

Frye, N. K., & Breaugh, J. A. (2004). Family friendly policies, supervisor support, work family conflict, family work conflict, and satisfaction: A test of a conceptual model. *Journal of Business and Psychology, 19 (2)*, 197–220.

Gajendran, R. S., & Harrison, D. A. (2007). The good, the bad, and the unknown about telecommuting: Meta-analysis of psychological mediators and individual consequences. *Journal of Applied Psychology, 92 (6)*, 1524–1541.

Galinsky, E., Bond, J. T., Sakai, K., Kim, S. S., & Giuntoli, N. (2008). *2008 National Study of Employers*. New York: Families and Work Institute.

Giga, S., & Cooper, C. L. (2005). The development of psychological contract in organizations: Implications for work and family life. In: E. E. Kossek & Lambert. S. J (Eds.), *Work and life integration: Organizational, cultural and individual perspectives* (pp. 429–444). Mahwah, NJ: Lawrence Erlbaum.

Geurts, S. A. E., Beckers, D. G. J., Taris, T. W., Kompier, M. A. J., & Smulders, P. G. W. (2009). Work time demands and work–family interference: Does work time control buffer the adverse effects of high demands? *Journal of Business Ethics, 84*, 229–241.

Glass, J. (2004). Blessing or curse? Work–family policies and mother's wage growth over time. *Work and Occupations, 31 (3)*, 367–394.

Goff, S. G., Mount, M. K., & Jamison, R. L. (1990). Employer supported child care, work/family conflict and absenteeism: A field study. *Personnel Psychology, 43 (4)*, 793–809.

Golden, T. D., Veiga, J. F., & Simsek, Z. (2006). Telecommuting's differential impact on work–family conflict: Is there no place like home? *Journal of Applied Psychology, 91 (6)*, 1340–1350.

Gray, M., & Tudball, J. (2003). Family-friendly work practices: Differences within and between workplaces. *Journal of Industrial Relations, 45 (3)*, 269–291.

Green, F. (2001). It's been a hard day's night: The concentration and intensification of work in late twentieth-century Britain. *British Journal of Industrial Relations, 39 (1)*, 53–80.

Greenhaus, J. H., & Beutell, N. J. (1985). Sources of conflict between work and family roles. *Academy of Management Review, 10 (1)*, 76–88.

Greenhaus, J. H., & Powell, G. N. (2006). When work and family are allies: A theory of work family enrichment. *Academy of Management Review, 31 (1)*, 72–92.

Grover. S., & Crooker, K. (1995). Who appreciates family responsive human resource policies: The impact of family friendly policies on the organizational attachment of parents and non parents. *Personnel Psychology, 48 (2)*, 271–288.

Grzywacz, J. G., Almeida, D. M., & McDonald, D. A. (2002). Work–family spillover and daily reports of work and family stress in the adult labor force. *Family Relations, 51(1)*, 28–36.

Grzywacz, J. G. & Carlson, D. S. (2007). Conceptualizing work–family balance: Implications for practice and research. *Advances in Developing Human Resources, 9 (4)*, 455–471

Grzywacz, J. G., & Marks, N. F. (2000) Reconceptualizing the work–family interface: An ecological perspective on the correlates of positive and negative spillover between work and family. *Journal of Occupational Health Psychology, 5 (1)*, 111–126.

Higgins, C. A., Duxbury, L. E., & Lyons, S. T. (2010). Coping with overload and stress: Men and women in dual-earner families. *Journal of Marriage and Family, 72 (4)*, 847–859.

Hill, E. J. (2005). Work–family facilitation and conflict, working fathers and mothers, work–family stressors and support. *Journal of Family Issues, 26 (6)*, 793–819.

Hill, E. J., Erickson, J. J., Holems, E. K., & Ferris, M. (2010). Workplace flexibility, work hours, and work–life conflict: Finding an extra day or two. *Journal of Family Psychology, 24 (3)*, 349–358.

Hill, E. J., Ferris, M., & Martinson, V. (2003). Does it matter where you work? A comparison of how three work venues (traditional office, virtual office, and home office) influence aspects of work and personal/family life. *Journal of Vocational Behavior, 63 (2)*, 220–241.

Hughes, D., Galinsky, E., & Morris, A. (1992). The effects of job characteristics on marital quality: Specifying linking mechanisms. *Journal of Marriage and Family, 54 (1)*, 31–42.

Jacobs, J. A., & Gerson, K. (2004). *The time divide: Work, family and gender inequality*. Cambridge, MA: Harvard University Press.

Jager, A. K. (2002). Households, work and flexibility: The Netherlands. In: C. Wallace (Ed.), *HWF Research Report by Countries*. Vienna: HWF Research Consortium.

Johnson, S., Li, J., Kendall, G., Strazdins, L., & Jacoby, P. (2013). Mothers' and fathers' work hours, child gender, and behavior in middle childhood. *Journal of Marriage and Family, 75 (1)*, 56–74.

Judiesch, M. K., & Lyness, K. S. (1999). Left behind? The impact of leaves of absence on managers' career success. *Academy of Management Journal, 42 (6)*, 641–651.

Kelliher, C., & Anderson, D. (2010). Doing more with less? Flexible working practices and the intensification of work. *Human Relations, 63 (1)*, 83–106.

Kelly, E. L., Moen, P., & Tranby, E. (2011). Changing workplaces to reduce work family conflict: Schedule control in a white collar organization. *American Sociological Review, 76 (2)*, 265–290.

Kinnunen, U., & Mauno, S. (1998). Antecedents and outcomes of work–family conflict among employed women and men in Finland. *Human Relations, 51 (2)*, 157–177.

Klumb, P., Hoppmann, C., & Staats, M. (2006). Division of labor in German dual-earner families: Testing equity theoretical hypotheses. *Journal of Marriage and Family, 68 (4)*, 870–882.

Konrad, A. M., & Yang, Y. (2012). Is using work–life interface benefits a career-limiting move? An examination of women, men, lone parents, and parents with partners. *Journal of Organizational Behavior, 33 (8)*, 1095–1119.

Kossek, E. E. (2005). Workplace policies and practices to support work and families. In: S. M. Bianchi, L. M. Casper, & R. B. King (Eds.), *Work, family, health and well-being* (pp. 97–116). Mahwah, NJ: Lawrence Erlbaum.

Kossek, E. E., Barber, A., & Winters, D. (1999). Using flexible schedules in the managerial world: The power of peers. *Human Resource Management, 38 (1)*, 33–46.

Kossek, E., & Ozeki, C. (1998). Work–family conflict, policies, and the job–life satisfaction relationship: A review and directions for organizational behavior human resource research. *Journal of Applied Psychology, 83 (2)*, 139–149.

Kossek, E. E., Lautsch, B. A., & Eaton, S. C. (2006). Telecommuting, control, and boundary management: Correlates of policy use and practice, job control, and work family effectiveness. *Journal of Vocational Behavior, 68 (2)*, 347–367.

Kossek. E. E., Lewis, S., & Hammer, L. B. (2010). Work life initiatives and organizational change: Overcoming mixed messages to move from the margin to the mainstream. *Human Relations, 63 (1)*, 3–19.

Kraut, R. E. (1989). Telecommuting: the trade-offs of home work. *Journal of Communication, 39 (3)*, 19–47.

Kreiner, G. E. (2006). Consequences of work–home segmentation or integration: A person environment fit perspective. *Journal of Organizational Behavior, 27 (4)*, 485–507.

Kreiner, G. E., Hollensbe, E. C., & Sheep, M. L. (2009). Balancing borders and bridges: Negotiating the work–home interface via boundary work tactics. *Academy of Management Journal. 52 (4)*, 704–730.

Lambert, S. (2000). Added benefits: The link between work–life benefits and organizational citizenship behavior. *Academy of Management Journal, 43 (5)*, 801–815.

Lapierre, L. M., & Allen, T. D. (2006). Work supportive family, family supportive supervision, use of organizational benefits, and problem focused coping: Implications of work family conflict and employee well being. *Journal of Occupational Health Psychology, 11 (2)*, 169–181.

Lapierre, L. M., & Allen, T. D. (2012).Control at work, control at home, and planning behavior: Implications for work family conflict. *Journal of Management, 38 (5)*, 1500–1516.

Lapierre, L. M., Spector, P. E., Allen, T. D., Poelmans, S., Cooper, C. L., O'Driscoll, M. P., Sanchez, J. I., Brough, P., & Kinnunen, U. (2008). Family supportive organization perceptions. Multiple dimensions of work family conflict, and employee satisfaction: A test of model across five samples. *Journal of Vocational Behavior, 73 (1)*, 92–106.

Lewis, S. (2003). The integration of paid work and the rest of life: Is post industrial work the new leisure? *Leisure Studies, 22 (4)*, 343–355.

Lyness, K. S., & Judiesch, M. K. (2013). Gender egalitarianism and work life balance for managers: multisource perspective in 36 countries. *Applied Psychology: An International Review, 63 (1)*, 96–129.

Major, V. S., Klein, K. I., & Ehrhart, M. G. (2002). Work time, work interference with family, and psychological distress. *Journal of Applied Psychology, 87 (3)*, 427–436.

Maume, D. J., & Houston, P. (2001). Job segregation and gender differences in work–family spillover among white-collar workers. *Journal of Family and Economic Issues*, *22 (2)*, 171–189.

Mauno, S., Kinnunen, U., & Piitulainen, S. (2005b). Work–family culture in four organizations in Finland: Examining antecedents and outcomes. *Community, Work and Family*, *8 (2)*, 115–140.

Mauno, S., Kinnunen, U., & Pyykko, M. (2005a). Does work–family conflict mediate the relationship between work–family culture and self-reported distress? Evidence from five Finish organizations. *Journal of Occupational and Organizational Psychology*, *78 (4)*, 509–530.

Mauno, S., Kinnunen, U., & Ruokolainen, M. (2006). Exploring work and organization based resources as moderators between work–family conflict, well-being, and job attitudes. *Work & Stress*, *20 (3)*, 210–233.

McGinnity, F., & Calvert, E. (2008). Yuppie Kvetch? Work–life conflict and social class in Western Europe, ESRI, Working paper no. 239.

McNamara, T. K., Pitt-Catsouphes, M., Mata-Costa, C., Brown, M., & Valcour, M. (2013). Across the continuum of satisfaction with work–family balance: work hours, flexibility-fit, and work–family culture. *Social Science Research*, *42 (2)*, 283–298.

Mesmer-Magnus, J. R., & Viswesvaran, C. (2006). How family-friendly work environments affect work/family conflict: A meta-analytic examination. *Journal of Labour Research*, *26 (4)*, 555–574.

Moen, P., Lam, J., Ammons, S., & Kelly, E. L. (2013). Time worked by overworked professionals: Strategies in response to the stress of higher status. *Work and Occupations*, *40 (2)*, 79–114.

Mumford, K. A., & Budd, J. W. (2006). Family friendly practices in Britain: Availability and perceived accessibility. *Human Resource Management*, *45 (1)*, 91–110.

Netemeyer, R. G., Boles, J. S., & McMurrian, R. (1996). Development and validation of work–family conflict and family–work conflict scales. *Journal of Applied Psychology, 81 (1)*, 400–410.

Ng, T. W. H., & Sorensen, K. L. (2008). Toward a further understanding of the relationships between perceptions of support and work attitudes: A meta analysis. *Group Organization Management, 33 (1)*, 243–263.

Nomaguchi, K. M. (2007). Change in work–family conflict among employed parents between 1977 and 1997. *Journal of Marriage and Family, 71 (February)*, 15–32.

Noonan, M. C., & Glass, J. L. (2012). The hard truth about telecommuting. *Monthly Labor Review, (June)*, 38–45.

Offer, S. & Schneider, B. (2011). Revisiting the gender gap in time-use patterns: Multitasking and well-being among mothers and fathers in dual-earner families. *American Sociological Review, 76 (6)*, 809–832.

Perrons, D., Fagan, C., McDowell, L., Ray, K., & Ward, K. (2005). Work, life and time in the new economy. *Time & Society, 14 (1)*, 51–64.

Porter, G. (1996). Organizational impact of workaholism: Suggestions for researching the negative outcomes of excessive work. *Journal of Occupational Health Psychology, 1 (1)*, 70–84.

Pittman, J. F. (1994). Work/family fit as a mediator of work factors on marital tension: Evidence from the interface of greedy institutions. *Human Relations, 47 (2)*, 183–209.

Premeaux, S. F., Adkins, C. L., & Mossholder, K. W. (2007). Balancing work and family: A field study of multi-dimensional, multi-role work–family conflict. *Journal of Organizational Behavior, 28 (6)*, 705–727.

Prottas, D. J., Thompson, C. A., Kopelman, R. E., & Jahn, E. W. (2007). Work–family programs: Factors affecting employee knowledge and accuracy. *Personnel Review, 36 (2)*, 163–169.

Rantanen, M., Mauno, S., Kinnunen, U., & Rantanen, J. (2011). Do individual coping strategies help or harm in the work–family conflict situation? Examining coping as a moderator between work–family conflict and well-being. *International Journal of Stress Management, 18 (1)*, 24–48.

Rhoades, L., & Eisenberger, R. (2002). Perceived organizational support: A review of the literature. *Journal of Applied Psychology, 87 (4)*, 698–714.

Richman, A. L., Civian, J. T., Shannon, L. L., Hill, E. J., & Brennan, R. T. (2008). The relationship of perceived flexibility, supportive work–life policies, and use of formal flexible arrangements and occasional flexibility to employee engagement and expected retention. *Community, Work & Family, 11 (2)*, 183–197.

Roehling, P. V., Roehling, M. V., & Moen, P. (2001). The relationship between work–life policies and practices and employee loyalty: A life course perspective. *Journal of Family and Economic Issues, 22 (2)*, 141–170.

Rogier, S. A., & Padgett, M. Y. (2004). The impact of utilizing a flexible work schedule on perceived career advancement potential of women. *Human Resource Development Quarterly, 15 (1)*, 89–106.

Rothbard, N. P., Phillips, K. W., & Dumas, T. L. (2005). Managing multiple roles: Work–family policies and individuals' desires for segmentation. *Organization Science, 16 (3)*, 243–258.

Schieman, S., Milkie, M. A., & Glavin, P. (2009). When work interferes with life: Work–nonwork interference and the influence of work related demands and resources. *American Sociological Review, 74 (6)*, 966–988.

Shockley, K. M., & Allen, T. D. (2007). When flexibility helps: Another look at the availability of flexible work arrangements and work–family conflict. *Journal of Vocational Behavior, 71 (3)*, 479–463.

Sivatte, I., & Guadamillas, F. (2013). Antecedents and outcomes of implementing flexibility policies in organizations. *The International Journal of Human Resources Management, 24 (7)*, 1327–1345.

Smithson, J., Lewis, S., Cooper, C., & Dyer, J. (2007). Flexible working and the gender pay gap in the accountancy profession. *Work, Employment and Society, 18 (1)*, 115–135.

Snir, R., & Harpaz, I. (2012). Beyond workaholism: Towards a general model of heavy work investment. *Human Resources Management Review, 22 (3)*, 232–243.

Spain, D., & Bianchi, S. M. (1996). *Balancing act: Motherhood, marriage and employment among American women.* New York: Russell Sage.

Sutton, K. L., & Noe, R. A. (2005). Family friendly programs and work–life integration: More myth than magic? In: E. E. Kossek, & S. J. Lambert (Eds.), *Work and life integration: Organizational cultural and individual perspectives* (pp. 151–170). Mahwah, NJ: Erbaum.

Thomas, L. T., & Ganster, D. (1995). Impact of family supportive work variables on work–family conflict and strain: A control perspective. *Journal of Applied Psychology, 80 (1)*, 6–15.

Thompson, C. A., Andreassi, J. K., & Prottas, D. J. (2005). Work–family culture: Key to reducing workforce–workplace mismatch? In: S. M Bianchi, L. M. Casper, & R. B. King (Eds.), *Work, family, health, and well-being* (pp. 117–132). Mahwah, NJ: Lawrence Erlbaum.

Thompson, C. A., Beauvais, L. L., & Lyness, K. S. (1999). When work–family benefits are not enough: The influence of work–family culture on benefit utilization, organizational attachment, and work–family conflict. *Journal of Vocational Behavior, 54 (3)*, 392–415.

Thompson, C. A., Jahn, E. W., Kopelman, R. E., & Prottas, D. J. (2004). Perceived organizational family support: A longitudinal and multilevel analysis. *Journal of Managerial Issues, 16 (4)*, 545–565.

Thompson, C. A., & Prottas, D. J. (2006). Relationships among organizational family support, job autonomy, perceived control, and employee well-being. *Journal of Occupational Health Psychology, 10 (4)*, 100–118.

Townsend, Nicholas W. (2002). *The package deal: Marriage, work, and fatherhood in men's lives.* Philadelphia, PA: Temple University Press.

Valcour, M. (2007). Work-based resources as moderators of the relationship between work hours and satisfaction with work–family balance. *Journal of Applied Psychology, 92 (6)*, 1512–1523.

Voydanoff, C. (2004). The effects of work demands and resources on work-to-family conflict and facilitation. *Journal of Marriage and Family, 66 (2)*, 398–412.

Wang, P., & Walumbwa, F. O. (2007). Family friendly programs, organizational commitment, and work withdrawal: The moderated role of transformational leadership. *Personnel Psychology, 60 (2)*, 397–427.

Wayne, J. H., Casper, W. J., Matthews, R. A., & Allen, T. D. (2013). Family-supportive organization perceptions and organizational commitment: The mediating role of work–family conflict and enrichment and partner attitudes. *Journal of Applied Psychology, 98 (4)*, 602–622.

Wharton, A. S., & Blair-Loy, M. (2006). Long work hours and family life: A cross national study of employees' concerns. *Journal of Family Issues, 27 (3)*, 415–436.

White, M., Hill, S., McGovern, P., Mills, C., & Smeaton, D. (2003). "High-performance" management practices, working hours and work–life balance. *British Journal of Industrial Relations, 41 (2)*, 175–195.

Whittington, K. B. (2011). Mothers of invention? Gender, motherhood, and new dimensions of productivity in the science profession. *Work and Occupations, 38 (3)*, 417–456.

Williams, J. C., & Boushey, H. (2010). The three faces of work–family conflict. Washington DC: Center of American Progress. Retrieved July 13, 2013 (www.americanprogress.org/1ssues/2010/01/pdf/threefaces.pdf).

Winslow, S. (2005). Work–family conflict, gender, and parenthood, 1977–1997. *Journal of Family Issues, 26 (6)*, 727–755.

Yeung, J. W., Sandberg, J. F., Davis-Kean, P. E., & Hofferth, S. L. (2001). Children's time with fathers in intact families. *Journal of Marriage and Family, 63 (1)*, 136–154.

12

WORKAHOLISM IN A DYNAMIC WORKFORCE

Shahnaz Aziz, Kevin Chaney, and Justin Raines

For over four decades, workaholism has been a commonplace term used in popular culture to depict individuals who are addicted to work. Oates (1971) first created the term *workaholic* to describe a person whose addiction and compulsion to work, or uncontrollable need to work incessantly, impedes multiple life functions. The term has since grown in familiarity and been used more often in the media, on the Internet, and in the research literature. People typically view "workaholics" as hardworking employees who are devoted to their careers. Furthermore, workaholism has a positive connotation in our society and many believe that being a workaholic is a prerequisite to a successful career. The concept of workaholism has become engrained in North American culture and is now an accepted way of life—as Spruell (1987, p. 44) states, "workaholism is the most rewarded addiction in our culture."

Compared to other organizational behavior topics, empirical study in the area of workaholism has somewhat trailed its popular culture usage for a variety of reasons. First, researchers have struggled to agree upon a definition of workaholism (Buelens & Poelmans, 2004; Burke, 2001a; Scott, Moore, & Miceli, 1997). Second, the most commonly used measures of workaholism are methodologically flawed and often criticized for their lack of validity and reliability (Ersoy-Kart, 2005; McMillan, Brady, O'Driscoll, & Marsh, 2002). Last, researchers (e.g., Burke, 2000; Aziz & Zickar, 2006) have not been able to convince society that the behavioral component of workaholism, working excessively, can lead to negative outcomes—instead, organizations prefer their employees to work longer hours, which presumably leads to financial gains for both the organization and the employee.

The increasing number of hours that comprise a typical workweek, coupled with the rise in the use of technology in organizations, has made workaholism a relevant problem. Additionally, the modern workforce is becoming more diverse, so it can be difficult for employers to understand the sectors of the workforce that are at increased risk for developing workaholism. Therefore, by investigating individual differences that might impact the development of workaholism, employers are better prepared to deal with the negative consequences of the construct. In turn, the result is a greater understanding of the workaholism syndrome as a whole.

Recently, there has been growing interest in exploring how employees' behaviors and attitudes in the workplace change depending on individual differences, such as their career stage and generation membership (e.g., Burke, 2001b; Gursoy, Mair, & Chi, 2008). Managers and employees alike need to effectively interact, motivate, and communicate with individuals in different career stages and from different generations in the workplace. The absence of this understanding could result in work stress, loss of productivity, and lower job satisfaction (Kupperschmidt, 2000). In addition, employers need to be aware of potential career stage or generational differences that influence the development of workaholism in order to mitigate the likelihood of its development.

In this chapter, we will discuss workaholism in a dynamic workforce. That is, we will explore the role of demographics and workaholism by examining career stage and generation membership. Similarly, certain professions are underrepresented in this area of study. Therefore, we will describe the role of workaholism in samples other than white-collar professionals—that is, people in artistic occupations will also be discussed. Specifically, we will first provide an overview of workaholism and then expand upon the existing literature by describing how career stage and generational differences might affect workaholism. Next, we will summarize preliminary research on workaholism's association with these two variables, including limitations in this area of study, as well as conclusions. Finally, we will discuss workaholism in artistic workers, including preliminary research on workaholism in artists, practical implications, as well as directions for future research.

Overview of Workaholism

Despite the use of the term *workaholism*, researchers have struggled to agree on what compromises the construct. Perhaps workaholism is simply an extreme case of an already recognized construct, such as job involvement or organizational commitment. Several attempts have been made to answer this question, but have resulted in different conclusions. Some believe that workaholics can have a positive influence on organizations, as workaholics are committed, hardworking employees (Machlowitz, 1980). From this perspective, it seems that employers should attract, recruit, and retain this type of worker. However, others view workaholism negatively (e.g., Burke, 2000; Porter, 1996). If it is true that workaholics are perfectionists who are unable to delegate work and work cooperatively with others, then they are unlikely to be productive employees. Based on this outlook, employers should avoid workaholics and discourage a culture of workaholism. Clearly, these contrasting viewpoints make choosing an organizational strategy difficult. While there is disagreement on whether workaholism is a desirable or undesirable trait, currently, researchers see it as an addictive work habit that interferes with an individual's health, happiness, and/or personal relationships (Aziz & Zickar, 2006; Burke, 2000; Robinson, 1996).

One of the most widely used and agreed upon definitions of workaholism was developed by Spence and Robbins (1992). They claimed that employees who are addicted to work should be divided into subcategories rather than fall under the umbrella term of workaholic. They measured three distinct components of workaholism: work involvement, work drive, and work enjoyment. Work involvement is the extent to which individuals commit themselves to a project and make constructive use of their time. Work drive is the individual's internal motivation to work. Work enjoyment is the pleasure individuals derive from working. These facets were considered to be independent of one another, as a person could be high on one component, yet low on another. Using a cluster analysis technique, Spence and Robbins established subcategories for employees, with workaholics defined as high on work involvement and work drive, but low on work enjoyment.

Another common definition of workaholism comes from Robinson (1989), who defined workaholism as "the overindulgence in and preoccupation with work, often to the exclusion and detriment of the workaholic's health, intimate relationships, and participation in child rearing" (Flowers & Robinson, 2002, p. 517). Robinson's Work Addiction Risk Test (WART) measures workaholism according to his definition. Flowers and Robinson (2002) conducted a principle components analysis on the WART and found it to be comprised of five factors, three of which validly differentiated workaholics from non-workaholics (i.e., compulsive tendencies, control, and impaired communication/self-absorption)—this three-factor structure has been replicated in other studies (Clarke, Lelchook, & Taylor, 2010).

Schaufeli and Taris (2004) developed the Dutch Work Addiction Scale (DUWAS), which conceptualizes workaholism as a two-dimensional construct that is comprised of working excessively (WE) and working compulsively (WC). Each of these scales originated from the WART and Spence and Robbins's triad of workaholism. It is of note that the DUWAS also distinguishes workaholism from work engagement.

To reach a compromise to the workaholism definition debate and to expand on previous delineations, workaholism has also been theorized as a syndrome (Aziz & Zickar, 2006; Vodanovich & Piotrowski, 2006).

A syndrome is a term used to describe a regularly occurring group of symptoms that comprise a disease where the full condition has not yet been defined (Aziz & Zickar, 2006). In their cluster analysis of Spence and Robbins's (1992) triad of workaholism, Aziz and Zickar (2006) found empirical support for the notion that workaholism should be conceptualized as a syndrome. Specifically, they identified a cluster of individuals that corresponded to the workaholic profile with the symptoms of high work involvement, high work drive, and low work enjoyment. Similarly, Vodanovich and Piotrowski (2006) suggested the workaholism syndrome moves through certain stages and deteriorates over time. In its early stage, workaholic behaviors form due to individual differences, responsibilities, and stress, but they do not disrupt the workaholic's daily functioning. Eventually, these behaviors intensify and become recurrent, ultimately interfering with the individual's functioning. When the full syndrome emerges, work reinforces the individual's behavior and consumes the individual's life, and the individual becomes dysfunctional, neglecting all other aspects of life (e.g., family, relationships, and personal health; Vodanovich & Piotrowski, 2006).

Career Stages and Workaholism

There has been growing interest in the relationship between career stages and an employee's attitudes and behaviors in the workplace. A career stage is defined as job sequences or career patterns that individuals progress through during their working lives, similar to the concept of life stages (Lynn, Cao, & Horn, 1996). The underlying assumption of this area of research is that people advance through certain career stages in their work lives, with each stage marked by different work attitudes, behaviors, needs, and values.

There have been numerous models of career development. For example, researchers have used biosocial life cycles, family or procreation cycles, and work/career cycles (Lynn et al., 1996). The biosocial life cycle divides adult development into overlapping yet distinct eras (e.g., early adulthood, middle adulthood, late adulthood), taking into account biological, psychological, and social aspects into defining these periods (Levinson, 1978). The family or procreation cycle divides stages in terms of the roles within the family (e.g., independence, marriage, parenting, launching adult children). The work/career cycle breaks down stages of development into the focus of one's career (e.g., establishment, advancement, maintenance) (Schein, 1978). Although the biosocial life model is the most popular conceptualization, it is less applicable to studying managerial careers (Mount, 1984). Consequently, the three-stage model of work/career cycles is deemed as most appropriate for measuring the work attitudes and behaviors of professionals. The first stage, establishment, is the process of gaining competence and acceptance among peers and leaders. The second stage, advancement, is characterized by the newly competent employee shifting his/her career focus on upward mobility, promotion, greater responsibility, and increased autonomy. The last stage, maintenance, is where the individual's concentration shifts away from competition with peers and turns to the development of others as well as the organization (Mount, 1984).

Trying to determine the optimal way to measure career stages has been a challenging task. Individual age, organizational tenure, position tenure, professional or occupational tenure (Lynn et al., 1996), and self-report measures such as the Career Concerns Inventory (CCI; Maio, Lund, & Evans, 2009) have typically been used to assess career stages. While the CCI seems to be the most comprehensive measure of career stage, empirically, it has performed relatively poorly and its length (56 items) could result in a lower response rate due to respondent fatigue (Maio et al., 2009). In short, there is no widely agreed upon way of measuring career stage. As a result, some researchers have used a self-selection categorical approach to successfully assess career stage (e.g., Flaherty & Pappas, 2002; Maio et al., 2009).

The self-selection categorical method is an effective and succinct way of measuring career stage (Flaherty & Pappas, 2002). Having employees categorize themselves allows them to account for their own career perceptions and concerns. Individuals can go through various career stages more than once as a result of an organizational or job change. This trend has become increasingly more common in today's organizations, thereby making simpler measures of career stage (e.g., individual age) less accurate (Lynn at al., 1996). For these reasons, it seems that self-categorization is a more appropriate measure of career stage than individual age, organizational tenure, and position tenure.

Research findings on career stages have suggested that individuals go through significant changes at these career crossroads. Adler and Aranya (1984) found that among employees in the same field, those at different career stages varied in work needs, attitudes, and work preferences. As a general trend among those under the age of 60, the more advanced the career stage, the stronger the level of work needs, the higher the job satisfaction, the stronger the organizational and professional commitment, and the more conventional the work preferences. While those over the age of 60 showed stronger security needs, higher organizational and professional commitment, and more conventional preferences than people in earlier stages, higher-order needs and job satisfaction were at significantly lower levels.

There is evidence that one's career stage can correlate with facets of workaholism. Research suggests that work involvement is influenced by career stage. Specifically, Slocum and Cron (1985) found in a sample of salespeople that work involvement increased as individuals' careers developed—those in the maintenance stage had significantly higher ratings of work involvement than individuals in the advancement stage. Organizational commitment also increased as individuals' careers advanced, as those in the maintenance stage reported greater levels of organizational commitment than did individuals in the establishment and advancement stages. Similarly, in a sample of primarily 36–45-year-old professionals, Burke (2001a) found that employees at higher levels of the organization reported greater work involvement. Those at higher organizational levels also reported spending more hours per week working than employees lower in the organization. It also seems that career stages have a positive relationship with another facet of workaholism, work enjoyment. Mount (1984) investigated managers' satisfaction across career stages and found that those in the establishment stage were more satisfied with most aspects of their jobs compared to managers in the other two stages. Collectively, these results, as well as the possibility that older workers are more healthy, satisfied, and committed than younger workers, seem to suggest that the more advanced the career stage, the higher the level of workaholism.

Generational Differences and Workaholism

Researchers, managers, and employees are increasingly becoming interested in how to interact with people from different generations in the workplace. Although Kupperschmidt's (2000) theory that generational differences in personality, values, and attitudes exist is popular in the media, relatively little empirical research has investigated this topic. The notion of generational differences is important because managers need to be able to interact, motivate, and communicate effectively with employees, regardless of their generation. The absence of this understanding could result in work stress, loss of productivity, and lower job satisfaction (Kupperschmidt, 2000).

A generation can be defined as "a group of people or cohorts who share birth years and experiences as they move through time together, influencing and being influenced by a variety of critical factors" (Kupperschmidt, 2000, p. 66). In turn, these groups of people develop personality characteristics, values, attitudes, preferences, and behaviors that are specific to their generational cohort. While people within a generational cohort can have individual differences between one another, generational characteristics are typically generalizations (Kupperschmidt, 2000).

Drawing the boundaries between generations can be difficult. The two generational cohorts that make up the majority of the workforce today are Baby Boomers and Generation X, while Generation Y is the up and coming generation. The boundaries for Baby Boomers are commonly drawn between 1945, when World War II ended, and the mid-1960s, when the birth rate declined. Those individuals born after the post-World War II baby boom are Generation X, and are born from the mid-1960s to the late 1970s. The generation entering adulthood and thus the workforce now is the Baby Boomers' children, or Generation Y (Kupperschmidt, 2000). Using the methods of Smola and Sutton (2002) and Hess and Jepsen (2009), the following terms and boundaries will be used hereafter in this chapter: Baby Boomers (born 1946–1964), Generation X (born 1965–1979), and Generation Y (born 1980–1994).

Baby Boomers lived through a time of great social change and political unrest. Memorable events for the Boomers include the Vietnam War, the Civil Rights Movement, and the assassinations of John F. Kennedy and Martin Luther King, Jr. Baby Boomers also grew up in a time of growing consumerism and wealth. Furthermore, Boomers are often stereotyped as being focused and dedicated to their work, which results in them staying with the same organization throughout their careers, and at times neglecting their families in favor of work (Stawiski, Gentry, & Baranik, in press; Kupperschmidt, 2000).

Generation X was shaped by U.S. economic problems such as the oil crisis in 1973, the 1979 energy crisis, Black Monday, and the savings and loan crisis. They also witnessed the AIDS epidemic, the Cold War, and the War on Drugs. In addition, they grew up in a time where divorce became commonplace. In short, this generation experienced great economic uncertainty and incessant change. Consequently, Generation X is generally thought of as independent, less dedicated to their organization, and more likely to frequently change jobs. They are also less focused on their work and believe work–life balance is important (Stawiski et al., in press; Kupperschmidt, 2000).

Generation Y is marked by the use and prevalence of digital technology, media, and communication. They experienced communication tools such as email, texting, and instant messaging, as well as the rise of social networking sites such as Facebook and Twitter. This generation has faced difficult economic times either while in the early stages of their careers or while on the verge of entering the job market. They watched the dot-com bubble burst, and the housing market collapse, and are enduring the aftermath of the financial crisis of 2007–2010. Generation Y has been nicknamed the "Peter Pan" generation, for their reputation of delaying their passage into adulthood. While Generation Y is just entering the workforce, and struggling to do so with high unemployment rates, it is important that organizations understand the tendencies for this up-and-coming generation (Cennamo & Gardiner, 2008; Stawiski et al., in press).

Research suggests that generational differences may also exist in the workplace. Of particular importance, these differences relate to some important correlates of workaholism, namely, work–life balance. For example, Sullivan, Forret, Carraher, and Mainiero (2009) found that Generation X reported a higher need for work–life balance than Baby Boomers. In short, Boomers "live to work" and Generation Xers "work to live." Generation Xers want a life outside of work, as they are not likely to sacrifice their lives for the organization (Gursoy, Mair, & Chi, 2008). Consequently, Generation X employees may not feel as driven or be as involved in their jobs because of their strong desire to balance work with other aspects of their lives.

A recent review of the literature on generational differences in work attitudes has revealed that Generation Y, to an even greater extent than Generation X, tends to value leisure and work–life balance (Twenge, 2010). Generation X, and especially Generation Y, usually see their work as less central to their lives, highly value leisure, seek freedom, and are not as willing to work hard. In addition, Generation Y is "more likely to value time off and less likely to value work for work's sake" (Twenge, 2010, p. 204). In a similar study, it was found that Generation Y values freedom more than Generation X and Baby Boomers (Cennamo & Gardner, 2008). Thus, it seems there is a generational trend developing, in which younger generations tend to value leisure, freedom, and work–life balance more than previous generations. So, while both Generations X and Y share similar attitudes and values toward work, it seems that Generation Y has a more extreme stance than Generation X. As a result, Generation Y might have lower levels of workaholism than Generation X and Baby Boomers.

Generational membership may also account for an employee's commitment and motivation to work. For instance, Baby Boomers are willing to be patient and earn their promotions and rewards, and they are committed to their organizations. On the other hand, Generation X employees believe they should receive recognition immediately through title, praise, promotion, and pay (Gursoy, Mair, & Chi, 2008). Perhaps Generation Xers feel a sense of entitlement for recognition, as they do not feel the need to work for their rewards and promotions, potentially indicating they are less driven to work and less job-involved than Boomers. As a result, Baby Boomers might have higher levels of workaholism than Generation X and Generation Y.

One possible reason behind these differing attitudes towards commitment and patience is the recent transformation from a traditional organizational career to what is now being called the *protean career*. The protean career is the process whereby individuals are managing their career, not the organization. Individuals are in charge of their own career choices, and development and job security have become virtually nonexistent. Organizations are in a constant state of flux and must be smaller and faster in order to respond to changing conditions. Thus, individuals must be flexible and adaptive in their careers as well (Hall & Moss, 1998).

Baby Boomers may be more willing to be patient and committed because the traditional organizational career model rewarded these behaviors. However, younger generations, such as Generation X, may have adapted to the more modern protean career path and realize that being committed and patient in a single organization is less likely to pay off.

Kanai, Wakabayashi, and Fling (1996) looked at age differences and workaholism among blue-collar workers (e.g., factory workers, sales employees) using Spence and Robbins's (1992) definitional framework. Age is typically used to determine generation membership, so these results provide some insight into generational differences as well. Their findings showed that work drive was lowest among those individuals less than 24 years old and greatest for participants 40 years of age and older. Similarly, work enjoyment increased as age increased and was the highest for those over 50 years old. One interesting trend found among age group means was that as age increased, a transition occurred from unengaged workers (low on work involvement, work drive, and work enjoyment) to enthusiastic workaholics (high work involvement, work drive, and work enjoyment) (Kanai et al., 1996).

Preliminary Research on Workaholism, Career Stages, and Generational Differences

In a recent study by Chaney and Aziz (2012), workaholism was investigated among a wide-ranging sample of employees, thereby capturing all generations and career stages of interest. Their results indicate that, in general, career stage was not a major contributor to the prevalence of workaholic behavior. Perhaps the current weak job market has created anxiety in employees where, regardless of career stage, they are more driven and involved in their work in order to keep their jobs. Also, due to the transition of traditional organization-led career paths into the protean career, where individuals independently manage their own career paths, employees may exhibit workaholic behaviors in order to succeed in their careers across all career stages. Furthermore, because there is no single agreed-upon method of measuring career stage, perhaps the method used by Chaney and Aziz (i.e., self-categorization) was insufficient for measuring career stage accurately enough to detect differences across career stages.

Career stage, however, contributed to one component of workaholism, namely control. While the overall scales of workaholism were not significant, Flowers and Robinson (2002) have shown that the control subscale is the greatest driving aspect separating workaholics from nonworkaholics. The control facet is described as being frustrated when tasks go awry. Thus, their results suggest that those in the maintenance stage are less frustrated by complications than those in the establishment and advancement stages. Chaney and Aziz's (2012) interpretation is that those in the maintenance stage are focused on developing the organization rather than themselves; therefore, personal difficulties with work tasks do not directly frustrate their goals. Conversely, given that those in the establishment and advancement stages are focused on becoming more competent and gaining responsibilities, respectively, complications with work tasks are more closely tied to their personal goals. Thus, their self-efficacy and self-esteem are more negatively influenced and perhaps they feel more frustration as a result.

The study results of Chaney and Aziz (2012) also suggest that generation does not have a major impact on the incidence of workaholism. Again, perhaps the current weak job market has created anxiety in employees, in that all employees are equally driven and involved in their work in order to keep their jobs. In addition, evolution into the protean career has become a reality in today's workplace, thereby affecting all generations. Thus, employees may exhibit workaholic behaviors equally, regardless of their generation. Finally, email was used as the method of recruitment in the Chaney and Aziz study—perhaps there is a systematic difference between the Baby Boomers who use email and those who do not, in that if they use email, they are more similar to the younger generations.

In sum, results of the Chaney and Aziz (2012) study suggest that neither generation membership nor career stage affect overall levels of workaholism, as there were no significant differences among the groups on two separate measures of workaholism. However, there were significant differences on the control subscale of the WART for both generation membership and career stage. This finding opens up the door for future investigation into these observed differences, as perhaps certain aspects of workaholism can vary among different generations and career stages. Although the total scales of workaholism did not indicate any significant differences among the groups, findings with the control subscale of the WART suggests that in the future, differences in these groups may be present.

Practical Implications

The lack of significant differences in workaholism between generations and career stages implies that no generation or career stage is exempt from, or particularly vulnerable to, the effects of workaholism and its correlates. This is an important finding in itself, as managers need to mitigate the likelihood of its development equally *across* generations and career stages by establishing workaholism awareness and interventions on their entire workforce. At the same time, organizations should be aware that younger generations, particularly Generation Y, and earlier career stages, mainly establishment and maintenance, are especially high on feelings of control. For organizations, this means that this segment of the workforce is vulnerable to feeling frustrated when tasks go awry. In order to combat this feeling, managers should be prepared to give younger generations and employees in earlier career stages greater organizational support to cope with their frustrations. Ideally, this support would include supervisors tailoring their management style to these employees, as well as the use of Employee Assistance Programs. Developing a protocol for employees who feel particularly frustrated with work tasks would also be an appropriate intervention to implement in organizations.

Limitations in Generational and Career Stage Research

Both generational and career stage research inherently have some limitations. First, there is still no consensus on how to measure these constructs. For generation, researchers differ on the years used to operationalize the various generations, making it difficult to generalize across studies, which may explain some of the inconsistent findings in this line of research. In future research, perhaps generation should be assessed with age in conjunction with another measure, such as having participants identify historical events that have affected their lives. Similarly, career stage has been measured using multiple methods (e.g., position tenure, career concerns inventories). Chaney and Aziz (2012) used a self-selection method to assess career stage. While this method has been shown to be effective and succinct (Flaherty & Pappas, 2002), thereby increasing response rate and lowering respondent fatigue, future research should use more comprehensive measures of career stage.

Another limitation in this domain of research is the cross-sectional design used in most studies. This is particularly problematic for generational research, as it is challenging to separate the effects of age and generation without utilizing a longitudinal design. Certainly, generations and individuals go through changes during their lives, and if data were captured multiple times, these changes could be accounted for. Similarly, career stage research also involves how individuals age and go through long-term changes throughout their careers, thus it suffers from the same limitation as generational research. Therefore, future research should employ longitudinal research designs.

Conclusions in Generational and Career Stage Research

Similarities in the prevalence of workaholism across generations and career stages suggest that organizations can benefit by selecting interventions that discourage workaholism for *all* employees, regardless of generation membership or career stage. While they will continue to be important concepts within work attitudes and behaviors, the current research highlights that these generational and career stage differences may have less of an effect than is widely assumed. However, Chaney and Aziz (2012) found a difference whereby individuals in the younger generations and earlier career stages had higher feelings of control. Managers can put this information to use by ensuring greater organizational support is provided to this segment of their workforce. Generation Y is only just beginning to enter the workforce and the next generation, Generation Z, will be entering the workforce in the near future. It is important that researchers continually examine these generations' work values, attitudes, and behaviors so that managers can communicate and tailor their interventions to these different groups of workers.

Workaholism in Artistic Workers

A PsycINFO database search on workaholism research reveals that certain careers are underrepresented in this area of study. While white-collar professionals have a healthy representation (Aziz & Zickar, 2006; Burke, 2001b; Burke & Koksal, 2002), blue-collar workers are notably less represented (Kanai et al., 1996). Additionally, although workaholism in organizations has been explored, and workaholism in self-employed workers has been touched upon (Gorgievski, Bakker, & Schaufeli, 2010; Morales, 2009; Snir & Harpaz, 2004; Taris, Geurts, Schaufeli, Blonk, & Lagerveld, 2008), no research to date has examined workaholism in artistic careers. According to Abbing (2002) and Menger (1999), many professional artists are self-employed. This view is echoed by the National Endowment for the Arts (2008a), who report that as many as 56 percent of visual artists identify themselves as being self-employed, indicating a fundamental difference between white-collar workers and artists since fewer than 10 percent of the general labor force consider themselves to be self-employed. Thus, this difference between self-employed and salaried workers bears exploration due to its potential influence on work habits, as well as possible implications for nonwork life.

The importance of studying artists and their work behaviors is underscored by their presence in the workforce. According to a report issued by the National Endowment for the Arts (2008a) based primarily on U.S. Census data and billed as "the first nationwide look at artists' demographic and employment patterns in the 21st century" (National Endowment for the Arts, 2008b, p. 1), artists comprised 1.9 million workers or 1.4 percent of the American workforce and are one of the largest occupation groups in the country just behind active-duty and reserve personnel in the U.S. military. They represent a larger group than the legal profession (lawyers, judges, and paralegals) or medical doctors (physicians, surgeons, and dentists), which are more extensively represented in workaholism literature. Limited access to the artist population could be to blame, as could the notion that "white-collar professionals are typically associated with workaholism" (Aziz & Zickar, 2006, p. 55). Yet it seems apparent that although the size of the artistic community gives it extraordinary income ($70 billion annually), with respect to numbers, artists depict a powerful labor force whose economic contributions go largely unrecognized not only by the general public and the government (National Endowment for the Arts, 2008a), but by researchers as well. By limiting the scope and influence of workaholism to just white-collar jobs, researchers have neglected a population that may provide insight into the comprehensive understanding of this construct and its correlates.

Preliminary Research on Workaholism in Artists

The increasing relevance of workaholism in the modern working world, as evidenced by the rise in number of hours worked per week and the growing concern for employee well-being, reinforces the need for additional research on workaholism in terms of its antecedents and correlates. As such, investigation of a diverse set of careers serves to further complete the nomological net and to enhance our understanding of the workaholism syndrome as a whole.

Weber and Aziz (2011) sought to expand our knowledge of workaholism by investigating obsessive-compulsive behavior and work/nonwork interference, known correlates of workaholism. They compared these two variables with workaholism in a traditional white-collar sample and a nontraditional artistic sample, ranging from sculptors to painters, to actors to musicians. In comparing the relationships between obsessive-compulsive behavior, work/nonwork interference, and workaholism in both samples, a broader understanding of the workaholism syndrome may be reached by investigating careers that have, up until now, been largely overlooked in the literature. Their results did not reveal any difference between these two groups on workaholism, hours worked, and work interference with personal life. However, Weber and Aziz (2011) found a significant difference between the two groups on work enhancement of personal life such that self-employed artists scored higher, but no significant difference on obsessive-compulsive behavior.

Additional results showed significant differences between white-collar professionals and artists on work enjoyment and the control facet of the WART measure, such that artists scored higher on work enjoyment and white-collar professionals scored higher on control. In fact, Shalley, Gilson, and Blum (2000) and Runco (1995) found that more creative and autonomous jobs, such as artists, are related to higher job satisfaction. A breakdown of these groups by self-employment status revealed that being self-employed was a significant factor in determining work enhancement of personal life. These results reinforce the study of artists' work behaviors as important areas for future research involving work/nonwork balance. Also of note, self-employed workers tend to be more passionate about work in that they are higher on work engagement and working excessively than non-self-employed (i.e., salaried) workers (Gorgievski, Bakker, & Schaufeli, 2010). This finding suggests that the job characteristics of self-employed workers lend them to exhibit self-motivation rather than stress.

Practical Implications

The similarities found between white-collar professionals and artists imply that artists are not immune to the influence of workaholism and its correlates. Therefore, managers should consider that workaholism and work interference with personal life are not solely problems that affect traditional white-collar employees, but they may also impact a diverse group of workers, such as artists. With this knowledge in hand, managers can better prepare their artistic employees to deal with the adverse effects of workaholism through awareness and intervention programs.

Moreover, as evident in the Weber and Aziz (2011) study, organizations and small businesses alike can draw from the positive influence associated with self-employment, namely, work enhancement of personal life. By applying principles and characteristics of the self-employed occupations, such as increased autonomy and flexible work schedules, to salaried jobs, the positive personal life outcomes and increases in healthy work/nonwork balance might be realized for a broader group of workers.

Directions for Future Research on Workaholism in Artists

Future research on workaholism in the artist population should examine more artistic occupations, including artistic groups who are more closely tied to computers, such as graphic designers—doing so might enhance the generalizability of the results. Also, increasing the scope of the current research and examining more diverse careers may yield additional differences between white-collar employees and artists.

Future research should also explore the control facet of the WART, which was significantly different between white-collar employees and artists. Researchers could seek to paint a better picture of how workaholism appears in each of these populations through the use of qualitative data analysis, peer interviews, or the application of additional measures of workaholism. It is possible that distinct occupations may express workaholism in different ways, and the control subscale may be a start to exploring potential differences.

Concluding Remarks on Workaholism and Artists

The absence of a significant difference between white-collar professionals and artists on workaholism seems to disprove the myth that workaholic behaviors only affect white-collar employees. Artists, despite numbering approximately two million in the United States, have long gone unrecognized in their contributions and have been excluded from work-related research. Their significant numbers, power as an economic generator, and positive contributions to modern society make artists a group who can not only contribute to Industrial/Organizational (I/O) Psychology as a discipline, but also serve to benefit from I/O research.

Artists are essentially a foreign entity in the current stream of workaholism research. Their high work enjoyment and work enhancement of personal life may help to further our understanding of job satisfaction and work/nonwork balance as we know it today. Further research on the artist population might reveal some of their secrets to gaining satisfaction from work and may help to bring those practices to other fields, which do not enjoy such benefits from their jobs. Although inclusivity is not necessarily the *modus operandi* of the artist, it is clear that psychologists, artists, and non-artists stand to benefit from artists being included in I/O research.

References

Abbing, H. (2002). *Why are artists poor? The exceptional economy of the arts.* Amsterdam: Amsterdam University Press.

Adler, S., & Aranya, N. (1984). A comparison of the work needs, attitudes, and preferences of professional accountants at different career stages. *Journal of Vocational Behavior, 25*, 45–57.

Aziz, S., & Zickar, M. J. (2006). A cluster analysis investigation of workaholism as a syndrome. *Journal of Occupational Health Psychology, 11*, 52–62.

Buelens, M., & Poelmans, S. A. Y. (2004). Enriching the Spence and Robbins' typology of workaholism: Demographic, motivational and organizational correlates. *Journal of Organizational Change Management, 17*, 440–458.

Burke, R. J. (2000). Workaholism in organizations: Psychological and physical well-being consequences. *Stress Medicine, 16*, 11–16.

Burke, R. J. (2001a). Workaholism components, job satisfaction, and career progress. *Journal of Applied Social Psychology, 31*, 2339–2356.

Burke, R. J. (2001b). Predictors of workaholism components and behaviors. *International Journal of Stress Management, 8*, 113–127.

Burke, R. J., & Koksal, H. (2002). Workaholism among a sample of Turkish managers and professionals: An exploratory study. *Psychological Reports, 91*, 60–68.

Cennamo, L., & Gardner, D. (2008). Generational differences in work values, outcomes and person-organization values fit. *Journal of Managerial Psychology, 23*, 891–906.

Chaney, K., & Aziz, S. (2012). Managing a dynamic workforce: The influence of generation membership and career stage on workaholism. Unpublished Master's thesis, East Carolina University, Greenville, NC.

Clark, M. A., Lelchook, A. M., & Taylor, M. L. (2010). Beyond the big five: How narcissism, perfectionism, and dispositional affect relate to workaholism. *Personality and Individual Differences, 48*, 786–791.

Ersoy-Kart, M. (2005). Reliability and validity of the Workaholism Battery (Work-BAT): Turkish Form. *Social Behavior and Personality, 33*, 609–618.

Flaherty, K. E., & Pappas, J. M. (2002). The influence of career stage on job attitudes: Toward a contingency perspective. *Journal of Personal Selling & Sales Management, 22*, 135–143.

Flowers, C. P., & Robinson, B. (2002). A structural and discriminant analysis of the Work Addiction Risk Test. *Educational and Psychological Measurement, 62*, 517–526.

Gorgievski, M. J., Bakker, A. B., & Schaufeli, W. B. (2010). Work engagement and workaholism: Comparing the self-employed and salaried employees. *The Jounal of Positive Psychology, 5*, 83–96.

Gursoy, D., Maier, T. A., & Chi, C. G. (2008). Generational differences: An examination of work values and generational gaps in the hospitality workforce. *International Journal of Hospitality Management, 27*, 448–458.

Hall, D., & Moss, J. E. (1998). The new protean career contract: Helping organizations and employees adapt. *Organizational Dynamics, 26*, 22–37.

Hess, N., & Jepsen, D. M. (2009). Career stage and generational differences in psychological contracts. *The Career Development International, 14*, 261–283.

Kanai, A., Wakabayashi, M., & Fling, S. (1996). Workaholism among employees in Japanese corporations: An examination based on the Japanese version of the workaholism scales. *Japanese Psychological Research, 38*, 192–203.

Kupperschmidt, B. (2000). Multi-generation employees: Strategies for effective management. *Health Care Manager, 19*, 65–76.

Levinson, D. J. (1978). *The seasons of a man's life.* New York: Knopf.

Lynn, S. A., Cao, L., & Horn, B. C. (1996). The influence of career stage on the work attitudes of male and female accounting professionals. *Journal of Organizational Behavior, 17*, 135–149.

Machlowitz, M. M. (1980). *Workaholics: Living with them, working with them.* Reading, MA: Addison-Wesley.

Maio, C., Lund, D. J., & Evans, K. R. (2009). Reexamining the influence of career stages on salesperson motivation: A cognitive and affective perspective. *Journal of Personal Selling & Sales Management, 29*, 243–255.

McMillan, L. H. W., Brady, E. C., O'Driscoll, M. P., & Marsh, N. (2002). A multifaceted validation study of Spence and Robbins' (1992) Workaholism Battery. *Journal of Occupational and Organizational Psychology, 75*, 357–368.

Menger, P. M. (1999). Artistic labor markets and careers. *Annual Review of Sociology, 25*, 541–574.

Morales, L. (2009, 26 August). *Self-employed workers clock the most hours each week.* Retrieved October 20, 2010 from gallup.com: www.gallup.com/122510/self-employed-workers-clock-hours-week.aspx

Mount, M. K. (1984). Managerial career stage and facets of job satisfaction. *Journal of Vocational Behavior, 24*, 340–354.

National Endowment for the Arts. (2008a). *Artists in the workforce: 1990–2005.* Washington, DC: Library of Congress Cataloging-in-Publication Data.

National Endowment for the Arts. (2008b). *Artists in the workforce: 1990–2005, executive summary.* Washington, DC: Library of Congress Cataloging-in-Publication Data.

Oates, W. (1971). *Confessions of a workaholic: The facts about work addiction.* New York, NY: World Publishing.

Porter, G. (1996). Organizational impact of workaholism: Suggestions for researching the negative outcomes of excessive work. *Journal of Occupational Health Psychology, 1*, 70–84.

Robinson, B. E. (1989). *Work addiction.* Deerfield Beach, FL: Health Communications.

Robinson, B. E. (1996). The psychosocial and familial dimensions of work addiction: Preliminary perspectives and hypotheses. *Journal of Counseling and Development, 74*, 447–452.

Runco, M. (1995). The creativity and job satisfaction of artists in organizations. *Empirical Studies of the Arts,* 13, 39–45.

Taris, T. W., Schaufeli, W. B., Hoogenhuyze, C. L. P., & Zon, A. (2003). Workaholism, stress and health: Development and validation of a Dutch workaholism scale. *Gedrag & Gezondheid, 31*, 2–18.

Schein, E. H. (1978). *Career dynamics: Matching individual and organizational needs.* Reading, MA: Addison-Wesley.

Scott, K. S., Moore, K. S., & Miceli, M. P. (1997). An exploration of the meaning and consequences of workaholism. *Human Relations, 50*, 287–314.

Shalley, C. E., Gilson, L. L., & Blum, T. C. (2000). Matching creativity requirements and the work environment: Effects on satisfaction and intentions to leave. *The Academy of Management Journal,* 43, 215–223.

Slocum, J. W., & Cron, W. L. (1985). Job attitudes and performance during three career stages. *Journal of Vocational Behavior, 26*, 126–145.

Smola, K., & Sutton, C. D. (2002). Generational differences: Revisiting generational work values for the new millennium. *Journal of Organizational Behavior, 23*, 363–382.

Snir, R., & Harpaz, I. (2004). Attitudinal and demographic antecedents of workaholism. *Journal of Organizational Change Management, 17*, 520–537.

Spence, J. T., & Robbins, A. S. (1992). Workaholism: Definition, measurement, and preliminary results. *Journal of Personality Assessment, 58*, 160–178.

Spruell, G. (1987). Work fever. *Training & Development Journal, 41*, 41–45.

Stawiski, S. A., Gentry, W. A., & Baranik, L. E. (In press). Can employees of every age have it all? Examining the relationship between work-life balance and promotability for Baby Boomers and Generation X. In S. E. Sullivan, & S. Gayle Baugh (Eds.), *Research in careers: Finding balance.* Charlotte, NC: Information Age Publishing.

Sullivan, S. E., Forret, M. L., Carraher, S. M., & Mainiero, L. A. (2009). Using the kaleidoscope career model to examine generational differences in work attitudes. *The Career Development International, 14*, 284–302.

Taris, T. W., Geurts, S. A., Schaufeli, W. B., Blonk, R. W., & Lagerveld, S. E. (2008). All day and all of the night: The relative contribution of two dimensions of workaholism to well-being in self-employed workers. *Work & Stress, 22*, 153–165.

Twenge, J. M. (2010). A review of the empirical evidence on generational differences in work attitudes. *Journal of Business and Psychology, 25*, 201–210.

Vodanovich, S. J., & Piotrowski, C. (2006). Workaholism: A critical but neglected factor in O.D. *Organization Development Journal, 24*, 55–60.

Weber, R., & Aziz, S. (2011). The artistic worker versus the white-collar professional: Workaholism, work/nonwork interference and enhancement, and obsessive-compulsive behavior in two samples. Unpublished Master's thesis, East Carolina University, Greenville, NC.

13

HEAVY WORK INVESTMENT, BRIDGE EMPLOYMENT, AND THE TRANSITION TO RETIREMENT

Kenneth S. Shultz and Deborah A. Olson

The concept of retirement has evolved dramatically in recent decades. For example, while the notion of "working in retirement" has been viewed as an oxymoron in the past, retirement is no longer tantamount to a lack of paid employment (Shultz & Wang, 2011). Instead we see older workers today redefining what it means to be "retired." More often than not, being retired now includes continued work investment in some form, particularly in the early stages of the retirement process. This continued, but often somewhat reduced, work investment is referred to as bridge employment. In fact, Cahill, Giandrea, and Quinn (2006) estimated that approximately 60 percent of older workers in the United States engaged in some form of bridge employment before exiting the workforce. Engaging in bridge employment has been found to have both physical and psychological benefits for retirees, depending on the type of bridge employment retirees engage in (Zhan, Wang, Liu, & Shultz, 2009). As a result, the concept of bridge employment is comprehensively explored in this chapter.

In addition, the retirement process itself has become a blurred, rather than a crisp demarcation. That is, most workers today no longer work full time until their last day of work and then retire the next day to full time leisure pursuits. In fact, a recent survey of over 6,000 older workers aged 45 and older in the United States indicated that 71 percent planned to engage in some form of paid employment during retirement (Merrill Lynch, 2013). Thus, we are seeing a longer, drawn-out retirement process where individuals continue to work for a wide range of reasons (e.g., devotion to their career, use of their talents, feelings of contribution to others, financial). Therefore, in this chapter we integrate Snir and Harpaz's model of HWI (Snir & Harpaz, 2012) with the concept of worker retirement in order to better understand the transition workers make from full time work to retirement at the end of their careers and how HWI can impact the retirement process. Both situational and dispositional forms of HWI are explored in terms of how they impact the retirement transition process, as well as retirement adjustment and related outcomes. The various theories and models of retirement (e.g., role theory, rational choice theory, continuity theory, and life course perspective) are juxtaposed with the HWI concept, along with related theories and models such as the selective optimization with compensation (SOC) model of aging and the emphasis on the use of one's talents from the individual and leadership development literature.

The Changing Nature of Mid and Late Careers

Historically, mid and late career has been viewed as a time of maintenance and decline in work involvement, as well as ongoing learning and development, since the emphasis was on the inevitable transition to retirement (Wang, Olson, & Shultz, 2013). Traditionally, retirement signified the end of work related activities and roles, with the emphasis being on leisure and family/community pursuits that were often separate and distinct from work related career activities. The focus was on how to find pursuits to keep busy and engaged in the way that traditional work roles filled one's day (Ekerdt, 1986). However, newer models of career development (e.g., the protean career model [Hall, 2004], boundaryless career model [Arthur & Rousseau, 1996], and kaleidoscope career model [Maniero & Sullivan, 2005]) more accurately frame the evolution that has occurred to a more dynamic interplay between work and retirement. Specifically, it is more often the norm that individuals in their mid and late careers remain engaged in learning new skills, expanding their talents, and continue to make strategic contributions to their organizations (Wang et al., 2013).

For example, the protean career model posits that workers in the 21st century are taking control of their own careers, rather than relying on organizational leaders to determine what their next job will be or when they will retire (Hall, 2004). The factors in this model define the significance of an individual's values, preferences, and career, as well as life goals, rather than arbitrarily set meaningless timelines for ending one's career and taking full retirement (e.g., linked to the age when full Social Security and pension benefits can be collected every month). Relatedly, in describing the Kaleidoscope Career Model, Maniero and Sullivan (2005) discuss the ABCs of Kaleidoscope careers. Specifically, A is for *Authenticity*, B is for *Balance*, while C is for *Challenge*. They note that while all three components are present across career stages, *Challenge* is most prominent at the early career stage, while *Balance* is the focus of the mid career stage. At late career stages, *Authenticity* becomes the driving force in one's career aspirations. Thus, individuals in their mid and late careers can and do continue to make strategic contributions to their organizations by adjusting their career goals as they progress through their careers (Wang et al., 2013).

In addition, it is not unusual for today's older workers in their mid and late career to change not only jobs, but employers and occupations as well during the ages that are traditionally associated with retirement. In fact, the concept of encore careers has become more popular among the baby boom cohort (Freedman, 2007). Older workers engaging in encore careers often retire from their career jobs, only to pursue a second career in a field that they view as having more social value (e.g., working for an NGO) or that more fully allows them to use their talents and strengths in their work (Buckingham & Clifton, 2001). As a result, older workers may retire several times throughout their work life (Shultz & Wang, 2011). In fact, a recent survey of over 6,000 individuals in the US aged 45 and older (Merrill Lynch, 2013) reported that 51 percent of respondents hope to work in a whole different career field after they retire rather than continuing in the same career field.

We must be careful, however, not to treat all older workers as having similar motives and goals related to their work. For example, a study of older workers by the Metlife Mature Market Institute (2006) indicated that while most workers in the 55–59 age range continue to work primarily for financial reasons, those older workers in the 66–70 age range cited the desire to "stay active and engaged" (72 percent), "opportunity to do meaningful work" (47 percent), and "enjoying the social interaction with colleagues" (42 percent) as the top three reasons why they continue to work, despite being eligible for Social Security and pension benefits. These older workers also indicated a desire to stay engaged and connected with work, but with reduced stress by engaging in alternative work arrangements, including being self-employed, part time work, downshifting to similar, but less stressful jobs, and so called "portfolio" positions.

The Changing Nature of Retirement

As noted earlier, retirement is no longer tantamount to a lack of paid employment. Instead, we see that retirement is a very individualized process (Shultz & Wang, 2011) that often includes some form of continued employment, at least in the beginning stage of the retirement process. The other key factor to note is that retirement is indeed a process that takes place over many years, beginning with distal notions of retirement imagining and anticipating what retirement might be like, progressing to more proximal and definitive decisions regarding the timing and form that retirement might take. Thus, it is no longer only a matter of deciding *when* to retire, but those approaching retirement must also determine *what* form their retirement will take (Adams & Rau, 2011); which today often means continued work investment in some form.

Several major theories dominate the retirement literature according to a recent review by Wang and Shultz (2010). The most prominent theories regarding retirement discussed by Wang and Shultz include role theory, image theory, rationale choice theory, expectancy theory, theory of planned behavior, continuity theory, social context theory, and the life course perspective. It is beyond the scope of this chapter to discuss each of these retirement related theories. Therefore, instead we focus on just three of the most prominent retirement related theories that would be most germane to a discussion of HWI: role theory, continuity theory, and the life course perspective. Both role theory and continuity theory focus on how individuals generally adapt as they age. As a result, both theories provide a sensible framework when applied to understanding how individuals progress through and adapt to retirement (von Bonsdorff & Ilmarinen, 2013) and how HWI may influence, and be influenced by, this process.

Role theory (e.g., Ashford, 2001) proposes that individuals engage in various roles (e.g., worker, spouse, parent, community citizen) throughout their life. As we age and begin to approach retirement, the various roles one engages in may begin to shift and take on more or less importance in one's life. Thus, someone who is a HWI individual may have difficulty making the transition from the full time worker role to the grandparent or community citizen roles since so much of their identity has been invested in the worker role. Accordingly, role theory focuses on the role changes that individuals go through as they transition into and through retirement. To the extent that older workers are able to successfully transition and adapt to new roles as they approach and move through retirement, their adjustment to their new retirement role is likely to be better.

Conversely, continuity theory (Atchley, 1989, 1999) stresses the significance of consistency or continuity, rather than change, that older workers are able to maintain as they age and transition into retirement. That is, how do older workers use their past experiences to adapt and adjust to the changes associated with aging, particularly with regard to retirement decision making, the transition to retirement, and the retirement adjustment process? This has traditionally been a somewhat easier task for white collar and professional workers, compared to blue collar skilled and unskilled workers, given the formers' typical higher education levels (Wang & Shultz, 2010). As one would guess, dispositional HWI individuals would likely strive to maintain their HWI in order to maintain consistency as they transition to retirement. Von Bonsdorff and Ilmarinen (2013) recently juxtaposed the concept of workability (i.e., the ability of older workers to maintain their ability to work by striking the balance between their resources and job demands) with continuity theory by suggesting that older workers will only be able to maintain continuity (and possibly HWI) if they are able to maintain their workability as they age.

The life course perspective (Elder, 1995), which many view as a meta-theory (e.g., Wang et al., 2009), integrates factors from many of the other theories of retirement. The life course perspective considers retirement in terms of one's broader life history and the contextual factors that surround the retirement decision making and adjustment process. These individualized life histories and contextual factors work together to shape the pathways that individuals take to enact and adjust to the retirement transition process. Previous workforce participation patterns and histories, general work and leisure preferences and routines, as well as significant life events (e.g., death of a spouse, late life divorce, and onset of a major chronic health condition) will all impact the paths individuals take as they approach, and transition through, retirement. Individual factors such as health and financial status, as well as transition related abilities and skills also fall within the framework of the life course perspective. The life course perspective also emphasizes the interconnectedness of the various life spheres of work, family, and social life. Thus, it is the unique and individualized combination of factors that emanate from our various life spheres, and the broader organizational and societal context, that impact our decisions of whether, and if so how, to continue to invest in work given all the other aspects of their development and what is most salient for individuals in their late career.

Another important theory to consider when examining retirement is the Theory of Selection, Optimization, and Compensation; or SOC for short (Baltes & Rudolph, 2013). Similar to the life course perspective, SOC is also considered a lifespan development meta-theory, which incorporates elements of various other theories of aging. Baltes and Rudolph recently applied the SOC model to examine how older workers can maintain successful performance as they age, thus allowing them to maximize their choices with regard to voluntary retirement. They also discuss how the SOC model can both be applied to retirement decision making, as well as demonstrate how engaging in SOC strategies are related to positive adjustment once retired. Thus, to the extent that continued HWI is viewed as a desirable outcome in retirement, engaging in SOC strategies can help older workers achieve that outcome by maximizing one's available resources (e.g., mental, physical, and environmental) at a given point in time.

Within the SOC model, selection refers to individuals identifying and setting goals. This selection, or focusing, can occur as a result of one's own choosing (e.g., choosing to focus on a limited number of goals after the birth of a grandchild) or due to loss of an internal or external resource (e.g., postponing early retirement due to loss of a spouse). Once the goals are solidified through selection, the next step is optimization.

Optimization is the acquisition, refinement, and use of various means to achieve the goals identified during selection. So, for example, an older worker may set the goal to become more savvy in the use of social media and so attend a training session on the use of social media in the workplace in order to gain new knowledge in that area. Finally, compensation refers to working to maintain a certain level of functioning when faced with developmental losses. For example, an older worker may compensate for reduced short-term memory by engaging in mnemonic strategies to compensate for worsening memory. Compensation becomes more prominent in the SOC model as we age given that chronic health conditions continue to accumulate and worsen with each passing year.

For those individuals who have HWI throughout their career (i.e., dispositional HWI), their selection of goals may be more focused on work related accomplishments, which in turn impact their strategies to optimize their performance as well as the intensity of how they compensate for what they might view as needed to continue to perform at a high level. An example of the selection of work focused development goals for late career workers may be to develop/expand their use of social media to accomplish specific work related goals. For workaholics (Snir & Harpaz, 2012), in their attempts to expand their understanding of social media they may develop a *presence* on many sites and network widely to learn from "digital natives" regarding what they can do to optimize their outcomes at work through incorporating a wide range of social media sites and applications. This could turn into the compulsion to be constantly online and plugged in 24/7 so that they do not miss anything and to prove to themselves and others that they are just as digitally adept as individuals in their 20s.

This could be contrasted with the activities of older workers who are work devoted and are seeking approaches to continue to use social media as a tool to maintain their performance and optimize their work. For older workers who have work devotion, they would tend to use social media as a way to continue to expand the results they accomplish and use it as another tool to expand their work role and ability to contribute to their organizations' goals. In this case, the workaholic and work devoted older workers may both engage in similar behaviors, for similar reasons, but the impact of their HWI on the quality of their life and overall balance is quite different.

We posit that addiction to technology may have similar behavioral manifestations regardless of age. As Snir and Harpaz (2012) so clearly state, workaholics and work devoted individuals both have HWI, but have different outcomes based on the choices that they make in response to internal drives and dispositional factors. One key concept that we believe is linked to the behavioral choices of those who are *work involved*, is whether or not they are able to use their talents at work regularly to achieve results that are important (Buckingham & Clifton, 2001). In this context, *talents* are defined as naturally reoccurring actions, thoughts, and feelings that are related to strong performance and the ability to consistently perform at a high level. Using one's talents is linked to engagement with the tasks and activities and results in the desire to consistently seek out those situations and activities in the future (Csikszentmihalyi, 1990; Seligman, 2002; Wagner & Hartner, 2006). The investment that individuals have made in developing their talents over the course of their life through engagement in both work and nonwork activities and passions is an important dispositional factor that impacts choices and decisions made by older workers.

Heavy Work Investment and the Importance of Using Talents for Older Workers

Individuals who are *work devoted* and have continuously invested in developing and learning throughout their career report that they are able to use their talents at work regularly to accomplish important outcomes—important to both the individuals and the organizations they are working for (Wagner & Hartner, 2006). For those individuals who are work devoted, understand their own talents and how to optimally use them to achieve specific results, they tend to perform at higher levels when compared to individuals who do not understand their own talents (Haralalka & Tung, 2012). Older workers, who have developed their understanding of themselves and know how to best use their talents, are important human capital assets for organizational leaders to continue to invest in and support. By doing so, older workers will continue to reap the benefits of the investments they have made in developing and enhancing their talents and continue to contribute to organizational results, and thereby remain engaged and motivated in their work.

To facilitate the ongoing effectiveness of older workers, it is important to understand what they share in common with workers of all ages. Relying on stereotypes of older workers (e.g., they resist learning new skills) can have a negative impact on older workers' self-perceptions (Cappelli & Novelli, 2010). For example, an individual in her 60s who has made heavy investments in her education and ongoing training over the course of her career and is passionate about her work (i.e., work devoted), may develop symptoms of a workaholic as she attempts to prove to others that she can continue to contribute at a high level to her team and the organization overall. For example, the Center for Creative Leadership (CCL) reported that differences across generations may be more based on stereotyping and media anecdotes than actual patterns in performance levels of workers, which can be systematically measured (DePinto, 2003). With a sample of over 3,000 leaders that represented five different generational cohorts, their research showed that there were more similarities reported across generational lines than differences. Specifically, individuals in all generations reported that: 1) based on their role, having flexible scheduling options to complete their work was important; 2) they were developing new skills and knowledge through the work they were doing; 3) they believed that people only remained working at their organizations as long as the work they were doing was using their talents; and 4) they received great satisfaction based on the accomplishments that they achieved through their work. In this sample, individuals reported strong engagement and enjoyment in their roles, but for older workers the feelings of engagement and satisfaction were the strongest. For older workers, being engaged through continuing to learn skills that allowed them to make significant contributions to their organizations was important for retention. In this study by CCL, older workers also reported that they believed they were secure in their positions and they believed that their current position utilized their talents and was consistent with their interests. These factors contribute to the willingness of older workers to continue to invest in their work and develop their talents in a way that contributes to their individual success, as well as the success of the organization overall (Wagner & Hartner, 2006).

Clearly, the human resource practices utilized by organizational leaders impact the well-being and performance levels of their employees. As individuals age, they are motivated by different work related outcomes and, therefore, the importance of different human resource practices clearly changes with age. For example, the importance of promotion opportunities and the ability to take on higher levels of leadership are less important for older workers (Baltes, Staudinger, & Lindenberger, 1999; Kanfer & Ackerman, 2004). Specifically, Kooij, Guest, Clinton, Knight, Jansen, and Dikkers (2013) found that older workers were more engaged and committed to their work when they were given ongoing opportunities to engage in developmental activities and formal training. They also found that older workers sought out opportunities for job enrichment to continue to invest in the development of their talents and expand their ability to make important contributions to the organization. Organizational human resource practices that offer job enrichment and developmental opportunities were linked to greater levels of well-being and higher levels of performance for older workers (Kooij et al., 2013). This research result supports the importance of organizational leaders continuing to provide opportunities for older workers who have made a HWI to develop their talents and contribute to the organization's success.

Situational Impacts on HWI: What Can Organizational Leaders Do to Engage the Work Devoted Older Workers?

Organizational leaders can implement specific practices to ensure that older workers are able to use their talents every day. Unfortunately, research has shown that leaders do not consistently focus on how to optimize the use of their employees' talents at work to optimize performance and engagement (Buckingham & Clifton, 2001; Haralalka & Tung, 2012; Wagner & Hartner, 2006). Specifically, research by Haralalka and Tung shows that only about 20 percent of individuals use their talents on a regular basis at work. However, individuals who are using their talents at work more consistently seek out opportunities to expand their skills and knowledge to develop their ability to apply their talents to achieve important results.

To optimize the situational context, leaders must begin by clarifying expectations. Older workers, like all employees, need to understand what is expected of them every day and how their work will be measured. To complete their work effectively, they also need to have the proper materials and equipment to complete their work to the established level of expectation. Older workers also need to be able to determine if they have everything they need to do their best work every day. Taken together, clear expectations, shared understanding of how work outputs will be measured, and having the right tools to complete one's work daily will make a positive impact on older workers' internal locus of control and willingness to continue to make the investments, in terms of both time and effort, to optimize their work outcomes.

Organizational leaders can also facilitate the positive outcomes for HWI workers by asking specific questions of their older workers to draw out their ideas and insights based on their years of experience and accumulated wisdom. For example, managers can focus on asking specific questions to elicit ideas about how to build new processes and programs to improve performance and strategies to help individuals develop their talents in order to achieve higher levels of organizational results (Buckingham & Clifton, 2001). Also, within the situational context, the actions of the leader make a significant impact on how older workers respond to and interact with others. Specifically, being praised or acknowledged regularly for one's work and contributions makes a significant impact on one's feeling of importance and significance in a team or organization (Goulston, 2013).

Going beyond development activities, older workers need to communicate what they find energizing about their work. Their managers can support them by providing them with opportunities to complete that type of work regularly. This is called *job crafting* and is a process that can be used by organizational leaders to ensure that older workers are able to fully utilize their talents by organizing their work and tasks around their talents. Job crafting is a process that acknowledges the heavy work investments that individuals have made by organizing the job tasks and responsibilities in a manner that allows individuals to do what they do best every day (Wrzesniewski, Berg, & Dutton, 2010). Also, organizational leaders can identify opportunities to create jobs for older workers that allow them to continue to be engaged in work that is important to the organization and uses the talents of the individual, but does not require the full time commitment of the older worker. This unique form of crafting jobs creates opportunities for bridge employment so that the individual can remain engaged in work activities and the organization continues to receive the value of his/her performance while s/he transitions into retirement.

Bridge Employment, Heavy Work Investment, and the Transition to Retirement

While various definitions of bridge employment exist, most agree that bridge employment consists of some kind of paid employment, either year round part time or full time, or seasonal employment, working as an employee or self-employed (Cahill, Giandrea, & Quinn, 2013). The key is that bridge employment occurs after retirement from a career job, thus bridging the gap between full time career employment and full time leisure retirement. As a result, bridge employment is similar to related concepts such as phased retirement; however, the latter typically requires staying in the same job with the same employer, but transitioning to retirement over a several year period by reducing one's hours and/or work load. A good example of phased retirement is the Faculty Early Retirement Program (FERP) that many colleges and universities offer tenured faculty members to ease in to retirement by gradually reducing their teaching, research, and/or service requirements. Conversely, if a faculty member were to fully retire from his/her tenured position, but then teach part time at a community college or start up a part time consulting business linked to his/her area of expertise, then that would be an example of bridge employment. Of course there is often nothing precluding the individual from first engaging in phased retirement and then engaging in bridge employment.

The primary antecedents and consequences of bridge employment are just starting to become better known. For example, Wang, Zhan, Liu, and Shultz (2008), using a large nationally representative sample with longitudinal data, found that individual attributes (e.g., age, education level, health status, financial situation), job related psychological variables (e.g., work stress, job satisfaction), family related variables (e.g., marital status, marital quality), and retirement planning related variables (e.g., thoughts regarding retirement), all impacted whether or not an individual engaged in bridge employment versus retiring, and for the former, the type of bridge employment engaged in (i.e., career versus non-career bridge employment). In a follow-up study using the same data set, the same authors (this time as Zhan et al., 2009) examined consequences associated with various forms of bridge employment. The results of their analyses indicated that engaging in either career related or non-career related bridge employment was associated with fewer major diseases (e.g., heart disease, cancer, lung disease) and functional impairment (e.g., difficulty bathing, dressing, climbing stairs) compared to those who fully retired. In addition, those who engaged in career bridge employment also experience significantly better mental health outcomes (e.g., fewer depressive symptoms) compared to either full retirement or non-career bridge employment. These results are particularly noteworthy in that they were based on longitudinal data that controlled for prior physical and mental health status.

Two other recent studies also looked at the antecedents of bridge employment. First, Pengcharoen and Shultz (2010) found that work related factors of job involvement and schedule flexibility, as well as the nonwork related factors of certainty of retirement plans, attitudes toward retirement, and job seeking self-efficacy all distinguished the various employment statuses (e.g., completely retired, partly retirement, and not retired at all) of older workers over a ten-year period. Meanwhile, Gobeski and Beehr (2009) found that retirees who had skills specifically related to their career job were more likely to work in a career-related bridge job than to fully retire or to engage in a bridge job that was not related to their careers. In addition, retirees who previously held career jobs with intrinsically motivating job characteristics were more likely to engage in a career-related bridge job than to retire fully, and retirees who had experienced work strain in their career job were more likely to engage in a bridge job not related to their former career than to engage in a career bridge job. Thus, it is clear that a wide variety of individual, job related, and family related variables combine to influence bridge employment decisions, as well as bridge employment outcomes.

Central to this chapter is how HWI may impact the bridge employment decision, as well as the outcomes or consequences of engaging in bridge employment. Snir and Harpaz (2012) note that the predictors of HWI include background factors (e.g., gender, parenthood, education level), external predictors (e.g., basic financial need, employer demands), as well as internal factors (e.g., an addiction to work, passion for work). Many of these same predictors also impact bridge employment decisions (Gobeski & Beehr, 2009; Wang et al., 2008; Wang et al., 2009). Snir and Harpaz also noted that HWI consists of both a time dimension (e.g., how *much* you work) as well as an effort dimension (e.g., how *hard* you work). When older workers choose to engage in bridge employment, they are making a conscious decision to reduce how much they work, but not necessarily how hard they work. For older workers who continue to use their talents in their work, they remain engaged and invest the needed time to accomplish important results. In fact, some individuals who make the transition from a hectic career job to bridge employment may even find they are able to be more focused without the competing demands that often come with full time positions. For example, Kim and Feldman (2000) found that professors at research universities who opted to engage in an early retirement program found that they enjoyed teaching more than they would have thought, and were more heavily invested in the teaching role than prior to beginning the early retirement program (e.g., engaging in bridge employment).

Most important for the present discussion are the two major types of HWI, namely situational (e.g., employer directed, financial needs-based) and dispositional (e.g., workaholism, work devotion). While both situational and dispositional HWI may impact bridge employment and retirement decisions, dispositional HWI is likely to have the longer and stronger impact on the outcomes associated with retirement and/or engaging in bridge employment. For example, a situational factor (e.g., a sudden increase in work load imposed on an older worker toward the end of her career) may influence her to decide to retire and engage in bridge employment or dispositional factor (e.g., work devotion may lead to staying with an employer by engaging in bridge employment) may influence an older worker to engage in bridge employment. However, notice that in the case of situational HWI the impetus was negative (e.g., feeling forced out). Conversely, when the precipitator for engaging in bridge employment is dispositional, the impetus is of a positive nature (e.g., the desire to stay connected with the current employer and use their talents to accomplish important results). Thus, the disposition impetus to engage in bridge employment is likely to be more positive and facilitate the health and well-being of the older worker compared to the situational impetus.

When examining dispositional forms of HWI it is important to clearly distinguish HWI from conceptually related, but somewhat distinct, concepts such as work engagement, work enthusiasm, work centrality, job involvement, work enjoyment, and job satisfaction. While all of these concepts share some common themes or components, the two key dimensions of heavy time and effort investment in work are key distinguishing factors that differentiate HWI from these other conceptually related constructs. As a result, when looking at the unique influence of dispositional HWI on retirement and bridge employment decisions, it is important to focus on these distinguishing factors of heavy time and effort investment. By its nature, bridge employment typically involves a reduction in both time and effort (both physical and mental) investment in work. However, dispositional HWI individuals may have a more difficult time imposing these reductions than either situational HWI or non-HWI individuals. In fact, Snir and Harpaz (2012) note, "Moreover, when unemployed or retired, they [dispositional heavy work investors] may need more psychological counseling" (p. 239).

Snir and Harpaz (2012) also discuss the outcomes of HWI. First, they note that HWI can result in positive, mixed, or negative outcomes. In addition, these effects or outcomes can be short, intermediate, or long term. Finally, the outcomes can have their influence at multiple levels including at the individual (e.g., health, work satisfaction), family (e.g., experienced work–family conflict), and/or work (e.g., productivity) levels. Thus, the nature of the outcomes associated with HWI may in turn influence both individuals' decisions regarding retirement and bridge employment (both whether to engage in bridge employment, and if so, what types of bridge employment to engage in), as well as one's adjustment to such decisions.

In a recent theoretical paper on adjustment to retirement, Wang, Henkens, and van Solinge (2011) note that, "Retirement from work is one of the major life course transitions in late adult life" (p. 204). Wang et al. conclude that a resource-based dynamic perspective is the best way to predict and understand individuals' adjustment to retirement. The resources they discussed included physical, cognitive, emotional, motivational, financial, and social resources that the person transitioning through retirement has access to. To the extent that older workers approaching retirement are heavy work investors, such resources will interact with other key factors (e.g., job attachment, organizational climate, psychological resilience) to impact how well they transition through and adjust to retirement.

For example, an older worker with a strong work ethic and organizational member role perception (which is common in HWI individuals) is likely going to have a more difficult time transitioning to the family member and community member roles that become more prominent in retirement compared to an individual who finds their job to be burdensome or overly stressful. In the latter case, retirement often serves as a reprieve from an undesirable work situation. However, for older workers who are work devoted and have found opportunities to engage their talents on a regular basis at work, they could continue to make investments in terms of time and effort to use their talents to achieve outcomes they value for their families, communities, and themselves (Seligman, 2002). As those individuals retire, they will be more successful in reaping the benefits of their HWI and have fewer negative health and relationship outcomes when compared to their counterparts who were workaholics and lacked a clear understanding of how their talents can be used to achieve important outcomes in retirement.

Directions for Future Research

Below we discuss several potential avenues for future research to better understand how HWI, bridge employment, and retirement interrelate.

- *Integrate the HWI and bridge employment literatures.* The work force continues to age globally. This demographic reality has implications for both individuals and organizational leaders. Specifically, organizational leaders spend billions of dollars annually on training and development processes to facilitate the development of employees and ensure that they possess the skills that optimize job performance (Noe, 2008). In turn, individuals who have made a heavy investment in both time (to learn, develop, and refine job related talents) and effort (going beyond the standard requirements to develop new processes and approaches to accelerate their performance), may have more desire to engage in bridge employment as they transition into retirement. Further research needs to be conducted to understand the differences in outcomes for the individuals who are workaholics (addicted to the activities associated with their work) versus those who are work devoted (and seek to have bridge employment tasks and projects that link directly to their talents and allow them to do their best work because it is their passion). Specifically, are those who are classified as workaholics willing to take a wider range of bridge employment opportunities offered by their organization while those who are work devoted seek out specific bridge employment opportunities that are congruent with their talents? As a result, they may not accept bridge employment jobs with their current organization if they can find tasks and projects that they are passionate about at another organization.

  Since many organizational leaders are not proactive in addressing the knowledge management needs of their organization, can bridge employment be used as a process to gather the needed information from older workers before they retire (Chaudhuri & Ghosh, 2012)? Beyond establishing documentation, further research can be conducted on the effectiveness of older workers as a coach or mentor to assist new/younger workers in taking over their positions. This can be particularly important for organizational leaders to consider in important knowledge positions and client relationships (where bringing in a "new person" and transiting the long term relationship with a client can be a challenging process).
- *Differences in engagement between organizational leaders and HWI older employees.* Given the importance of external reinforcement and the concern about others' perceptions for those who express

workaholic forms of HWI, the impact of those dispositional tendencies on reactions of their managers needs to be more fully researched. Specifically, those individuals who are reliant on external reinforcement from their managers may be viewed as more "high maintenance" and difficult to manage. While they may be willing to work hard and invest the time, their need for approval and attention may be qualitatively different when compared to those who could be categorized as work devoted. Those individuals who are more self-aware of their own talents and know where and how they can contribute most to achieving organizational and team goals may be easier to manage and develop over time (Cappelli & Novelli, 2010). Also, they may be more efficient in completing their work in terms of the required time and resources invested since they are working within their area of talent and have developed skills and can apply their knowledge more consistently to achieve high levels of performance (Buckingham & Clifton, 2001). Further research is needed to identify if managers respond differently to HWI older workers who are workaholics versus those who can be classified as work devoted.

- *Examine the longitudinal effects of disposition and situation on HWI individuals' retirement transition and decision making process.* Additional research is also needed to examine the significant work and nonwork related events that impact the career development and progression of HWI individuals over time (Damman, Henkens, & Kalmijn, 2013). For example, are there specific challenging life events that occur (e.g., parenthood, health problems with family members, financial challenges) that can lead individuals to change their dispositional HWI type from workaholic to work devoted (or vice versa) over time? Which life events impact individuals in a significant way so that they re-evaluate their dispositional tendencies and make changes that result in them evolving from work devoted to workaholic? Can significant negative events trigger those individuals who are passionate about their work to become workaholics? Can situational factors lead a work devoted person away from the type of jobs that use their talents and lead them to make choices to engage in work primarily for financial reasons with little concern for their talents and passions? Viewed longitudinally, for those individuals who become workaholics for the purposes of making money once they retire, do they purposefully and consciously make choices when they retire to engage in work and activities that utilize their talents again and for which they feel passion? These are important questions to ask in order to better understand the impact on individuals who are work devoted versus workaholic in terms of their perceived effectiveness in transitioning to retirement.

References

Adams, G. A., & Rau, B. L. (2011). Putting off tomorrow to do what you want today: Retirement planning. *American Psychologist, 66,* 180–192.

Arthur, M. B., & Rousseau, D. M. (1996). *The boundaryless career: A new employment principle for a new organizational era.* New York: Oxford University Press.

Ashford, B. (2001). *Role transitions in organizational life: An identity-based perspective.* Mahwah, NJ: Lawrence Erlbaum.

Atchley, R. C. (1989). A continuity theory of normal aging. *Gerontologist, 29,* 183–190.

Atchley, R. C. (1999). *Continuity and adaptation in aging: Creating positive experiences.* Baltimore, MD: The Johns Hopkins University Press.

Baltes, B. B., & Rudolph, C. W. (2013). The theory of selection, optimization, and compensation. In M. Wang (Ed.), *The Oxford handbook of retirement* (Ch 7, pp. 88–101). New York: Oxford University Press.

Baltes, P. B., Staudinger, U. M., & Lindenberger, U. (1999). Lifespan psychology: Theory and application to intellectual functioning. *Annual Review of Psychology, 50,* 471–507.

Buckingham, M., & Clifton, D. O. (2001). *Now, discover your strengths.* New York: The Free Press.

Cahill, K. E., Giandrea, M. D., & Quinn, J. F. (2006). Retirement patterns from career employment. *Gerontologist, 46,* 514–523.

Cahill, K. E., Giandrea, M. D., & Quinn, J. F. (2013). Bridge employment. In M. Wang (Ed.), *The Oxford handbook of retirement* (Ch 19, pp. 293–310). New York: Oxford University Press.

Cappelli, P., & Novelli, B. (2010). *Managing the older worker: How to prepare for the new organizational order.* Boston, MA: Harvard Business Review Press.

Chaudhuri, S., & Ghosh, R. (2012). Reverse mentoring: A social exchange tool for keeping the boomers engaged and millennials committed. *Human Resource Development Review, 11,* 55–76.

Csikszentmihalyi, M. (1990). *Flow: The psychology of optimal experience.* New York: Harper & Row.

Damman, M., Henkens, K., & Kalmijn, M. (2013). Late-career work disengagement: The role of proximity to retirement and career experiences. *Journals of Gerontology, Series B: Psychological Sciences and Social Sciences, 68,* 455–463.

DePinto, R. (2003). *Emerging leaders research survey summary report.* Center for Creative Leadership, Greensboro, NC. Downloaded on May 14, 2013 from www.ccl.org/leadership/pdf/research/elsummary.pdf

Ekerdt, D. J. (1986). The busy ethic: Moral continuity between work and retirement. *The Gerontologist, 26,* 239–244.

Elder, G. H. (1995). The life course paradigm: Social change and individual development. In P. Moen, G. H. Elder, & K. Luscher (Eds.), *Examining lives in contexts: Perspectives on the ecology of human development* (pp. 101–139). Washington, DC: American Psychological Association.

Freedman, M. (2007). *Encore: Finding work that matters in the second half of life.* New York: Public Affairs, Perseus Book Group.

Gobeski, K. T., & Beehr, T. A. (2009). How retirees work: Predictors of different types of bridge employment. *Journal of Organizational Behavior, 30*, 401–425.

Goulston, M. (2013). *How to give a meaningful "thank you"*. Harvard Business Review, HBR Blog Network. Downloaded on May 20, 2013 from http://blogs.hbr.org/cs/2013/02/how_to_give_a_meaningful_thank.html

Hall, D. T. (2004). The protean career: A quarter century journey. *Journal of Vocational Behavior, 65*, 1–13.

Haralalka, A., & Tung, L. C. (2012). *Why strengths matter in training*. Gallup Management Journal, New York, NY. Downloaded on May 14, 2013 from http://businessjournal.gallup.com/content/153341/Why-Strengths-Matter-Training.aspx

Kanfer, R., & Ackerman, P. L. (2004). Aging, adult development and work motivation. *Academy of Management Review, 29*, 440–458.

Kim, S., & Feldman, D. C. (2000). Working in retirement: The antecedents of bridge employment and its consequences for quality of life in retirement. *Academy of Management Journal, 43*, 1195–1210.

Kooij, D. T. A., Guest, D. E., Clinton, M., Knight, T., Jansen, P. G. W., & Dikkers, J. S. E. (2013). How the impact of HR practices on employee well-being and performance changes with age. *Human Resource Management Journal, 23*, 18–35.

Mainiero, L. A., & Sullivan, S. E. (2005). Kaleidoscope careers: An alternate explanation for the opt-out revolution. *Academy of Management Executive, 19*, 106–123.

Merrill Lynch (2013, May). *Americans' perspectives on new retirement realities and the longevity bonus: A 2013 Merrill Lynch Retirement Study, conducted in partnership with Age Wave*. New York: Merrill Lynch Wealth Management. Downloaded May 6, 2013 from http://wealthmanagement.ml.com/publish/content/application/pdf/GWMOL/2013_Merrill_Lynch_Retirement_Study.pdf

Metlife Mature Market Institute (2006, March). *Living longer, working longer: The changing landscape of the aging workforce – A Metlife study*. Metlife Mature Market Institute, Westport, CT. Downloaded March 2, 2013 from www.metlife.com/assets/cao/mmi/publications/studies/mmi-studies-living-longer.pdf

Metlife Mature Market Institute (2012, April). *Transitioning into retirement: The Metlife study of Baby Boomers at 65*. Metlife Mature Market Institute, Westport, CT. Downloaded March 2, 2013 from www.metlife.com/assets/cao/mmi/publications/studies/2012/studies/mmi-transitioning-retirement.pdf

Noe, R. A. (2008). *Employee training and development*. New York: McGraw-Hill Irwin.

Pengcharoen, C., & Shultz, K. S. (2010). The influences on bridge employment decisions. *International Journal of Manpower, 31*, 322–336.

Seligman, M. E. P. (2002). *Authentic happiness*. New York: The Free Press.

Shultz, K. S., & Wang, M. (2011). Psychological perspectives on the changing nature of retirement. *The American Psychologist, 66*, 170–179.

Snir, R., & Harpaz, I. (2012). Beyond workaholism: Towards a general model of heavy work investment. *Human Resource Management Review, 22*, 232–243.

von Bonsdorff, M. E., & Ilmarinen, J. (2013). Continuity theory and retirement. In M. Wang (Ed.), *The Oxford handbook of retirement* (Ch 6, pp. 73–87). New York: Oxford University Press.

von Bonsdorff, M. E., Shultz, K. S., Leskinen, E., & Tansky, J. (2009). The choice between retirement and bridge employment: A continuity theory and life course perspective. *International Journal of Aging and Human Development, 69,* 79–100.

Wagner, R., & Hartner, J. K. (2006). *12: The Elements of Great Managing.* New York: Gallup Press.

Wang, M., Adams, G. A., Beehr, T. A., & Shultz, K. S. (2009). Career issues at the end of one's career: Bridge employment and retirement. In S. G. Baugh & S. E. Sullivan (Eds.), *Maintaining focus, energy, and options over the life span* (pp. 135–162). Charlotte, NC: Information Age.

Wang, M., Henkens, K., & van Solinge, H. (2011). Retirement adjustment: A review of theoretical and empirical advancements. *American Psychologist, 66,* 204–213.

Wang, M., Olson, D. A., & Shultz, K. S. (2013). *Mid and late career issues: An integrative perspective.* New York: Routledge Academic Press.

Wang, M., & Shultz, K. S. (2010). Employee retirement: A review and recommendations for future investigation. *Journal of Management, 36,* 172–206.

Wang, M., Zhan, Y., Liu, S., & Shultz, K. S. (2008). Antecedents of bridge employment: A longitudinal investigation. *Journal of Applied Psychology, 93,* 818–830

Wrzesniewski, A., Berg, J. M., & Dutton, J. E. (2010). Turn the job you have into the job you want. *Harvard Business Review, 88,* 114–117.

Zhan, Y., Wang, M., Liu, S., & Shultz, K. S. (2009). Bridge employment and retirees' health: A longitudinal investigation. *Journal of Occupational Health Psychology, 14,* 374–389.

14

WORK ADDICTS' ATTRIBUTIONS ABOUT COMPANY-SUPPLIED SMARTPHONES

Gayle Porter

Introduction

The importance of quality human resource (HR) management is not merely a matter of establishing the right practices. Research has shown that positive outcomes depend on how those practices are interpreted by employees. If employees assign meaning to HR actions and decisions that are contrary to that intended by the organization, it may lead to employee reactions that are contrary to that organization's strategy and related objectives. Supplying smartphones to employees is one current issue and one decision shown in recent research to exact a variety of interpretations. While work addicts—identified here through measure of perfectionism—did not show significant variation from other employees in larger statistical analysis, finer analysis of specific sub-categories of responses gives some suggestion for topics that are worth additional research attention.

People and Performance

A number of scholars have written about the importance of the human factor in creating a competitive market advantage—with emphasis on either individual strengths (human capital) or the ties among a network of employees (social capital). Pfeffer drew popular attention to the link between people and performance in 1998, and numerous authors have built on the idea since then. In addition to recommendations for action by immediate managers, the HR function within an organization creates a focus on people-related policies and practices that can either facilitate or hinder organizational performance.

General advice often stresses the importance of a strategic approach and clear matching of HR practices to the overall business strategy (e.g.,

Ulrich and Brockbank, 2005). Overall firm performance was linked to HR practices when employees had a common, shared interpretation of actions (in the desired direction to match strategy), creating a strong organizational climate (Bowen & Ostroff, 2004). Along with the importance of an overall coherent and supportive policy structure, comparison of how employees perceive very specific HR decisions and practices also has shown to be important in past research. For example, customer-contact employees who believed pay is handled fairly were more productive and displayed more prosocial behaviors in both prescribed and extra-role behavior (Chebat, Babin, & Killias, 2002).

Attributions about HR Practices

In contrast to the positive potential referenced earlier, when there is variation in attributions about HR practices, the impact shows in employee attitudes and behaviors and through to customer satisfaction. Nishi, Lepak, and Schneider (2008) explored these relationships, looking at the firm's management as sometimes being a passive recipient of external forces—for example, actions being taken solely for the reason of union compliance. Employees' interpretation of this as the cause for a practice would be categorized as their having made an external attribution, the organization's action driven by an external causal factor. Internal attributions, more relevant to this discussion, are not driven directly by an external body such as a union. Decisions and actions stemming from internal causation can be interpreted by employees as focused either on strategic goals or on an employee-oriented philosophy. Additionally, a particular practice can be seen as either commitment-focused or control-focused.

In the Nishi et al. (2008) reporting, these dimensions of internal attributions are offered in a 4×4 matrix. For example, based on an HR strategic emphasis, the commitment-focused attribution could be a commitment to service quality; or, the strategic emphasis from a control-focused perspective could be cost reduction. The employee-oriented philosophy along with commitment-focused action would express concern for employee well-being, while that philosophy and a control-focus would suggest exploiting employees. This is reminiscent of a 1995 study of 456 hospital workers in which employees viewed the use of contingent workers as a decision based on either gaining staffing flexibility without overburdening the full-time workers (concern for regular employees), or cost savings by avoiding payment of benefits and severance packages (Porter, 1995). In that research, the organization's motive was crossed with perceptions regarding the quality of the contingent workers, and examined for ethical implications.

Here, the organization's motives are represented in two comparisons, which when placed on vertical and horizontal axes create the four quadrants shown in Figure 14.1. This adaptation of the Nishi et al. matrix emphasizes the organization's intended message and shows the likely climate outcomes, adding notations on interpretations related to technology adoption. Particularly when looking across a general population (i.e., not in one organization) it also seems intuitive that individuals might have more negative reaction to some combinations as they are described.

Starting from the basis of social attribution theory (Fiske & Taylor, 1991) and continuing into HR study of attitudes and behavior (Huselid, 1995; Jackson & Schuler, 1995), research has long shown employees make attributions about the company's intention based on particular decisions. In spite of the strength potential of a strong climate, wherein perceptions are shared among employees (Bowen & Ostroff, 2004), the Nishii et al. (2008) research approach indicated that not only can the attributions vary but, also, they may differentially impact attitudes and behaviors. Nishii's study highlighted here suggests emphasis on individual differences with implications of impact on overall organizational outcomes.

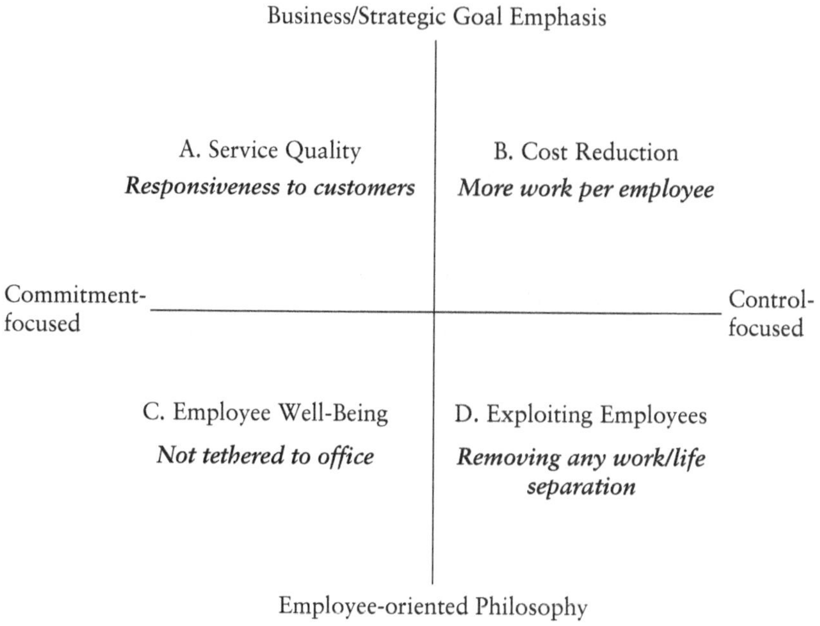

Figure 14.1 Adaptation of typology from Nishii et al. (2008) with addition of notes on application to technology adoption

Decision to Supply Smartphones

Global business increasingly requires some degree of monitoring, if not involvement, around the clock. Customers, suppliers, and business partners are spread across multiple time-zones. Problem situations, as well as routine decision-making, require attention beyond the traditional end of day. Technology allows a means to address these competitive demands, without spending 24 hours a day at the office. Smartphones allow for calls, text messages, email, and internet linking to information of the company and beyond. If employee use of smartphones can facilitate better ease of operations, one decision on the table for many companies is whether it would be advantageous to *supply* smartphones to employees. The offer of a company-supplied phone (or lack of offer) is a decision employees will interpret in different ways. Further, as described above, that interpretation may or may not match the intent with which the company made their decision.

We can use the Nishii et al. framework for internal attributions to consider this technology adoption decision. Within Figure 14.1, there are added notations in italics to show how this would translate into consideration of such mobile technology. In quadrant A, the strategic goal combined with a commitment-focus has been identified as service quality. Employees with smartphones are capable of being responsive to customers' questions and/or problems even when away from the office. Shifting to quadrant B, strategic goal combined with control-focus, reflects that anytime/anywhere situation as one in which cost reduction is accomplished through expectation of more hours worked per employee. Quadrant B might also cover efficiencies gained through use of this tool, but research has shown that smartphone users tend to work more hours than non-users and often report that their hours have increased since they began use (Porter, 2009).

Quadrant C, combining an employee-oriented philosophy with commitment-focus, is the concern for employee well-being. Because a smartphone enables handling work tasks without being in a specified location, this can free up the employee for family situations, which might range from emergency doctors' appointments to simply having the freedom to be present at children's sporting events or school performances. This consideration for the employee's life outside of work could be viewed as a very positive contribution to personal well-being, even if there are occasional interruptions of personal time that accompany this new flexibility.

When that employee-oriented philosophy is combined with a control-focus, the flexibility shifts from being a benefit to the employee to a situation in which the individual is considered to always be on call for work needs. The interruptions are not occasional but, rather, a persistent assumption of being not just available but actively involved in work at all hours. There no longer is any time set aside for family only, no separation between what used to be office hours and clearly defined non-work time.

Although the Nishii et al. research (2008) identified these as fairly discrete categories, the application of their attribution differences to use of smartphones provides a good example of how very similar information can be the foundation for differing attributions. For example, a company might offer to supply smartphones to a specific group of employees, with message content that references being able to respond to customer needs whether in the office or at another time/place; the customer will not have the frustration of being referred to a new contact person, and happier customers lead to continuing business. This message can be seen as driven by concern for service quality (responsiveness) or cost reduction (no need for back-up personnel as the customer can reach the primary contact person at any time). It suggests there may be freedom of time and place during the workday but also hints that the primary contact person must always be available.

In earlier research, most people reported that smartphone usage made them more productive (Porter, 2009). One subject in the study said that he had not become more productive—he was always a highly productive worker and the smartphone just made it easier for him to be so. However, the vast majority claimed higher productivity even though, as referenced previously, many of them had also increased their working hours. Clearly, there are differences across individuals as to how a specific decision and related outcomes will be interpreted. In the usage applied here, the quadrants show some amount of potential overlap rather than being discrete categories.

Bowen and Ostroff (2004) pointed out that employees look for consistency in HR messages—consistency with the organization's value-demonstrative actions, with other HR practices that should fit with the current consideration, and with the experience in that organization over time. While the general culture of the organization will provide some commonality, each employee's personal situation has likely also created slightly different experiences across time. Whether a decision to supply smartphones is interpreted as shown in one quadrant or another, thus, might differ from person to person based on one or two individual past experiences.

Another individual difference could be personality. Lane and Manner (2010) demonstrated a relationship between some personality traits related to ownership and use of smartphones. It might be inferred from their results that personality would also influence individuals' reaction to their employer furnishing a smartphone for their use. Other individual differences might also come into play, and there is much opportunity for research investigating what personal factors would be most relevant. If the attributions being made are not consistent among employees and/or not the impressions desired by the company, HR could enhance performance outcomes by identifying the reasons and taking corrective action. If a particular group of employees is not in sync, it would be beneficial to know that.

One group of interest would be those addicted to their work. The recognition of tech-addiction has led to speculation that technology and work are mutually reinforcing addiction patterns (Porter & Kakabadse, 2006). Any adoptions of additional technology in the workplace, therefore, would suggest potential outcome differences comparing work addicts to other employees. This study provided a chance to explore whether this potential for later outcome differences might also be reflected in employees' interpretation of the company decision to supply or not supply smartphones.

Work Addicts' Attribution Tendencies

Researchers have begun giving more attention to work intensification (e.g., Green, 2004), the tendency to expect not only more work generally from employees but also greater amounts work within the same period of time. Within a related study of heavy work investment, Snir and Harpaz (2009) explain that this increase in both time and effort can be situational or dispositional. Further, the dispositional aspect has subtypes, one being the negative variation referred to as work addiction or workaholism (used here as synonymous terms). Without digressing into the debates over terminology, the discussion here will focus on work addiction as an extreme of heavy work investment and one that stems from an internal drive—a dispositional difference, rather than situational or external demands (Harpaz & Snir, 2003; Mudrack, 2004; Porter, 1996; Schaufeli, Taris, & van Rhenen, 2008; Schaufeli, Taris, & Bakker, 2008).

The essence of what makes a workaholic was captured in the phrase from Burke's (2006) chapter title, "It's not how hard you work buy why and how you work hard." Departing from that to a fairly cynical view of outcomes, the remaining question might be, "why should the company care?" Hard-working employees are viewed as an asset and organizational leadership may not want to question that too deeply. Burke (1999) identified four work outcomes that correlated to workaholism: intent to quit (higher in workaholics), work satisfaction, career satisfaction, and future career prospects (these last three being lower in workaholics).

When the long hours and intensity about work are taken at face value, an employer might have less concern about the individual's satisfaction and future prospects than the fact that it appears the workaholic individual is out-performing others on standard performance metrics. The only one of the four outcomes in Burke's results that would cause immediate alarm might be the intent to quit. However, Schaufeli, Taris, and van Rhenen (2008) found workaholics were committed to the organization, similar to engaged workers. This research was an extensive examination to compare burnout, engagement, and workaholism. Whereas burnout and engagement were revealed as opposites, workaholism shared some related features with each of the other two. For example, the similarities with burnout extend to negative outcomes such as health issues, which would be an organizational concern tied to both attendance and expense of health benefits (see also Porter, 2006 on patterns of workaholic health experience).

The similarity to burnout also appeared in relation to poor social functioning, often less of a concern for the organization's managers on a daily basis. As individuals, managers might sympathize with an employee's disintegrating marriage and social life but, typically, not to the extent of lowering work demands or lessening deadline pressure. Many managers rose to their current position through workaholic habits and, while sympathetic, consider these sacrifices the unfortunate cost of career success—their own and their subordinates' following behind.

An earlier paper to highlight concerns from the organization's perspective focused on the typical patterns of addiction that would impair workplace interactions long before the onset of burnout (Porter, 1996). Although many standard measures of performance, including long hours on the job, would suggest a positive situation from the organization's viewpoint, the (work) addict's high need for control, inability to share/delegate work, and an escalating need to prove worth through work accomplishments could do more damage in the long run. A workaholic will create demand for more work (Schaufeli et al., 2008), even to the extent of allowing or even causing crisis situations (Porter, 1996) and be a source of stress among other workers battling to work with—or around—the workaholic's addiction behaviors (Porter, 2001).

The added question for discussion here is whether workaholics, as a group, will display identifiable attitude differences that might also be of concern to the employer. In particular, negativity can be not only detrimental to that one individual's performance but also expressed to others and can become a factor in group functioning. The proliferation of social media opportunities broadens the impact of expressed dissatisfaction so that it is no longer just a concern for the immediate work group and can even extend easily beyond the boundaries of that organization. The example pursued here is whether workaholics cluster on the type of attribution they make as to why their organization does or does not supply smartphones. Both decisions carry the opportunity for negative interpretations.

As with any research question, expectations should be based on existing knowledge. Schaufeli et al. (2008) reported one unexpected finding in their research, that workaholism was associated with reported lack of job resources. Perhaps workaholics are drawn to organizations that have sparse resources (providing more needed work), or they are simply more inclined to negative attributions based on the feeling that no one else shares their sense of heightened responsibility (Porter, 1996). Referring back to Figure 14.1, workaholics are often characterized as having a high need for control, which could result in their projecting that tendency onto others and placing their attributions on the right hand side—the more negative views—in this comparison.

Drawing from a larger study on use of smartphones, this was explored through analysis of responses on an open-ended question in which respondents commented on why their company did or did not supply smartphones. The total sample was 627 full-time employed subjects, of which 271 (43 percent) reported being current users of smartphones. Of those users, 241 (89%) were using phones supplied by their employer. In this study, a four-item scale of perfectionism was used as proxy for workaholism. It is worth noting that not all perfectionists are workaholics, but most workaholics show strong perfectionist tendencies, and this scale has been used as a work addiction proxy in previous studies (cf. Porter, 2006).

Items in the perfectionism scale reflect heightened responsibility for work such as, "most people are not as aware as I am of the need for attention to detail," and "others cannot work as well as I do." This perfectionist measure was not correlated with age, gender, or education, but was significantly related to (1) hours of active use of smartphone, (2) the belief that use of a smartphone enhances performance, (3) having been told by others that they sometimes get "carried away" in use of smartphone (although not significantly related to own belief of whether they get carried away).

When those using company-supplied smartphones were asked, "What is the strongest message being relayed by your company in supplying smartphones to employees?" The responses clustered into these general comments:

- it's a tool for assigned job tasks—referencing efficiency, productivity, or contact (corresponding to quadrant A in Figure 14.1, plus some suggestion of quadrant C when contact included both with customers and with boss, central office or service departments)
- to make one ALWAYS accessible/available/aware (emphasis suggestive of quadrant B or D)
- so can work all the time (quadrant B or D)
- make employees' lives easier (quadrant C)
- indicates status/level or importance of particular job function (not relevant to comparisons in Figure 14.1).

Those whose companies did not supply smartphones were similarly asked, "What is the strongest message being relayed by your company in not supplying . . . ?" and elicited responses in these categories:

- not needed/appropriate for the work (implications for quadrant A, as seemingly based on something of this type and does not apply in their current organization)
- cost issues (quadrant A or B, in that cost would exceed gain)
- would be bad for employees (quadrant D)
- give other support instead (not clear fit to Figure 14.1).

Note that these categorizations of comments were assigned prior to considering comparisons from Nishii et al. (2008), but later reviewed for the application of comment clusters to those quadrants. However, a high proportion of them can be related to the elements differentiated in Figure 14.1, showing general fit to broad consideration of HR practices and employee attributions.

More about Work Addicts and Smartphone Use

Some people have developed addictive behaviors related to use of technology, for example the need to have email always available or a drive to continually be adding enhancements to existing devices, beyond what is driven by actual need. According to Porter and Kakabadse (2006), "overindulgence in one behavior often occurs alongside another addiction" (p. 541), or one may serve as a trigger to a second addiction (Miller, 1980). For example, excess drinkers often also smoke heavily, and smokers tend to drink a lot of coffee. As technology becomes increasingly ubiquitous in the workplace, excess work and use of technology will become even more tightly linked. The two addictions would be mutually reinforcing. Work addicts can use the technology to facilitate around the clock work; technology addicts can use work demands to justify always being connected to their devices.

From this perspective, one might expect workaholics to want the facilitating technology and, perhaps, make a more negative attribution, if they felt the company was withholding it. On the other hand, recalling the work of Schaufeli et al. (2008), workaholics might actually be—or maintain an attribution that they are—working in an organization that supplies less support. Although that situation may offer the added perception that the individual has to work harder to do the job without support, that condition benefits the workaholic indirectly, but might still be cause for negative comment.

Here is a strong example of what happens with even exploratory research, when the existing literature does not clearly define what the appropriate expectations would be. In studies of workaholism, there has long been debate over definition and measurement, and a number of efforts to show the universalism of the construct by extending study to cultures outside the US. While each piece of research adds valuable information to the overall phenomenon, the continual need to justify the topic for study has limited attention given to the vast branching of implications to workaholic behavior, especially in moving from the individuals' outcomes to those of direct and immediate concern to the companies where they work. Because there is less attention to specifics of organizational impact, researchers are still inferring what attitudes and resulting behaviors to expect.

In the exploration of this data, respondents with scale scores of 3.5 to 5.0 (N = 278) were counted as high in perfectionism; others (N = 349) were low to moderate in perfectionism. Running correlation with these two identified groups, there was no clear difference in the overall categorized comments. There were no notable differences in where the high perfectionists work when comparing size of company or scope of operations (multinational, national, regional, local). Again, high perfectionism did not relate to age, gender, or education.

In the full sample (N = 627), 271 of the respondents were smartphone users (43 percent); of those users, 149 (55 percent of users) had phones supplied by their company. The number of respondents making up the high perfectionism group was 278, of which 114 were smartphone users (41 percent); of those users, 61 (54 percent) had phones supplied by their company. As shown in Table 14.1, the moderate to low perfectionism group percentages were very similar to those of the high perfectionists. On this one measure, pertaining specifically to being supplied smartphones, the previous research observation that workaholics tend to work in situations with fewer resources was not upheld.

Rather than abandon the data after lack of summary statistical results, a more qualitative analysis revealed sub-topics of interest that may be useful in formulating future research. Looking beyond just the categorizations, a small difference was noted in the cost-related comments about

Table 14.1 Comparison of Users and Proportions of Company Supplied Based on Perfectionism Scale Scores

	Total Sample	*Smartphone Users*	*Proportion Supplied*
High Perfectionists	278	114 (41%)	61 (54% of users)
Mod-Low Perfectionists	347	157 (45%)	88 (56% of users)
Total*	622	271 (44%)	149 (55% of users)

*differences in sample total due to missing responses

why a company does not supply phones. Fifty-four people answered with reference to cost or expense issues, 25 as high perfectionists and 29 low to moderate. Fairly equal numbers responded with phrases such as "not cost-justified," that the "company can't afford" to supply, or very general cost references. As shown in Table 14.2, there are two types of comments that tended to separate high perfectionists from others. One is the brief but emphatic (use of exclamation point) note that the company is "too cheap!" While it is only two subjects, this harsher style of comment on lack of willingness to supply phones came only from the high perfectionists (here representing the most likely workaholics). This might be the venting of frustration over a company policy that is hindering indulgence in technology as a facilitating second addiction.

The reverse is true of the five people who attributed the company's decision not to supply phones to it being the employees' responsibility to pay. No one in the high perfectionism group expressed that this was the employees' responsibility—all five were in the low to moderate perfectionism group. This might be a belief that the main benefit of having a phone is convenience for the employee in either personal freedom or ease of meeting job requirements, the commitment-focused side of Figure 14.1. As earlier speculated, workaholics (generally high perfectionists) might tend toward control-focused ideas, so that cost issues would not be interpreted this way. Additionally, if perfectionists believe they are more conscientious and capable than other people, they might feel they are owed more by the company and be less inclined toward the idea of paying for their own smartphone.

Another interesting comparison can be made on the responses regarding companies' not supplying phones because it's better for the employees. Only seven people in the total sample referenced employee benefit

Table 14.2 Workaholic Smartphone Users' Cost-Related Attributions for the Company Not Supplying Smartphones

	High Perfectionists	*Low-Moderate Perfectionists*
Not cost-justified	5	4
Company can't afford	6	6
Company doesn't want to pay	1	1
Employees' responsibility to pay	–	5
Too cheap!	2	–
General cost references	11	13
Total responding	*25*	*29*

as a reason not to supply phones, but six of the seven were in the high perfectionist group. Of those six respondents, four identified their rank as executive/officer/top level; one self-identified as senior level (the next category) and one as a mid-level manager. High perfectionists were fairly equally represented across all organizational levels. So, the proportion of perfectionist top-level executives was not higher than the proportion at other organizational levels but, on this question, higher ranking people were strongly represented in both being high on perfectionism, as well as explaining this decision in terms of consideration for employee benefit. Little interpretation can be offered at this time as to why high perfectionists would claim a "not-supply" company decision is for employee benefit except, perhaps, that high perfectionists' control-orientation causes them to want employees on site, but they rationalize the decision in this way. More research on this question could illuminate whether there is, in fact, a common reasoning among work addicts and, if so, the basis of that reasoning.

Two additional questions on the survey reflect difference between high perfectionists and others. Considering the potential of exploiting employees by supplying smartphones (the right hand side of Figure 14.1), these two items were included to assess whether people felt pressured to accept a smartphone if the company supplied it. Anecdotally, people had confided prior to this research that they foresaw higher work requirements and elimination of any work/life separation as being the unavoidable outcomes of having a company-supplied phone but also felt they had to accept a phone, if offered, to protect their job and/or career. The first item related to this concern asked whether employees could decline the offer of a phone without jeopardizing their current job. Across the total sample, 72 people said no, one could not decline without jeopardizing their job. Seventy-one of those 72 people were in the high perfectionist group.

The second item, similarly, asked whether employees could decline an offer of a company-supplied smartphone without jeopardizing their promotion potential. In the total sample, 75 people said no; 67 of them were high on perfectionism. It is difficult to surmise why perfectionists/workaholics would be more inclined to say there was jeopardy attached to declining offer of a company-supplied phone. Possibly, it is simply laying the groundwork for continuing or building up excess work time. Although workaholics are driven by an inward desire to work, they respond to complaining friends and family with claims of outside pressures. Again, not all perfectionists gave this response, but the vast majority of those who reported perceived jeopardy were high perfectionists. Are they consciously building an excuse for more work? Is it an unconscious tendency to create greater work demands? Or, is something else entirely leading to this pattern? Because these subjects are from a general population and not a single company, the responses of job and career jeopardy could be accurate for the specific companies where these respondents are employed. If so, wouldn't this suggest a high number of the people working in that type of environment are high perfectionists? Schaef and Fassel, in 1988, considered the impact of self-selection in creating entire organizations of workaholics. When the people who choose not to share in the addictive patterns leave the organization, and other workaholics find it an attractive, enabling environment, the overall culture takes on that dysfunctional heavy work investment as the norm (Schaef & Fassel, 1988).

Although the individual comment categories contained small numbers and were, therefore, not conducive to elaborate statistical analysis, looking at shadings of emphasis within the categories revealed some interesting differences. New research with the specific goal of comparing workaholics to non-workaholics would likely result in slightly different categories of open-ended responses and create more meaningful examination of the attitudes that might be more common to people with this negative type of heavy work investment.

From the current exploration, there are few conclusions and each leads to additional questions. First, perfectionists seemingly gravitate to companies that are less likely to offer company-supplied smartphones. This might extent to supply of general resources. The remaining question is on what basis does this gravitation occur? Is it a conscious choice or one that happens without awareness? Second, only a handful of people said a "not-supply" decision was for the benefit of the employees, but nearly all of these were high-perfectionists and at high organizational level. Many questions would follow this observation. Is it a bogus reason offered by policy setters who really want to keep employees on-site and more under direct control? Are these high-ranking perfectionists sincere in this reasoning, based on their personal experience of excess work and the related sacrifices?

Another conclusion might relate to the initial results discussed previously—that perfectionists/workaholics may be slightly harsher in expressing cost restraints as reason for not supplying smartphones; or, at least those harsher in their comments fell into the perfectionist classification. Do perfectionists feel higher frustration levels at being denied technology advancements, or are they naturally harsher in criticisms based on their incredibly high standards for self and others?

At this point, the work is not developed enough to provide clear guidelines for practice, although it is hoped that practitioners might see enough to become interested in pursuing related work within their own organizations. In the coverage offered here, the subjects spanned multiple companies and industries across geographic boundaries. The type of survey discussed here provides some indication of what might be common among workaholics. However, in-depth work in a single organization would be needed to reveal whether that group constitutes a problem for that company to deal with in terms of alignment of employee attitudes with firm level strategy and operating philosophies. Only with organization-specific information can a specific HR department formulate new policies—or at least new discussions—around issues such as supplying new technology.

The Nishii et al. (2008) framework for attributions made about HR practices provided one framework from which to consider whether workaholics as a group share particular tendencies in making attributions. Others can be found as alternative bases for building discussions. Only a sampling of possible future research questions is offered here. The readers who immediately think of competing explanations have taken an important first step in developing a research agenda related to the workaholic extreme of heavy work investment.

References

Bowen, D. E. & Ostroff, C. (2004). Understanding HRM—firm performance linkages: The role of the "strength" of the HRM system. *Academy of Management Review, 29*(2), 203–221.

Burke, R. J. (1999). It's not how hard you work but how you work hard: Evaluating workaholism components. *International Journal of Stress Management, 6*(4), 225–239.

Burke, R. J. (2006). Workaholic types: It's not how hard you work buy why and how you work hard. In R. J. Burke (Ed.), *Research Companion to Working Time and Work Addiction* (pp. 173–192). Cheltenham: Edward Elgar.

Chebat, J., Babin, B., & Kollias, P. (2002). What makes contact employees perform? Reactions to employee perceptions of managerial practices. *International Journal of Bank Marketing, 20*(7), 325–332.

Green, F. (2004). Why has work effort become more intense? *Industrial Relations, 43*(4), 709–741.

Harpaz, I. & Snir, R. (2003). Workaholism: Its definition and nature. *Human Relations, 56*(3), 291–319.

Lane, W. & Manner, C. (2010). The impact of personality traits on smartphone ownership and use. *International Journal of Business and Social Science, 2*(17), 22–28.

Miller, P. M. (1980). Theoretical and practical issues in substance abuse assessment and treatment. In W. R. Miller (Ed.), *The Addictive Behaviors: Treatment of Alcoholism, Drug Abuse, Smoking and Obesity* (pp. 265–290). New York: Pergamon Press.

Mudrack, P. E. (2004). Job involvement, obsessive-compulsive personality traits, and workaholic behavioral tendencies. *Journal of Organizational Change Management, 17*(5), 490–508.

Nishii, L. H., Lepak, D., & Schneider, B. (2008). Employee attributions of the "why" of HR practices: Their effects on employee attitudes and behaviors, and customer satisfaction. *Personnel Psychology, 61*(3), 503–545.

Pfeffer, J. (1998). *The Human Equation: Building Profits by Putting People First*. Boston: Harvard Business Review Press.

Porter, G. (1995). Ethical Considerations in the Use of Contingent Employees. Paper presented at the International Conference Promoting Business Ethics. New York, NY, November 1995.

Porter, G. (1996). The organizational impact of workaholism: Suggestions for researching the negative outcomes of excessive work. *Journal of Occupational Health Psychology, 1*(1), 70–84.

Porter, G. (2001). Workaholic tendencies and the high potential for stress among co-workers. *International Journal of Stress Management, 8*(2), 147–164.

Porter, G. (2006). Profiles of workaholism among high-tech managers. *Career Development International, 11*(5), 440–462.

Porter, G. (2009). Implications of Employer-Sponsored Connectivity Devices (research report SR 01 09; available to members at www.worldatwork.org/waw/adimLink?id=32005). Scottsdale, Ariz.: WorldatWork.

Porter, G. & Kakabadse, N. K. (2006). HRM perspectives on addiction to technology and work. *Journal of Management Development, 25*(6), 535–560.

Schaef, A. W. & Fassel, D. (1988). *The Addictive Organization.* San Francisco: Harper.

Schaufeli, W. B., Taris, T. W., & Bakker, A. B. (2008). It takes two to tango: Workaholism is working excessively and working compulsively. In R. J. Burke & C. L. Cooper (Eds.), *The Long Work Hours Culture: Causes, Consequences and Choices* (pp. 203–225). Bingley: Emerald Group.

Schaufeli, W. B., Taris, T. W., & van Rhenen, W. (2008). Workaholism, burnout, and work engagement: Three of a kind or three different kinds of employee well-being? *Applied Psychology: An International Review, 57*(2), 173–203.

Snir, R. & Harpaz, I. (2009). Cross-cultural differences concerning heavy work investment. *Cross-Cultural Research, 43*(4), 309–319.

Ulrich, D. & Brockbank, W. (2005). *The HR Value Proposition.* Boston: Harvard Business Press.

Part 4

FUTURE DIRECTIONS IN CONCEPTUALIZATION AND RESEARCH OF HEAVY WORK INVESTMENT (HWI)

15

IS WORK ADDICTION A PROPER LABEL FOR HIGH WORK INVESTMENT HABITS?

Gayle Porter

Publications on workaholism have traditionally begun with discussion of different views on outcomes being positive, negative, or both. To alleviate some of this confusion, some authors have used the term "work addiction" to indicate their positioning on the negative outcome side of this debate. Others question whether it is appropriate to use the word addiction when there is not a physiological root cause, as with alcohol and drugs. While there is general acceptance of some behaviors as pathological, such as gambling (APA, 2000), there is ongoing debate on use of the term addiction. This controversy is not limited to study of workaholism but, rather, repeats in research on internet use, shopping/buying, sex, gambling, indoor tanning, and other involvements that become difficult to self-regulate. The goal of this chapter is to review some conclusions about the terminology of addiction from various fields of study and, further, to consider what research on workaholism might look like if actually pursued under the premise of addiction.

What Is Workaholism . . . Again?

Recently, Snir and Harpaz (2012) explained Heavy Work Investment—consisting of both time and effort—as having subtypes, one being the negative dispositional difference they have titled workaholism. Working within that framework bypasses the arguments on good versus bad workaholism, placing it clearly on the side of a behavior with negative connotation. Not too long ago, in reviewing research on workaholism, McMillan, O'Driscoll, and Burke (2003) considered it "fair to critique much of the present research as biased in favour of pathological interpretation" (p. 183). If we read the term "biased" to simply mean showing preference, rather than an unfair prejudice, they were reflecting the trend in workaholism research to be moving toward the addiction view.

There have always been two camps among researchers—those who consider the meaning of workaholism to mean heavy work hours but with good or bad outcomes, and those who consider the definition of workaholism to be excess work in spite of bad outcomes. My work falls into the second camp; the negative consequences are part of the definition. I view this in terms of comparison to drinking. If the goal is to research heavy alcohol consumption, one might correctly include good and bad outcomes of alcohol consumption. However, if the goal is to research alcoholism, defined as drinking in excess even when negative outcomes are apparent, the focus on negative outcomes is the logical choice. Correspondingly, one can research working long hours and look at both good and bad outcomes. But, if the goal is to look at working in excess even when negative outcomes are apparent, it is logical to exclude positive outcomes from the research.

That entire debate will not be repeated here. Snir and Harpaz (2012) have offered a resolution. They placed the issue into a large picture of Heavy Work Investment (HWI). While the overall model allows for researching both positive and negative sides to HWI, they place the workaholic as *one type* of Heavy Work Investor, exhibiting a behavior pattern that "does not stem from external predictors or from a passion for work, but from addiction to work" (2012, p. 5). In this model positioning, they follow the growing trend (or prevalent bias, if you prefer) to consider workaholism and work addiction as synonymous terms. The benefit of working within Snir and Harpaz's framework is that we can simply take the word workaholic and that long-term debate out of the discussion entirely. The people who devote great time and energy to their work are displaying heavy work investment; those who do so on the negative side of the dispositional comparison are displaying work addiction. I'm personally happy with this resolution and will work within this frame although, out of habit, I sometimes interchange workaholism and work addiction as synonymous terms.

Yet, there is more to determining appropriateness of the label work "addiction" than simply placing it in a model or noting growing acceptance in recent years. The approach here will be to consider the addiction label along with related issues as they have been debated in study of other behavioral concerns. If we want to call it work "addiction," are there topics and approaches we should be including in order to equate our work to other addiction research? Some of this discussion will be historic, some of it contemporary, all of it relevant to how we view excess work.

Multi-disciplinary Views

Over time, there has been a great deal of attention paid to the topic of addiction—some from predicted disciplines but some from writers that are not typically reviewed as related literature. Considering a broad range of perspectives can add richness to the topic. Following are short notations on work done by various professionals relating to addiction.

Physicians

Drug dependence is known to have physiological elements. In a recent lecture, Dr. Carl Christensen (2012) describes the effects of decreased dopamine and abnormal receptors that link to addiction. However, he does not talk exclusively about drug users. For example, his visuals include brain scans of overeaters, as well as cocaine dependent subjects. The general conclusion is that addicts have an abnormal response to reward. Although it seems somewhat counter-intuitive, the addicts seem to "like" their chosen substance less and therefore pursue more of it in order to achieve the same feeling of reward that non-addicts could get from smaller amounts.

A 1997 report from the Institute of Medicine (IOM) focused on dispelling myths related to addiction. In that report, they clarify the medical diagnosis as "compulsive use . . . accompanied by impairment in health or social functioning" (IOM, 1997, p. 13). They also highlight "tolerance," which means that over time, either more frequent or higher doses of a drug are needed in order to achieve a result that previously was achieved with less. Although this book was written specifically to address drug and alcohol addictions, they also highlight contributing behavioral factors, as well as social and environmental, along with the biological. Because of the interaction of factors, they recommend that treatment should integrate knowledge from all applicable disciplines.

To some people, the physiological aspect of addiction is imperative for use of that terminology; in their view, if there is no physical dependence, it should not be called an addiction (e.g., Rachlin, 1990; Walker, 1989). Continuing research is providing medical evidence that behavioral excesses relate to similar brain activity. For example, Brewer and Potenza (2008) review the neuropathological bases of impulse control disorders (ICD), and find that there are "multiple similarities between ICDs and substance addictions," so they consider it accurate to consider ICDs such as pathological gambling (or shopping, or internet use, etc.) as behavioral addictions. Goudriaan, Oosterlaan, de Beurs, and Van den Brink (2004) similarly discussed reward pathways in the brain that support the idea of non-substance addictive behaviors. Considering various diagnostic instruments, Albrecht, Kirschner, and Grusser (2007) conclude that "clinical perception as well as the increasing amount of scientific investigations emphasize the commonalities of substance-related and non-substance related behavioral addictions" (p. 8).

Economists

The perspective referenced here as coming from economists would also fall into what others might categorize as a cognitive theory. It emphasizes a rational approach in which choice of behavior is based on maximizing utility. In their theory of rational addiction, econometricians Becker and Murphy (1988) proposed that utility calculations would include both current time and future—short-term and long-term. Applying their view to alcohol, drugs, and smoking, as well as working, eating, and other activities, they warned that those most likely to reach the harmful addiction stage were people who are present-oriented, who have a tendency to discount the future. In their mental calculations they over-state the current benefits and discount future problems.

This will continue into the tolerance cycle of addiction, wherein "increasing amounts of the particular activity are required to achieve the former effects" (Griffiths, 2005). The initial calculation was current pleasure against possible negatives at some unidentified time in the future. As the initial high wears off and withdrawal begins, the calculated current need is even greater—more (substance or behavior) is needed now for the same level of benefit on which past calculations were based.

This type of research is pursued by people classified as behavior economists, who tend to agree that over-emphasizing gratification today while distorting or discounting future consequences is a sign of self-control problems (O'Donoghue & Rabin, 1999). The withdrawal sign of addiction is the immediate pain when the addictive substance or behavior is eliminated. In addition, whatever substance or behavior has taken over the person's thoughts lessens the probability that individual will make a truly rational choice. O'Donoghue and Rabin (1999) call this "consumption-induced myopia" (p. 172). It becomes increasingly difficult to give consideration to anything beyond the immediate felt need, and how to satisfy that need.

This approach to understanding addiction—maximizing utility—is not exclusive to substance addictions. The cognitive process can be easily applied to what has come to be called behavioral addictions. From the psychiatric community, Brewer and Potenza (2008) offer the medical explanation of how the amygdala receives serotonergic and dopaminergic input, affecting the processing of memory (particularly that of past emotional reactions), thus influencing decision-making. They also continue the discussion into "overtraining" of behaviors. Once a particular behavior becomes a conditioned response, it shifts from being goal-directed to being habit. For example, something once pursued for pleasure is done habitually without the same concern for that original goal. Continuation of these habits in the presence of negative consequences is an addiction.

The approach of the economists, that these behaviors begin with actual calculation of utility (as distorted as those calculations may be), is complemented by other professionals' explanations of how this cognitive process then shifts into addictive behavior.

Philosophers

The idea of calculating utility is represented in literature of philosophers, as well. The priority given to immediate gratification is considered failure to invest in the necessary reflection to realize that the addictive behavior is not beneficial in the long-run (Gjelsvik, 1999). According to Watson (1999), the acquired appetite is considered non-natural, i.e. one that does not contribute to a person's flourishing. Philosophers also comment on utility calculations as being degraded due to the tolerance factor, an accelerating level of need to maintain the current benefit as utility. This is a vicious cycle of "repeated acts with a total sum of negative consequences" (Waal & Morland, 1999, p. 132). With true and accurate consideration, this should be recognized as a suboptimal choice for not only the individual but also that person's family and the broader society.

This theme of non-natural appetite is similar to psychiatric use of the term egodystonic to classify behaviors that are in conflict with personal goals and do not support the individual's ideal self-image. (Egosystonic is the term for being in harmony with goals and ideal self-image.)

The point of interest here is not that people from different disciplinary backgrounds have come up with diverse ideas but, rather, that the ideas explaining addiction are either similar or highly complementary across their approaches.

Psychologists

Far more work has been done related to addictions in the field of psychology than either economics or philosophy. Discussions often include just the physicians' medical studies and the psychologists for the nonphysiological issues. Because psychology as a profession includes clinical considerations, these professionals as a group are interested in treatments options as well as furtherance of theories. Therefore, they have both considered a broad range of theories and considered integrative approaches to the topic of addiction.

Prior to the 1960s, there was need to classify alcoholism as something other than law-breaking or violating morality—to maintain the seriousness without labeling it crime or sin (Orford, 1985). One response was to categorize alcoholism as a disease, but that lost favor over time. The disease perspective positioned the addict as powerless, to the point of implying that behavior change was not possible. Similarly, abuse of drugs and/or alcohol was once viewed as a personality disorder, but the 1980 version of the Diagnostic and Statistical Manual (DSM) (APA, 1980), identified it as a more treatable problem of behavior (Miller, 1980). The DSM-IV-TR (APA, 2000 text revision) recognized pathological gambling as an impulse control disorder (ICD), rather than calling it a behavioral addiction. In fact, the word addiction is not used in the manual for substances either. Instead, there is categorization of Substance Use Disorders (SUD) with sub-categorizations by the specific substance (Potenza, 2006). In anticipation of the DSMV update, the classification of behavioral addictions was a topic of discussion but without much change being realized in terminology of the new manual (cf. Grant, Potenza, Weinstein, & Gorelick, 2010). Overall, the ICD label is the closest behavioral category to an addiction state.

Backing up to a look at how the problem develops, Alexander and Hadaway (1982) proposed the comparison of exposure versus adaptation in how addiction develops (writing specifically on opiate addiction). The exposure approach posits that initial use leads to additional use, and then even more use. Each occurrence creates a stronger habit until it reaches a state of addiction. This has some similarity to the aspect of the utility calculations in that each re-calibration of utility weights the current benefit more heavily and the future consequences less. In contrast, their adaptation perspective is based on the idea that drug use is initiated as a way to alleviate distress, to supply a coping mechanism. They parallel overeating and Type A behavior as two non-substance coping mechanisms that could also be harmful to the individual's long-term functioning.

The balancing of benefits and costs is covered by numerous authors. Terming "use" as indulgence in excessive appetites, the "opposing tendencies toward restraint versus appetite" are a balancing of incentives against disincentives (Orford, 1985, p. 167). Excess is considered deviant, whereas restraint and conforming to moderation is more socially acceptable. The understanding of this distinction comes through social learning, or messages provided by interaction with other people as to social acceptability of behavior (e.g., Bandura, 1977). Whether considering substance abuse or behavioral excess, this perspective brings factors of the environment clearly into play, as one person might have a very different social referent group to another.

The consideration of self-efficacy, belief in one's capability to successfully complete a task, is another application of Albert Bandura's work. Two separate aspects of self-efficacy are important in relapse prevention—the individual's choice of what task they feel confident to attempt and how long they will persevere at that task (Miller, 1980). High relapse rates are common, but lack of belief that one can really succeed with the change make it even more likely that one will relapse. Treatment programs such as Cognitive Behavioral Therapy try to change beliefs and the accompanying self-statements, in order to impact the behaviors based on those beliefs (Christensen, 2012). One study on smoking relapse showed substantial differences on self-efficacy, with higher scores belonging to the maintainers, i.e. the non-relapse group (Prochaska, Crimi, Lapsanski, Martel, & Reid, 1982).

A summary article covering several perspectives on addiction (Johnson, 1999) offered overviews of the neurobiological, coping mechanism, and object-related dynamics as three separate but complementary explanations. The neurobiological concept repeats concerns of the medical approach, referencing dopamine neurotransmission, along with psychological processes. Key to this approach is the incremental adaptation of the neural system, reaching a point at which "the pleasure of addictive behaviors becomes irrelevant" (Johnson, 1999, p. 793). The now permanently hypersensitized neural system simply "wants" the stimulus. As a biological process, this is entirely separate from cognitive calculations of benefits and costs or any other thought process.

Johnson explains the coping mechanism of addiction as related to the individual's early life and failure to develop self-care capacity: "Addicted persons cannot regulate self-esteem or relationships, or provide themselves with caring" (Johnson, 1999, p. 795). Use of drugs, alcohol, or even smoking then becomes a self-medication to help tolerate unpleasant feelings. Johnson also cites Dodes' (1990) writings on helplessness, which state is alleviated temporarily by enacting the addiction, doing something that gives a false sense of controlling the situation. Dodes connects this to a narcissistic vulnerability that leads to feeling overwhelmed.

Johnson's third perspective, the object-related dynamics, positions addictive behaviors as a means to maintain connections. Once a pleasurable activity is identified and experienced, the person becomes progressively unable to self-regulate. This person creates a protective psychological system of denial about the excess, to enable continuance despite unfavorable consequences. The object of the addiction is protected. While there may be contributing influences in genetic pre-disposition or social supports, this is essentially a psychological dependency focused on the relationship between the person and the object of the addiction. This approach covers not only the psychological component of drug and alcohol use but also addiction levels of behaviors such as eating, shopping, working, or making love.

Johnson considers the three perspectives presented here to have overlapping aspects and to provide, in consolidation, a comprehensive framework. Here we see the person-oriented approach of psychology shifting to full-scale concern of psychoanalytic processes. In order to help a patient struggling with addiction, broader consideration of multiple approaches and the combination of those approaches is demonstrated through clinical examples.

Business/Organization/Management Researchers

The field of Organization Behavior is heavily informed and influenced by psychology. In fact, many of the researchers focused on behavior in business organizations are industrial/organizational psychologists, the others predominantly having education and experience in business management. Therefore, it would be highly repetitious to re-insert the psychology studies here, even though it would be appropriate placement in many cases. Business researchers study alcohol and drug abuse issues under headings such as employee wellness, absenteeism, and even productivity. While substance abuse certainly does exist in the workplace, and is of concern to business leaders, the attention to drugs and alcohol is not exclusive to business organizations. This section will be distinct in its direct reference to the study of work as the specific object of the addiction.

Burke (2008) consolidated earlier empirical work across multiple industries, to explore different sources of work motivation that he labeled passion and addiction. This was essentially an adaptation of Spence and Robbins' (1992) variations comparing enjoyment in work to feeling driven to work. Burke found that passion and addiction were related, possibly indicating the commonality of high investment in the work. However, passion and addiction were very different in their relationship to outcomes. Passion related to more positively to psychological health and job satisfaction, while addiction had more negative associations.

Borrowing again from research in psychology, the idea of why people work the way they do (e.g., passion or addiction) can also be explained in terms of a self-determination theory of motivation (cf. Deci, 1980). In the self-determination framework, people tend to be either motivated by internal desire for growth and development (intrinsic), or motivated by external rewards (extrinsic). Individuals who are overly reward-oriented may face additional risk of work addiction in their dependence on external recognition.

In the work setting, rewards such as pay, promotion, office size and location, and other "perks" are signs that an individual is valued by that organization. This can bolster self-esteem for the work addict, although only for a short time, and then even greater rewards are needed to reach that same level of good feelings (Porter, 1996), the tolerance cycle of needing more to replicate even temporary benefit. Studies on self-determination theory have shown positive outcomes related to people who are motivated by intrinsic goals, such as well-being and person growth, and negative outcomes related to extrinsic goals, such as money (e.g., Kasser & Ryan, 1993). Further, low sense of well-being may be related to seeking enhancement through extrinsic goals and, thus, become a cycle that is difficult to break.

One of the most influential writers on addiction to work is Bryan Robinson, a counselor specializing in marriage and family therapy. His influence on research in the business environment includes development of one of the most widely used instruments for measuring workaholism, the Work Addiction Risk Test (WART) (Robinson and Phillips, 1995). He has also written numerous books on work addiction (e.g., Robinson, 2013) and related topics such as stress. His work has an individual focus, but those researching organizational concerns have successfully used the WART instrument for identifying prevalence of work addiction in specific companies and professions (e.g., Schaufeli et al., 2008; Taris et al., 2005).

The other frequently used measure of workaholism derives from the work of Spence and Robbins (1992) that was referenced earlier. Their instrument provided a differentiation between people who are highly work involved and enjoy their work versus those who are highly involved but working at that level because they are internally driven (the specification typically used for work addicts).

Although both can be used to identify workaholic tendencies, and both are influencing ongoing research, the development was slightly different. Again, the issue of clinical application comes into discussion. Robinson's WART was developed for research but also with clinical use in mind. It measures an overall tendency but also contains descriptive phrasing that can be directly used for counseling the work addicted individual. The Spence and Robbins instrument was first published in a study to differentiate sub-groups of people by identification of their relationship to their work. The work addicts are identified as a statistical collective. No evidence has been found of clinical application of use in providing feedback to individuals to address the problem if they fall into the workaholic category. This is not to say it couldn't be used in that way, but that organizational applications have not included that.

This leads to making the point that study of work addiction has been a dynamic collection of work from other disciplines, many of which focus on treatment concerns, while other components have been developed specific to the work environment. Published papers focused on the business context often have "implications for practice." However, the focus has been primarily on documenting the existence of work addiction (and debating definitions) with very little study of how this information has been successfully used in any practical follow-up. If we are serious about it being an addiction, is it adequate to continue exploration only in terms of identifying groups and correlating to possible outcomes of interest? Theoretical study of the addiction phenomenon is important. Still, if we want it to be assigned the seriousness of other addictions, we might need to extend our look at negative outcomes to include action implications more rigorously.

This is not to say that managers all become therapists, which would be ill-advised if not actually dangerous. In preparation for a survey study on referral of workaholics to Employee Assistance Programs (EAPs), Porter and Herring (2006) met with a focus group of EAP professionals to discuss how likely it was that anyone would be referred by managers to their program for workaholism. The group had many examples of referrals that fell into the working definition of workaholism but unanimously agreed that it would be very rare for the terminology to appear. Most likely, the person came to them due to interpersonal conflicts in the workplace or stress-related issues. They were referred for the symptoms without managers' using the terminology that the EAP professionals knew could tie it all together.

At about that same point in time, work moved forward in differentiating between work engagement and work addiction (Schaufeli, Taris, & Bakker, 2006). This type of research will have a big impact on better awareness that everyone who appears to be working hard is not doing so in the optimal manner. Work has become more intense (Green, 2004) in time and effort requirements, so there is increased need to spot which workers are hard-working in a sustainable way in contrast to those who are hard-working in a destructive way. As we broaden our research on the topic, there is a great deal of literature on other behavioral addictions that can be of use and some of this might frame better practical use of the information.

A Behavioral Addiction Sampler

The stated second goal of this chapter was to consider what research might look like if the idea of workaholic behavior were seriously pursued under that premise of addiction. The work noted as follows on other behavioral or process addictions offers suggestions that could be useful to further discussion of workaholism as a behavioral addiction. This is not intended to be a comprehensive literature review on any of the behaviors mentioned. Rather, it is a sampling that reveals certain commonalities. In the final section, summary comments will highlight a few key implications from these commonalities and potential future directions for research.

Gambling

Recognition in the DSM-IV-TR (without addiction specification), as well as popular recognition, has resulted in more research related to gambling than other behavioral addictions. Most of the work cited earlier with reference to brain functioning that is similar between behavioral and substance addiction has been conducted with emphasis on gambling, although the articles often acknowledge a range of comparable activities that do not involve drugs or alcohol. Termed pathological gambling, the DSM classification is that of impulse control disorder (APA, 2000). Potenza (2006) makes suggestions for more effective classification, noting the strong similarities of pathological gambling and substance use disorders (DSM terminology used instead of addiction). He notes elements of addiction to include craving to indulge in the behavior, inability to fully control choice to engage in the behavior, and "continued behavioral engagement despite adverse consequences" (p. 143). Citing the diagnostic criteria for substance dependence—"interference in major areas of life functioning, tolerance, withdrawal, and repeated unsuccessful attempts to cut back or quit" (p. 144)—he also notes the need for differentiating problem use from pathology, as is done with separation of substance abuse and dependence.

Goudriaan et al. (2004) also outline similarities between addictive behaviors such as gambling and the dysfunctional self-regulation of substance abuse. They call for exploration into different subgroups of problem gamblers—not good versus bad gamblers, but subgroups such as type of gambling preferred by problem gamblers. They also concluded that frequency does not seem to be a satisfactory criterion for whether gambling is a problem, similar to the idea that addiction to work cannot be differentiated by the number of hours alone.

Technology-Related

Recent attention to addictive behaviors has shifted toward use of technology, sometimes phrased in other ways but increasingly focused on internet use as it has become not only widely available but also a growing part of many people's day to day lives. Armstrong, Phillips, and Saling (2000) studied internet addiction, comparing scores on a variety of scales to measure (1) internet related problems, (2) addiction potential, (3) self-esteem, and (4) sensation-seeking/impulsivity. As with much behavior addiction research, the internet addiction items were reworded versions of DSM IV criteria for substance abuse. They found a link between low self-esteem and addictive behavior but did not see the expected impulsivity connection to heavier internet use.

Overuse of the computer and/or internet can have negative consequences as both time and attention is drawn away from school, family, and other relationships. Ng and Wiemer-Hastings (2005) considered the question of whether internet functions as an avoidance of social interaction or simply a different form. They did this through comparing users of massive multiplayer online role playing games (MMORPGs) versus users of offline video games. In MMORPGS, there is need for collaboration with others as the game progresses, combining social and competitive aspects, whereas offline games seemed to serve as distraction or relief from social interactions. From their results, these authors speculate that MMORPG players have a more anti-social or introverted perspective on social life, so that they find the game environment "more pleasant and satisfying than what occurs in the real world" (Ng & Wiemer-Hastings, 2005, p. 112). Although they spend more time engaged in the activity, these MMOPRG players indicated they would find fun elsewhere if this activity did not exist. Even though they played for long hours, lost sleep due to extended play, and had been told by others they spend too much time with it, the authors felt they did not exhibit behaviors of addicts, they simply preferred this style of social interaction.

Beard (2005) reviewed assessment potentials for use of internet that had become uncontrollable and damaging to other aspects of life. After a quick overview of the biological, psychological, and social views on problematic use of the internet, he reviews assessment instruments, often containing identification of depression, self-esteem issues, and withdrawal difficulty. Here the clinical emphasis comes up, as Beard recommends an interview format as the best tool for assessment, and offers more than 70 questions as screening samples. He acknowledged that use of the term addiction was under debate and would likely continue to be so for some time into the future. The three articles highlighted here show how diverse writings are on the topic.

Added concerns have been proposed in the overlap between addiction to technology and addiction to work (Porter & Kakabadse, 2006). The availability of small devices that allow work at any time from any location enables the work addicted person to indulge in that behavior (and hide it from others?) far more conveniently than ever in the past. On the other hand, a person addicted to using their technology can respond to complainers that it is work related and, therefore, cannot be criticized. In an interesting twist on this, the 1998 study by Young to compare dependent (addicted) users and non-dependent, defined usage as that done outside of school or work requirements. That definition served the purposes of her study, and she was able to show the self-regulation, relationship, and other problems expected among the dependent group. However, it highlights the tendency to "excuse" behavior when it can be justified by work, without looking more closely at whether it still might be considered excessive. In the years since Young's study, technology in the workplace has increased exponentially, so that new research would be appropriate, considering what usage is a requirement.

Others

Gambling has received extensive attention over the years due, in part, to the diagnostic categorization given by the APA. Technology has received strong attention more recently, as it has rapidly become a ubiquitous part of life, and we see high levels of use among many in the general population. Still, there is a much broader range of behaviors being studied and treated under the addiction terminology. A few examples are included briefly here to acknowledge that range.

Shopping/Buying

In line with the examples of gambling and technology, research on excess buying indicates the term addiction is appropriate (e.g., Clark & Calleja, 2008). As a repetitive, maladaptive behavior, buying provides a brief high or feeling of euphoria. Characteristically, the problem can be recognized through buying impulses dominating thoughts and feelings, inability to control the behavior, euphoric feelings at the time of purchase that quickly disappear—all general signs of addiction. The activity of buying provides the temporary high but the purchased merchandise is not needed and often later discarded. Making their case for the terminology, these authors submit that "widening of the concept of addiction to include behavioral addictions does not attest disillusionment for the concept but recognition of its power and utility" (Clark & Calleja, 2008, p. 637).

Indoor Tanning

Anxiety symptoms, but not depression, predicted whether recreational tanners would fall into the addicted group—young adults who excessively use this behavior for improved mood and socialization, despite dangers of skin cancer (Mosher & Danoff-Burg, 2010). The self-reports of this study also showed a relationship between tanning at an addiction level and greater use of alcohol, marijuana, and other substances.

Pathological Grooming

Both generic and environmental forces, and their interaction, are influential in development of pathological grooming, which includes hair pulling, skin picking, and severe nail biting. Each of these can be detrimental to daily quality of life. As with other behaviors discussed in this chapter, there is ongoing disagreement about terminology. The psychobiological mechanisms offering positive reinforcement seem to "overlap with those involved in addiction to substances" (Stein, Chamberlain, & Fineberg, 2006). The onset of these behaviors provides some pleasurable sensation, following either lack of arousal or negative feelings. These authors recommend an A-B-C Model, "affect regulation, behavioral addiction, and cognitive control" (p. 824), as the most effective of current approaches.

Sex

Much of the research on addiction to sex dates back to the 1980s and early 1990s. However, there is renewed interest in the overlap of sex and internet, which is chosen here to include sex on the list of behavioral addictions, as well as point out issues of discussion when two addictions are concurrent. Internet sex was explained by Griffiths (2001) using the familiar addiction characteristics of craving, mood modification, tolerance (needing progressive amounts to achieve good feelings), withdrawal symptoms, conflict in other (non-internet) relationships, and likelihood of relapse after attempts to quit. Although, at the time of this article, there were very few empirical studies, issues were posed about low self-esteem (particularly related to body image), male/female differences in type of internet used for sexual activities, and whether the issue is really sex addiction through the mechanism of the internet or a sub-category of internet addiction.

Summary

In each case of behavioral addictions, we see very similar comments about the correspondence to substance addictions, not just in the psychological processes but also now the neurobiological functioning. While it is unlikely the official diagnostic manuals will catch up to this trend in the near future, it is clear that professionals studying each of the highlighted topics are increasingly comfortable using the term addiction to describe the excess behavior that continues despite having become harmful to individuals' daily functioning. Researchers who study work behavior that similarly fits the criteria would be in line with their colleagues in other disciplines by using the term work addiction.

Implications for Ongoing Research

Admittedly, some of the sections in the chapter include sporadic editorializing on what might be done to supplement or augment research on the topic of work addiction. Rather than repeat those, a few more will be added.

There is a time when gaining support for a topic requires establishing its separateness, and then a time when study needs to re-incorporate with the surrounding world. In addiction research, there is very often discussion about comorbidity among addictions—indoor tanning with alcohol and drug use, smoking and alcohol consumption, and so on. There is also belief that recovery from one addiction can result in simply replacing it with another, such as recovering alcoholics becoming very heavy smokers. Much existing research has focused on substantiating that work addiction exists and that it is different from working long hours due to enjoyment, passion, or engagement. The time is ripe for bringing work addiction research into better alignment with that on other behavioral addiction.

As is often the case, researchers do what seems to be highly related work coming from different starting points, and it takes some time for these researchers to acknowledge and begin to utilize the similarities for shared advancement. It is a positive sign that researchers previously focused on other behavioral or process addictions have begun to include work addiction as another category, along with gambling, shopping, eating, internet, or sex addictions (e.g., Andreassen et al., 2012; Griffiths, 2005; Sussman et al., 2011). However, it seems to be unidirectional at this point—researchers of other behavioral addictions are beginning to include work addiction, but there is little evidence of researchers of work addiction giving more attention to other addictive behaviors.

Additionally, Andreassen et al. (2012) recently added another measurement potential to the research on workaholism, the Bergen Work Addiction Scale, which includes a suggested cut-off for categorization of workaholism. Early work shows good psychometric properties and supporting relationships to other work addiction measures. A difference here is that it is a work related scale developed by researchers using seven core elements identified for addiction more generally. It remains to be seen whether work addiction researchers will adopt this as another popular measure in their investigations. This is not to say the Bergen Scale is the ultimate measure of work addiction, but those serious about the addiction approach to excess work would be well advised to at least consider this as another tool. The commonly used work addiction measures do not seem to have crossed into use by researchers on other addictions, and it might be interesting to pursue that possibility, as well.

What additional learning might be available through looking at not just outcomes but the influences of parallel addictions outside the workplace or whether work addiction is replacing another excess? This latter possibility seems likely as other addictions, unless they are successfully hidden, carry social disapproval. Work addiction, because hard work is highly valued in our society, may be the safest haven for those able to make the transition. In a comprehensive review of addiction literature, Sussman et al. (2011) found the category of addiction to work had no studies in which there was examination of co-occurrence with other addictions. Although the number of work addiction studies was small compared to qualifying studies of alcohol or drug, overeating, internet, or sex addiction, the lack of research on comorbidity identifies a potential area of research. If other addiction research often includes this aspect, and work addiction is a proper reference, this missing piece in the research needs some attention.

In another comprehensive article, McMillan et al. (2003) looked for implications related to addiction—both physical and psychological. They included learning theory, trait theory or personality, cognitive theory, and family systems. Their conclusion after reviewing recent literature was that the best promise for future research was under the topics of learning and personality. The work reviewed in this chapter would suggest some refinement of those general categories. First, learning and especially social learning is clearly important to development of work habits and habits can cross the line into addiction. That process has been referenced here in both neural pathways and cognitive or psychological adaptations. It could be extremely valuable to focus on that crossing point when the enjoyment or goal has faded but the habitual activity continues and grows.

In terms of personality or individual traits, there seems to be some hesitation to bring family, self-concept, and other related topics into the discussion of workplace behavior. Managers are still expected to treat employees based on demonstrated performance, not analyze their troubled childhood or vary decisions based on someone's level of self-esteem. We recognize the importance of self-efficacy in the work environment and try to train employees to have task-specific confidence in their abilities. Still, personal topics much beyond that are harder to directly apply. However, tracking personal background and traits can be useful, and much study of addiction in other fields has included some element of self-concept. If specific issues can be identified as strongly tied to existing work addiction or likely development, that knowledge might inform actions that can influence employee selection or educational processes before people become workforce members. A broad array of potential scales are available that can be incorporated into future research specific to work addiction (e.g., Judge, Erez, Bono, & Thoresen, 2003).

The social acceptance of excess work has always been a hurdle in research and selling organizational leaders on the importance of recognizing and dealing with work addiction. In the Johnson (1999) description of object-related addiction, he references protecting the object of the addiction, which has strong implications in the workplace. Protecting the supply of ever-increasing amounts of work is contrary to the need for greater efficiency. This may be the strongest approach for gaining the attention of managers, but it requires research done with practical application in mind. Again, this is not an argument against any other type of study but, rather, to point out that there is a great deal of room for application-oriented research. As attention to positive work engagement grows, the contrast effect should be very useful to more fully explore the underlying nature of work addiction.

This chapter considered historic views of addiction, along with contemporary approaches, from the perspective of how this knowledge related to potential organizational actions to alleviate the negative side of heavy work investment. The overall conclusion is that, yes, work addiction is a proper label, but much would be gained from expanding our knowledge of research on other addictions, both substance-based and behavioral, to support this stand.

References

Albrecht, U., Kirschner, N. E. & Grusser, S. M. (2007). Diagnostic instruments for behavioural addiction: An overview. *GMS Psycho-Social-Medicine, 4*, 1–11.

Alexander, B. K. & Hadaway, P. F. (1982). Opiate addiction: The case for an adaptive orientation. *Psychological Bulletin, 92*, 367–381.

Andreassen, C. S., Griffiths, M. D., Hetland, J. & Pallesen, S. (2012). Development of a work addiction scale. *Scandinavian Journal of Psychology, 53*, 265–272.

APA—American Psychiatric Association (1980). *Diagnostic and Statistical Manual of Mental Disorders (DSM-III)*. Washington, DC: American Psychiatric Association.

APA—American Psychiatric Association (2000). *Diagnostic and Statistical Manual of Mental Disorders (DSM-IV-TR)*. Washington, DC: American Psychiatric Association.

Armstrong, L., Phillips, J. G. & Saling, L. L. (2000). Potential determinants of heavier internet usage. *International Journal of Human-Computer Studies, 53*, 537–550.

Bandura, A. (1977). Self-efficacy: Toward a unifying theory of behavior change. *Psychological Review, 84*, 191–215.

Baumeister, R. F. & Vohs, K. D. (2004). *Handbook of Self-Regulation: Research, Theory and Applications*. New York: Guilford Press.

Beard, K. W. (2005). Internet addiction: A review of current assessment techniques and potential assessment questions. *CyberPsychology & Behavior, 8*, 7–14.

Becker, G. S. & Murphy, K. M. (1988). A theory of rational addiction. *Journal of Political Economy, 96*, 675–700.

Brewer, J. A. & Potenza, M. N. (2008). The neurobiology and genetics of impulse control disorders: Relationships to drug addictions. *Biochemical Pharmacology, 57*, 63–75.

Burke, R. J. (2008). Work motivations, satisfactions, and health: Passion versus addiction. In R. J. Burke & C. L. Cooper (Eds.) *The Long Work Hours Culture: Causes, Consequences and Choices*. Bingley: Emerald, pp. 227–251.

Christensen, C. (2012). Physiology of addiction. Accessed May 29, 2013 from www.slideshare.net/jschwartz/the-physiology-of-addiction-february-2012

Clark, M. & Calleja, J. (2008). Shopping addiction: A preliminary investigation among Maltese university students. *Addiction Research and Theory, 16*, 633–649.

Deci, E. L. (1980). *The Psychology of Self-determination*. Lexington, MA: D.C. Heath.

Dodes, L. M. (1990). Addiction, helplessness, and narcissistic rage. *Psychoanalytic Quarterly, 59*, 398–419.

Frisch, M. B. (2006). *Quality of Life Therapy: Applying a Life Satisfaction Approach to Positive Psychology and Cognitive Therapy*. New York: Wiley.

Gjelsvik, O. (1999). Freedom of will and addiction. In J. Elster (Ed.) *Addiction Entries and Exits*. New York: Russell Sage Foundation, pp. 3–28.

Goudriaan, A. E., Oosterlaan, J., de Beurs, E. & Van den Brink, W. (2004). Pathological gambling: A comprehensive review of biobehavioral findings. *Neuroscience and Biobehavioral Reviews, 28*, 123–141.

Grant, J. E., Potenza, M. N., Weinstein, A. & Gorelick, D. A. (2010). Introduction to behavioral addictions. *The American Journal of Drug and Alcohol Abuse, 36*, 233–241.

Green, F. (2004). Why has work effort become more intense? *Industrial Relations, 43*, 709–741.

Griffiths, M. (2001). Sex on the Internet: Observations and implications for Internet sex addiction. *The Journal of Sex Research, 38*, 333–342.

Griffiths, M. (2005). A "components" model of addiction within a biopsychosocial framework. *Journal of Substance Use, 10*, 191–197.

IOM—Institute of Medicine (1997). *Dispelling the Myths about Addiction: Strategies to Increase Understanding and Strengthen Research*. Washington, DC: National Academy Press.

Johnson, B. (1999). Three perspectives on addiction. *Journal of the American Psychoanalytic Association, 47*, 791–815.

Judge, T. A., Erez, A., Bono, J. E. & Thoresen, C. J. (2003). The core self-evaluations scale: Development of a measure. *Personnel Psychology, 56*, 303–331.

Kasser, T. & Ryan, R. M. (1993). A dark side of the American dream: Correlates of financial success as a central life aspiration. *Journal of Personality and Social Psychology, 65*, 410–422.

McMillan, L. H. W., O'Driscoll, M. P. & Burke, R. J. (2003). In C. L. Cooper & I. T. Robertson (Eds.) *International Review of Industrial and Organizational Psychology, 2003, Vol. 18*. Sussex: Wiley.

Miller, W. R. (1980). Theoretical and practical issues in substance abuse assessment and treatment. In W. R. Miller (Ed.) *The Addictive Behaviors: Treatment of Alcoholism, Drug Abuse, Smoking, and Obesity*. Oxford: Pergamon Press, pp. 265–290.

Mosher, C. E. & Danoff-Burg, S. (2010). Addiction to indoor tanning: Relation to anxiety, depression, and substance use. Accessed May 24, 2013 from http://archerm.jamanetwork.com.

Ng, B. D. & Wiemer-Hastings, P. (2005). Addiction to the internet and online gaming. *CyberPsychology & Behavior, 8*(2), 110–113.

O'Donoghue, T. & Rabin, M. (1999). Addiction and self-control. In J. Elster (Ed.) *Addiction Entries and Exits*. New York: Russell Sage Foundation, pp. 3–28.

Orford, J. (1985). *Excessive Appetites: A Psychological View of Addictions*. New York: Wiley.

Porter, G. (1996). The organizational impact of workaholism: Suggestions for researching the negative outcomes of excessive work. *Journal of Occupational Health Psychology, 1*, 70–84.

Porter, G. & Herring, R. A. III (2006). The unlikely referral of workaholics to an employee assistance program. In R. J. Burke (Ed.) *Research Companion to Working Time and Work Addiction*. Cheltenham: Elgar, pp. 242–269.

Porter, G. & Kakabadse, N. K. (2006). HRM perspectives on addiction to technology and work. *Journal of Management Development, 25*, 535–560.

Potenza, M. N. (2006). Should addictive disorders include non-substance-related conditions? *Addiction, 101*(Suppl. 1), 142–151.

Rachlin, H. (1990). Why do people gamble and keep gambling despite heavy losses? *Psychological Science, 1*, 294–297.

Robinson, B. E. (2013). *Chained to the Desk: A Guidebook for Workaholics, Their Partners and Children and The Clinicians Who Treat Them*. New York: New York University Press.

Robinson, B. E. & Phillips, B. (1995). Measuring workaholism: Content validity of the work addiction risk test. *Psychological Reports, 77*, 657–658.

Schaufeli, W. B., Taris, T. W. & Bakker, A. B. (2006). Dr Jekyll or Mr Hyde? On the differences between work engagement and workaholism. In R. J. Burke (Ed.) *Research Companion to Working Time and Work Addiction*. Cheltenham: Elgar, pp. 193–217.

Schaufeli, W. B., Taris, T. W. & Bakker, A. B. (2008). It takes two to tango: Workaholism is working excessively and working compulsively. In R. J. Burke & C. L. Cooper (Eds.) *The Long Work Hours Culture: Causes, Consequences and Choices* (pp. 203–226). Bingley: Emerald.

Snir, R. & Harpaz, I. (2012). Beyond workaholism: Towards a general model of heavy work investment. *Human Resource Management Review, 22*, 232–243.

Spence, J. T. & Robbins, A. S. (1992). Workaholism: Definition, measurement, and preliminary results. *Journal of Personality Assessment, 38*, 160–178.

Stein, D. J., Chamberlain, S. R. & Fineberg, N. (2006). An A-B-C Model of habit disorders: Hair-pulling, skin-picking, and other stereotypic conditions. *CNS Spectrums, 11*, 824–827.

Sussman, S., Lisha, N. & Griffiths, M. (March, 2011). Prevalence of the addictions: A problem of the majority or the minority? *Evaluation & the Health Professions, 34*, 3–56.

Taris, T. W., Schaufeli, W. B. & Verhoeven, L. C. (2005). Workaholism in the Netherlands: Measurement and implications for job strain and work–nonwork conflict. *Applied Psychology: An International Review, 54*, 37–60.

Waal, H. & Morland, J. (1999). Addiction as impeded rationality. In J. Elster (Ed.) *Addiction: Entries and Exits*. New York: Russell Sage Foundation, pp. 120–148.

Walker, M. B. (1989). Some problems with the concept of "gambling addiction": Should theories of addiction be generalized to include excessive gambling? *Journal of Gambling Behavior, 5*, 179–200.

Watson, G. (1999). Discorded appetites: Addiction, compulsion, and dependence. In J. Elster (Ed.) *Addiction: Entries and Exits*. New York: Russell Sage Foundation, pp. 3–28.

Young, K. S. (1998). Internet addiction: The emergence of a new clinical disorder. *CyberPsychology and Behavior, 1*, 237–244.

16

APPLYING THE BIOPSYCHOSOCIAL MODEL TO EXAMINE CROSS-CULTURAL SIMILARITIES AND DIFFERENCES IN HEAVY WORK INVESTMENT BEHAVIORS AND OUTCOMES

Marina Astakhova and Mary Hogue

Work plays an increasingly important role in the lives of employees in today's competitive, global economy. Not only is work taking on a more central role in the lives of employees, but the way it is conducted differs greatly from previous decades. People today interact with others from all over the world in a way they never have before. There has been an upsurge of demographic diversity within organizations along with an intensified expansion of international business collaborations, both of which make an understanding of the effect of culture on organizational behavior and outcomes crucial (Lee & Ramaswami, 2013; Tsui, 2007). The increased centrality of work in individuals' lives has contributed to the phenomenon known as heavy work investment (HWI), which occurs when a considerable investment of time and effort is directed toward work (Astakhova & Hogue, forthcoming; Snir & Harpaz, 2009). While research is beginning to examine the influence of culture on HWI (e.g., Snir & Harpaz, 2006), to date, such research has been sparse and fragmented, and perhaps most importantly, findings are equivocal.

For example, when researchers examine cultural effects on HWI, sometimes they find cultural similarities, and other times they find differences. To illustrate, researchers find a rather robust cultural similarity in hours worked per week such that among workers in Belgium, Israel, Japan, the Netherlands, and the USA, the hours worked per week are higher for women over men, for married women over unmarried women, and for private-sector workers over public-sector employees (Snir & Harpaz, 2006). Conversely, researchers find differences in the hours per day devoted to work such that Japanese workers spend a significant amount of their waking hours working (Snir & Harpaz, 2006), deriving a great deal of satisfaction from doing so (Ishiyama, & Kitayama, 1994), while European workers devote more of their time to those non-work activities that Westerners might consider the simple "pleasures" of life (Levine, 1997), including outdoor physical activities and travelling (Alesina, Glaeser, & Sacerdote, 2005). Unlike Europeans, Japanese and Americans are reluctant to go on vacation as they perceive that vacation time may have a negative impact on their job stability and career success (Richards, 1999). Given this evidence, it remains unclear whether HWI experiences are similar or different across cultures.

These seemingly equivocal findings could be due to the fact that as yet, we have no meaningful, theoretically grounded framework for understanding the role of culture in HWI. In this chapter we provide such a framework. We begin with the definition that culture is a collective programming of the mind that distinguishes one group of people from another (Hofstede, 2011). Researchers view culture as a boundary condition beyond which specific "theory does not apply" (Edwards, 2008, p. 172) as well as a contingency variable such that the influence of culture is often dependent on other factors (Allaire & Firsirotu, 1985). To understand the role of culture in HWI, we need a theoretical framework that can be used across cultural boundaries and will facilitate understanding of particular factors upon which the influence of culture is contingent.

Thus, we focus on the framework of the biopsychosocial (BPS) model, which suggests that understanding human experience involves consideration of biological, psychological, and social factors (Engel, 1977). The application of this model to HWI initially occurred as a means of creating a typology that would allow a systematization and integration of the various forms and outcomes of HWI that exist in the literature (Astakhova & Hogue, forthcoming). The logic is that differential influence from biological, psychological, and social factors has a direct impact on HWI, and we are suggesting that even before that happens, the biology, psychology, and social factors are, themselves, affected by culture.

Culture

Culture has been described in many ways across various fields of study (see Kitayama & Cohen, 2010, for a thorough review). According to Lee and Ramaswami (2013), culture involves the community to which the individual belongs. This community can occur at a societal, regional, or national level. In management studies, culture is generally described in terms of value dimensions that are examined across nations (Hofstede & Hofstede, 2005; McSweeney, 2002).

Values are conceptions of what is desirable, and as such, values guide human behavior (Schwartz, 1994, 1999). Numerous classifications of human values exist (e.g., Hofstede & Hofstede, 2005; House et al., 2004; Schwartz, 1999). Among these, the Hofstede (1980) classification remains the most comprehensive and widely cited (Tung & Verbeke, 2010). Originally, Hofstede identified four primary dimensions, later adding a fifth and then a sixth (Hofstede, 2011). His dimensions are individualism/collectivism, masculinity/femininity, uncertainty avoidance, power distance, future orientation, and indulgence/restraint. Each of these has been linked to various work-related behaviors and outcomes, with individualism/collectivism one of the most widely studied (McSweeney, 2002) and one that has been linked to HWI (Way & Lieberman, 2010).

Individualism/collectivism is characterized by four defining attributes (Triandis, 1995). It involves: 1) the definition of the self by personal/independent or collective/interdependent aspects; 2) the prioritization of individual or group-based goals; 3) an emphasis on rational exchange versus communal relatedness; and 4) the importance of personal attitudes versus group norms as determinants of social behavior. The core element of *individualism* is the assumption that individuals are independent of one another existing in a loosely knit network (Oyserman, Coon, & Kemmelmeier, 2002). The emphasis is on self-reliance, and a desire to be unique. The core element of *collectivism* is interdependence and a tightly knit relational network (Hofstede & Hofstede, 2005). The emphasis is on interdependence, belongingness, pursuing common goals with others, and maintaining harmonious relationships (Hofstede & Hofstede, 2005).

Interestingly, when researchers examine the impact of individualism/collectivism on HWI, the link between the two is not always clear, with some researchers suggesting collectivistic values bring increased HWI (Scholz et al., 2002) and others arguing that HWI is fed by individualistic values (Schor, 1991). This controversy may be due to a lack of consideration of the contingent influence of culture (and by extension, the contingent influence of cultural dimensions), and a lack of understanding of those factors on which the influence of culture is contingent.

We are proposing that culture and its various dimensions influence the behaviors and outcomes of HWI by influencing one or more of the factors of the BPS model. To provide an in-depth explanation of this argument, we focus on one dimension, individualism/collectivism, and we encourage the reader to extrapolate from that to begin thinking of how this model might be applied to understand additional cultural dimensions and their influences on HWI.

Biopsychosocial Model

The BPS model suggests that factors related to biology, psychology, and the social context all play a role in shaping human experience (Engel, 1977), including influencing the behaviors and outcomes associated with HWI (Astakhova & Hogue, forthcoming). Biological factors involve the individual's anatomy and genetics, which means that these remain relatively stable during the individual's life. Psychological factors include the complex influences of behavior, emotions, and cognition. These are more flexible than biological factors and may show higher variability within an individual over time. Finally, social factors involve aspects of the social context such as norms or work policies, thus being most flexible in their influence relative to either biological or psychological factors.

The BPS framework provides a means of classifying HWI into three major types: workaholic HWI (W-HWI); situational HWI (S-HWI); and pseudo HWI (P-HWI), with each type having its own, unique pattern of influence from the three factors in the model (Astakhova & Hogue, forthcoming). W-HWI is closely aligned with clinical manifestations of addiction. Therefore, the influence of biology is strongest, which can lead to compulsive behaviors such as reluctance to disengage from work (McMillan & O'Driscoll, 2004). The influence of biology is diminished in S-HWI relative to the impact of both psychology and social factors. Thus, S-HWI behaviors can fluctuate, ranging from opportunistic work investment behaviors driven by the psychological need for self-gratification to fickle work investment behaviors aimed at satisfying a particular situational demand such as receiving a bonus in time to pay bills. Finally, P-HWI involves behavioral engagement without internal commitment. In other words, in P-HWI the person puts on the façade of HWI, so biological and psychological engagements are weak, and the influence of social factors is strongest.

Numerous outcomes can be associated with HWI, including those that involve the person's physical and psychological well-being, as well as relationships and work productivity. In each case, both positive and negative outcomes can occur (Astakhova & Hogue, forthcoming). In addition, stress can be elevated (Scott et al., 1997) or reduced (Burke & Fiksenbaum, 2009). Well-being can be improved (Burke & Fiksenbaum, 2009) or deteriorate as work and life become imbalanced (Aziz & Cunningham, 2008). Effects on productivity might be enhanced through additional work effort (Machlowitz, 1980) or diminished as employees become overworked (Ng et al., 2007). One point made by Astakhova and Hogue (forthcoming) in their initial application of the BPS model to HWI is that it is not always easy to determine whether outcomes of HWI will be positive or negative. A consideration of culture may improve such predictions, as culture is often the lens through which personal experiences are perceived.

In this next section, we apply the BPS model to HWI in the context of culture. In doing so, we note a sampling of examples of the effect that individualistic versus collectivistic culture can have on various biological, psychological, and social factors that affect HWI. We discuss how various forms of biological, psychological, and social factors bring about differences in the behavioral manifestations of HWI and the outcomes associated with it. It is important to note that as this is the seminal application of BPS to the cultural context of HWI, we often do not have directly applicable literature from which to draw (e.g., there has been no direct examination of the genetic components of HWI). Where direct examinations are possible, we use these to illustrate our points. Where direct examinations are unavailable, we draw from related literature to demonstrate how those concepts can be applied to HWI.

Biopsychosocial Model in the Culture Context

With respect to its effect on human behavior, culture is often viewed as a broader macro-level context that may alter or even overwrite the influences of other micro-level effects (Erez & Gati, 2004). For example, an expatriate from the U.S. to China may need to learn more about how to work in groups and be sensitive to group members' interests and needs. Thus, culture affects the people within the collective, and in a recursive way, the people within the group shape and reinforce culture. Figure 16.1 presents this recursive relationship.

As this figure shows, we are proposing that culture exerts influence on the biology, psychology, and social context of people living within it. In turn, biological, psychological, and social factors influence all forms of

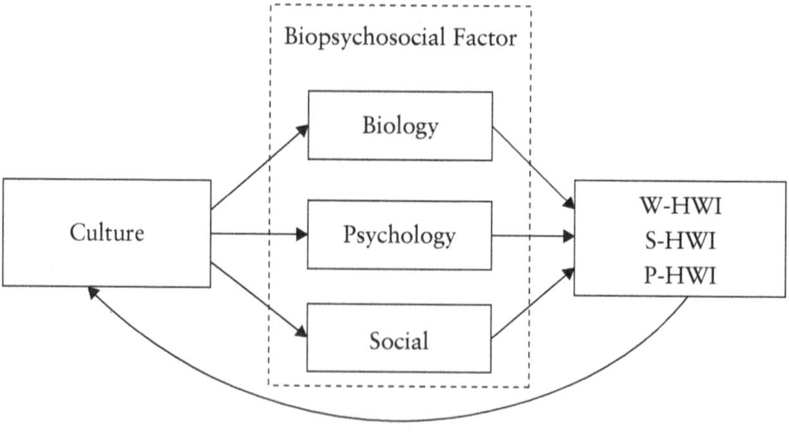

Figure 16.1 Culture, biology, psychology, social factors, and HWI

HWI, with HWI-related behaviors and outcomes serving to shape and reinforce the culture within which they exist.

Biological Factors, HWI, and Culture

Understanding how culture affects biology to result in differences in HWI may seem counterintuitive to many who believe that the biological foundations of behavior are similar across people, but a closer look at the literature shows this may not always be the case. The prominent reasoning supporting the argument for invariance in the effect of biological factors across cultures is that biological influences on human behavior are generated at the atomic or molecular levels (Cacioppo et al., 2000). These provide "cultural universals" (Rindos, 1986, p. 319) stemming from the basic genetic template that we all share. This means that the influence of biology on HWI will be more consistent than the influences of either psychology or the social context, but it does not necessarily mean that it results in complete uniformity.

Another line of research coming from cultural neuroscience posits that biology and culture work together in many important ways (Kitayama & Cohen, 2007). Cultural neuroscientists suggest that cultural variation in biological influences may occur due to a number of evolutionary processes, such as natural selection and genetic drift (Chiao & Ambady, 2007). Genetic drift is the process of genetic fluctuation that results in the formation of a new phenotype with modified biological characteristics (Keinan et al., 2007). Genetic drift may occur in the face of selective pressures such as the influences of a particular culture that can increase the frequency of specific alleles (i.e., gene forms that arise by mutation) allowing the individual to "fit" the culture. In other words, different cultural practices can actually bring about genetic changes within the people of the culture. For example, research suggests that the lactase gene, the enzyme that breaks down lactose in milk, is found in nearly 80 percent of people from the U.S. and Europe but is absent in the Bantu of South Africa and in most Chinese populations (Balter, 2005). Similar genetic changes can impact HWI.

HWI Behaviors

Biological influences on HWI are most prominent in W-HWI, which is similar to an addiction (Astakhova & Hogue, forthcoming). Most addictive behaviors, including workaholism, share several commonalities, such as salience or importance in the person's life, mood modification, tolerance, withdrawal symptoms, conflict, and relapse (Griffiths, 2010). Although there have been no direct examinations of the cultural neuroscience of workaholism, to understand how it might work, we can look to research on another addiction-related process, that of the serotonin and opioid neurotransmitter systems.

Differences exist in certain alleles affecting the serotonin and opioid neurotransmitter systems of the brain among those in collectivistic cultures versus individualistic cultures (Way & Lieberman, 2010). These have been dubbed "social sensitivity alleles" as they impact emotional responsiveness to social experiences (Way & Lieberman, 2010). Relative to individualistic cultures, social sensitivity alleles are more common in collectivistic cultures where hard work and effort are more highly valued than personal ability (Scholz et al., 2002). The emphasis on work effort over work ability may have brought about the genetic drift resulting in increased social sensitivity alleles, and these may actually set the stage for W-HWI. This possibility is supported by research findings that in Japan (Shimazu et al., 2011) and China (Van Beek et al., 2012), both highly collectivistic cultures (Hofstede & Hofstede, 2005), workers tend to consistently and more widely gravitate towards W-HWI while in the U.S., a more individualistic country (Hofstede & Hofstede, 2005), the workaholic form of HWI is less prevalent.

HWI Outcomes

Research generally shows that relative to workers in individualistic countries, workers in collectivistic countries tend to have greater life satisfaction (Way & Lieberman, 2010). In fact, even when HWI clearly fits the definition of workaholism, as it does in Japan, workers generally report high levels of job satisfaction (Oishi et al., 2006). Such findings have been explained by the fact that collectivistic cultures emphasize enduring relationships and social support within the group (Way & Lieberman, 2010), and we are suggesting that it may also be due to the presence of social sensitivity alleles. These alleles may make the experience of W-HWI subjectively different for the worker in a way that is construed as good and thereby results in positive outcomes, where the same may not be true for workers in whom the same alleles are either not present or are less prominent.

Research also generally shows increased stress among people in individualistic countries (Alesina, Glaeser, & Sacerdote, 2005; Bergeron & Schneider, 2005). As work in the individualistic countries of the West increasingly incorporates collectivist principles of teamwork (Baker, Day, & Salas, 2006) while also maintaining individualism at the national level, without the buffer of the social sensitivity allele, negative outcomes may be produced. In fact, research shows that aggression is increased among stressed workers in such countries (Van Beek, Hu, Schaufeli, Taris, & Schreurs, 2012).

Psychological Factors, HWI, and Culture

Psychological factors include cognition, affect, and behavior and may manifest in expressions of temperament and personality (Astakhova & Hogue, forthcoming). These factors are generally less stable than biological factors and more stable than social factors. Stability is found in processes such as working memory, in which capacity and processing appear to be similar across cultures (Hedden et al., 2002) and personality, with traits such as those found in the Big Five model and self-esteem existing across various cultures (e.g., Endo et al., 2000; Poortinga et al., 2002). Cross-cultural flexibility in psychological processes can stem from the interplay of genes and environment (Triandis & Suh, 2002), and flexibility in S-HWI can stem from the interplay of psychology and the social context (Astakhova & Hogue, forthcoming).

Culture impacts all aspects of psychology (Triandis, 1994). One important area for considering the influence of culture on psychology is in self-construal. As noted previously, self-definition differs in individualistic versus collectivistic cultures with individualism tending to bring an independent self-view and collectivism bringing an interdependent self-view (Markus & Kitayama, 1991; Triandis, 1995). These views can influence personality such that individualists develop more independent personalities and collectivists care more about fitting in, and these views can also impact the types of behaviors in which those in individualistic versus collectivistic cultures are motivated to engage (Markus & Kitayama, 1991), including behaviors related to HWI. Moreover, these cultural differences in how people see themselves will influence perceptions about and experiences of various outcomes tied to HWI.

HWI Behaviors

Viewing oneself as an individual or as a member of a group can influence both emotions and personality. Emotions are generally given greater priority in individualistic relative to collectivistic cultures (Mesquita & Markus, 2004). This is because emotions provide feedback about the correspondence of one's personal needs and goals with the actual state of affairs (Schimmack & Diener, 1997). A focus on personal needs fits the individualist orientation, rendering emotions less important in collectivistic cultures wherein following cultural norms and showing oneself to be a valuable group member outweigh the maximizing of personal pleasure (Suh et al., 1998). With respect to personality, there is a significant link between cultural dimensions and personality traits (Hofstede & McCrae, 2004). Individualism leads people to want to be noticed for their individual attributes (Markus & Kitayama, 1991), so it is positively linked with extraversion (Hofstede & McCrae, 2004). In collectivistic cultures individuals view themselves as interdependent, so they become less self-reliant and less competitive relative to those living in individualistic cultures (Triandis, 2001).

These differences in the psychology of people within the culture can lead members of each group toward different behavioral manifestations of S-HWI. Given the difference of importance placed on emotions within these cultures, passion toward work may develop in workers in individualistic cultures in a way it may not in collectivistic cultures so that passion-driven S-HWI would be more prevalent in individualistic cultures and compliance-related or necessity-driven S-HWI would be more widespread among employees in collectivistic cultures. Evidence from existing studies supports this, showing, for example, that the work attitudes of employees in the U.S. are readily driven by internal ambitions and passion (Richie et al., 1997) while those of Japanese people are driven by socio-cultural influences and require time to be internalized (Schallert et al., 2004).

HWI Outcomes

This influence of self-views can be seen in HWI outcomes as well. A relational–interdependent self-construal is the tendency to think of oneself in terms of relationships with close others (Cross et al., 2000). An independent self-construal is more common within an individualistic, not collectivistic culture leading people in individualistic cultures to value self-promotion and favor personal gain (Cross et al., 2000). Such individuals defend their interests and achieve favorable outcomes by taking action, confronting others, and speaking up. In other words, individuals with an independent self-construal are likely to use primary control strategies, in which they attempt to change the situation to fit their own needs (Chun et al., 2006). For example, individualists will most likely perceive involvement in workaholic behaviors as the opportunity to obtain extrinsic benefits, such as income and hierarchical career progress and career acceleration. Excessive work will contribute to their personal sense of power and esteem (Baruch, 2011).

On the other hand, those with an interdependent self-construal, such as is common in collectivistic cultures, have a greater prevention focus, valuing information that might warn of potential losses (Chun et al., 2006). They prefer close alignment and harmony with others, and to achieve that, individuals in collectivistic societies will use secondary control strategies in which they attempt to change themselves to adjust to the situation/group (Cross et al., 2000). In this way, through their constant urge to please the in-group (i.e., organization members), these individuals achieve positive psychological states through forms of HWI that promise favorable organizational rather than individual outcomes. For example, collectivists are shown to be committed to their organizations and to exert considerable time and effort to assure organizational success (Ramamoorthy & Flood, 2002).

Social Factors, HWI, and Culture

Social factors represent the role of the social context in determining an individual's behavior (Burke et al., 2009). While biological and psychological factors are the internal forces that influence an individual's behavior, social factors work externally, making them extremely flexible relative to both psychological and biological factors. The influence of social factors on HWI is most prominent in S-HWI and P-HWI relative to W-HWI (Astakhova & Hogue, forthcoming). The social context involves both formal and informal social rules. Formal rules include explicit policies and procedures within an organization, while informal rules include implicit organizational climate and norms.

A fundamental difference that exists between members of individualistic versus collectivistic societies is in their conceptions of goals and their adherence to norms. Not only do individualists focus on independent goals while collectivists focus on group goals, each group also differs in the meanings they assign to goal achievement. Members of individualistic societies tend to attribute success or failure to the individual, seeing it as relatively stable and immutable, while members of collectivistic societies tend to attribute success or failure to the context, which is less stable and more changeable (Triandis, 1994). Also, members of collectivistic societies place greater value on rules and norms relative to the value placed by members of individualistic societies. As rules and norms take on greater importance, they are likely to be given prominence within the situation and be adhered to with a conviction that would not exist when they do not have the same importance. These cultural differences in goals, rules, and norms will impact both behavioral manifestations and outcomes associated with S-HWI and P-HWI.

HWI Behaviors

National culture has a direct influence on organizational practices within a country (Hofstede, 2011). One such practice involves the rules associated with rewards. These rules can involve the *type* of extrinsic rewards available and the *method* by which rewards are allocated. Organizations use rewards to motivate workers, and to be motivating, a reward must be valued (Porter & Lawler, 1968). Because values differ between individualistic and collectivistic societies, workers in each society will find some types of rewards to be more motivating than others. For example, in individualistic cultures, one's standing as an individual is very important (Kurman, 2001). The focus is on individual determinants of performance rather than congruence with the in-group (Eisenberg, 1999). As such, workers are motivated through, and direct their behavior toward, types of rewards that are individual-based such as personal recognition, increased salary, and promotion (Hewlett & Luce, 2006; Suh et al., 1998). Such rewards will drive HWI for members of individualistic societies in a way that other types of rewards such as team harmony or life-long job security might not. These types of rewards are more likely to motivate and direct the behavior of members of collectivistic societies wherein group incentives are common within organizations and favored by employees (Eisenberg, 1999; Ray, 1986).

This difference carries over to method of reward allocation. Rewards can be allocated according to an equity rule in which they are distributed by input such that those individuals who produce more work receive more reward, or they can be allocated according to an equality rule in which members receive an equal distribution, such as when members of a group that generated a unified work product are paid equally. Research shows that the equity rule tends to prevail when a group's primary goal is economic performance and the group is not concerned with group harmony, while the equality rule tends to be salient when a group is primarily concerned with relational harmony among the members (Kim et al., 1990). The fact that individualistic countries present a preference for equity over equality in reward allocation, and the converse is true in collectivistic countries (Sama & Papamarcos, 2000), implies that in individualistic societies, S-HWI behaviors will most likely be prevalent when organizational policies create an equitable distribution of rewards and will be suppressed by organizational culture and policies oriented toward equality.

HWI Outcomes

In the same way that culture influences formal social factors such as rules, it also influences informal factors such as norms, and these can impact various HWI-related outcomes. Two common work-related norms that are affected by culture are related to seeking social support and to social loafing. Relative to workers in collectivistic cultures, workers in individualistic cultures generally have fewer opportunities to receive personal support (Kurman, 2001). An infrequency of availability of social support networks will not allow the development of a norm for seeking support. Instead, a norm of self-reliance will develop. In collectivistic cultures, social support systems are rich and interconnected (Kaufman et al., 2004), with the protection and involvement of managers in the personal lives of employees commonplace (Butler & Burchase, 2004). The prevalence of such support systems provides many opportunities to seek support, thereby strengthening the development of a norm for doing so. In this way, people from collectivistic cultures who have readily available access to this kind of help are generally resilient in the face of negative circumstances (Kaufman et al., 2004) and less likely to suffer from negative HWI outcomes such as stress, exhaustion, and burnout (Shimazu et al., 2010).

Not only does individualism/collectivism influence the development of norms, it also impacts the likelihood that group members will follow the group's norms. As previously noted, members of collectivistic societies generally follow norms more fervently than do members of individualistic societies (Triandis, 1994). Social loafing is defined as reduced performance of individuals who act as part of a group rather than alone (Harkins & Petty, 1982). Social loafing is an aspect of P-HWI. In this, a worker creates the façade of working while letting others perform the actual labor, and as a deviant work behavior, most cultures have norms specifying that such behavior is not acceptable. Because group norms have a stronger effect on members of collectivistic societies versus individualistic societies, this norm should result in a reduced amount of social loafing among collectivists versus individualists. Research supports this claim showing that workers in individualistic societies often work to maximize self-gain, even if that means relying on the efforts of others (Earley, 1989). As a form of P-HWI, social loafing may result in increased conflict among group members, with the type of conflict differing for individualistic and collectivistic societies. In individualistic societies, social loafing may be increased by one worker's desire to maximize self-gain. That may threaten another worker's opportunity to maximize her or his self-gain, thus increasing conflict over resources. In an individualistic society, social loafing may be reduced, but when it occurs, it may be experienced more profoundly. Workers may believe their coworker is not upholding his or her obligation to the group, and this may be experienced as a personal affront, thus increasing relational conflict.

In sum, culture impacts factors related to biology, psychology, and the social context in a way that influences the behaviors and outcomes tied to HWI. By using the BPS model, we were able to integrate cross-cultural findings to provide a way of understanding the contingent effect that culture has on HWI.

Implications and Directions for Future Research

We have suggested that the impact of culture on HWI occurs through its effect on the biology, psychology, and social factors of people within the society. We illustrated that argument by exploring the impact of the value dimension, individualism/collectivism, on the three factors within the BPS model. Heretofore, researchers have understood *that* culture plays a role in HWI; through our application of the BPS model, we provide an explanation of *how* culture plays its role. This perspective has a number of important theoretical and practical implications.

First, the chapter underscores the need to conceptualize HWI by viewing it through the lens of national culture. Without such a consideration, our understanding of HWI is constrained. Although culture is generally viewed as bounded by national borders, rather than focusing solely on geographic differences, cultural influences can best be understood through an examination of shared values within a collective. Because the influence of culture on human behavior often outweighs the influence of individual differences (Erez & Gati, 2004), its consideration in understanding HWI is crucial. Triandis (1994) notes that as Northwest Europe and North America have been the centers of industrial development, they have also been the center of psychology-based research into work-related phenomena. He further notes that despite creating the foundation for an overwhelming majority of such research, the population in these areas is only roughly 15 percent of the world's population. It is impossible to create a full understanding of any phenomenon related to human behavior by studying only 15 percent of the population. Thus, it is crucial to explore the impact of culture whenever attempting to understand human experience.

As part of a new world order in which people are increasingly encountering others from different nations, such as expatriates or multi-national businesses, understanding cross-cultural differences and similarities is ever more important (Snir & Harpaz, 2006). Further, as culture is both a product and a shaper of human behavior, it becomes both an antecedent and a consequence of HWI, raising several implications for researchers. We examined only one dimension of culture, individualism/collectivism, but many more dimensions exist, and for a full understanding of the role of culture in HWI, these should be explored as well, both conceptually as we did in this chapter and empirically to determine the relative strength of various dimensions with respect to HWI across different cultures. An interesting and important question that might be explored is how dimensional similarities and difference influence HWI in various cultures, exploring whether certain cultural dimensions exert greater influence on biology, psychology, or social factors and how that plays out with respect to the various forms of HWI.

Also, we contrasted individualism and collectivism, leading to the demonstration of many cross-cultural differences, but as we noted at the outset, cross-cultural similarities exist as well, and these also provide useful information for understanding HWI. Further, differences and similarities can exist within the various cultural dimensions (Triandis, 1995). For example, collectivistic/individualistic values may vary in strength within a single culture (Astakhova, DuBois, & Hogue, 2010). Thus, culture is a complex construct comprised of many dimensions with each dimension containing a complexity of its own that should be explored with respect to its direct influences on factors of the BPS model and, through that, its indirect influences on HWI.

Moreover, our discussion of the role of culture in HWI focused on national culture, but culture exists at the levels of society, social class, organization, and occupation (Hofstede, 2011). This presents important forms of shared thinking among people and so presents a myriad of opportunities for future research to examine both similarities and differences at these levels of culture, for a complete understanding of HWI requires a grasp of both cultural similarities and differences (Snir & Harpaz, 2006).

Second, by using the BPS model as a guiding framework, the chapter offers a systemic approach to examining the role of culture on HWI. Such an approach allows practical and theoretical explanations of the interconnections between culture and HWI, thereby potentially enriching the types of research questions to be explored as well as providing a theoretical grounding for hypothesis development. Previous research has examined BPS-related variables outside of the framework of the BPS model. For instance, Snir and Harpaz (2004) found that the number of hours worked is positively related to the psychological variable of occupational satisfaction and negatively related to the psychological variable of work centrality. Also, Liang and Chu (2009) found a causal influence of the psychological variable of personality and the contextual variable of organizational inducements on excessive work. As future research is guided by the BPS model, many more antecedents to HWI can be identified and explored.

The challenge that future researchers may attempt to resolve is how empirical tests may capture the complex interplay of biological, psychological, and social factors within people of a given culture. As the triad of factors often results in a variety of HWI manifestations (Astakhova & Hogue, forthcoming), it will be particularly interesting to examine the mediated, recursive relationship that we propose exists among culture, factors, of the BPS model, and HWI. Moreover, it is possible that the three factors of the BPS model work together to influence HWI, rather than working in the seemingly independent fashion suggested by our model. For example, while emotions (psychology) and norms (social) may each have an independent effect on HWI as previously discussed, they also may work together. It is possible that people may have an emotional reaction to particular norms that produces an interactive effect on HWI. This possibility should also be examined in future research.

Finally, some practical implications of a culturally sensitive understanding of HWI should also be noted. This knowledge will benefit the organizations that either have a culturally diverse workforce or are exploring opportunities to expand to a different country. Perceptions of workaholic behaviors as "just all good" have become obsolete because of the known negative outcomes of excessive work for both individuals and organizations (Kiechel, 1989). The question that remains is *when*, or under what circumstances, HWI may be good, bad, or both (Astakhova & Hogue, forthcoming). By increasing their cultural sensitivity and knowledge of cross-cultural organizational phenomena (Gelfand et al., 2007), managers would better understand cultural influences on HWI, and its positive, negative, or variable outcomes.

For example, as our discussion shows, in order to foster healthy HWI at work in collectivistic cultures or among workers from collectivistic societies who are working in other countries, a consideration of the BPS model suggests that managers might need to be aware of possible genetic buffers to the negative effects of HWI, consider the interdependent self-construals of their workers, and put into practice some form of group-based reward system. On the other hand, in order to foster healthy HWI at work in individualistic cultures or among workers from individualistic societies working in other countries, managers might want to be aware that these workers may not have a genetic buffer against the negative effects of HWI, are likely operating from an independent self-construal, and will be motivated by independent reward systems. In order to tame HWI behaviors that produce negative outcomes, managers in individualistic countries should create support systems and get more involved in assisting overworked, stressed, and burned out employees. In collectivistic societies, managerial involvement may be less critical as the employee's group members (e.g., co-workers) may serve as a "correcting mechanism" for self-destructing HWI behaviors.

Conclusion

In sum, this chapter has explored how the biopsychosocial influences on HWI can be examined through the lens of national culture. In particular, we demonstrated how the cultural dimension of individualism/collectivism may have a contingent impact on W-HWI, S-HWI, and P-HWI and their associated outcomes. The application of the biopsychosocial model to understand cultural influences on HWI provides a useful framework that allows a systematic and theoretically guided approach to synthesizing existing and future research on cross-cultural HWI. Most importantly, we hope that the ideas presented in this chapter will stimulate future research in the area of cross-cultural HWI that remains largely neglected.

References

Alesina, A., Glaeser, E., & Sacerdote, B. (2005). Work and leisure in the U.S. and Europe: Why so different? *NBER Macroeconomics Annual*, 11278, April.

Allaire, Y., & Firsirotu, M. E. (1985). Theories of organizational culture. *Organizational Studies*, 5, 193–226.

Astakhova, M., & Hogue, M. (forthcoming). A heavy work investment typology: A biopsychosocial framework. *Journal of Managerial Psychology*.

Astakhova, M., DuBois, C. Z., & Hogue, M. (2010). A typology of middle managers in modern Russia: An intracultural puzzle. *International Journal of Intercultural Relations*, 34, 527–539.

Aziz, S., & Cunningham, J. (2008). Workaholism, work stress, work–life imbalance: Exploring gender's role. *Gender in Management: An International Journal*, 23, 553–566.

Baker, D. P., Day, R., & Salas, E. (2006). Teamwork as an essential component of high-reliability organizations. *Health Services Research*, 41, 1576–1598.

Balter, M. (2005). Evolutionary genetics. Are humans still evolving? *Science*, 309, 234–237.

Baruch, Y. (2011). The positive wellbeing aspects of workaholism in cross cultural perspective: The chocoholism metaphor. *Career Development International*, 16, 572–591.

Bergeron, N., & Schneider, B. H. (2005). Explaining cross-national differences in peer-directed aggression: A quantitative synthesis. *Aggressive Behavior*, 31, 116–137.

Burke, N. J., Joseph, G., Pasick, R. J., & Barker, J. C. (2009). Theorizing social context: Rethinking behavioral theory. *Health Education & Behavior*, 36(Suppl. 1), 55S–70S.

Burke, R. J., & Fiksenbaum, L. (2009). Work motivations, work outcomes, and health: Passion versus addiction. *Journal of Business Ethics*, 84, 257–263.

Butler, B., & Purchase, S. (2004). Personal networking in Russian post-Soviet life. *Research and Practice in Human Resource Management*, 12, 34–60.

Cacioppo, J. T., Berntson, G. G., Sheridan, J. F., & McClintock, M. K. (2000). Multi-level integrative analyses of human behavior: Social neuroscience and the complementing nature of social and biological approaches. *Psychological Bulletin*, 126, 829–843.

Chiao, J. Y., & Ambady, N. (2007). Cultural neuroscience: Parsing universality and diversity across levels of analysis. In S. Kitayama & D. Cohen (Eds.), *Handbook of cultural psychology* (pp. 237–254). New York: Guilford Press.

Chun, C., Moos, R. H., & Cronkite, R. C. (2006). Culture: A fundamental context for the stress and coping paradigm. In P. T. P. Wong & L. C. J. Wong (Eds.), *Handbook of multicultural perspectives on stress and coping* (pp. 29–53). Dallas, TX: Spring.

Cross, S. E., Bacon, P. L., & Morris, M. L. (2000). The relational interdependent self-construal and relationships. *Journal of Personality and Social Psychology*, 78, 791–808.

Earley, P. S. (1989). Social loafing and collectivism: A comparison of the United States and the People's Republic of China. *Administrative Science Quarterly*, 34, 565–581.

Edwards, J. R. (2008). Person–environment fit in organizations: An assessment of theoretical progress. *Academy of Management Annals*, 2, 167–230.

Eisenberg, J. (1999). How individualism–collectivism moderates the effects of rewards on creativity and innovation: A comparative review of practices in Japan and the U.S. *Creativity and Innovation Management*, 8, 251–261.

Endo, Y., Heine, S. J., & Lehman, D. R. (2000). Culture and positive illusions in close relationships: How my relationships are better than yours. *Personality and Social Psychology Bulletin*, 26, 1571–1586.

Engel, G. L. (1977). The need for a new medical model: A challenge for biomedicine. *Science*, 196, 129–136.

Erez, M., & Gati, E. (2004). A dynamic, multi-level model of culture: from the micro level of the individual to the macro level of a global culture. *Applied Psychology: An International Review*, 53, 583–598.

Gelfand, M. J., Erez, M., & Aycan, Z. (2007). Cross-cultural organizational behavior. *Annual Review of Psychology*, 58(1), 479–514.

Griffiths, M. D. (2010). The role of context in online gaming excess and addiction: Some case study evidence. *International Journal of Mental Health and Addiction*, 8, 119–125.

Harkins, S. G., & Petty, R. E. (1982). The effects of task difficulty and task uniqueness on social loafing. *Journal of Personality and Social Psychology*, 43, 1214–1229.

Hedden, T., Park, D. C., Nisbett, R., Ji, L.-J., Jing, Q., & Jiao, S. (2002). Cultural variation in verbal versus spatial neuropsychological function across the life span. *Neuropsychology*, 16, 65–73.

Hewlett, S. A., & Luce, C. B. (2006). Extreme jobs: The dangerous allure of the 70-hour work week. *Harvard Business Review*, 84, 49–59.

Hofstede, G. (1980). Motivation, leadership, and organization: Do American theories apply abroad? *Organizational Dynamics*, 8, 42–63.

Hofstede, G. (2011). Dimensionalizing cultures: The Hofstede model in context. *Online Readings in Psychology and Culture*, 2(1). Retrieved from http://scholarworks.gvsu.edu/orpc/vol2/iss1/8 on May 15, 2013.

Hofstede, G., & Hofstede, G. J. (2005). *Culture and organizations: Intercultural cooperation and its importance for survival. Software of the mind* (2nd ed.). New York: McGraw–Hill.

Hofstede, G., & McCrae, R. R. (2004). Personality and culture revisited: Linking traits and dimensions of culture. *Cross-Cultural Research*, 38, 52–88.

House, R. J., Hanges, P. J., Javidan, M., Dorfman, P. W., & Gupta, V. (Eds.) (2004). *Culture, leadership and organizations: The GLOBE study of 62 societies*. Thousand Oaks, CA: Sage.

Ishiyama, F. I., & Kitayama, A. (1994). Overwork and career-centered self-validation among the Japanese: Psychosocial issues and counseling implications. *International Journal for the Advancement of Counseling*, 17, 167–182.

Kaufman, J., Yang, B. Z., Douglas-Palumberi, H., Houshyar, S., Lipschitz, D., Krystal, J. H., & Gelernter, J. (2004). Social supports and serotonin transporter gene moderate depression in maltreated children. *Proceedings of the National Academy of Sciences*, 101, 17316–17321.

Keinan, A., Mullikin, J., Patterson, N., & Reich, D. (2007). Measurement of the human allele frequency spectrum demonstrates greater genetic drift in East Asians than in Europeans. *Nature Genetics*, 39, 1251–1255.

Kiechel, W., III (1989, April). The workaholic generation. *Fortune*, 119, 50–62.

Kim, K., Park, H., & Suzuki, N. (1990). Reward allocations in the United States, Japan, and Korea: A comparison of individualistic and collectivistic cultures. *Academy of Management Journal*, 33, 188–198.

Kitayama, S., & Cohen, D. (2010) *Handbook of cultural psychology*. New York: Guilford Press.

Kurman, J. (2001). Self-enhancement: Is it restricted to individualistic cultures? *Personality and Social Psychology Bulletin*, 12, 1705–1716.

Lee, Y.-T., & Ramaswami, A. (2013). Fitting person–environment fit theories into a national cultural context. In A. L. Kristof-Brown & J. Billsberry (Eds.), *Organizational fit: Key issues and new directions* (pp. 222–240). Chichester: Wiley-Blackwell Publishing.

Levine, R. (1997). Financial development and economic growth: Views and agenda. *Journal of Economic Literature*, 35, 688–726.

Liang, Y., & Chu, C. (2009). Personality traits and personal and organizational inducements: Antecedents of workaholism. *Social Behavior and Personality*, 37, 645–660.

Machlowitz, M. (1980). *Workaholics: Living with them, working with them.* Reading, MA: Addison-Wesley.

McMillan, L. H. W., & O'Driscoll, M. P. (2004). Workaholism and health: Implications for organizations. *Journal of Organizational Change Management*, 17, 509–519.

McSweeney, B. (2002). Hofstede's model of national cultural differences and their consequences: A triumph of faith—a failure of analysis. *Human Relations*, 55, 89–118.

Markus, H. R., & Kitayama, S. (1991). Culture and the self: Implications for cognition, emotion, and motivation. *Psychological Review*, 98, 224–253.

Mesquita, B., & Markus, H. R. (2004). Culture and emotion: Models of agency as sources of cultural variation in emotion. In N. H. Frijda, A. S. R. Manstead, & A. H. Fischer (Eds.), *Feelings and emotions: The Amsterdam symposium* (pp. 341–358). Cambridge: Cambridge University Press.

Ng, T. W. H., Sorensen, K. L., & Feldman, D. C. (2007). Dimensions, antecedents, and consequences of workaholism: A conceptual integration and extension. *Journal of Organizational Behavior*, 28, 111–136.

Oishi, S., Diener, E., & Lucas, R. E. (2006). The optimum level of well-being: Can people be too happy? *Perspectives on Psychological Science*, 2, 346–360.

Oyserman, D., Coon, H., & Kemmelmeier, M. (2002). Rethinking individualism and collectivism: Evaluation of theoretical assumptions and meta-analyses. *Psychological Bulletin*, 128, 3–72.

Poortinga, Y. H., van de Vijver, F., & van Hemert, D. A. (2002). Crosscultural equivalence of the Big Five: A tentative interpretation of the evidence. In R. R. McCrae & J. Allik (Eds.), *The Five–Factor Model of personality across cultures* (pp. 273–294). New York: Kluwer Academic/Plenum Publishers.

Porter, L. W., & Lawler, E. E. (1968). What job attitudes tell about motivation. *Harvard Business Review*, 46, 118–126.

Ramamoorthy, N., & Flood, P. (2002). Employee attitudes and behavioral intentions: A test of the main and moderating effects of individualism–collectivism orientations. *Human Relations*, 55, 1071–1096.

Ray, C. A. (1986). Corporate culture: The last frontier of control. *Journal of Management Studies*, 23, 287–297.

Richards, G. (1999). Vacations and the quality of life. *Journal of Business Research*, 44, 189–198.

Richie, B. S., Fassinger, R. E., Linn, S. G., Johnson, J., Prosser, J., & Robinson, S. (1997). Persistence, connection, and passion: A qualitative study of the career

development of highly achieving African American-Black and White women. *Journal of Counseling Psychology*, 44, 133–148.
Rindos, D. (1986). The evolution of the capacity for culture: Sociobiology, structuralism, and cultural selectionism. *Current Anthropology*, 27, 315–326.
Sama, L. M., & Papamarcos, S. D. (2000). Hofstede's I-C dimension as predictive of allocative behaviors: A meta-analysis. *International Journal of Value-Based Management*, 13, 173–188.
Schallert, D. L., Reed, J. H., & Turner, J. E. (2004). The interplay of aspirations, enjoyment, and work habits in academic endeavors: Why is it so hard to keep long-term commitments? *Teachers College Record*, 106, 1715–1728.
Schimmack, U., & Diener, E. (1997). Affect intensity: Separating intensity and frequency in repeatedly measured affect. *Journal of Personality and Social Psychology*, 73, 1313–1329.
Scholz, U., Gutierrez-Dona, B., Sud, S., & Schwarzer, R. (2002). Is general self-efficacy a universal construct? Psychometric findings from 25 countries. *European Journal of Psychological Assessment*, 18, 242–251.
Schor, J. (1991). *The overworked American: The unexpected decline of leisure*. New York: Basic Books.
Schwartz, S. H. (1994). Are there universals in the content and structure of values? *Journal of Social Issues*, 50, 19–45.
Schwartz, S. H. (1999). A theory of cultural values and some implications for work. *Applied Psychology: An International Review*, 48, 23–47.
Scott, K. S., Moore, K. S., & Miceli, M. P. (1997). An exploration of the meaning and consequences of workaholism. *Human Relations*, 50, 287–314.
Shimazu, A., Demerouti, E., Bakker, A. B., Shimada, K., & Kawakami, N. (2011). Workaholism and well-being among Japanese dual-earner couples: A spillover-crossover perspective. *Social Science & Medicine*, 73, 399–409.
Shimazu, A., Schaufeli, W. B., & Taris, T. W. (2010). How does workaholism affect worker health and performance? The mediating role of coping. *International Journal of Behavioral Medicine*, 17, 154–160.
Snir, R., & Harpaz, I. (2004). Attitudinal and demographic antecedents of workaholism. *Journal of Organizational Change Management*, 17, 520–536.
Snir, R., & Harpaz, I. (2006). The workaholism phenomenon: A cross-national perspective. *Career Development International*, 11, 374–393.
Snir, R., & Harpaz, I. (2009). Cross-cultural differences concerning heavy work investment. *Cross-Cultural Research*, 43, 309–319.
Suh, E., Diener, E., Oishi, S., & Triandis, H. C. (1998). The shifting basis of life satisfaction judgments across cultures: Emotions versus norms. *Journal of Personality and Social Psychology*, 74, 482–493.
Triandis, H. C. (1994). *Culture and social behavior*. New York: McGraw-Hill.
Triandis, H. C. (1995). *Individualism and collectivism*. Boulder, CO: Westview.
Triandis, H. C. (2001). Individualism–collectivism and personality. *Journal of Personality*, 69, 907–924.
Triandis, H. C., & Suh, E. M. (2002). Cultural influences on personality. *Annual Review of Psychology*, 53, 133–160.
Tsui, A. S. (2007). From homogenization to pluralism: International research in the academy and beyond. *Academy of Management Journal*, 50, 1353–1364.

Tung, R. L., & Verbeke, A. (2010). Beyond Hofstede and GLOBE: Improving the quality of cross-cultural research. *Journal of International Business Studies*, 41, 1259–1274.

Van Beek, I., Hu, Q., Schaufeli, W. B., Taris, T. W., & Schreurs, B. H. J. (2012). For fun, love, or money: What drives workaholic, engaged and burned-out employees at work? *Applied Psychology: An International Review*, 61, 30–55.

Way, B. M., & Lieberman, M. D. (2010). Is there a genetic contribution to cultural differences? Collectivism, individualism and genetic markers of social sensitivity. *Social Cognitive and Affective Neuroscience*, 5, 203–211.

17

BRING YOUR PARENTS TO THE JOB INTERVIEW

Intergenerational Similarity in (Heavy) Work Investment

Raphael Snir

Introduction

Heavy Work Investment

Snir and Harpaz (2012), who introduced the concept of Heavy Work Investment (HWI), maintain that *both* long hours and substantial effort are its core dimensions. Effort means the amount of either physical or mental energy allocated to work (Becker, 1985). They distinguish two major types of heavy work investment. The first is situational, stemming from external and uncontrollable predictors. At least in the short range, external predictors such as basic financial needs (e.g., to support one's family, pay debts), and a demanding supervisor or organizational culture (e.g., the overtime culture in high-tech organizations, and among hospital physicians) are uncontrollable. The second major type of heavy work investment is dispositional, stemming from personal characteristics. Snir and Harpaz (2012) further distinguish two subtypes of dispositional heavy work investment, for instance workaholism, which is based on an addiction to work (an internal, negative, uncontrollable, and stable predictor), and work devotion as an expression of a passion for work (an internal, positive, controllable, and stable predictor). Work devotion is similar to Spence and Robbins's (1992) concept of work enthusiasm, as well as to the concept of work engagement, which refers to a positive, fulfilling, work-related state of mind characterized by vigor, dedication, and absorption (Schaufeli, Shimazu, & Taris, 2009; Schaufeli, Taris, & Bakker, 2006). According to Snir and Harpaz (2012), the difference between addiction and passion for work is similar to the distinction of Vallerand, Blanchard, Mageau, Koestner, Ratelle, Leonard, and Gagne (2003) between Obsessive Passion and

Harmonious Passion. Obsessive Passion occurs when individuals feel compelled to engage in an activity because of internal contingencies that control them; whereas Harmonious Passion occurs when individuals have freely accepted an activity as important to them without any contingencies attached to it.

In this chapter, I explore intergenerational similarity in personality traits, values, attitudes, and behavior in general; and the two-dimensional parental role in this respect. Later on, I address specifically intergenerational similarity in work investment with the emphasis on heavy work investment subtypes, discuss its possible implications, and outline research dilemmas and future directions.

Intergenerational Similarity in Personality Traits, Values, Attitudes, and Behavior

Psychologists, sociologists, and others have been interested in parent–offspring similarity for a long time, and have calculated many parent–offspring correlations for personality traits and attitudes since the 1930s (Loehlin, 2005). Parental intergenerational transmission, which refers to the transfer of personality traits, values, attitudes, and behavior from parents to children, is considered one of the major causes of intergenerational similarity. The present section provides a brief review of recent studies on intergenerational similarity in personality traits, attitudes, and behavior.

To examine the relationships between personality traits over generations, a cross-sectional study was conducted for fathers and mothers of school-age children of grades 5–9. Personality traits (e.g., novelty seeking, self-directedness) measured by the Temperament and Character Inventory (TCI) were transmitted from the parents to the children (Kitamura, Shikai, Uji, Hiramura, Tanaka, & Shono, 2009). In another personality study, regression analyses revealed that athletes' self-oriented perfectionism; was predicted by parents' self-oriented perfectionism; athletes' other-oriented perfectionism was predicted by parents' other-oriented perfectionism; and athletes' socially prescribed perfectionism was predicted by parents' socially prescribed and other-oriented perfectionism (Appleton, Hall, & Hill, 2010).

In the following description of studies, I address attitudes in their broader sense, including decisions and intentions.

Dohmen, Falk, Huffman, and Sunde (2009) used measures of risk attitudes for a sample of more than 3,000 children and their parents. They provided a strong indication that parents who stated they were more willing to take risks had children with similar attitudes. The correlation between children's risk attitudes with those of both mothers and fathers was statistically significant.

Using a sample of mother–child pairs from the National Longitudinal Survey of Youth 1979, Farré and Vella (2013) studied the intergenerational transmission of attitudes regarding women's roles. They found that a mother's attitudes had a statistically significant effect on those of her children. They also found a strong association between the attitudes of sons in their youth and their wives' labor supply as adults. Wight (2008) also examined the relationship between parents' gender-role attitudes and their children's subsequent gender-role attitudes as adults. Overall, it was found that attitudes remained stable across generations, particularly from mothers to children.

Using data from the German Socioeconomic Panel (GSOEP), Knoll, Riedel, and Schlenker (2012) found that children are highly influenced by their father's job. About 23 percent of the participants in their sample had chosen the same occupation as their fathers. Laspita, Breugst, Heblich, and Patzelt (2012) drew on cross-cultural theory and the Global Leadership and Organizational Behavior Effectiveness project to develop a model for the transmission of entrepreneurial intentions within families in different cultures. Using data on more than 40,000 individuals from 15 countries, they showed that beyond the transmission of entrepreneurial intentions from parents to children, grandparents—directly, or "indirectly" through the parents—impacted the offspring's intentions.

Finally, with regard to behavior, Wilhelm, Brown, Rooney, and Steinberg (2008) examined the correlation between the generosity of parents and the generosity of their adult children using regression models of adult children's charitable giving. They found the religious giving of parents and children strongly correlated—as closely as their income and wealth.

Liefbroer and Elzinga (2012) maintain that research on intergenerational transmission tends to focus on the transmission of specific behaviors from parents to children, and stress the importance of studying the intergenerational transmission of *behavioral patterns* as well. They examined the similarity in demographic trajectories of parents and children. Their results showed that intergenerational transmission of demographic trajectories occurred despite major changes in the incidence and timing of family-related events (e.g., marriage and childbearing) across generations. A comparison of the average similarity of parent–child pairs with that of dyads consisting of unrelated persons from the parental and child generations showed that the similarity of the latter group was about 20 percent lower than that of parent–child pairs.

The following section elaborates the ways in which parents transmit their personality trait, values, attitudes, and behavior to their children.

Intergenerational Transmission of Personality Traits, Values, Attitudes, and Behavior: The Two-dimensional Parental Role

A basic question in social sciences is the degree to which children's personality, values, attitudes, and behavior are influenced by genes (familial and general), environment, and the interaction of the two. According to Loehlin (2005), some have emphasized the role of mechanisms centered on learning, such as imitation and identification, in accounting for parents–child similarity. For example, work values develop through interaction and identification with various socializing agents, as well as through the individual's experiences in family, school, and work settings (Kohn & Schooler, 1969; Super, 1957; Schwarzweller, 1959). If individuals see that other family members (e.g., parents, spouses, siblings, significant others) work excessively, they may have a tendency to treat their own work in the same manner because they are influenced by such important role models (Machlowitz, 1980). Among socializing agents, parents are the primary and potentially most influential ones, at least during early and middle stages of vocational development, since they are the principal worker models with which their children identify and whose attitudes and values they internalize (Super, 1957; Williams, 1972). Parents' attitudes as regard to work and employment and their work experiences shape the development of their children's work attitudes (e.g., Barling, Dupre, & Hepburn, 1998; Loughlin & Barling, 1998). Moreover, parents have a preference for endowing children with attitudes similar to their own and exert effort in order to shape their children's endowments (Fernandez, 2007). This preference also affects parents' marriage choices, causing them to seek out a spouse with similar attitudes, in order to avoid distortions in the child's attitudes (Dohmen, Falk, Huffman, & Sunde, 2009).

On the other hand, behavior geneticists have pointed out that insofar as the genes influence the development of personality traits and attitudes in each generation, the fact that parents and children share genes can also contribute to their similarity (Loehlin, 2005). Their most frequently cited result is that genetic factors explain some 50 to 60 percent of the variation in adults' IQ, while family environment explains little of the variation in it. The numbers are somewhat similar for decompositions of the variance of educational attainment (Sacerdote, 2008). Overall, it seems that in ordinary intact families parents serve as *both* social and biological agents for their children.

Intergenerational Similarity in Work Investment

Altonji and Dunn (2000) found strong similarities within families in work hours that run along gender lines and are due primarily to linkages in work preferences. Toledo (2005) examined the intergenerational persistence of work hours between fathers and sons in the USA. Using data from the Panel Study of Income Dynamics, he found a strong persistence in the permanent component of hours worked, which was mostly explained by the intergenerational correlation of leisure preferences. Based on data from a sample of 3,169 adult women in the 2002–2004 wave of the Netherlands Kinship Panel Study, van Putten, Dykstra, and Schippers (2008) found that women raised by a working mother work about two more hours per week than those raised by a homemaking mother. Olivetti and Patacchini (2012) explored the intergenerational determinants of women's work choices. For a recent cohort of women, they found a general positive relationship between the labor supply of mothers and daughters.

Concerning workaholism specifically, Machlowitz (1980) found that some workaholics in her study followed in the footsteps of their workaholic parents. Robinson (1998) claimed that children of workaholics tend to become high achievers to gain their parents' approval. Adult children of workaholics showed a greater tendency than adult children of non-workaholics to be workaholics themselves (Navarette, 1998; Searcy, 2000). Statistically significant relationships were found between college students' perceived parental workaholism and their own workaholism (Chamberlin & Zhang, 2009). Finally, Kravina, Falco, De Carlo, Andreassen, and Pallesen (2013) found that fathers' scores on working excessively were positively related to their adult children's level of workaholism.

The above findings add to the growing evidence that parental behaviors during childhood have long-reaching consequences for children's behaviors, also in the realm of work investment. Hence:

Proposition 1: *There is a positive relation between a parent's work investment in the formative years and his/her same-sex adult child's current work investment.*

Zumbuehl, Dohmen, and Pfann (2013) found that parents who invest more in the upbringing of their children have offspring who are more similar to them with respect to risk and trust attitudes and thus transmit their own attitudes more strongly. Min, Silverstein, and Lendon (2012) examined how the quality of intergenerational relationship moderates the strength of intergenerational transmission of religious beliefs and gender role attitudes over the life course. They addressed this question using the 1971 and 2000 waves of the Longitudinal Study of Generations (LSOG). Their sample consisted of 775 parent–child dyads in which parents' age averaged 44 years in 1971 and their offspring's age averaged 48 years in 2000. They found that the quality of the parent–child relationship strengthened the contemporaneous transmission of religious beliefs and the lagged transmission of gender-role attitudes. The transmission of these attitudes was considerably weaker and less stable over time than it was for religious orientation, but tended to have a lagged impact under conditions of high solidarity. In a similar manner,

Proposition 2: *The relation between a parent's work investment in formative years and his/her adult child's current work investment is stronger if the child–parent relationship during the formative years was profound and positive.*

Dispositional heavy work investors are more likely to be attracted to demanding jobs, to be selected by organizations for such jobs, and to keep these jobs even when less demanding jobs are available, due to their personal characteristics. Moreover, they may maintain their HWI even in the absence of financial justification to work at all. On the other hand, situational heavy work investors are likely to reduce their HWI when they have the opportunity to do so. For instance, needy heavy work investors may work less if their financial pressures ease. Similarly, employer-directed heavy work investors may quit their current jobs during an economic upswing in favor of other, less demanding, occupational alternatives (Snir & Harpaz, 2012). Snir and Harpaz (2012) also maintain that dispositional heavy work investors are likely to experience higher degrees of both positive affect (e.g., pleasure derived from the successful completion of a task, or a promotion) and negative affect (e.g., frustration due to a setback on an important project, or forced retirement) as a reaction to work-related events, than are situational heavy work investors.

In sum, a dispositional investor parent serves as a much more behaviorally consistent and emotionally involved role model of HWI for his/her child, than a situational investor does. Accordingly,

Proposition 3: *An adult child's likelihood of being a heavy work investor is stronger if his/her parent was a dispositional heavy work investor than if his/her parent was a situational one.*

Operant conditioning (Skinner, 1938) is a type of learning in which an individual's behavior is modified by its outcomes, which may reinforce or inhibit recurrence of that behavior. According to McMillan and O'Driscoll (2008), an operant condition implies that workaholism develops where it leads to desired outcomes, and thus dominates high earning, high-status jobs. Hence, if HWI, regardless of its causes (dispositional or situational), leads to pleasant outcomes (e.g., a sense of accomplishment, peer approval, and organizational rewards) it will be repeated, as one attempts to re-experience the pleasing outcomes. Moreover, according to the rationale of social learning theory (Bandura, 1977) in such circumstances one also has a greater likelihood of serving as a potent role model in the work domain for one's children, due to one's influence by virtue of being a parent, and the fact that one's behavior is rewarded. Hence:

Proposition 4: *An adult child's likelihood of being a heavy work investor is stronger if his/her parent's heavy work investment in the formative years had positive outcomes than if it had negative outcomes, regardless of the causes.*

Workaholics were found to have lower levels of satisfaction with aspects of work (e.g., job, career), non-work (e.g., family, friends), and psychological well-being, in contrast to work enthusiasts across countries and occupations (e.g., Bonebright, Clay, & Ankenmann, 2000; Burke & Fiksenbaum, 2009a, 2009b). In three recent studies comparing work engagement and workaholism, the former was associated with one's own better psychological and physical health, job and family satisfaction, and job performance. In addition, among dual-earner couples one's work engagement was associated with one's partner's better engagement. By contrast, workaholism was associated with one's own poor psychological and physical health, job and family satisfaction, work–family balance, and job performance. Furthermore, workaholism was associated with one's partner's poor work–family balance (Shimazu, 2012).

The studies cited do not necessarily imply that HWI due to negative dispositional causes such as workaholism has only negative outcomes, or that HWI due to positive dispositional causes such as work devotion has only positive outcomes. However, since workaholism is mainly associated with negative outcomes, and work devotion mainly with positive outcomes, a work-devoted parent has a higher likelihood of serving as a potent role model for his/her children. Hence:

Proposition 5: *An adult child's likelihood of being a heavy work investor is stronger if his/her parent's heavy work investment in the formative years was due to positive dispositional causes than if it was due to negative dispositional causes.*

HWI may have different outcomes for the parties concerned (i.e., the individual, his/her family and workplace, and society). Moreover, the outcomes for a specific party are not necessarily uniform (Snir & Harpaz, 2013). For example, one's family may enjoy a high material standard of living due to one's paid overtime. On the other hand, one's HWI may interfere with family. Consequently, one can devote less time and attention to one's children. In case of mixed outcomes of work investment, viewing them on the bottom line as positive or negative constitutes a subjective perception of an objective reality. Hence:

Proposition 6: *A child's perception of the nature of his/her parent's work investment outcomes in the formative years mediates the relation between these outcomes and the adult child's current work investment.*

Among the personality traits that may encourage HWI are Type A Behavior Pattern (Seybold & Salomone, 1994), and some dimensions of obsessive-compulsive personality (namely obstinacy, orderliness, rigidity, and superego: Mudrack, 2004). Clark et al. (1996) also found workaholism positively related to compulsiveness (r = 0.41), as well as to the higher order ('Big Five') trait of conscientiousness (r = 0.53). Aziz and Tronzo (2011) found a positive correlation between conscientiousness and Spence and Robbins' (1992) three workaholism components (work involvement, work drive, and work enjoyment).

Some attitudes may also predict HWI. For example, Snir and Harpaz (2004) found that respondents with a high level of occupational satisfaction worked more hours per week than those with a low level of occupational satisfaction. On the other hand, people with a high level of family centrality worked fewer hours per week than those with a low level of family centrality. Snir and Harpaz (2006) examined the workaholism phenomenon from a cross-national perspective through representative samples of the labor force in Belgium, Israel, Japan, Netherlands, and the USA. The following finding has remained stable across nations: respondents with a high level of work centrality worked more hours per week than did those with a low level of work centrality. Douglas and Morris (2006) suggested that a low preference for leisure due to experience of boredom during leisure activities is positively related to working long hours.

Since (1) in ordinary intact families there is a parent–offspring similarity in personality traits and attitudes that may stem from both social and biological factors, and (2) some personality traits and attitudes may predict HWI, there follows:

Proposition 7a: *An adult child's work-related personality variables (such as conscientiousness) mediate the relation between the parent's work-related personality variables and the adult child's work investment.*

Proposition 7b: *An adult child's work-related attitudes (such as work centrality) mediate the relation between the parent's work-related attitudes and the adult child's work investment.*

Implications

This chapter adds to the theoretical discussion on intergenerational similarity, focusing specifically on the work domain. In this section the practical implications of intergenerational similarity in work investment are elaborated.

Selection of Job Candidates

Sierra Atlantic, an American company with operations in India, requires all Indian job applicants to bring their parents to work with them for an introduction to the company. Sierra Atlantic took the step to influence these parents, who have more sway over their children's career choices than do their American counterparts, in the hope that it would be translated into increased company loyalty in their children (Cooper, 2004). True, the notion of implementing such a step in Western societies is quite far-fetched. However, in the search for candidates for demanding jobs, gathering information about their parents' work investment patterns as a part of a biodata questionnaire seems like a good idea.

Organizational Policy Regarding Work Hours

Organizations start serving as a major socialization agent for their employees only in their adulthood. By then, people are usually less susceptible to attempts at attitudinal or behavioral change (Snir, Harpaz, & Ben-Baruch, 2009). Accordingly, the effectiveness of policies designed to encourage working long hours on the one hand, or a work–life balance on the other, is questionable. Indeed, Russo and Waters (2006) found that workaholics, in contrast to their enthusiastic workaholic counterparts, did not experience easing of the work–family conflict with increased access to flexible scheduling. In view of the findings on intergenerational similarity in respect of work hours (e.g., Altonji & Dunn, 2000; Toledo, 2005), organizational interventions to increase/reduce employees' work hours need to be strong and pervasive to overwhelm earlier parental influence.

Breaking the Workaholic Vicious Cycle

According to a recent literature review (Sussman, 2012), workaholics experience relatively high work–family conflict and negative life outcomes including high perceived stress, low self-esteem, low life satisfaction, sleeping difficulties, career dissatisfaction and poor performance, delay of planned retirement, work burnout, and ill-health. Snir and Harpaz (2012) maintain that negative personal work/non-work outcomes (e.g., burnout and stress) are highest among workaholics and needy heavy work investors, lowest among work-devoted investors, and in between among employer-directed heavy work investors. On the other hand, positive personal work/non-work outcomes (e.g., work and life satisfaction) are lowest among workaholics and needy heavy work investors, highest among work-devoted investors, and in between among employer-directed heavy work investors. Hence, workaholism seems to be a problematic HWI subtype.

In view of the findings concerning intergenerational similarity in workaholism (e.g., Chamberlin & Zhang, 2009; Kravina, Falco, De Carlo, Schou Andreassen, & Pallesen, 2013), proper measures should be taken at *early* stages of one's work career to decrease the risk of intergenerational transmission of workaholism. Such measures include identifying those at risk of becoming workaholics and those who are already workaholics, as well as implementation of therapeutic interventions (such as participation in Workaholics Anonymous meetings, psychotherapy, and time-management training).

Research Dilemmas and Future Directions

In this section, several research dilemmas and future directions concerning intergenerational similarity in work investment are presented.

Which Parent is the Most Influential?

Which parent has the strongest influence over the adult child's work investment: the father, the mother, or the same-sex parent?

The relatively few studies on this topic provide evidence of same-sex parent influence (e.g., Altonji & Dunn, 2000; Olivetti & Patacchini, 2012; van Putten, Dykstra, & Schippers, 2008). Snir and Harpaz (2012) claim that gender is among the most relevant background predictors of HWI. For example, in a cross-national study, workaholism was found to be primarily a male phenomenon (Snir & Harpaz, 2006). On the other hand, Wharton and Blair-Loy (2002) state that employed women in the industrialized world continue to bear more responsibility for family and children than do their male counterparts so they are more often considered candidates for a part-time job. Drago, Wooden, and Black (2006) found that women are relatively rare among those who work long hours, especially long-hours volunteers (those who prefer to work long hours). Snir, Harpaz, and Ben-Baruch (2009) found that a contrasting parenthood effect on men and women prevails even in the demanding high-tech sector, where women are expected to work long hours and play down their care-giving activities. Fathers invested more weekly hours in work than childless men, whereas mothers invested fewer weekly hours in work than childless women.

However, the literature on work-related issues in general provides mixed findings concerning parental influence. For example, Wiese and Freund (2011) found that same-sex parents served as main role models for the adolescents' own plans regarding their future work involvement, whereas opposite-sex parents served as models for the preferred degree of work participation for the adolescents' future life partners. On the other hand, Wijting, Arnold, and Conrad (1978) found that at earlier ages (grades 6, 9, and 10) there was greater similarity in work values between children and their same-sex parents, but older (grade 12) boys and girls were most similar to their fathers. Van de Werfhorst, De Graaf, and Kraaykamp (2001) found an association between the fields of study of father and child, which appeared to be particularly strong in general, teacher/educational, and agricultural fields. This association was hardly affected by other family characteristics. Finally, in a recent study on elite junior athletes, it was found that the intergenerational transmission of perfectionism between parents and their athletic child was not limited to same-sex, parent–child dyads (Appleton, Hall, & Hill, 2010).

In practical terms, it is recommended if possible to compare an adult child with both parents on investments in work. Alternatively, the adult child should be compared with the parent whom he/she *perceives* as the more influential of the two in regard to his/her investment in work.

The Relative Weight of Social and Biological Parental Influences

Research on the relative weight of social and biological parental influences on their adult child's work investment is practically nonexistent; therefore future research on this topic is clearly needed. Currently, I have referred to two studies concerning relevant work-related variables (occupational choices and conscientiousness).

Time investment in work has proved positively related to holding a professional or managerial position (Jacobs & Gerson, 1997). To separate effects related to genetic factors (nature) and parental education or role models (nurture), Knoll, Riedel, and Schlenker (2012) determined the persistence of occupational choices among generations separately for children who grew up with their biological fathers and for those who did not. Their results suggest that nurture especially plays a decisive role in explaining the choice of one's occupation.

Loehlin (2005) compiled a table of 1,279 correlations between a parent and a child on some personality traits or attitudes, based on 59 samples from the published literature. He differentiated four parent–child categories: (1) parent–child in ordinary intact families, (2) parent–child in adoptive families, (3) birth parent and his/her adopted-away child, and (4) a monozygotic twin and his/her twin's child. In the first category the parent serves as both biological and social agent, and in the second category as social but not biological agent. The third and the forth categories were merged, as reflecting cases in which genes are shared but not family environments. The Big Five Model taps five basic personality dimensions, among them conscientiousness. A highly conscientious person is responsible, organized, dependable, and persistent; hence, this dimension is highly relevant regarding HWI (e.g., Aziz & Tronzo, 2011). Loehlin (2005) reported that mean parent–child correlations on conscientiousness were low: 0.9 for the biological and social parent–child type, 0.2 for the social but not biological type, and 0.11 for the biological but not social type.

Bidirectional Influence in Parent–Child Relationships

De Mol and Buysse (2008) described the theoretical development in the domain of parent–child relations. By the classical unidirectional approach, parents are seen as the only active agents, and children are regarded as passive recipients of parental influence. By a second unidirectional approach, although the influence of children on their parents is recognized, it concerns effects that do not entail much active involvement on the part of the child (e.g. the child's age, gender, and temperament). The bidirectional approach stresses the co-occurrence of both directions of influence—from parent to child and from child to parent, and the equal agency (i.e., the human capacity for initiating purposeful behavior to influence the other, and the ability to interpret and construct meanings out of relational experiences) of parents and children. Moreover, Kuczynski and Parkin (2007) maintain that agency and bidirectional influence in parent–child relationships must be understood in the context of an intimate long-term relationship.

Based on the bidirectional approach, it is possible that those who became parents in their twenties not only influence their children's future work habits, but are also influenced in their later work career by their adult children's current work habits. Hence, intergenerational similarity in work investment among such parent–child dyads might be created due to *bidirectional* influence.

Perceptual Biases

Selective perception is the tendency to interpret selectively what one sees, on the basis of one's interests, needs, background, experience, and values. This tendency may provide a possible alternative explanation for Chamberlin and Zhang's (2009) finding that students who perceived their parents as more workaholic actually scored higher on their own level of workaholism. As they speculated, this finding could also mean that students who are more workaholic themselves merely tend to *perceive* their parents as being more workaholic, while the parents may not actually be workaholic. Indeed, Appleton, Hall, and Hill's (2010) finding that athletes' perceptions of their parents' perfectionism, but *not* parents' self-reported perfectionism, emerged as a significant predictor of athletes' own perfectionism may constitute an indication for the need to address the issue of selective perception bias as a possible artificial inflator of intergenerational similarity.

Accordingly, we should prefer objective measures of work hours and effort to assess intergenerational similarity in work investment. Yet, since such measures are not always available, taking a multi-source approach (e.g., using both self-reports and acquaintance reports concerning the focal person: Aziz & Zickar, 2006) is strongly recommended (Snir & Harpaz, 2012).

Finally, conducting a longitudinal study (i.e., assessing the parent's work investment in his/her child's formative years at Time 1, and the adult child's work investment at Time 2) is preferable to conducting a cross-sectional study due to the possible retrospective bias in both self-reports and acquaintance reports concerning the parent's work investment in his/her child's formative years.

Intergenerational Differences and Their Possible Sources

This chapter focuses on intergenerational similarity in general and particularly in work investment. Note however that there is a large body of literature focusing on low intergenerational similarity or even intergenerational *differences*. For example, based on parent–child personality correlations compiled by Loehlin (2005), a parent and a child do not resemble each other very much. He found that the average r in ordinary intact families, in which the parent serves as both biological and social agent for his/her child, was 0.13.

Much attention has been paid to intergenerational differences in work values, attitudes, and behaviors (e.g., Alsop, 2008; Filipczak, 1994; Kupperschmidt, 2000; Parry & Urwin, 2009; Smola & Sutton, 2002). For instance, in a study with American respondents, Smola and Sutton (2002) found that Generation X-ers' work values were significantly different from those of Baby Boomers. They were generally found to be less loyal to the company and more "me"-oriented. At the same time, there were indications of a more idealistic attitude to work among Generation X-ers. They felt more strongly that working hard was an indication of one's worth. On the other hand, Parry and Urwin (2011) claim that given the multitude of problems found in the evidence on intergenerational differences in work values, it is not clear what value the notion of generations has for practitioners.

In a study on childhood workaholism and Type A behavior in school-age children, no relationship was found between parental workaholism and child Type A behavior as rated by parents, as well as children's self-perceived workaholism (Robinson & Kelley, 1999). However, one may claim that childhood workaholism and Type A behavior are not necessarily indicative of one's future work investment as an adult.

Disregarding age effects and the macro-level economic situation may account for observed intergenerational differences in general and in work investment particularly.

Disregarding Age Effects

The term "age effects" refers to the changing views, attitudes, and behaviors of individuals as they mature (Parry & Urwin, 2011). For example, students' values change as they move from middle school to high school, to college and into the workforce (Walsh, Vacha-Haase, Kapes, Dresden, Thomson, & Ochoa-Shargey, 1996). Rhodes (1983) reported that work attitudes, values, and satisfaction change as workers pass through career stages. Furnham (1990) suggested that the relationship between age and Protestant Work Ethic beliefs may be curvilinear, peaking around the age of 60. Smola and Sutton (2002) found that work values change to some extent as workers grow older. Accordingly, a comparison between a parent's work investment and his/her adult child's work investment at *different* ages or career stages may artificially result in observed intergenerational differences. As Twenge, Campbell, Hoffman, and Lance (2010) maintain, researchers should isolate intergenerational differences from age differences.

Macro-Level Economic Situation

One of the two major dimensions of cross-cultural variation is linked to the transition from an industrial society to post-industrial societies, which brings about a polarization between survival and self-expression values. The unprecedented wealth that has accumulated in advanced societies during the past generation means that an increasing share of the population has grown up taking survival for granted. Thus, priorities have shifted from an overwhelming emphasis on economic and physical security toward an increasing emphasis on subjective well-being, self-expression, and quality of life (Inglehart & Welzel, 2013). This notion has both cross-national and intergenerational implications.

Assuming that values affect behavior, Snir and Harpaz (2009) expected and indeed found cross-national differences: work investment was heavier and situational heavy work investors were more likely to be common in societies where survival values are important, as compared to societies where self-expression values are important. On the other hand, since they conceptualized work devotion as an expression of one's passion for work, Snir and Harpaz (2009) expected and indeed found that work-devoted persons were more likely to be common in societies where self-expression values are important than in societies where survival values are important.

Wide intergenerational value changes will be found in societies that have experienced a long period of rising economic and physical security. Young people will be much more likely than old people to prioritize well-being values over survival values. This reflects the fact that the young experienced greater security in their formative years than the old. Conversely, the difference between the values of young and old will be small or nonexistent in societies that have experienced relatively little increase in per capita income (Inglehart, 1997). Again, assuming that values affect behavior, a larger intergenerational difference in work investment will be found in rich and secure societies than in impoverished societies. Future research should address this topic.

Overall, the present chapter signifies the need to empirically explore the nature of the relation between investments in work of parents and their children. The chapter also outlines possible sources of intergenerational similarity in work investment, describes its possible practical implications, and presents several research dilemmas and future directions concerning this similarity.

References

Alsop, R. (2008). *The trophy kids grow up: How the millennial generation is shaking up the workplace.* San Francisco, CA: Jossey-Bass.

Altonji, J.G. and Dunn, T.A. (2000). An intergenerational model of wages, hours, and earnings. *The Journal of Human Resources,* 35(2), 221–258.

Appleton, P.R., Hall, H.K., and Hill, A.P. (2010). Family patterns of perfectionism: An examination of elite junior athletes and their parents. *Psychology of Sport and Exercise,* 11(5), 363–371.

Aziz, S. and Tronzo, C.L. (2011). Exploring the relationship between workaholism facets and personality traits: A replication in American workers. *The Psychological Record,* 61(2), 269–286.

Aziz, S. and Zickar, M.J. (2006). A cluster analysis investigation of workaholism as a syndrome. *Journal of Occupational Health Psychology,* 11(1), 52–62.

Bandura, A. (1977). *Social learning theory.* New York: General Learning Press.

Barling, J., Dupre, K.E., and Hepburn, C. G. (1998). Effects of parents' job insecurity on children's work beliefs and attitudes. *Journal of Applied Psychology,* 83(1), 112.

Becker, G.S. (1985). Human capital, effort, and the sexual division of labor. *Journal of Labor Economics,* 3 (Supplement), S33–S58.

Bonebright, C.A., Clay, D.L., and Ankenmann, R.D. (2000). The relationship of workaholism with work–life conflict, life satisfaction, and purpose in life. *Journal of Counseling Psychology,* 47(4), 469–477.

Burke, R.J. and Fiksenbaum, L. (2009a). Work motivations, work outcomes, and health: Passion versus addiction. *Journal of Business Ethics,* 84 (Supplement 2), 257–263.

Burke, R.J. and Fiksenbaum, L. (2009b). Work motivations, satisfactions, and health among managers: Passion versus addiction. *Cross-Cultural Research,* 43(4), 349–365.

Chamberlin, C.M. and Zhang, N. (2009). Workaholism, health, and self-acceptance. *Journal of Counseling and Development,* 87(2), 159–169.

Clark, L.A., Livesley, W.J., Schroeder, M.L., and Irish, S.L. (1996). Convergence of two systems for assessing specific traits of personality disorder. *Psychological Assessment,* 8(3), 294–303.

Cooper, C. (October 28, 2004). Mandatory: Bring your parents to the job interview. Sierra Atlantic's new spin on keeping Indian employees from job hopping. http://news.cnet.com/8301-10784_3-5431356-7.html (accessed December 27, 2013).

De Mol, J. and Buysse, A. (2008). The phenomenology of children's influence on parents. *Journal of Family Therapy,* 30(2), 163–193.

Dohmen, T., Falk, A., Huffman, D., and Sunde, U. (2009). The intergenerational transmission of attitudes. *CESifo DICE Report,* 7(1), 8–12.

Douglas, E.J. and Morris, R.J. (2006). Workaholic, or just hard worker? *Career Development International,* 11(5), 394–417.

Drago, R., Wooden, M., and Black, D. (2006). *Long work hours: Volunteers and conscripts* (Melbourne Institute Working Paper No. 27/06). Victoria, Australia: Melbourne Institute of Applied Economic and Social Research, the University of Melbourne.

Farré, L. and Vella, F. (2013). The intergenerational transmission of gender role attitudes and its implications for female labour force participation. *Economica,* 80(318), 219–247.

Fernandez, R. (2007). Culture and economics. In S. Durlauf and L. Blume (Eds.), *New Palgrave dictionary of economics, second edition.* Basingstoke and New York: Palgrave Macmillan.

Filipczak, B. (1994). It's just a job: Generation X at work. *Training,* 31(4), 21–27.

Furnham, A. (1990). *The Protestant work ethic: The psychology of work-related beliefs and behaviours.* New York: Routledge.

Inglehart, R. (1997). *Modernization and postmodernization: Cultural, economic and political change in 43 societies.* Princeton, NJ: Princeton University Press.

Inglehart, R. and Welzel, C. (2013). The WVS cultural map of the world. www.worldvaluessurvey.org/wvs/articles/folder_published/article_base_54 (accessed 20 March, 2014).

Jacobs, J.A. and Gerson, K. (1997). *The endless day or the flexible office: Working hours, work-family conflict, and gender equity in the modern workplace.* A report to the Alfred P. Sloan Foundation.

Kitamura, T., Shikai, N., Uji, M., Hiramura, H., Tanaka, N., and Shono, M. (2009). Intergenerational transmission of parenting style and personality: Direct influence or mediation? *Journal of Child and Family Studies,* 18(5), 541–556.

Knoll, B., Riedel, N., and Schlenker, E. (2012). *He's a chip off the old block: The persistency of occupational choices among generations.* Stuttgart: University of Hohenheim.

Kohn, M.L. and Schooler, C. (1969). Class, occupation and orientation. *American Sociological Review,* 34, 659–678.

Kravina, L., Falco, A., De Carlo, N.A., Andreassen, C.S., and Pallesen, S. (2013). Workaholism and work engagement in the family: The relationship between parents and children as a risk factor. *European Journal of Work and Organizational Psychology,* (ahead-of-print), 1–9.

Kuczynski, L. and Parkin, M. (2007) Agency and bidirectionality in socialization: Interactions, transactions, and relational dialectics. In J.E. Grusec and P.D. Hastings (Eds.), *Handbook of socialization* (pp. 259–283). New York: Guilford Press.

Kupperschmidt, B. (2000). Multigenerational employees: Strategies for effective management. *Health Care Manager*, 19, 65–76.

Laspita, S., Breugst, N., Heblich, S., and Patzelt, H. (2012). Intergenerational transmission of entrepreneurial intentions. *Journal of Business Venturing*, 27(4), 414–435.

Liefbroer, A.C. and Elzinga, C.H. (2012). Intergenerational transmission of behavioural patterns: How similar are parents' and children's demographic trajectories? *Advances in Life Course Research*, 17(1), 1–10.

Loehlin, J.C. (2005). Resemblance in personality and attitudes between parents and their children. In S. Bowles, H. Gintis, and M.O. Groves (Eds.), *Unequal chances* (pp. 192–207). New York: Russell Sage Foundation.

Loughlin, C.A. and Barling, J. (1998). Teenagers' part-time employment and their work-related attitudes and aspirations. *Journal of Organizational Behavior*, 19(2), 197–207.

Machlowitz, M. (1980). *Workaholics. Living with them, working with them.* Reading, MA: Addison-Wesley.

McMillan, L. and O'Driscoll, M. P. (2008). The wellsprings of workaholism: A comparative analysis of the explanatory theories. In R.J. Burke and C.L. Cooper (Eds.), *The long work hours culture: Causes, consequences and choices* (pp. 85–111). UK: Emerald Group Publishing.

Min, J., Silverstein, M., and Lendon, J. P. (2012). Intergenerational transmission of values over the family life course. *Advances in Life Course Research*, 17(3), 112–120.

Mudrack, P.E. (2004). Job involvement, obsessive-compulsive personality traits, and workaholic behavioral tendencies. *Journal of Organizational Change Management*, 17(5), 490–508.

Navarette, S. (1998). *An empirical study of adult children of workaholics: Psychological functioning and intergenerational transmission.* Unpublished doctoral dissertation, California Graduate Institute, Santa Barbara.

Olivetti, C. and Patacchini, E. (2012). *Mothers and friends: Intergenerational preference transmission and women's work choices*. Unpublished paper.

Parry, E. and Urwin, P. (2009). *Tapping into talent*. London: CIPD.

Parry, E. and Urwin, P. (2011). Generational differences in work values: A review of theory and evidence. *International Journal of Management Reviews*, 13(1), 79–96.

Rhodes, S. (1983). Age-related differences in work attitudes and behavior: A review and conceptual analysis. *Psychological Bulletin*, 93(2), 328–367.

Robinson, B.E. (1998). The workaholic family: A clinical perspective. *The American Journal of Family Therapy*, 26(3), 65–75.

Robinson, B.E. and Kelley, L. (1999). School age workaholic children: Type A behaviors, self-esteem, anxiety and locus of control. *Early Child Development and Care*, 158(1), 43–50.

Russo, J.A. and Waters, L.E. (2006). Workaholic worker type differences in work–family conflict: The moderating role of supervisor support and flexible work scheduling. *Career Development International*, 11(5), 418–439.

Sacerdote, B. (2008). *Nature and nurture effects on children's outcomes: What have we learned from studies of twins and adoptees?* Hanover, NH: Dartmouth College and NBER.

Schaufeli, W.B., Shimazu, A., and Taris, T.W. (2009). Being driven to work excessively hard: The evaluation of a two-factor measure of workaholism in the Netherlands and Japan. *Cross-Cultural Research,* 43(4), 320–348.

Schaufeli, W.B, Taris, T.W., and Bakker, A.B. (2006). Dr Jekyll or Mr Hyde? On the differences between work engagement and workaholism. In R.J. Burke (Ed.), *Research companion to working time and work addiction* (pp. 193–217). Northampton, MA: Edward Elgar.

Schwarzweller, H.L. (1959). Value orientations and educational and occupational choices. *Rural Sociology,* 24(4), 246–256.

Searcy, E.A. (2000). *Adult children of workaholics: Anxiety, depression, family relationships, and risk for work addiction.* Unpublished master's thesis, University of South Australia.

Seybold, K.C. and Salomone, P.R. (1994). Understanding workaholism: A review of causes and counseling approaches. *Journal of Counseling and Development,* 73(1), 4–10.

Shimazu, A. (March 20, 2012). *Is working hard good or bad for employee well-being? The distinctiveness of work engagement and workaholism.* The 30th International Congress on Occupational Health. Cancun, Mexico.

Skinner, B.F. (1938). *The behavior of organisms: An experimental analysis.* New York: Appleton-Century-Crofts.

Smola, K.W. and Sutton, C.D. (2002). Generational differences: Revisiting generational work values for the new millennium. *Journal of Organizational Behavior,* 23(4), 362–382.

Snir, R. and Harpaz, I. (2004). Attitudinal and demographic antecedents of workaholism. *Journal of Organizational Change Management,* 17(5), 520–536.

Snir, R. and Harpaz, I. (2006). The workaholism phenomenon: A cross-national perspective. *Career Development International,* 11(5), 374–393.

Snir, R. and Harpaz, I. (2009). Cross-cultural differences concerning heavy work investment. *Cross-Cultural Research,* 43(4), 309–319.

Snir, R. and Harpaz, I. (2012). Beyond workaholism: Towards a general model of heavy work investment. *Human Resource Management Review,* 22(3), 232–243.

Snir, R. and Harpaz, I. (2013). The challenge of heavy work investment. In R. Burke, S. Fox, and C. Cooper (Eds.), *Human frailties: Wrong turns on the road to success* (pp. 165–179). Farnham: Gower Publishing.

Snir, R., Harpaz, I., and Ben-Baruch, D. (2009). Centrality of and investment in work and family among Israeli high-tech workers: A bicultural perspective. *Cross-Cultural Research,* 43(4), 366–385.

Spence, J.T. and Robbins, A.S. (1992). Workaholism: Definition, measurement, and preliminary results. *Journal of Personality Assessment,* 58(1), 160–178.

Super, D.E. (1957). *The psychology of careers.* New York: Harper & Row.

Sussman, S. (2012). Workaholism: A review. *Journal of Addiction Research & Therapy,* S6, 1–10.

Toledo, M. (2005). *On the intergenerational persistence of work hours.* Job market paper. University of Rochester.

Twenge, J.M., Campbell, S.M., Hoffman, B.J., and Lance, C.E. (2010). Generational differences in work values: Leisure and extrinsic values increasing, social and intrinsic values decreasing. *Journal of Management,* 36(5), 1117–1142.

Vallerand, R.J., Blanchard, C., Mageau, G.A., Koestner, R., Ratelle, C., Leonard, M., and Gagne, M. (2003). Les passions de l'ame: On obsessive and harmonious passion. *Journal of Personality and Social Psychology,* 85(4), 756–767.

van de Werfhorst, H.G., De Graaf, N.D., and Kraaykamp, G. (2001). Intergenerational resemblance in field of study in the Netherlands. *European Sociological Review,* 17(3), 275–293.

van Putten, A.E., Dykstra, P.A., and Schippers, J.J. (2008). Just like mom? The intergenerational reproduction of women's paid work. *European Sociological Review,* 24(4), 435–449.

Walsh, B.D., Vacha-Haase, T., Kapes, J.T., Dresden, J.H., Thomson, W.A., and Ochoa-Shargey, B. (1996). The values scale: differences across grade levels for ethnic minority students. *Educational and Psychological Measurement,* 56(2), 263–275.

Wharton, A.S. and Blair-Loy, M. (2002). The "overtime culture" in a global corporation: A cross-national study of finance professionals' interest in working part-time. *Work and Occupations,* 29(1), 32–63.

Wiese, B.S. and Freund, A.M. (2011). Parents as role models: Parental behavior affects adolescents' plans for work involvement. *International Journal of Behavioral Development,* 35(3), 218–224.

Wight, V.R. (2008). *The intergenerational transmission of gender-role attitudes and behavior: How do parents matter?* Unpublished doctoral dissertation, University of Maryland.

Wijting, J.P., Arnold, C.R., and Conrad, K.A. (1978). Generational differences in work values between parents and children and between boys and girls across grade levels 6, 9, 10, and 12. *Journal of Vocational Behavior,* 12(2), 245–260.

Wilhelm, M.O., Brown, E., Rooney, P.M., and Steinberg, R. (2008). The intergenerational transmission of generosity. *Journal of Public Economics,* 92(10), 2146–2156.

Williams, T.H. (1972). Educational aspirations: Longitudinal evidence on their development in Canadian youth. *Sociology of Education,* 45(2), 107–133.

Zumbuehl, M., Dohmen, T., and Pfann, G. (2013). *Parental investment and the intergenerational transmission of economic preferences and attitudes.* IZA Discussion Paper No. 7476.

Epilogue

THE CURRENT STATE OF HEAVY WORK INVESTMENT AND FUTURE DEVELOPMENTS

Itzhak Harpaz

This part of the book commences by showing how central work is for human beings and its relation to the current state of heavy work investment. It moves on to discuss a host of negative outcomes associated with heavy work investment, in contrast to a small number of positive ones. Achieving a balance between work and life, particularly family, is suggested as an approach to cope with and alleviate some of the possible destructive consequences of heavy work investment. Next, based on Snir and Harpaz's (2012) model, a typology of heavy work investment is presented, identifying four basic types of employees. Then, some essential methodological and conceptual research needs, which have potential for improvement, are identified. Finally, the present state of heavy work investment concept is assessed, with the conclusion that at present it is still in its early stages.

Work Centrality

The role of work in life cannot be disregarded. Individuals spend a great deal of time on preparation for work or on bettering their status through education and training. The importance of work has varied throughout history; in modern industrial societies work plays a central role in people's lives and in satisfying economic, psychological, and social needs. Several studies have shown that work is second only to family among various life aspects (Harpaz & Meshoulam, 2010; MOW-International Research Team, 1987). We obtain another indication of the importance of work through observing individuals' disheartenment, reaction, and agony in situations where they are forced to quit working on account of mandatory retirement age or the misfortune of unemployment. Moreover, a survey of 21 different studies among employed respondents conducted in eight countries found that a clear majority would continue to work even in the absence of any further need to earn money (Harpaz, 2004). A study of people who won substantial amounts of money in US lotteries revealed that 85 percent continued working even without any financial need to do so (Arvey, Harpaz, & Liao, 2004).

The prominence of work is manifested by these initial accounts. Yet the borderline between need to work, the functions of work for individuals, and amount of time people currently invest in work, seems rather blurry. Average annual hours actually worked per person have decreased globally since the mid-1800s, when a working day could range from 10 to 16 hours six days a week, amounting to at least 2,880 annual hours (Chase, 1993). For most people at that time, heavy work investment for sustenance and survival seems to have been the norm. In 2012, the average annual working hours in OECD countries for individuals was 1,765. Lee, McCann, and Messenger (2007) estimate that approximately 614 million people (about 22 percent of the global workforce) work more than 48 hours a week. So apparently, while countless people were investing many hours at work, paradoxically, according to the International Labour Organization, about 200 million individuals around the world were out of work.

Negative Outcomes of Heavy Work Investment

Once the essence of this volume is perceived, the reader, who may be quite familiar with the concept of heavy work investment (HWI), will realize that focusing just on working hours is not sufficient to fully portray HWI. Hours worked is only one of its components, yet it is the most observable, relatively easy to measure, and its impact cannot be ignored. Moreover, there is a void concerning the "effort" component of HWI; therefore, this section will present some studies showing negative outcomes of heavy work investment, particularly pertaining to its lengthy work hours.

With regard to working excessively, Caruso (2006) reports several problems associated with long work hours such as sleep deprivation, poor recovery after work effort, mental and physiological dysfunction, fertility problems, and injuries. Caruso (2006) contends that working long hours has some detrimental consequences for family relationships, including late marriage and late childbirth, and also reports that children of heavy workers suffer from excessive weight. There is also a considerable price tag affecting the community, namely blunders caused by exhausted workers that take a toll on individuals and organizations, medical errors that may result in fatalities, and car and work accidents that may cause disasters and environmental hazards, to name just a few (Caruso, 2006).

Barton and Folkard (1993) found that an average working time of 48 hours or more a week caused workers to suffer greater mental and physical health problems, such as anxiety, cardiovascular ailments, digestive disorders, and neuroses, than those who worked fewer hours. Wagstaff and Sigstad Lie (2011) found that working more than eight hours a day increased the risk of accidents. Furthermore, the risk of being involved in accidents on jobs entailing 12 hours a day is double that of working only eight hours.

Kawakami, Araki, Takatsuka et al. (1999) found an increased risk of noninsulin-dependent diabetes mellitus among employees who worked more than 50 hours of overtime a month. Another Japanese study (Hayashi, Kobayashi, Yamaoka, & Yano, 1996) showed that systolic blood pressure was significantly higher among individuals who worked an average of 60 hours overtime a month in contrast to a control group who worked an average of 30 hours overtime monthly.

Several other studies conducted with Japan's labor force revealed some very disturbing outcomes associated with working an extreme number of daily hours (10–11 or more). Sokejima and Kagamimori (1998) discovered an association of the latter with an increased risk of myocardial infarction. Nakanishi, Yoshida, Nagano et al. (2001) found that long work hours were associated with increased risk of developing hypertension. Finally, the Japanese term of "karoshi" (*karo*—overwork, *shi*—death) reflects an extreme case of extensive overtime, which may be associated with death or permanent disability from cardiovascular and ischemic heart diseases caused by working 3,000–3,500 hours (!) a year (Hayashi et al., 1996). It is believed that tens of thousands of Japanese become seriously ill or die from overwork each year (Herbig & Palumbo, 1994).

Besides symptoms of illness or ailments, long working hours have been associated with poor lifestyle habits such as heavy smoking, alcohol consumption, inadequate diet, sleep disorders, and lack of exercise (e.g., van der Hulst, 2003). These behaviors themselves can lead to health problems. Likewise, studies of overtime have identified fatigue as an important factor in the working-hours–health relationship (Sparks, Cooper, Fried, & Shirom, 1997).

Positive Outcomes of HWI

In contrast to the negative outcomes of HWI, it is difficult to perceive its positive ones. Yet, it is interesting that some publications, particularly in Australia, contend that HWI (its long hours dimension) has some favorable effects. For example, Wooden and Loundes (2001, in Weston, Gray, Qu, & Stanton, 2003) revealed that the majority of individuals in Australia who work 49 or more hours per week state that they are satisfied with their working hours and declare that they do not want to change them. Data from the International Social Sciences Survey Australia disclosed that long working hours did not negatively affect men's satisfaction with their marriage or with their children (Kelley, 2001). Persons working 49–59 hours per week and those working 60 or more hours per week depicted greater job satisfaction and contentment with their earnings than those working only 35–48 hours. Kelley (2001) argues that the high levels of gratification men derive from work is perhaps one of the explanations why they tend to stay at work for so many hours.

Work–Life Balance

In contrast to HWI and its possible negative outcomes, there is a consensus that a balance between work and life, particularly one's family, is of the utmost importance. A theme gaining prominence in the last two decades, among researchers as well as organizations, is the creation of a better balance between work and life, particularly one's personal life. Role conflict is a major problem facing individuals in modern societies, a significant number of them belonging to one's role set. This may include co-workers, parents, spouses, friends, caregivers of elderly relatives, school parents, church congregations, clubs, volunteers in the community, etc. Individuals also need to reserve time in their lives to attend to their own physical and mental well-being. Needless to say, achieving balance among all these competing roles and functions can be challenging.

As with many other aspects in the current world of work, it should be individuals' responsibility to take care of their lives, as most likely no one else will. They have to be aware of this, and be accountable for maintaining the required balance, or else suffer the ominous consequences: strain on their personal relations with their spouses, children, and other family members. They may also forfeit relations with close friends and relatives, and not have adequate leisure time for any non-work activities. They may not have any life other than work. In many instances it is beyond the power of employees to maintain the desirable balance. Employing organizations must institute progressive employment policies, which consider employees' needs and desire for achieving balance (Kossek, Pichler, Bodner, & Hammer, 2011; Stier & Sella-Dotan, Chapter 11). Moreover, without specific organizational policies providing favorable family benefits, it is practically impossible to achieve work–life balance. Thus, a growing number of organizations have considered the impact that work–life balance has on their employees as well as on their bottom line, and currently offer them a whole range of benefits.

Conspicuous in this regard are European states, particularly Scandinavian countries. According to the European Working Hours Act of April 2007, there is a maximum of 60 hours of work a week, and various restrictions on overtime and nightshift lengths (Euronline, 2013). The European Quality of Life survey, conducted by Eurofound (2013), revealed increasing support for more flexible working time arrangements, as well as allowing women greater opportunities to advance both family and career plans. Men could also reduce their formal working time so as to assume more family responsibilities. Many countries (mainly in northern Europe) also provide paid paternity leaves.

The *2012 National Study of Employers* conducted by SHRM's Families and Work Institute (Matos & Galinsky, 2012) provides the most recent data on current US employers' perspectives on HWI. It discloses that unlike in the past, American employers now provide their employees with more options to choose the times and places to work, but fewer alternatives to full-time work (Matos & Galinsky, 2012). The study was previously conducted in 1998, 2005, and 2008, covering a nationwide sample of 1,126 employers. The changes in the provision of flexible work options from 2005 to 2012 included an increase in employers' range of options that allow employees to better manage the times and places to work. These include flex time, flex place, choices in managing time, and daily time off when important needs arise. In contrast, employers have reduced their range of options that allow for employees spending significant amounts of time away from full-time work. These include moving from part-time to full-time and back again, and flex career options such as career breaks for personal or family responsibilities. Similarly, the maximum length of caregiving leaves offered to new fathers following childbirth, new adoptive parents, and employees caring for seriously ill family members, has also shortened since 2005.

While SHRM's findings are encouraging, it seems that efforts to achieve a more meaningful and effective work–life balance in the US need some significant improvements and still have a long way to go, as compared with the European situation.

A Typology of Heavy Work Investment

The state of research and writings on HWI as presented in this volume may be summarized and depicted by a typology presented in Figure 18.1.

Basically, this typology adheres to Snir and Harpaz's (2012) model as described in Chapter 1 of this volume. Snir and Harpaz (2012) distinguish two basic categories of heavy work investment, *situational* and *dispositional*. The former represents a work environment that is learned by individuals, who tend to socialize and adjust to it, sometimes against their will. In contrast, the latter embodies an uncontrollable internal orientation, springing from within the individual, who is conceivably related to one's personality. Thus, we can further classify the *focus* or *source of control as external or internal* to the individual involved. Facets of HWI may as well be associated with *positive* or *negative* consequences. On the one hand, the positive aspect denotes a possible favorable or happy work

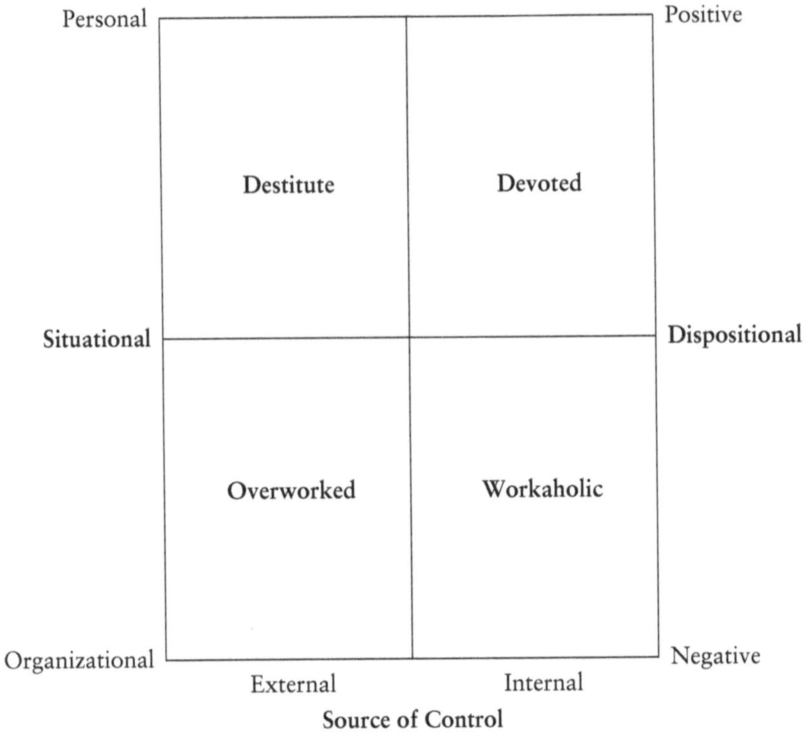

Figure 18.1 A typology of heavy work investment

state of affairs. In contrast, the negative attribute designates gloomy and even detrimental consequences associated with HWI.

Four major basic categories can be identified within the suggested typology of heavy work investment. The first category, perhaps best known in association with HWI, is the notion of workaholism, hence "workaholic" employees. Like some other addictions it is a negative dispositional and uncontrollable concept, stemming from within the individual. It has been given other negative connotations such as obsessive passion (Houlfort, Vallerand, & Laframboise, Chapter 3) and negative (affect) emotions (Shamai, Chapter 10). Abundant publications portray its deleterious outcomes, including obsessive-compulsive traits. Andreassen, Ursin, and Eriksen (2007) contend that workaholism is related to stress concerning health condition, burnout (Schaufeli, Taris, & van Rhenen, 2008), and a negative association between workaholism and life satisfaction (Aziz & Zickar, 2006). These are also mentioned in Sussman's (2012) extensive literature review, and in addition he revealed that workaholism exacerbates work–family conflict, as well as yielding other unfavorable outcomes such as low self-esteem, lower job and life satisfaction, poor job performance, sleep deprivation, and other health problems.

The second category is a positive dispositional notion of individuals who are work "devoted," this being the most outstanding buoyant outcome of HWI. It is the positive clone of workaholism, mostly typified by happy enthusiastic and passionate employees. Other researchers have termed it work engagement (van Beek, Taris, & Schaufeli, Chapter 6), harmonious passion (Houlfort, Vallerand, & Laframboise, Chapter 3), and positive (affect) emotions (Shamai, Chapter 10). Work devotion is perceived as a positive mental experience portrayed by vigor and dedication to work (Schaufeli, Shimazu, & Taris, 2009). Although individuals may feel weary following a long work day, they tend to express it as a pleasant experience along with a sense of accomplishment. Virtually all studies on work devotion accentuate its advantages (Bakker, Albrecht, & Leiter, 2011).

The third category is a situational organizational type termed "overworked," designating a state of affairs external to individuals, and to some extent beyond their power. Organizational norms are imposed on employees, compelling them to conform to a dominant culture that promotes working long hours; this is the case in such organizations as law firms, hospitals, hi-tech companies, etc. (Burke, 2006; Gaba & Howard, 2002). These also evince situations where management, implicitly or explicitly, compels employees to work long hours (Clarkberg & Moen, 2001; Golden & Wiens-Tuers, 2005). Any attempt to deviate from this type of HWI usually encounters fierce opposition by such employing organizations.

The fourth category of HWI type is the external, personal, "destitute" or needy employee. This is a situational state caused by personal circumstances and obligations that necessitate individuals to provide for their own or their families' basic needs. They end up working long hours or having to hold more than one job. Financial need has been a fundamental motive for working since the time when a monitory reward was established as an official form of incentive for work. The more one needs it, the harder and longer one is inclined to work (Smith Major, Klein, & Ehrhart, 2002).

While four basic HWI types are presented in this typology, note that in reality some overlap may transpire among them. Specifically, these should be treated merely as some initial general propositions, and should be further conceptualized, studied, and empirically tested, prior to any generalizations being made.

Research Directions and Future Needs

An examination of the current state of heavy work investment, as well as the contents of this volume, reveal some vital research needs. Some are methodological, others conceptual; all have the potential for contributions to and advancement of the state of the art.

Measurement

Presently there are at least ten measures utilized by various researchers to measure similar constructs with different methods (Nimon and Aguilar, Chapter 5). In some cases little is known about the psychometric values of these measures. Moreover, very few are based on theoretical conceptualization; many are based on college students' samples (Andreassen, Chapter 4). Relying on data provided by such studies could therefore be risky. It seems that this state of affairs is typical of developmental stages of new fields. There is a great need for agreement on constructs, definitions, and validations of measurements before one may move ahead. Finally, future research needs to be carried out on the measurement of HWI, including all its subcomponents (workaholism being only one of them), for a substantive contribution to this field to be made and for it to move to a higher level.

Cross-Cultural Comparative Research

Studies of a cross-cultural comparative nature focusing on HWI are rare. If we want to advance the HWI construct, we have to move in the comparative direction as well. Research in this area needs to be based on a theoretical background, and its outcomes should move toward advancement of theoretical conceptualizations. Marina Astakhova and Mary Hogue (Chapter 16) make an important input by proposing a theoretically-grounded framework for understanding the role of culture in HWI.

Longitudinal Research

Conspicuous by their paucity in the domain of HWI are longitudinal studies, as is also noticeable in the present volume. This lacuna is apparent in management and behavioral sciences in general, not only in HWI studies. Longitudinal research can shed light on the evolution of HWI and advance our comprehension of issues such as causality. The dearth of an overtime research design also prevents progress in inter-generational research, as it is an intricate task to isolate the effects of age and generation (Aziz, Chaney, & Raines, Chapter 12) as well as individuals' transition into retirement (Shultz & Olson, Chapter 13). Yet such research may also assist in improving our understanding of some major concepts related to HWI, such as personality, particularly as regards workaholism, which can greatly benefit from overtime analysis, as suggested by Aziz and Burke (Chapter 2).

Heavy Work Investment of Parents and Their (Adult) Children

Research on inter-generational similarity/difference in workaholism or HWI in general is scant (see Aziz, Chaney, & Raines, Chapter 12), nor has the possible transmission of parents' HWI patterns to their children been studied systematically or comprehensively (Snir, Chapter 17). Social learning theory asserts that behavior can be learned by observation and replication of significant others (Bandura, 1977). If individuals perceive their parents as heavy work investors, they may develop a tendency to treat their own work in the same manner, since parents serve as foremost role models (Machlowitz, 1980). Future studies should focus on one of the background predictors of HWI model: family relations. How similar or different are parents' and their children's HWI patterns? Is HWI "contagious"? Such research may enhance our understanding of this phenomenon and the role of parents in the development of particular work behavior patterns among their children.

Heavy Work Investment and Health-Related Outcomes

A growing body of research focuses on negative outcomes of workaholism and health-related issues, or the link between long working hours and health problems, as presented earlier in this Epilogue. Also, quite a few findings concern the association between long working hours and increased likelihood of burnout and illness (Schaufeli, Taris, & van Rhenen, 2008). Conversely, reference to the "effort" dimension of heavy work investment is insufficient. Moreover, few data exist on the difference among the outcomes of the four main types of heavy work investment in Snir and Harpaz's (2012) model: "workaholics," "work-devoted," "employer directed," and "needy."

Conclusion

The concept of "heavy work investment" pervades this volume as a phenomenon expressing changes in the nature of employment in the modern era. The origins of this notion can be traced to the concept of "workaholism" coined by Oates (1971), who defined it as compulsive need that is not controlled by a person and drives an individual to work so excessively as to possibly harm health and impair personal life or social functioning. This concept gained attention in the popular press and for many years lacked consistent research in accordance with scientific criteria. Data on workaholism were mostly collected by mental health researchers, and were classified as negative, based on conversations with workaholics and their families (e.g., Naughton, 1987; Oates, 1971; Robinson, 1999; Schaef & Fassel, 1990). Their main contribution was to shed light on the person's mental state, family, and workaholic lifestyle. The downside of this approach was tagging this phenomenon as a mental disorder, thus limiting research to a theoretical framework focusing on pathologies. Since then substantial progress has been made by several authors who published articles based on reliable and valid measures, including Spence and Robbins (1992), Robinson (1999), Schaufeli et al. (2009), and Andreassen, Griffiths, Hetland, and Pallesen (2012). In contrast to the negative side, other studies have emphasized the positive aspects of the drive to work. They saw it as a dispositional motive that causes enthusiasm and passion in one's work behavior, perceiving it as a source of pleasure, self-fulfillment, and existential meaning (e.g., Machlowitz, 1980; McMillan & O'Driscoll, 2006).

It is apparent in the present volume that both aspects of the sphere HWI are replete with related concepts denoting some overlapping or analogous concepts, as depicted in Figure 18.2.

This phenomenon is perhaps typical of developing fields, and is probably an outcome of incongruity in definitions of concepts and utilization of different measurement instruments.

These distinctions between the negative and positive contrasting HWI approaches formed the background that prompted us to move "beyond workaholism" and apply the concept of heavy work investment, as presented in Chapter 1 of this volume (Snir & Harpaz, 2012).

The occasion of publishing a special volume of articles on heavy work investment may serve as a podium attempting to assess the present state

Concept	Positive	Negative	Authors
HWI (types)	Work devotion	Workaholism	Snir & Harpaz (Chapter 1)
HWI	Engagement	Workaholism	van Beek, Taris, & Schaufeli (Chapter 6)
Passion	Harmonious Passion	Obsessive Passion	Houlfort, Vallerand, & Laframboise (Chapter 3)
Affective Happiness	Positive (affect) emotions	Negative (affect) emotions	Shamai (Chapter 10)

Figure 18.2 Some overlapping concepts in heavy work investment

of this concept. A useful framework for this evaluation is Reichers and Schneider's (1990) three-stage model for describing the evolution of scientific constructs: (1) concept introduction and elaboration; (2) concept evaluation and augmentation; (3) concept consolidation and accommodation. It seems that the HWI concept is too novel, and has not yet matured to achieve all three stages. Currently we seem clearly positioned at the first stage, that of "concept introduction and elaboration." This stage is characterized by attempts to establish legitimacy for the research domain, a process initiated through articles, or a publication like the present one, to edify students and scholars on the concept. Research in the field focuses primarily on the HWI domain's definition, importance, and value for illuminating organizational phenomena with the purpose of informing the community on these issues (Reichers & Schneider, 1990). Early data are presented to strengthen the argument that the concept represents a real phenomenon. The HWI concept appears to be still in its infancy and has still to spend some time at the first stage before being able to move forward; so it is too early to discuss the next two stages in Reichers and Schneider's (1990) framework of the evolution of scientific constructs. We trust that the present volume will challenge researchers in this field to take it upon themselves to remedy some of the deficiencies and research needs that have emerged, thereby moving us ahead in the evolution of the heavy work investment construct.

References

Andreassen, C.S., Griffiths, M.D., Hetland, J., and Pallesen, S. (2012). Development of a work addiction scale. *Scandinavian Journal of Psychology,* 53, 265–272.

Andreassen, C.S., Ursin, H., and Eriksen, H.R. (2007). The relationship between strong motivation to work, "workaholism", and health. *Psychology and Health,* 22, 615–629.

Arvey, R.D., Harpaz, I., and Liao, H. (2004). Work centrality and post-award work behavior of lottery winners. *The Journal of Psychology,* 138, 404–420.

Aziz, S. and Zickar, M.J. (2006). A cluster analysis investigation of workaholism as a syndrome. *Journal of Occupational Health Psychology,* 11, 52–62.

Bakker, A.B., Albrecht, S.L., and Leiter, M.P. (2011). Key questions regarding work engagement. *European Journal of Work and Organizational Psychology,* 20, 4–28.

Bandura, A. (1977). *Social learning theory.* Englewood Cliffs, NJ: Prentice Hall.

Barton, J. and Folkard, S. (1993). Advancing versus delaying shift systems. *Ergonomics,* 36, 59–64.

Burke, R.J. (2006). Workaholic types: It's not how hard you work but why and how you work hard. In R.J. Burke (Ed.), *Research companion to working time and work addiction* (pp. 173–192). Northampton, MA: Edward Elgar

Caruso, C. (2006). Possible broad impacts of long work hours. *Industrial Health,* 44, 531–536.

Chase, E. (1993). *The brief origins of May Day. Industrial Workers of the World.* www.iww.org/history/library/misc/origins_of_mayday (retrieved November 28, 2013).

Clarkberg, M. and Moen, P. (2001). Understanding the time-squeeze. Married couples' preferred and actual work-hour strategies. *American Behavioral Scientist,* 44, 1115–1136.

Herbig, P.A. and Palumbo, F.A. (1994). Karoshi: Salaryman sudden death syndrome. *Journal of Managerial Psychology,* 9, 11–16.

Eurofound (2013). *European Quality of Life Surveys.* www.eurofound.europa.eu/areas/qualityoflife/eqls/index.htm (retrieved November 15, 2013).

Euronline (2013). *New Working Hours Act places fewer restrictions on working hours.* www.eurofound.europa.eu/eiro/2007/05/articles/nl0705029i.htm (retrieved November 15, 2013).

Gaba, D.M. and Howard, S.K. (2002). Fatigue among clinicians and the safety of patients. *New England Journal of Medicine,* 347, 1249–1255.

Golden, L. and Wiens-Tuers, B. (2005). Mandatory overtime work in the United States: Who, where, and what? *Labor Studies Journal,* 30, 1–25.

Harpaz, I. (2004). To work or not to work: Winning the lottery and the wish to continue working. *Human Resources,* 193, January, 20–26 [Hebrew].

Harpaz, I. and Meshoulam, I. (2010). The meaning of work, employment relations, and strategic human resources management in Israel. *Human Resource Management Review,* 20, 212–223.

Hayashi, T., Kobayashi, Y., Yamaoka, K., and Yano, E. (1996). Effect of overtime work on 24-hour ambulatory blood pressure. *Journal of Occupational & Environmental Medicine,* 38, 1007–1011.

Kawakami, N., Araki, S., Takatsuka, N., Shimizu, H., and Ishibashi, H. (1999). Overtime, psychosocial working conditions, and occurrence of non-insulin dependent diabetes mellitus in Japanese men. *Journal of Epidemiology Community Health,* 53, 359–363.

Kelley, J. (2001). Consequences of working long hours. *Australian Social Monitor,* 4, 99–102.

Kossek, E.E., Pichler, S., Bodner, T., and Hammer, L.B. (2011). Workplace social support and work–family conflict: A meta-analysis clarifying the influence of general and work–family-specific supervisor and organizational support. *Personnel Psychology,* 64, 289–313.

Lee, S., McCann, D., and Messenger, J.C. (2007). *Working time around the world: Trends in working hours, laws, and policies in a global comparative perspective.* London: Routledge.

Machlowitz, M. (1980). *Workaholics. Living with them, working with them.* Reading, MA: Addison-Wesley.

Matos, K. and Galinsky, E. (2012) *2012 National Study of Employers.* SHRM's Families and Work Institute. http://familiesandwork.org/site/research/reports/NSE_2012.pdf (retrieved November 15, 2013).

McMillan, L.H.W., and O'Driscoll, M.P. (2006). Exploring new frontiers to generate an integrated definition of workaholism. In R.J. Burke (Ed.), *Research companion to working time and work addiction* (pp. 89–107). Northampton, MA: Edward Elgar.

Nakanishi, N., Yoshida, H., Nagano, K., Kawashimo, H., Nakamura, K., and Tatara, K. (2001). Long workings hours and risk for hypertension in Japanese male white collar workers. *Journal of Epidemiology & Community Health*, 55, 316–322.

Naughton, T.J. (1987). A conceptual view of workaholism and implications for career counseling and research. *Career Development Quarterly*, 6, 180–187.

Oates, W. (1971). *Confessions of workaholic: The facts about work addiction.* New York: World Publishing.

Reichers, A.E. and Schneider, B. (1990). Climate and culture: An evolution of constructs. In B. Schneider (Ed.), *Organizational climate and culture* (pp. 5–27). San Francisco: Jossey Bass.

Robinson, B.E. (1999). The Work Addiction Risk Test: Development of a tentative measure of workaholism. *Perceptual and Motor Skills*, 88, 299–310.

Schaef, A.W. and Fassel, D. (1990). *The addictive organization: Why we overwork, cover up, pick up the pieces, please the boss & perpetuate sick organization.* San Francisco: Harper Row.

Schaufeli, W.B., Shimazu, A., and Taris, T.W. (2009). Being driven to work excessively hard: The evaluation of a two-factor measure of workaholism in the Netherlands and Japan. *Cross-Cultural Research*, 43, 320–348.

Schaufeli, W.B., Taris, T.W., and van Rhenen, W. (2008). Workaholism, burnout, and work engagement: Three of a kind or three different kinds of employee well-being? *Applied Psychology: An International Review*, 57, 173–203.

Smith Major, V., Klein, K.J., and Ehrhart, M.G. (2002). Work time, work interference with family, and psychological distress. *Journal of Applied Psychology*, 87, 427–436.

Snir, R. and Harpaz, I. (2012). Beyond workaholism: Towards a general model of heavy work investment. *Human Resource Management Review*, 22, 232–243.

Sparks, K., Cooper, C., Fried, Y., and Shirom, A. (1997). The effect of hours of work on health: A meta-analytic review. *Journal of Occupational and Organizational Psychology*, 70, 391–408.

Spence, J.T. and Robbins, A.S. (1992). Workaholism: Definition, measurement, and preliminary results. *Journal of Personality Assessment*, 58, 160–178.

Sokejima S. and Kagamimori, S. (1998). Working hours as a risk factor for acute myocardial infarction in Japan: Case control study. *British Medical Journal*, 317, 775–780.

Sussman, S. (2012). Workaholism: A review. *Journal of Addiction Research & Therapy*, Supl. 6, 1–10.

van der Hulst, M. (2003). Long workhours and health. *Scandinavian Journal of Work, Environment, & Health*, 29, 171–188.

Wagstaff, A.S. and Sigstad Lie, J.-A. (2011). Shift and night work and long working hours: A systematic review of safety implications. *Scandinavian Journal of Work, Environment, & Health*, 37, 173–185.

Weston, R., Gray, M., Qu, L., and Stanton, D. (2003). *The impact of long working hours on employed fathers and their families*. Australian Institute of Family Studies. http://flosse.fahcsia.gov.au/fahcsiajspui/handle/10620/3540 (retrieved December 22, 2013).

INDEX

Note: Page numbers in *italics* are for tables.